Bonded by Evolution

Bonded by Evolution

*What We've Got Wrong About
Love and Connection*

PAUL EASTWICK

Cornerstone Press

CORNERSTONE PRESS

UK | USA | Canada | Ireland | Australia
India | New Zealand | South Africa

Cornerstone Press is part of the Penguin Random House group of companies whose addresses can be found at global.penguinrandomhouse.com

Penguin Random House UK,
One Embassy Gardens, 8 Viaduct Gardens, London SW11 7BW

penguin.co.uk

First published in the US by Crown,
an imprint of Penguin Random House LLC, New York 2026
Published in the UK by Cornerstone Press 2026
001

Copyright © Paul Eastwick, 2026

The moral right of the author has been asserted

Wedding rings icon on part openers from Shutterstock/Erta.
Hold-punched memo paper in figure 9.1 on pages 230 from Shutterstock/hoad.

No part of this book may be used or reproduced in any manner for the purpose of training artificial intelligence technologies or systems. In accordance with Article 4(3) of the DSM Directive 2019/790, Penguin Random House expressly reserves this work from the text and data mining exception.

Text designer: Aubrey Khan

Printed and bound in Great Britain by Clays Ltd, Elcograf S.p.A.

The authorised representative in the EEA is Penguin Random House Ireland, Morrison Chambers, 32 Nassau Street, Dublin D02 YH68

A CIP catalogue record for this book is available from the British Library

ISBN: 978–1–529–91055–1 (hardback)
ISBN: 978–1–529–91056–8 (trade paperback)

Penguin Random House is committed to a sustainable future for our business, our readers and our planet. This book is made from Forest Stewardship Council® certified paper.

For Isa,
and the world you deserve

· CONTENTS ·

Author's Note ix

Preface xi

INTRODUCTION
On the Market 1

PART 1
The Lies We're Told About Love

CHAPTER 1
Measuring Desirability 25

CHAPTER 2
Real and Overblown Gender Differences 51

CHAPTER 3
Marriage Material? 76

PART 2
The Science of Close Relationships

CHAPTER 4
Attachment Part 1: Bonds of Support 105

CHAPTER 5
Attachment Part 2: The Biases That Bind 126

CHAPTER 6
Compatibility, Fickle Beast 147

CHAPTER 7
Relationships as Creative Chaos 169

PART 3
Finding Connection in the Real World

CHAPTER 8
Moving Online 193

CHAPTER 9
Disrupting the Manosphere 213

CHAPTER 10
Real Relational Solutions 236

CONCLUSION
Gender, Love, and Evolution 253

Acknowledgments 257

Appendix A 261

Appendix B 263

Notes 265

Index 323

· AUTHOR'S NOTE ·

This is a nonfiction book about research on attraction and close relationships, and it reflects my view of the state of the scientific evidence at this moment in time. I recount many of my own experiences in this book, and I have recounted these experiences honestly and to the best of my memory. When these experiences involved other people, I changed their names and other peripheral details to preserve their anonymity. Throughout this book, I also describe many case studies of couples. To protect their privacy, elements of their backstories have been revised or have been blended with other people's experiences.

· PREFACE ·

When I tell people that I work at the University of California, Davis, they naturally ask what I teach. The answer raises eyebrows.

For nearly a decade, I have taught an undergraduate course on romance—roughly six hundred students per year. Upon learning this fact about me, people sometimes transition to skeptical questions: Am I a dating coach at one of our nation's flagship university systems? I quickly reassure them that my class is nothing of the sort. In fact, the field of "attraction and close relationships" is the branch of research psychology that I know best—my academic home.

The class itself is sprawling, as psychology classes go. I cover behavioral studies on initial attraction, studies on children's attachments to caregivers, studies about love, studies about conflict in couples, studies about sexual arousal, and studies about the physiological effects of a breakup. The class isn't just useful for psychology majors; my students include biology and human development and anthropology and economics majors, too. The science of attraction and close relationships spans all these different disciplines.

My class is different from other college classes in one particularly striking way: My students have been developing theories about romance long before they walk in. When they attend lectures about meiosis or James Baldwin or historical migration patterns in Eurasia, are their thoughts about those topics already so personal and so elaborated? Probably not. But write out my students' own love lives in full, and the pages would dwarf any textbook I might assign.

So by the time I meet my students, their romantic experiences are already deeply integrated into their sense of who they are. A few have had serious relationships; many let a good one get away. They're all still learning.

And they all have been rejected at one time or another, in heartbreaking fashion for some. The young woman, for example, who asked me one day after class: "At what point do I need to accept the fact that I'm not attractive?" She didn't ask me this question because she desperately wanted to be the center of attention at a party, or because her friends have more followers on Instagram. Her real question, I suspect, was the one that lurks for so many people, of every age and generation: "Will the process of finding and keeping a partner always feel this daunting, this grueling? Am I relationship material, and if not, is there anything I can do about it?" And the most anxiety-provoking and insidious misconception of them all: "Am I struggling because of something evolved or innate about me? Because if so, I'm screwed, right?"

I tried to answer her as best I could, by condensing the entire ten-week course into a tiny, reassuring soundbite. It came out as a splat; it's not easy to dismantle a lifetime of discouraging, biologically determinist messages in the passing period between classes. She smiled politely.

Of course we've all worried about these questions—and no genders are exempt. We've been fed it from every angle. Movies and stories and social media and, hell, the entirety of the Internet. "Are you a catch, or not? Take this short quiz to find out."

For many single people, these worries linger. People have increasingly turned to online dating in the hopes of finding a partner, and many times it helps. But the apps are exquisite in their ability to perpetually reinforce these same insecurities. They require you to compile what you have to offer—your appearance, your skills, your qualifications—and put yourself out there for other shoppers to peruse. You are something to be marketed—something with an inherent and agreed-upon value, like the price of corn on the commodity exchange. And every time a budding romance fizzles, people dust off their apps and think: "Ugh, I have to put myself back out there, don't I?"

Against this backdrop, I teach these students about the science. And science can be messy: one study showing this, a second study showing that, a hypothesis that everyone believes to be true but actually has very weak support. Using this shared pile of facts, a scientist must construct a coherent story that connects the pieces. There is no how-to manual for this part of the job, and a human being has to do it—human beings with ideas and beliefs and values and romantic experiences of their own. I have been at this for about twenty years, and only now am I starting to see how the pieces come together. This book is about that vision, based on the strongest contemporary scientific studies, and with a few embarrassing and reassuring stories tossed in for good measure.

Of course, I'm not the only one trying to assemble all of the puzzle pieces. Other scientists have ideas and beliefs and values and romantic experiences of their own, too. They have put the pieces together in a different way.

One popular vision comes from scientists in a field known as evolutionary psychology. It's an approach that has been very successful, and rightly so; these scholars have been demonstrating for decades how applying the logic of evolutionary biology to the human mind can lead to new psychological discoveries. Almost no practicing researcher today would argue against this basic principle—that natural selection shaped how we think—and I cover plenty of evolutionary psychological studies in my class, too.

But the way that evolutionary psychologists turned our shared pile of facts into their own vision of how human mating works? This is where I depart from them, and dramatically so. Their story is a familiar one: the idea that relationships are best depicted as a conflict between men and women, two kinds of organisms with distinct preferences and goals. Or the idea that romantic relationships are a negotiation between two parties offering value, extracting benefits, and attempting to maintain a competitive edge. Sitting at the center of it all: a person's personal "mate value"—their true, core desirability—to be leveraged on the mating market to get what they want and deserve. She's hot, he's rich, let's make a deal.

This book is for anyone who has felt that this popular scientific story of human mating is bleak—that if you look at it too directly or internalize it too deeply, you could become overwhelmed with cynicism and quit the whole gross spectacle. In fact, the evolutionary psychological narrative is warped and distorted. There is a more optimistic, more interesting, and more accurate *relational* evolutionary story that connects the scientific facts.

The real story is about how people evolved to form emotionally meaningful attachment bonds with each other, and how satisfying relationships stem from close interpersonal attunement and compatibility. Our evolutionary instincts don't prime us to chase the most attractive or highest-status partner we can find, nor do they push us to worry about the difference between our partner's mate value and our own. Rather, we crave attachment bonds with partners who can meet our needs in good times and bad. In the strongest bonds, we treat our partners as a safe haven by going to them for practical or emotional support. We seek assurances in the face of adversity and insecurity, and we don't "keep score" of who's contributing what or who's making bigger sacrifices when navigating career transitions, conflict, or the logistics of taking the dog to the vet. And when we encounter opportunities, we treat our partners as a secure base by using them as a springboard to learn, discover, and create—celebrating each other's successes, accumulating a shorthand of inside jokes and traditions, and forming a shared reality.

The interpersonal chemistry that creates this kind of bond has little to do with the surface-level traits that are top of mind for most people. We don't need to find someone who matches our pre-packaged perfect "type" or someone who speaks our love language, and there is no carefully calibrated mix of similarities and differences that could be captured by an algorithm. Instead, our ideas about what we want in a relationship have a way of evaporating in the face of rich, real-world impressions. The dynamics that cause a relationship to succeed or fail are perpetually changing and highly specific to a particular couple's story and history; they aren't bound to a set of traits that make someone a "good" or a "bad" partner. In the pages ahead, we'll explore how compatibility is largely constructed, in small, cumulative ways, over time: A relationship is what you make it, through trial and error and good fortune, regardless of how well two people fit together on paper.

This story of human bonding is true for women, for men, for LGBTQ folks, for heteroscxuals, for young people, for older people, for aromantics, for hopeless romantics. No groups are cut out.

This alternative vision of human relationships isn't all roses and puppies. Relationships are hard, building them from scratch can take forever, and they can fall apart with little warning. Everyone struggles, and everyone has their low points.

Even when the cold streaks end, the challenges remain because the entire process is fundamentally, deeply unpredictable. One person may think that you are hilarious (or charismatic, or impressively knowledgeable about nineties alternative rock), but no one else has ever placed such a priority on this specific feature of yours. You can spend all this time learning about what you have going for you, only to have it upended with a change of scenery. (How come none of your fellow paralegals seem impressed by your ability to recite Pavement and Cranberries lyrics?) We like different people for different reasons, which just adds to the chaos of it all.

But I say this with confidence: The idea that you have a romantic destiny—that you have a stable value as a partner, linked to your ability to use a specific gendered set of mating strategies, and a "type" who makes you happy—is one of the weakest ideas ever promoted by scientists. This book will tell you why you get to set this idea aside, replaced by the lessons of carefully conducted studies of real people trying to make their way in the romantic world and real couples trying their best to cultivate something meaningful and fulfilling. Some of the lessons are surprising; some of the lessons are frustrating;

most of them are a welcome antidote to contemporary "Men-and-women-hate-each-other-and-relationships-are-terrible" heteropessimism. After all, humans have been forming and maintaining romantic relationships—often happily—for hundreds of thousands of years. And if you're willing to dig in, the science of how and why we do it is inspiring.

· INTRODUCTION ·

On the Market

A punishing stretch of dating debacles in young adulthood prompted some deep reflection. A good friend suggested that, if I changed a few things about myself, I might have better luck next time. This friend also knew a couple of things about pickup artistry, and he was happy to help me become the best player I could be. All I needed to do was (1) get better clothes, (2) lift weights, (3) approach women with confidence, (4) tell them jokes (funny ones), (5) relax and stop trying so hard . . . and so on. I think we got to fifteen "things to improve" before I started to wonder if this was a helpful exercise.

"This feels fake. I need to do all this to date someone cool?" My friend assured me that, in fact, I did. I needed to boost my stats for someone to be into me because relationships are like a competitive market. "Those other guys—the ones sucking up all the attention—it comes easy for them. We're not 10s. But you and I can play in this game, too, with a little extra work."

This "mating market" concept is an appealingly simple and intuitive idea. As a potential mate, you have a value, and this value is determined by your attributes—traits like attractiveness, youth, status, confidence, intelligence, or wealth. The more attributes you bring to the table, the greater your *mate value*.

Your mate value determines how well you do on the market. It's nice for *you* that you've worked through your avoidance or self-esteem issues, but mate value is about what you do for *me*. That is, high-value people succeed because they have the attributes that other people desire in a partner. In heterosexual markets, women should be in high demand to the extent that they are attractive, and men should be in high demand to the extent that they have good earning potential. You can imagine different marketplaces for different kinds of partners, too. In a marketplace for short-term partners, people should be valued for their sexiness, and in a marketplace for long term partners, people should be valued for their ability to invest in and care for children.

The online dating landscape reinforces these ideas. People with attractive photos in their profile receive much more attention than people with unattractive photos (and this is especially true for women). People with higher levels of education and income receive more attention than people with lower levels (and this is especially true for men). Online dating is a market with dramatic levels of desirability inequality—a system of "haves" and "have-nots" that rivals the inequality in a kleptocracy.[1]

Many academics think that dating offline works this way, too; throughout the twentieth century, economists, sociologists, and psychologists described dating and marriage patterns using market-like concepts. Wealthy people historically operated within a mating market of other wealthy people, while the poor tried to sneak their way into the ballrooms. Scholars have wanted to understand how these so-called markets worked because they have real social consequences—when social circles are isolated, the rich only marry the rich, and wealth consolidates. The way that we form and maintain romantic relationships is fundamentally interwoven with every other thread of our social lives.[2]

The market metaphor for human mating appears ageless and powerful. Courtship patterns are not fair, and so it is only natural that modern-day daters feel as though they are looking for a product—or that they are one. But in the 1990s, scientists spawned another idea: Human mate choice might also be at the mercy of a *biological* market—deriving from something deep within our DNA. This evolutionary argument adds new complexities and anxieties.

INTRODUCTION 3

The EvoScript

I first encountered this argument at age fifteen in the form of one particularly alarming magazine cover. It was August of 1994, and I was on vacation with my parents in a small rental house in New Hampshire, where they'd stockpiled the requisite middle-class magazines of the day: *Newsweek*, *Vanity Fair*, and the occasional *National Geographic*. Several unread issues sprawled over the coffee table, and one day midway through the trip, I picked up a copy of *Time* magazine. On the cover, a broken wedding band floated aimlessly against a stark black background, along with a headline that declared INFIDELITY: IT MAY BE IN OUR GENES.

I froze. In our genes? Yikes.

I should add: At this same moment, my ex-girlfriend and my best friend were hooking up for the first time. Technically, she had already broken up with me, and certainly no wedding bands were involved. But the romantic misery radiating off the page felt personally tailored all the same. I was doomed.

This was my introduction to evolutionary psychology.

EVOLUTIONARY PSYCHOLOGY IS the study of human thought, preferences, and behavior, using Darwinian principles. Scholars of evolutionary psychology suggest that our tendency to like certain things, from fatty foods to trustworthy interaction partners, reflects our evolved legacy—the preferences we inherited from our ancestors because they helped us to survive and win reproductive competitions in the distant past.

In the nineties, evolutionary psychology was a scrappy underdog of a discipline, fighting for academic acceptance, and eager to take on a social-science mainstream that, at the time, rarely acknowledged biological processes like natural selection. Their point was simple and logical: If we accept the biological fact that our lungs and kneecaps had evolved to serve distinct functions, then it should also be true that different portions of our minds possessed ancient rationales. Over the ensuing decade, their ideas made major inroads in both academic and popular culture.

This *Time* magazine cover story (excerpted from Robert Wright's 1994 book *The Moral Animal*) was a distillation of hot-off-the-press evolutionary psychological research on intersexual conflict, infidelity, and the desire for sexual variety. Wright argued that, according to evolutionary psychology, relationships are unstable because people evolved to want more, more, more. This theory follows directly from the idea that dating is a competitive market: If the search for valuable traits is what motivated your partner to choose you in the first place, what happens when someone who outshines you comes along? (It turns out: She starts dating him while you read a *Time* magazine article.) Wright's view is that evolutionary psychology, in explaining how these impulses have evolved through natural selection, will help people accept the realities of sex and romance, and set more practical expectations.[3]

In the intervening thirty years, these ideas have coalesced into something that I call the EvoScript. The EvoScript describes "the way human mating works" according to the principles of Darwinian natural and sexual selection. It tells us that our preferences derive from our genes' impulses to propagate themselves, and so we pursue the partners who possess the traits that will best maximize the fitness of our potential offspring. It tells us that because men and women have faced different pressures over our evolutionary history, they have different impulses and desires. It tells us that human mating falls into two distinct categories—short-term and long-term—and that each type of encounter has its own set of rules and its own scoreboard of winners and losers.

Throughout the popular dating advice canon, you can find appeals to human nature with this scientific veneer. For example, from the 1995 mega bestseller *The Rules*, women learn that they need to be coy and play hard-to-get to have success with men. "We trust in the natural order of things—namely, that man pursues woman." His primitive mind won't let him fall for you unless he works for it, because there is a biological rationale for why easy women have no long-term value. According to the authors of *The Rules*, after you manage to lock him down, the games continue: "Don't initiate sex, even if you want it badly. Let him be the man, the aggressor in the bedroom."[4]

These ideas endured into the twenty-first century and continue to guide popular relationship advice for heterosexuals. Women hear that the biggest problem is securing any kind of commitment, given that men would rather be philandering. In 2024, relationship therapist Dr. Laura Berman explained (on Nick Cannon's show *Counsel Culture*): "Let's just talk about the science, okay? From an evolutionary perspective, those with the xy chromosome . . . [have a] core DNA-driven impulse perhaps to spread your genes as far and wide as you can." Men simply don't want to be tied down the way that women do, because according to the EvoScript, their ancestors achieved an edge hundreds of millions of years ago by getting some action on the side.[5]

Browsing through the great romance-themed TED Talks, you'll be reminded yet again that when it comes to love, men and women might as well be different species. Women, the late biological anthropologist Dr. Helen Fisher told you, "get intimacy from face-to-face talking. We swivel towards each other, we do what we call the 'anchoring gaze' and we talk. This is intimacy to women. I think it comes from millions of years of holding that baby in front of your face, cajoling it, reprimanding it, educating it with words." Not so for men, of course. "Men tend to get intimacy from side-by-side doing. As soon as one guy looks up, the other guy will look away. I think it comes from millions of years of . . . sitting behind the bush, looking straight ahead, trying to hit that buffalo on the head with a rock." The behaviors that we associate with men's and women's roles apparently derive from the sexes' distinct evolved abilities.[6]

And this kind of thinking has shaped pop culture, too. The beloved comedies of my young adulthood—*Clueless, Hitch, The 40-Year-Old Virgin*—vividly depicted how the process of becoming desirable is a project. As Hitch admonishes his unlucky-in-love clients: "'You' is a very fluid concept right now." This is why dating feels fake—if you want a relationship, you need to shape yourself into a particular gendered ideal. According to advice from users on Reddit, "dating is just sales," and you have to market yourself in a way that caters to the evolved preferences of your preferred gender.[7]

If you manage to get into a relationship, both men and women still have reasons to worry. A better-looking, more accomplished rival can always take your partner off your hands. On behalf of women, Reddit users ask: "What are the actual actionable things you can do as a woman to continually increase your mate value over time?"[8] On behalf of men, online personalities warn: "Men often don't want to tell their romantic partner that they're sick, or injured, or having difficulties at their job, or anything that indicates a loss of mate value. Because women initiate most breakups, and men don't want their partner to leave them."[9] The science supposedly says that couples with mismatched levels of desirability are historic rarities, so conceal your weaknesses or get dumped.

Supporters of the EvoScript present its conclusions as fact, and those who do not accept its conclusions are accused of being deceptive, far-left ideologues. Sherrie Schneider, author of *The Rules,* continued to proclaim in 2023 that "Dating is completely biological . . . biology has not changed," and to argue otherwise is to feed women lies.[10] According to popular podcast host Joe Rogan, challenges to evolutionary psychology reflect "a willful ignorance of the actual basic biological differences between men and women." Somewhere in the three decades since evolutionary psychology entered the public domain, its theories about the evolved differences between men and women have become reality, and to believe otherwise is, in Rogan's words, "deciding to believe a set of ideas that has no basis in science or fact".[11]

. . .

I doubt this is your first encounter with these ideas. You may find some of them extreme, and you may find others intuitive. Either way, for most people, the EvoScript is a real bummer.

The message that many of us have absorbed is that, like it or not, human beings live—and always have lived—in a hierarchy of romantic inequality. Each romantic rejection is a referendum on your true inherent value as a partner. The "haves" outcompete the "have-nots," and people are relentlessly on the lookout for a better mate. In this market, some people find mates and have children who inherit their attributes and preferences; others are left mateless, and their traits are weeded out. Your ancestors successfully navigated these challenges—that's why you're here today—but, depending on the attributes you possess, it's entirely possible that your evolved destiny is to be a weed.

The EvoScript has three central pillars. First is the idea that people have an inherent mate value—an intrinsic value (say, out of ten) that determines how successful they will be in the mating market. On this scale, higher numbers represent qualities such as better looks, more charisma, greater financial success, appealing talents—and these qualities contribute to a greater overall value as a romantic or sexual partner. People pursue (and eventually settle for) the mate with the best attributes who will accept them in return—the so-called 10s should match up with the 10s, which leaves the 9s to match up with the 9s, and so on until the 1s settle for the 1s. As evolutionary psychologist Dr. Geoffrey Miller puts it, mating is a game that features "men assessing women (unconsciously) as egg donors, and women assessing men (unconsciously) as sperm donors" in an attempt to maximize the genetic fitness of their unborn children.[12]

Imagine that you're in that precarious early dating phase with someone you're really into—the point where you keep saying to yourself "How lucky am I that *he* wants to spend time with me?" For one brief shining moment, you appear to be the chosen one. Then, like waking up from a dream, it all comes crashing down, with a text: "It's been great hanging out with you, but I realize that I'm looking for something else, and I feel like I'm wasting your time." Would you interpret your heartbreak as a reflection of your inherent (lower) value, like you'd flown too close to the sun? If so, congratulations, you've internalized the EvoScript.

The second pillar is that men and women have historically achieved reproductive success through different avenues, and so they evolved to prioritize different things out of their sexual and romantic relationships. For example, according to the EvoScript, men are more interested in sex than women, whereas women are more vigilant for signs of commitment. Men and women also supposedly differ substantially in the priority they place on physical attractiveness vs. earning potential in a partner, with men seeking partners with good looks and women favoring men who can provide. Some of these differences create considerable conflict in mixed-gender relationships, especially when it comes to sexual desire. Ultimately, men and women are so different in the evolutionary narrative that undergraduate students learn about men's and women's mating psychology in separate sections of textbooks.[13]

Imagine that you're a man in a new dating relationship. You've just learned that your whole team at work might be getting laid off next month. This news is beyond nerve-racking, and you have an impulse to confess the accompanying vulnerability and career-change anxieties to your new girlfriend. In your fantasies, she responds by saying that she doesn't really care what you do professionally, as long as you're happy doing it. But instead of opening up, would you invoke your best impression of a stone wall because women want stoic providers, not needy unemployed losers trying to "find their passion"? In doing so, you'd have internalized the EvoScript.

The third pillar is the vital, essential distinction between short-term and long-term forms of human mating. The key idea is that humans evolved a menu of distinct mating strategies, and chief among them are the short-term, sexy fling and the long-term committed partnership. Depending on what people are good at, they end up specializing in the pursuit of one or the other: She will take you home with her if you can boast confidently and compellingly over a couple of cocktails, but she will marry you if you have lofty ambitions. He will hook up with you if he thinks you're hot, but he will stay with you if he thinks his parents would approve of you. This principle also implies that people need to pick a strategy to fit their goals. If you want a wife, avoid the bars; if you want a husband, keep your legs closed.[14]

Imagine that you're a single woman, and you're out on a first date with a guy you met on Tinder. Drink number three has just arrived, and his hand keeps brushing yours. Does he want to go back to your place? You definitely want him to; in fact, you want more than just sex with him, and that's where you pause. You want to be girlfriend material, not "that Tinder girl." Would you assume that having sex with him *reduces* the likelihood of landing a long-term relationship with him, as if forming a relationship and indulging sexual desires are mutually exclusive? If so, welcome to the club, you've internalized the EvoScript.

Of course, evolutionary psychology did not invent these narratives wholesale. Women have long felt pressure to be attractive and youthful; to derive complete fulfillment from motherhood; to keep their own ambitions in check; to downplay their sexual desires; to watch their husbands closely around the younger competition. In the past, if you wanted to change this gendered world, you smashed the patriarchy. But the EvoScript posits that these pressures derive from ancient human nature. Unfortunately, it is not clear how you smash millions of years of evolution.

The EvoScript is taxing on men, too. It is a recipe for depression to learn that your poor romantic fortunes may stem from your nature as a permanent Darwinian loser. This understanding of evolutionary psychology has led to much bleaker ideas about mating and gender differences. Some men have turned to the flourishing collection of online spaces that includes men's rights activists, pickup artists, and "incels" (short for "involuntary celibates").[15]

Here, a twisted version of evolutionary psychology plays a role in the larger culture wars. For example, the ideology of the red pill purportedly "reveals" hard truths about the conflicting mating strategies of men and women (the "red pill" is a reference to the 1999 film *The Matrix*, in which characters take a literal red pill when they are ready to learn hard truths about how the world works—to have their eyes opened to an unsettling reality). In this community, men learn about the 80/20 rule, in which "a tiny percentage of genetically superior alpha guys hoard most hetero sex"; in other words, 80 percent of women desire only the top 20 percent of the men (the alphas), while men of middling attractiveness (the betas) compete for the few remaining women with their desperate "nice-guy" routines.[16] These communities have adapted the EvoScript in the service of misogynistic rhetoric, portraying themselves as hapless victims of women's evolved and unchecked impulse to obtain the most attractive and high-status mate possible. On the flipside, they believe that the feminists are hard at work curtailing men's own evolved impulses to pursue sex partners and assert their dominance.

At its most extreme, this ideology has been used to justify horrific acts of violence. Consider Alek Minassian, who drove a van into a Toronto crowd, killing ten people and injuring sixteen more, or Jake Davison, the self-described "loner" who killed five people in Plymouth in the United Kingdom in 2021 after filling incel forums on Reddit with descriptions of his feelings of frustration and hopelessness. Public intellectuals like Jordan Peterson explain these actions by consulting the EvoScript. According to Peterson, Minassian was angry because he was rejected, and he was rejected because "women will all only go for the most high-status men."[17] To influential men like Peterson, these are deep, unyielding, biological truths—as ancient as the lobster—and to argue otherwise is naïve and sentimental.

So the stakes are high with the way that we talk and think about our evolved nature, especially when it comes to deeply personal issues like love and sex. People have learned to have modest goals, and not to date above their station, and that sex and parenting are two distinct strategies, so they must pick a short-term or a long-term lane. The message of the EvoScript is, if you are heterosexual, do not trust the other gender, and watch your back because your interests are fundamentally misaligned.

But what if the EvoScript doesn't capture the way things actually are? Is there an antidote to the existing bleak story that inspires despair and anxiety (at best) and provides cover for misogyny and violence (at worst)? Is there an alternative underdog of a science that examines these same topics and comes to very different conclusions? Absolutely there is.

The Alternative to Marketplace Dating: Compatibility-Driven Bonding

Here's a thought experiment: You live with a small group of people on a remote island. You have everything you need to survive, but no way to connect with the rest of civilization. And in this group, your romantic options consist of five people who are approximately your age and your preferred gender. That's it. This is your pool, and ultimately, you and one of these five people need to pick each other.

Your first response might be: "I guess I'd have to settle, and I wouldn't be happy about it." I say: The dating apps have infected you. Yes, if you held tightly to the assumption that you had to show off and compete for the "best" partner, or to the assumption that you knew what attributes your partner absolutely had to have, then yes, you might be disappointed. But I bet you wouldn't approach remote-island love that way. First of all, you'd be getting to know these folks slowly and gradually over time, without necessarily thinking of them as potential partners. You also can't ghost after a weak first impression—where are you going to go, exactly? You'd be spending time with all of them, and, eventually, your experiences with each person would be unique; some uniquely meh, but some uniquely good. In this situation, you wouldn't have to worry about competing for the attention of strangers; you'd be perseverating on how you could re-create that butterfly-inducing moment you shared yesterday by the campfire.[18]

In other words, you'd wisely be paying attention to compatibility. Whose sense of humor clicks with yours? Whose smile makes you giddy in a way you can't quite explain? Who makes you feel at ease, or competent, or smart, or special? You'd be focused on the person right in front of you, and the feelings that their movements and facial expressions and quips and stories inspire. This kind of compatibility has to be experienced; it rarely leaps off the online dating profile, and it often doesn't manifest on a coffee date.

I like this thought experiment because it gets us far closer to our true evolved heritage. And it reveals the alternative to the EvoScript, which is that *humans form mating bonds by finding sexual and romantic compatibility in small networks*. You evolved to evaluate partners who you could talk to, and see, and touch. These were real people who were connected to existing social networks, who made you feel something—for good or for ill—and who shared a unique history with you.

There are two reasons why this framework is a better depiction of the human ancestral condition than the EvoScript. Firstly, we evolved in *very* small markets. Using evolutionary principles to understand human mating is a fantastic idea, but we have to consider the context in which humans actually evolved. Humans didn't evolve in an environment with large sexual marketplaces that would permit the "hot" people to dazzle us. Finding a partner wasn't about amassing choices and exploring options until you were able to select the most fertile, intelligent, and successful mate who would select you back. The idea that a person could select a mate from a large array of options is a recent innovation in our evolutionary history.

Humans evolved in small groups with a very limited number of mating choices. Among hunter-gatherers living in sub-Saharan Africa—whose lifestyle offers a reasonable approximation of the way that humans evolved—the average group size is about fifty people. That's pretty small. If you lived in this environment, you could have relationships with people in nearby groups; this would be a larger band of people (150 or so) that you would get to know over a period of years. You could end up pursuing one or more of them, in principle. But of these 150, about half would be your preferred gender, about half of the remaining set would be of reproductive age, and many of those left would be in a stable partnership already.[19]*

Ancestral humans, then, had a relatively small number of mating options. The deluge of eligible strangers that we experience today is

---

* There might be 500–1,500 people who speak your language that you could conceivably encounter from time to time; these people would be analogous to modern-day acquaintances. But they would be spread out across an area that was roughly the size of Connecticut. And remember: You're on foot.

highly novel, and online dating—competing for potential mates within a vast pool of complete strangers—is the antithesis of what we evolved to do. For highly desirable people to dominate a market, there need to be more options than what ancestral humans would have encountered.[20]

The second advantage of this new framework is that it recognizes that compatibility is central. The EvoScript says that some individuals are more desirable than others, and this inequality in mate value drives the way people behave in the market environment of romantic love. But this perspective sidelines *compatibility*, the way two people mesh or fit together as a pair. Two people might have equally desirable attributes, but they just don't work well together. Two other people might be quite mismatched in how appealing they are to strangers, but they fit together like a dream. The way that you feel about someone—initially, and especially over time—is barely about how appealing they are on paper. It's mostly about compatibility.[21]

We crave compatibility for two related reasons. The first is that compatibility facilitates *attachment,* which refers to a collection of features associated with strong emotional bonds—or "pair-bonds" in the language of evolutionary biologists. For example, when two people are bonded and attached, they feel less stressed when they are around each other, they tend to go to each other for support, and they rely on each other as they strive toward major life goals. Second, compatibility helps people to navigate *communal interdependence,* which refers to the way that two people handle each other's preferences and needs when faced with the complex realities of day-to-day life.

Attachment and communal interdependence are the two major factors that explain why some relationships work well and some do not. And critically, attachment and interdependence have virtually nothing to do with two people's mate value. Instead, if you want to know whether a relationship has the potential for attachment and interdependence, you have to know how compatible you are with someone. Or rather, you have to *feel* it, through repeated interaction, getting to know them, and seeing if you can find a way to integrate your needs and preferences. Compatibility is very hard to ascertain from a set of questionnaires or a dating profile; compatibility has to be curated, cultivated, and constructed.

EvoScript enthusiasts sometimes declare that mate value is the underlying source of compatibility. Specifically, some scientists claim that bonding derives from "identifying potential partners who possess a similar mate-value trajectory," or that couples who match in mate value are more likely to have lasting relationships.[22] But these assertions are baseless; as this book will show, the level of similarity in people's mate value doesn't predict much of anything, full stop. The fact that we're both 6s doesn't have anything to do with whether we're a compatible match.[23]

THROUGHOUT MY TEENAGE YEARS, as evolutionary psychology became more deeply embedded in our culture, I found that my reaction to it grew more and more ambivalent. On the positive side, I was moved by the way it connected the human experience to deep history and highlighted our connections with other animals. Wasn't it inspiring to think that other people had been navigating these same romantic challenges with the same social brain for hundreds of thousands of years? Maybe there are real opportunities for intervention, too: Perhaps progressive divorce laws and economic policies could intersect with our evolved psychology to produce happier marriages and happier children?

But at the same time, was it really true that every time someone doesn't want to date you, the decision results from a deep truth about where you fall in the mating hierarchy, rather than a simple matter of taste and timing? And wasn't it perplexing to think that the thrill of a mutual romantic spark was actually just a brief, delirious ceasefire in a perpetual battle between men and women?

Evolutionary psychology felt deeply thrilling and deeply wrong all at once, and I could not cleanly separate which part was thrilling and which part was wrong. A bit like hooking up with the ex of your best friend.

So in the early 2000s, driven by a frustration that this science was incomplete, I went to graduate school to study human mating. As my training progressed, I tried to glean all that I could from the writings of evolutionary psychologists themselves, as well as their critics. I read research in other disciplines, too—from anthropology to family studies to sexuality research—to get a sense of how scholars in those traditions understood human mating relationships. By taking the time to understand evolutionary psychology from both inside and outside of the field, I learned about its weaknesses.

These weaknesses stem from the way evolutionary psychologists had conducted their research studies—when compared with other disciplines, these approaches lacked rigor. When I dug into the specifics of these studies, I saw that evolutionary psychologists were typically conducting their research on deep questions about human mating and behavior by handing people surveys that asked things like how they felt about a person depicted in a photograph, or what they would do in a hypothetical mating-relevant scenario. Endless troves of studies claimed to be capturing the evolved basis of human desire by asking people questions like "How important is attractiveness to you in a romantic partner?" These studies are cheap to run, and they generate data that are easy to analyze. Relative to the typical pace of science, a researcher using this approach could confirm their predictions quickly, which then generates more publications, more grants, and more accolades. Academia has a perverse incentive structure: It can be costly to slow down and take the time to get the story right.

Nevertheless, I remained troubled by the shockingly large gap between what these studies were asking participants to do in the lab (like reading about an imaginary person) and human mating as it happens in the real world (which typically involves real people). Where were the studies showing what happens when potential romantic partners meet each other face-to-face? Where were the studies examining how people decide to form a relationship (or not) with a given person? Where were the studies that identified the factors that aid real-life romantic partners in maintaining their relationships over time? And then there are the challenges connecting this science to human mating as it (might have) actually unfolded in our ancestral past. Where were the studies that seriously grappled with the fact that the modern visual onslaught of potential partners has no parallel for our ancestors who lived in relatively small nomadic groups?

In fact, these kinds of labor-intensive studies exist in other disciplines. From the person perception tradition in social psychology, I learned how scientists study the way that people experience attraction for their real-life acquaintances and friends. From the close relationships tradition, I learned how scientists capture the way that real-life romantic couples affect each other on a day-to-day basis.[24]

But the EvoScript incorporated these approaches rarely (if at all). Evolutionary psychologists had developed a robust science around what people *say* they would do or *say* they would be attracted to. But natural selection does not act on what people say they would do in a hypothetical scenario. Darwin never advanced a theory about a "survival of the fittest" response to a fictional situation. If we want strong methods for an evolutionary science, they need to be based on what people would *actually* do and *actually* be attracted to.

As a result of these methodological issues, a reasonable person could be skeptical about whether evolutionary psychology can answer the question "How does human mating work?" Sorry, Joe Rogan: You can in fact be a scientist and raise questions about the centrality of gender differences in human mating.* By not paying sufficient attention to the distinction between what people say they want (their stated preferences) and what people actually want (their revealed preferences), the picture of human mating that has emerged from this field is deeply flawed.

---

* Although if you do raise questions, you risk being personally dismissed as unscientific. In the episode I quoted earlier, Rogan and his guest Dr. David Buss accuse my graduate school advisor, Dr. Alice Eagly, of engaging in grift and perpetrating anti-science delusions by mentoring students like me.

Homo sapiens, Bonded by Evolution

This book brings together different disciplines—including psychology, anthropology, and sociology—to challenge the especially grim tenets of the EvoScript and present an alternative vision of attraction and romantic relationships. This alternative revolves around compatibility-driven bonding. It is every bit as scientific and connected to evolutionary principles—arguably even more so—yet it yields strikingly different conclusions.

Part 1 critically examines the three central pillars of the EvoScript: Mate value, gender differences, and the short-term vs. long-term distinction. It explores why the importance of mate value in real-world contexts is relatively short-lived, and why men and women sometimes *say* they prefer different things, when in fact—with one or two exceptions—their *actual* preferences are extremely similar. We will also explore why pursuing a "short-term strategy"—playing the field, and trying to keep things casual—has remarkably little bearing on someone's long-term relationship prospects.

In part 2 we will review *relationship science,* a different evolutionary vision that focuses on pair-bonding and compatibility. I will show that people evolved to form emotionally meaningful attachment bonds, which prompt couples to look out for each other, push each other to greater heights, and unconsciously avoid tempting alternative partners. We will also explore compatibility, and we'll learn why it is essential to attraction and relationships. Compatibility is often puzzling and elusive, because it has little to do with the match between two people's traits and attributes. Instead, compatible relationships require that two people co-construct a coherent narrative about who they are as a couple—and that they work together to set up healthy rituals and patterns and help each other grow.

The final section of this book describes the implications of these different visions for the way that people approach dating and relationships in the twenty-first century. We will explore why online dating works well in some ways, but is a time-waster in others, and how it excels at being addictive and making us feel terrible about ourselves. I'll describe other online environments that have hijacked the EvoScript in recent years, purporting to use the science of human mating to justify a regressive and misogynistic ideology. Finally, this book will show that people have an easier time navigating the modern dating world when they spend their time cultivating (or even upending) their social networks rather than pursuing literal dates.

But before we begin dismantling the three pillars of the EvoScript, there are a few critical issues to be tackled. The first is about how scientists who study human mating approach relationships between two people who are the same gender or a different gender.

This book will interleave research that examines the romantic and sexual experiences of people with different sexual orientations. By and large, the factors that make for strong couples tend to be the same for mixed- and same-gender couples alike, and regardless of sexual orientation. Couples tend to be happier to the extent that they are responsive and attuned to each other; couples remain committed if they can constructively resolve conflicts and are lucky enough to sidestep stress; couples experience more conflict when they become parents.

Some differences do emerge: Perhaps because people in same-sex relationships are not bound by contemporary gender norms in the home, they commonly achieve equality in the way they divide chores and responsibilities (unlike mixed-gender couples, see figure i.1). And sexual minorities may encounter unique challenges: For example, gay men and lesbian women are more likely to be victims of stigma and prejudice, and these stressors may force them to keep their feelings or relationships secret. Trans men and women face particularly acute exclusionary forces in the dating arena.[25]

The EvoScript offers assertions about how heterosexual attraction and mixed-gender relationships reflect a psychology that people inherited from their distant ancestors. Therefore, for the most part, the research that supports this script has tended to ask men how they feel about women and women how they feel about men. Evolutionary psychology sometimes features sexual minorities, too—there are perspectives that explain the evolutionary origin and ancestral function of same-sex sexual attraction—but the EvoScript has mainly held lessons for what makes men appealing to women and what makes women appealing to men. Nevertheless, in this book, we will sometimes find that new lessons emerge when we highlight the relationships of sexual minorities and other couples who do not fit heteronormative scripts. This book ultimately contains useful takeaways for people of all genders and sexualities.[26]

The second critical issue is about how scientists draw conclusions from data in the first place. In some branches of science, we need to make binary "it's there" or "it's not there" decisions. For example, scientists often need to know whether a new vaccine provides immunity that exceeds some reasonable baseline. If the vaccine's effectiveness exceeds 50 percent, it's approved; otherwise, no approval.

But in attraction and relationships research, knowing that an effect "is there" (e.g., people who are stressed get in more fights with their partners) is often insufficient; we also need to know how big that effect is. For this reason, I'll often describe findings in terms of *effect sizes* with comparative language like "small," "medium," and "large" (figure i.1). Intuitively, you can think of small effects as "invisible to the naked eye," medium effects would be clear to you if you are paying close attention, and large effects should be pretty obvious to anyone. Effects in this research area only occasionally get bigger than "large," and if they are smaller than "small," they are unlikely to be terribly important.

If you (like me) think about the world in terms of probabilities, appendix A shows you how to translate small, medium, and large effect sizes into an intuitive guessing game. For our stress-fighting example: the effect of stress on relationship conflict is medium-size, which means that if you had a stressed couple and an unstressed couple in front of you, the odds that the stressed couple fights more often is about 65 percent (and the odds that the unstressed couple fights more often is about 35 percent).[27]

By focusing on effect sizes throughout this book, we will arrive at conclusions that are sounder, more nuanced, and better calibrated to the data. And—as we'll see with respect to the importance of mate

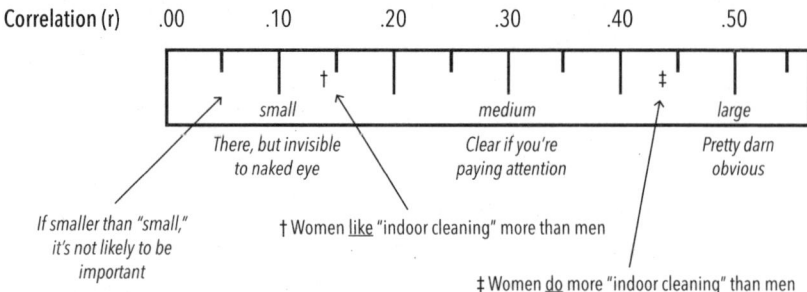

FIGURE i.1
Effect size "ruler" for research on attraction and relationships

Note: A correlation (r) is a type of effect size that describes how strongly associated two variables are. Correlations allow us to put different effects on the same common ruler. For example, in heterosexual couples, women are more likely to *do* the indoor cleaning than men ($r = .44$). This gender difference is fairly obvious. But do women *like* indoor cleaning more than men? Yes, but this effect is fairly small ($r = .14$), and you wouldn't really be able to notice it with the "naked eye."[28]

value in the next chapter—effect sizes illuminate how some forces in the real world affect attraction powerfully, some matter a little, and some barely matter at all.

I OPENED THIS CHAPTER with my friend's advice, which was in essence: "Nerd, improve thyself." His idea—that human mating takes place within a competitive market—is coherent. It's an idea that seems to fit many people's experiences. It's an idea that assuages the adult part of your brain that sternly says, "You can't always get what you want." It's an idea that appears at first glance to be backed up by science.

But surprisingly, the idea is spectacularly flawed. In the end, finding a partner who makes you happy has remarkably little to do with showing off—or landing a partner with—the right traits. This basic lesson will come up repeatedly throughout this book. Traits related to mate value aren't terribly important once two people get to know each other; almost anyone can be a good or a terrible long-term relationship partner, depending on the circumstances. The differences in what men and women actually want are quite small, and people don't really have a stable "type." The lingering presence of these ideas in our culture makes romantic success harder for many people than it needs to be. In fact, this book makes the scientific case that people who adopt the lessons of the EvoScript are *reducing* the likelihood that they will find a partner who makes them happy.

Your own traits matter *for you,* of course. If you are an avoidant or anxious person, you probably feel a gnawing skepticism about intimacy and romance. Your outlook means that, relative to a typical secure person, you probably don't find your relationships to be deliriously happy. But you are not fixed or immutable, either. When people seek therapy for their depression, for example, they typically find that their close relationships—romantic, platonic, and familial—improve across the board. And the right relationship can be transformative, turning a fearful and jaded person into a contented and optimistic one. Romantic luck and chaos are impressive forces, and no one's romantic destiny is predetermined.[29]

This book will illustrate how attraction is best depicted as a process of finding—and oftentimes creating—a compatible relationship within a small set of romantic options. Although the mating market is an inadequate metaphor for understanding human romantic relationships, we won't jettison it entirely; online dating is here to stay, and we need to understand what people are doing when they feel like mate shopping. And, surely, there are many people who have done quite well by acting as though the search for a mate is like perusing a marketplace; humans are extraordinarily flexible creatures, and we evolved the capacity to find love and sex in a staggeringly large variety of settings. Nevertheless, by understanding how humans have historically sought compatible partners in small networks, we can build a truly relational alternative to the EvoScript that provides a clearer—and brighter—picture of how attraction and relationships work.

· PART 1 ·

The Lies We're Told About Love

· 1 ·

Measuring Desirability

Here is a story about how I learned my place.

It is 1999, and I'm at Cornell University in upstate New York. The school is big enough to foster considerable anonymity, and the dazzling cold makes it easy to disappear under the requisite winter hat, scarf, and parka. On one such freezing morning in early November, a woman approaches me in the middle of the sidewalk. This is not a common occurrence. Did I drop something? Will I be asked to make a donation? Surely she has mistaken me for someone else? She exudes a social confidence that feels like a foreign language.

I quickly discover that she knows who I am; we went to the same high school. After fumbling awkwardly through the first few minutes of conversation, it finally occurs to me to blurt out that I have a car, since the easiest way to travel back to our hometown outside of Boston is a six-hour car trip. We exchange email addresses.

Anna is younger than me, but she possesses an uncommon level of sophistication. She is tall and striking; when she enters a room, the center of gravity shifts in her direction. She is fluent in Russian, she is a fan of classic films, and she writes poetry. She is friends with interesting people. On the 1–10 EvoScript scale of mate value, Anna is a 9.[*]

---

[*] Throughout this chapter, I deliberately use this 1–10 scale in the way that people (including evolutionary psychologists) might use the concept of mate value: as if it referred to a core, objective truth about a person's desirability as agreed upon by others. However, as we'll see, such judgments end up being largely—and in some cases near-totally—subjective.

I, on the other hand, would be considered a 6. I'm not bad-looking, but at this particular moment in my life I don't exercise much, so my physique can charitably be described as "doughy-adjacent." More problematic is that I have very little social cachet: I wake up early, dutifully attend all my classes, study hard, and spend any remaining free time with a small group of close friends. I'm a little too proud of the fact that I rarely go to parties, and when I do, I'll glom onto the one or two people I already know. I have not yet learned the fine art of mingling.

A drive home together over the holiday break gives Anna and me a chance to get to know each other. The conversation is easy; I initially award the credit to her charming lack of inhibition, but maybe I'm playing a role, too—I do seem to be making her laugh. We talk about exes and the Beatles and my pet gecko named Ringo. We make plans to hang out in person over the break. Cue butterflies.

And we do hang out. A lot. Whereas most month-long breaks reach a plateau of dreary sameness, this one is jam-packed. I go with her to buy her first guitar, and I teach her how to play. We get high and watch *Yellow Submarine*. She shares with me some poetry she has written, and I set it to music. Critically, whatever tiny crushes and flings she had mentioned previously all seem to be evaporating. It feels like I can't lose.

Or can I? On the one hand, we are spending a massive amount of time together. Not many women have ever wanted to spend this much time with me without being at least somewhat into me. She emails regularly, and she returns every voicemail that I leave for her. On the other hand, when it's just the two of us? She's not giving me any signals. If anything, she seems to know exactly how *not* to give off signals. She never touches my arm accidentally. She never catches my eye for too long. We watch *My Fair Lady;* she stays on her side of the couch. Wistfully, I stay on mine.

By January, it's becoming obvious that if something doesn't happen soon, we will retreat to our disconnected social circles. This is my biggest fear, because I have tremendous doubts about my ability to hack it in her universe. As I mentioned, she is friends with interesting people. And many of these interesting people are also men who are accomplished, charming, and *hot*. Men who are worldly like her and who thrive in her social milieu.

As we arrive back at school, we make plans to watch one of the remaining movies on her bucket list for me: *It's a Mad, Mad, Mad, Mad World*. I am initially delighted to see the three-and-a-half hour running time as we head up to her room.

Except now, the signals are crystal clear, and they are decidedly inauspicious. If I move in her direction, she moves away. She receives phone calls from other people, and she takes them. I retreat to a corner of her twin bed; wow, this movie is long. When it is over, I say good night and head home.

Later that same night, after I leave, she goes to hang out with some other friends. Within a couple of days, she has a new crush in her life that she is hooking up with. I won't lie: He's pretty damn good-looking.

LEARNING YOUR PLACE in the dating pool can be a brutal process. You come to understand your intrinsic mate value—whether you are an appealing 8 or a lackluster 3—through repeated rejection. Are you rejected by only the most desirable people, or by pretty much everyone? Your answer to this question feels like an indication of your rank: your position in the hierarchy of desirability. This feeling shapes the romantic risks that you take, the situations you walk into, and the speed with which you count yourself out. After all, rejection hurts. If you continually aim too high with your attentions and affections, you'll receive an extra dose of ridicule and mockery. Find your rank and stay put, or fry like Icarus.

According to this logic, I was a fool for thinking I had a shot with Anna. Put simply, Anna was more attractive than me and more socially skilled than me. Even though she enjoyed spending time with me, she could attract someone with a lot more value than what I had to offer. I never spent much time with the good-looking guy she fell for that January, but nevertheless, I was competing with him—and I lost. For anyone of any gender who has had the experience of being rejected for someone else, the EvoScript is the voice that says: "This is your core essence. You're just not desirable enough. Get used to it."

In some cases, that voice offers an even more sweeping indictment. In this story, it might tell me that I was a willing participant in my own swindling. It whispers that I was a useful tool in the short term to alleviate Anna's boredom, and I should have known better than to walk right into the friendzone. Aggrieved men online might point to stories like mine to gin up misogyny: Anna was just another attractive, popular woman who gets everything she wants in life and delights in making sure that beta males like me know my place.

This interpretation—that Anna is a winner and I am a loser in the marketplace of mating—distorts the specifics of this story, and more important, it distorts the abstract, generalizable lesson about how romantic attachments form and what sustains them. To understand why, we need to scrutinize—and disassemble—the mate value concept.

We All Have a Value

It is a basic fact in evolutionary biology that animals differ in something called *reproductive success*. Put simply, only some individuals of a given species produce offspring who survive to reproduce themselves. Critically, members of early human (and protohuman) groups who made prudent mate choices—perhaps by identifying mates who had high reproductive potential—sent their own genes forward into future generations and became our ancestors. The ones who made poor choices did not.

Animals are not clairvoyant; they cannot directly peer into the future and know which potential mates are destined to be reproductive champions. So they try to size it up as best they can, usually by assessing whether potential mates possess traits that have historically been decent signals of reproductive success. This set of trait judgments is what evolutionary psychologists mean by the term *mate value*.

The EvoScript proclaims that mate value lingers among humans living today: Even if you don't have any intention of reproducing anytime soon (or ever), you have nevertheless inherited the instinct to assess others' mate value, and you have a mate value yourself. My friend's "how not to be a dating loser" list from the introduction is a fine illustration of the mate value concept. The more you possess these desirable traits—like attractiveness, or confidence, or a good sense of humor—the more mate value you have. Possessing the trait doesn't need to be binary, of course; the sexier you are, the better. These traits could have different origins, too: Some traits may derive from your genetics; others might be acquired through hard work and persistence. Some, like status, could accrue with time; others, like youth itself, slowly fade. Critically, your mate value is an amalgamation of all these appealing traits at a given moment in time—your worth on the open market.

Traits do not need to be universally desirable across all contexts to be a part of someone's mate value. As an avid 8-bit Nintendo player in the early nineties, I fully understood that this skill added nothing to my mate value while attending junior high. In gamer communities today, it could well be an asset. In other words, cultures can shape whether a specific modern skill or trait is linked to broader attributes—someone's status, social skills, or value to the local group—which would have been a reliable signal of reproductive success in ancestral times.

When it comes to figuring out your own mate value, parallels with self-esteem are clarifying. People develop their sense of self-esteem by paying exceedingly close attention to what other people in their social environment are doing and thinking. You have learned about your own traits and skills by comparing yourself to your friends' and acquaintances' traits and skills. Relatedly, most people seek validation for what they bring to the table: It is a natural human experience to feel delighted when you sense acceptance from others, and it stings when you don't feel appreciated.[1]

People learn about their mate value through a similar process: by paying attention to the partners who desire them and the partners who don't. These experiences teach people where they fit in the hierarchy. For example, if members of your preferred gender repeatedly fawn over you because of your attractiveness, your confidence, or your charisma, you would surmise that your mate value is sky high, and you'd come to believe that you deserve the most desirable partners. But if you never receive positive feedback—or if you receive negative feedback—you'd likely come to believe the opposite. And in this system, some traits seem to matter more than others. Of course, it's not a bad thing to be seen as kind, trustworthy, smart, and dependable, but generally speaking, your sense of your mate value is especially tightly linked to your attractiveness and social potency.[2]

People carry this internalized sense of their value with them, and it affects their actual behavior. Studies that capture videos of actual first dates find that people who believe that they have high mate value (e.g., they strongly agree with statements like "Members of the opposite sex are attracted to me") behave in ways that generate a self-fulfilling prophecy. Specifically, these folks act more flirtatious when meeting new potential partners, which in turn makes them more popular. People with a high sense of mate value also tend to be choosier about who they are willing to date. In essence, when people feel like they have mate value, they act with confidence, and they set their sights higher.[3]

The EvoScript tells us that mate value shapes not just initial attraction—the people we are willing to consider romantically—but also our relationships once we do couple up. If two high-value mates are in a long-term relationship, then each needs to maintain their mate value, or risk losing their partner. Significant mate-value shifts within an existing couple—if one partner's physical attractiveness radically changes, or if one partner suddenly becomes much more successful or wealthy—are dangerous because the now-high-value partner is likely to seek out a new relationship that more accurately reflects their new status. In the narrative of EvoScript, no relationship is safe from the pressures of the market, and a relationship can only be happy and successful when couples are equally matched.

Mate value appears to explain the inner workings of celebrity relationships, as in the cliché that one person's meteoric rise (and positive shift in mate value) precipitates their decision to end a long-term relationship—even the relationship that supported their ascent in the first place (Harrison Ford, JLo, Jim Carrey, Lorde). Everyday folks spend vast amounts of time and energy trying to keep their faces and bodies looking good, not just to be healthy, but to appear youthful and therefore maintain their mate value (which declines with age, perhaps particularly for women). Influencers on social media have plenty of tips on hand. And when those tips don't actually work for people, and they sense that their mate value doesn't stack up, they're more likely to feel depressed and anxious, and they lower their romantic expectations accordingly or begin to feel concerned about their relationships.[4]

Mate value is thus tied to how we feel about ourselves: It reflects our personal history of translating the responses we get from others into romantic self-confidence. Our sense of our own mate value also shapes who we believe is deserving of our love (or sexual attention) and whose love we, in turn, deserve.

The Matching Phenomenon

According to the popular ideas in the EvoScript, the power of mate value is best illustrated by the *matching phenomenon:* the fact that dating and married couples tend to match on various traits that are connected to mate value. This phenomenon is clearest for physical attractiveness: That is, physically attractive people tend to date and marry other physically attractive people. As the explanation goes, people can afford to be as selective as their physical attractiveness level permits, and so they end up attracting a partner who is about as hot as they are. Recall that humans have supposedly inherited a tendency to maximize their own reproductive chances by pursuing the mates with the best traits. The matching phenomenon emerges, therefore, because people will choose—or settle for—the highest mate-value mate that they can get.

I demonstrate the depressing nature of the matching phenomenon to my students by using a classic evolutionary psychological classroom activity. I begin by giving each student a card with a random number ranging from 1 to 10. I then tell all my students to hold up their cards to their foreheads so that their number is in full view to their peers, but unseen to themselves. This card is their value, and each student's job is to form a mutual "match" with the highest-value partner who will accept them back.

A melee will then unfold, as everyone lurches toward the 9s and 10s. These magnificent specimens will quickly surmise that they must have done quite well in this lottery, and they'll turn to select each other. Those who do not pair off at this point will start checking out the prospective partners with middling values, hoping to catch a 6 or maybe a 7. The others find that people are still refusing to make eye contact, and they will no doubt feel a chill coming over them; how bad, they wonder, is their value exactly? Is it still possible to land a 5 or a 4? In the end, those students who had received a 1 or a 2 will settle for someone else at the bottom of the scale.[5]

Countless research studies demonstrate the scientific validity of the matching phenomenon, and the steps required to capture it are straightforward. First, a researcher would acquire photographs of some couples. Second, the researcher would ask independent "coders" to rate all the people in these photographs on, say, a 1–10 attractiveness scale.[*] Third, the researcher would calculate whether the two members of the couple tended to be similarly attractive. In general, studies like these find a degree of similarity that is halfway between medium and large on our ruler from the introduction (figure i.1).[6]

In everyday language, here is what "halfway between medium and large" means. Imagine a woman of average attractiveness, standing next to two men. Your job is to guess which of these two men is her current romantic partner. If you picked the man who was closest to

---

[*] In most studies, researchers measure physical attractiveness like this—holistically—because it offers the best window into people's subjective experiences of another person's aesthetic appeal. In principle, there are objective features that partially underlie these subjective judgments: symmetry, "averageness," expressive features, youthful features, prominent cheekbones for women, a prominent jawline for men, and so on. But the reality is that an amalgamation of these objective features still yields a less useful and less comprehensive measure of a person's attractiveness relative to the holistic human coders.

her attractiveness level, you would be correct about 70 percent of the time. (It would be the same odds if your job was to guess between two women standing next to one man.) A casual observer could detect an effect of that size, and that's why matching on physical attractiveness is probably not news to you.

As a way of explaining the inner workings of the mating market, this portion of the EvoScript is, for most people, quite dispiriting. As unreal as my classroom demo is—none of us really walk around with a number stuck to our heads—the concept of mate value appears to matter in real life for the two main reasons I have just articulated. First, people have a sense of how desirable they are to others, and they act accordingly in first-impression contexts. Second, they tend to date and marry other people who are similar to them in terms of their attractiveness.

These findings are real and reliable. But they are not the whole story.

The Social Relations Model

The notion that some people have high mate-value traits and others do not contains a vital but hidden assumption: Observers must *agree* who has the traits and who does not. Organisms who evolved to assess one another's traits for the purpose of anticipating future reproductive success would need to demonstrate a reasonable amount of consensus about who, in fact, has those traits. My matching phenomenon class demonstration works because the students' numbers were visible to others; had all the numbers been hidden from view, there would have been no matching at all, and the card would not have mattered. But in the real world, do other people agree about each other's mate value as easily as reading a number on someone's forehead? Not even close.

To understand how people assess mate value, we need a tool called the Social Relations Model (or SRM, for short). This tool comes from a research tradition that examines how people perceive and understand other people. The premise of the SRM is that any subjective judgment that one person makes about another person (e.g., "He is sexy" or "I want to date her" or "She has high mate value") is the sum of three factors: the consensus factor (the person the judgment is *about*), the selectivity factor (the person *making* the judgment), and the compatibility factor (the unique *combination* of the two people). The SRM is straightforward, but it is also truly profound: It might be the single most important concept in the science of human social relationships.[7]

When I was just getting to know Anna, I fell head over heels for her. The SRM says there are three factors that contributed to my feelings. The first one captures Anna's mate value; the second and third have nothing to do with it.

The first factor is that there was something especially desirable about Anna herself. I mentioned earlier that Anna was a 9 and that she was popular—people generally seemed to gravitate toward her. There is something about Anna that inspired head-over-heels feelings, and the implication here is that anyone else who knew her would have felt similarly. This is the consensus factor, and for mate value to matter, this factor must be prominent.

The second factor derives from the way I perceived people in general. I was head over heels, yes, but what does that say about me? Perhaps at that point in my life, I was so desperate to make a connection that I would have been super into any woman spending time with me. This is the selectivity factor.

The third factor is specifically about the combination of me and Anna. That is, perhaps there was something about her that was uniquely appealing to me, above and beyond her popularity (i.e., the consensus factor) and my desperation (i.e., the selectivity factor). This third element derived from the specific relationship that I had with her: I might have felt that she was uniquely amazing in a way that no one else did. This is the compatibility factor.

These three factors are not mutually exclusive; they work together and add up to the one whole "thing." In the case of Anna, that "thing" was "I am super into you," but the SRM says that all interpersonal judgments and feelings—positive, negative, or anywhere in between—can be broken down this way. I might evaluate Anna on traits like sexiness or confidence; you might be thinking about how much you want to spend time with Sarah; Jeff thinks his co-worker Bob is insufferable. The SRM always applies.

But the three ingredients are not necessarily equally important. To understand how this works, it's useful to think about a basic three-ingredient cocktail. To make a daiquiri, for example, you take three parts rum, two parts lime juice, and one part simple syrup. Out of six total parts, that's 50 percent rum, 33 percent lime juice, and 17 percent simple syrup. Once you mix them all together, you have one thing—a delicious daiquiri—but the three ingredients came together in particular amounts to create the whole drink.

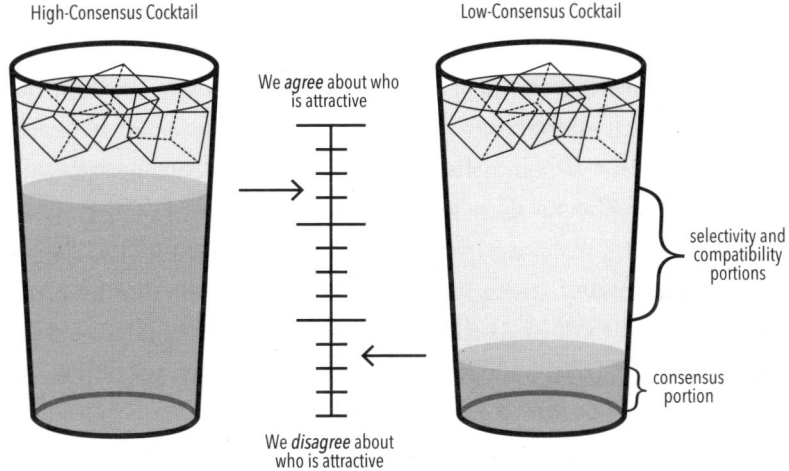

FIGURE 1.1

Consensus is one part of the attraction cocktail (hypothetical data)

Note: Sometimes attraction is a high-consensus cocktail, and sometimes attraction is a low-consensus cocktail. Less consensus (dark gray shading) means more room in the cocktail for selectivity and compatibility (light gray shading).

Attraction is a three-ingredient cocktail—the feelings we have for another person reflect some percentage of each of the consensus, selectivity, and compatibility factors. But the relative balance of these three factors can shift depending on the context. Since we're mainly concerned with mate value in this chapter, let's imagine that the consensus factor made up the largest (shaded) portion of the cocktail (the glass on the left in figure 1.1). In this case, we would mostly agree about who is attractive and who is not. Like my class demo card game, there is little room left in the top part of the glass for selectivity and compatibility to play a role. Alternatively, imagine that the consensus factor was a modest portion of the cocktail (the glass on the right in figure 1.1). In this case, we would barely agree about who is attractive and who is not; attraction would mostly consist of selectivity and compatibility.

Making matters even more challenging is that the three factors come together in your mind without any conscious awareness or intention; you can't grit your teeth, think really hard, and intuit the extent to which your feelings about someone's attractiveness are due to consensus or selectivity or compatibility. There's a simple reason why this is true: Knowing the proportions requires access to many other people's minds all at once, which the average person doesn't have. But enterprising scientists can collect the data and crunch the stats.

According to the EvoScript, the consensus portion of the attractiveness and romantic desirability cocktail should be the largest share—people *should* strongly agree who has mate value and who does not. It might not be as clear as a number on someone's forehead, but it should be in that ballpark. But a small consensus portion would indicate that mate value is murky and invisible, or that others seem not to be using mate value when they arrive at some judgment about how much they like you.

Running SRM studies can be time-intensive and complex. But going through all that work is worth it because the findings that emerge from this approach can be compared to some standard benchmarks for what counts as "large," "medium," or "small." That is, the findings can tell us whether attraction in a particular context is more like the large-consensus drink on the left (which would mean that mate value shapes attraction dynamics powerfully), or like the small-consensus drink on the right (which would mean that mate value has little practical importance for you and your life).[8]

One common approach is to ask people to judge the attractiveness of prospective partners they've never met. To illustrate: Picture a celebrity who you would rate as a 10. Now, ask your friends what they think of this person, and for the sake of argument, let's assume that these friends are commonly attracted to the same gender as you. Their ratings will reveal plenty of 10s, but surely some 8s and 9s, too. If you poll far and wide, maybe you'll get a handful of 7s or even a 6. Had you instead chosen a celebrity who you would rate as a 5, I suspect you'd find similarly strong levels of agreement in the 3–7 range. In other words, we *mostly* agree on who's hot, and we *mostly* agree on who's not. Agreement isn't perfect, but the ratings are certainly not evenly distributed across the scale. No one thinks your hottest pick is a 1.

In most cases, you have presumably never met these celebrities face-to-face; you're basing your judgments off of what you've seen in movies, on television and maybe Instagram. Most studies of human mating use pictures and videos, too. Sometimes they collect people's impressions of celebrities, but more commonly, these studies use realistic computer-generated faces, or photographs of everyday people. Often they look like what you see in figure 1.2.

FIGURE 1.2
Stimuli in a typical photo-rating design

Note: Photograph studies often ask people to rate faces like these. These photos are actually members of my laboratory, posing in the style of the faces used in a study by Dr. Hehman, Dr. Xie, and colleagues,[9] which came from the Chicago Face Database.[10]

The common thread here is that researchers ask people to evaluate targets they have never actually met and almost surely will never meet.

(*I* have met these two people. You likely have not.) The overwhelming majority of studies that have demonstrated the critical role of physical attractiveness uses these designs because such studies can be run fairly easily in a typical university research laboratory.

In these studies, consensus effects are reasonably strong. Participants show some agreement about who is attractive and who is not. In all the studies that have collected SRM data on ratings of photographs, the consensus portion is medium-to-large in size—check out the leftmost glass in figure 1.3. A value this large means that it would be hard not to notice that people tend to agree about who is attractive.

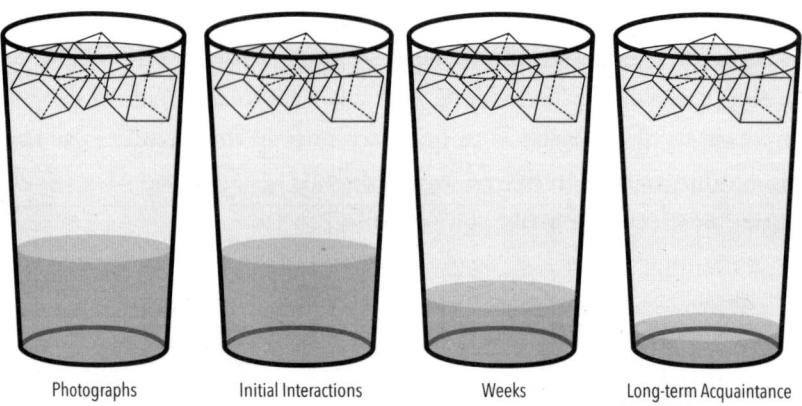

FIGURE 1.3
Consensus declines as people get to know each other (the real data)

Note: The dark gray shading in this figure illustrates the extent to which observers agree (i.e., consensus) when making physical attractiveness and romantic desire judgments about a person. The light gray shading is the portion due to selectivity and compatibility. Consensus in photographs and initial interaction settings is considered "medium to large" (but still not the majority share), consensus after knowing someone for weeks is "small," and consensus in long-term acquaintance settings is inconsequential. Estimates come from seventeen different studies.[11]

But even though the consensus factor is meaningful, it is still outweighed by the selectivity and compatibility factors. Notice how the dark shaded portion takes up far less than half of the leftmost drink in figure 1.3. Beauty is mostly in the eye of the beholder (the light gray portion), even when we behold photographs of strangers. A fascinating analysis by Dr. Johannes Hönekopp examined ratings of photographs of approximately two hundred men and women—not celebs, just regular people posing with neutral facial expressions—from the United States and Germany. Each face was evaluated on attractiveness by about forty volunteers in a study. For the vast majority of the faces (approximately 96 percent), *at least one* of these volunteers placed the face in the top half of his/her personal rankings, while someone else also placed the exact same face in the bottom half of his/her personal rankings. In other words, *all* the raters agreed "top half" or "bottom half" on merely 4 percent of the photographs. Even with a modest number of people eyeing you, odds are, someone thinks you're not half-bad.[12]

Nevertheless, consensus matters in settings where all you have to go on is a photograph. Hot men, and especially hot women, get plenty of attention in the form of swipes and messages when online dating. Mate value matters in this context, even if it is not the be-all and end-all, and even if there is far less agreement about mate value than reading a number on a person's forehead.

The consensus factor is also reasonably large when people meet face-to-face in real life, too. In figure 1.3, the portion due to consensus in initial face-to-face interactions is essentially the same as what you see for photographs. Again, this is a meaningful level of agreement: When people first meet each other, there are popular people and unpopular people. You will likely meet someone who is into you—when we conducted speed-dating research to study initial attraction, 96 percent of our speed-daters received at least one second date offer—but neither is the playing field level.

Mate Value Is Ephemeral

The thing is, most romantic relationships don't spring into existence after an initial interaction. We continue to evaluate how we feel about potential romantic partners as we get to know them over time. One recent study found that about *two-thirds* of romantic relationships grow out of long-term friendships, and the amount of time that passes between when people first meet and when they begin a dating relationship is almost always measured in weeks, months, or even years. (We'll revisit these counterintuitive facts many times throughout this book.) This protracted period of romantic suspense remains true even in the online dating age.* And in humans' ancestral past, given how rarely new people moved in and out of each other's lives, this extended pattern is likely to have been quite common.[13]

You can probably recall cases where someone seemed quite appealing at first: a chiseled jaw and a bright smile that won you over instantly. And then, as time passed, your impression changed. Maybe it was a subtle shift, as if every time you saw him, his appeal was a little weaker—like a distant echo of that first bolt of lightning. Maybe it was dramatic: After hearing his third off-color joke, you realized that his beady little eyes made him look like a comic book villain. Initial impressions can change, even when it comes to seemingly static properties like physical attractiveness.

Now add one additional ingredient, which is that the change might not happen the same way for all observers. Maybe your friend thought chiseled-jaw guy was dreamy at first, and she still thinks he's pretty dreamy. Your impression declined; your friend's remained positive. And neither of you are wrong, per se. You didn't change your opinion because you discovered chiseled-jaw guy's true mediocre nature; you discovered that he was not the "kind of hot" that appeals to you. This phenomenon isn't limited to people who initially seem appealing. Negative impressions can also grow more and more positive—at least for some subset of perceivers—over time.

In other words, as people get to know each other, we see shifts in their judgments. If these shifts differ from perceiver to perceiver, the implications for our understanding of mate value are dramatic. Think

---

* In one of the largest and most comprehensive studies on this topic, the *median* time between meeting someone and officially forming a relationship with them was thirty days for people who met online dating, and a full ninety days for people who met through other means. The *averages* were a whopping eight months and twenty-one months, respectively.

about it: Unless people all shift their impression the same amount in the same direction, disagreement will grow. Any agreement that perceivers exhibited when looking at photographs or in an initial face-to-face encounter will start to erode, as some people's impressions improve, some decline, and some stay the same. Altogether, the consensus portion should decline.

Evidence for this shift is also shown in figure 1.3. A study I conducted with my former graduate student Dr. Lucy Hunt examined how straight college students felt about their other-gender classmates in a small seminar with fifteen to twenty people. After these students got to know each other over a few weeks, the consensus portion dropped. Some perceivers saw 9s become 6s; some perceivers saw 2s become 5s; and some perceivers stayed true to their original opinions. Now, consensus was in the small-to-medium range (see the third cocktail glass in the figure), and this was true for both physical attractiveness judgments and romantic desire judgments.[14]

Critically, the shift doesn't stop after a few weeks. Studies have also examined these judgments in existing networks of friends and acquaintances—the context which spawns most relationships. If we take a snapshot of the consensus values in these settings, the values are in the zone of "not even small" effects. The tiny amount of consensus in that fourth cocktail glass in figure 1.3 means that if I think you're hot, someone else agrees with me a mere 53 percent of the time. This value barely beats 50/50 chance.[15]

This low level of agreement is astounding. These are people who really know you. They probably agree about how extroverted you are, how likely you are to order the jalapeño poppers, and how likely you are to start quoting *The Office* after two drinks. But they do not agree on your mate value; some of them think you're datable, and some of them don't. In this crowd, your mate value is an intangible mist.

The decline in consensus over time means that mate value is ephemeral. I'm not arguing that mate value isn't real; naturally, some people are initially more desirable than others. But regardless of how appealing someone seems to be on the surface, the effects of mate value dissipate as people get to know each other. The consensus of the snap judgments that people make about you is far less consequential than everything else in the attraction cocktail, which means that some prospective partners likely think you are a catch, especially as time passes. The EvoScript makes no mention of these low consensus numbers, and so it offers a mangled interpretation of the role of mate value.

I have focused mainly on consensus thus far, which is the formal foundation of the mate value concept. But if consensus is declining over time, something must be happening with the other SRM factors—selectivity and compatibility—to fill up the rest of the cocktail.

The selectivity factor reflects the fact that people carry around their own personal lenses that they use to view the world. I might be particularly open-minded, and so everyone looks datable to me. You, on the other hand, are notoriously selective, and you think most potential partners look like trolls. But critically, selectivity effects for attraction don't seem to trade off against consensus with increasing acquaintance—it probably isn't changing as consensus declines.[16]

That leaves the compatibility factor. Set aside how desirable everyone thinks you are (consensus) and how desirable I tend to find everyone (selectivity). The compatibility factor captures how I feel about you above and beyond all that. This compatibility factor is the nerdy, algebraic way of saying some people "fit" together, and some people don't.

SRM studies find that the compatibility factor is where we see the major trade-off against consensus with increasing acquaintance. That is, in a group of people who are getting to know each other, the portion due to consensus gradually declines, and the portion due to compatibility goes up. Put differently, in initial attraction contexts, consensus and compatibility are about equally important. But in long-term acquaintance contexts—once a few weeks or months have passed—the compatibility factor is quite powerful. If I know you well, most of my romantic feelings for you are about compatibility. In this context, your consensual hotness and my desperation probably can't explain why I'm super into you. Rather, I like you because I think that there is something unique about us; we work well together. For humans, beauty is in the eye of the continually reinterpreting beholder.[17]

The Fading Power of Physical Attractiveness

If a person's agreed-upon mate value begins to disappear as people get to know each other, we should see evidence for this shift in other subtle ways. One clear prediction is that the power and influence of physical attractiveness—the most central component of mate value—should weaken over time.

Earlier, we discussed the matching phenomenon with respect to desirable traits like physical attractiveness. That is, dating and married couples exhibit moderately to strongly similar physical attractiveness levels, presumably because the more attractive you are, the more you competed successfully with other suitors to win over an attractive partner in the first place. The ephemeral mate value idea generates the prediction that there should be conditions when the level of matching is higher or lower. Specifically, couples might show larger attractiveness mismatches if their relationship formed when the compatibility factor was dominant. Here is what we need to know, then: How well did the two members of the couple know each other *before they actually got together*?

Let's walk through it. In a situation where heterosexual people are just getting to know each other, the consensus factor is meaningful. I find it useful to draw parallels to the annual migration of U.S. adolescents to summer camp. At first, mate value should matter: Dating will be competitive because people will be especially likely to pursue the consensually attractive people. When relationships form under these circumstances, attractive people will pair up with attractive people, and unattractive people pair up with unattractive people. In these cases, the matching effect on attractiveness will be strong, just like the pairing game I conducted in my class.

But as the summer progresses, and our hypothetical adolescent camp attendees have gotten to know each other well, it should become less clear who the desirable partners are. The attractive single people shouldn't get to exert as much leverage on who they date, and some of the unattractive single people should have more opportunities to date people who are generally considered quite attractive. The level of physical-attractiveness matching in relationships that form at this later point in time should be weak; on an early August night, anything can happen! Lest my camp analogy seem fantastical and strange, remember that relationships commonly take time to form, like the study showing that two-thirds of couples described themselves as "friends first" before they started dating.[18]

The real-life studies fit my summer-camp narrative. One study from 2015 calculated the power of the attractiveness-matching effect depending on two related factors: How long couple members had known each other before getting together, and whether the couples described themselves as "friends first." Both measures showed the same thing: Attractiveness matching was large for couples who got together quickly or who were not friends first, but it was much smaller for couples who had known each other for a while beforehand or who were friends first. It is worth noting that the couples in this study mostly formed their relationships before online dating was so dominant. Attractiveness matching will likely be stronger in samples of couples who met on Tinder because online dating creates a more competitive marketplace. But the general principle still holds: If you are getting to know a large network of potential partners over time, your mate value is less likely to limit your prospects than if you are trying to hit up strangers.[19]

SO HOW MUCH of an advantage does attractiveness give someone in finding love? Consensually beautiful people certainly do tend to be popular; simply observe who gets the right swipes and who gets hit on at the club. When studies ask independent coders to rate a set of speed-daters on their level of attractiveness, the speed-daters who received higher marks tend to be more popular at the speed-dating event.[20]

But does physical attractiveness continue to exert large effects in the many relationships that form from existing friendships? It does not. In fact, physical attractiveness barely matters at all.

Recently, my colleagues and I collected and analyzed data examining the underexplored stretch of time after two people first meet, but before they form an actual relationship. In this study, around two hundred undergraduate students reported on over a thousand "crushes." The goal of the study was to capture and track the "I might be into this person" phenomenon—the potential romantic partners who float in and out of the lives of singles over the course of weeks and months. Had I been in this study in 1999, I would have started filling out surveys about Anna at some point during that fall.

Some participants reported especially high romantic interest in these crushes, and their interest remained high. Indeed, some of these crushes turned into dating relationships. In other cases, participants experienced only modest levels of interest in a given partner, or they lost interest quickly. But critically, the extent to which the people in our study were romantically interested in each crush was completely unrelated to whether the crush was hot or not. (As in the speed-dating studies, hotness was determined by a separate set of coders who rated photographs of the crushes.) The effect size was essentially zero—this consensus measure of coder-rated attractiveness had no ability to predict how the participants felt about their crushes. It wasn't that the crushes' attractiveness proved to be a liability; it was simply irrelevant. In other words, *mere weeks* after potential romantic partners meet each other, hotness seems to lose its magnetic pull.[21]

Mate value matters, but it matters most in the very specific context where people are forming initial impressions of each other. So yes, your subjective opinion about your own mate value is probably related to your social prowess *in initial interaction settings*—among people who don't know you. The longer you get to know other people, the less your mate value matters, and you can see the "winners and losers" phase begin to yield to the power of compatibility in a matter of weeks and just a handful of interactions. If you're widely considered hot, this news is actually not great for you, because your natural gifts will start to wear off. If others generally think you're unattractive, you might consider using this feature of human mating to your advantage: Cultivate your networks of friends and acquaintances, slowly and gradually.

Some people find the ephemeral mate value concept to be somewhat, if not extremely, counterintuitive. It might seem like I am telling people to ignore their personal observations of the world. Attractive people do acquire all sorts of social rewards: They receive more spontaneous help from strangers, and their bosses shower them with bigger raises at work. Unattractive people might find this hypothesis not particularly validating of their own personal experiences. They know perfectly well that fictionalized mismatched pairings are a sick joke. On *Parks and Recreation*, the Gayle and Jerry relationship was played for laughs: A guy this unattractive could not possibly land Christie Brinkley as a wife. It is debatably cruel for me to insinuate that these mismatched pairings represent the real world.[22]

Even if the importance of mate value declines with time, it does not disappear completely. In figure 1.3, the rightmost cocktail contains a dash of consensus, so even when people get to know each other, a trace of mate value remains. It won't be common for a 1 to date a 10.

On the other hand, pointing to hot couples as evidence of the importance of mate value is probably overstating the case. Consider the possibility that most of the hot couples that you know are actually not people you know personally, but celebrities, and these couples might not be an authentic reflection of the way human mating typically works. In order for two people to date, they have to meet each other in the first place. In contemporary Western societies, this means that we tend to meet similar people to ourselves. People live near others who are similar in terms of countless demographic factors—political orientation, education, religiosity, and race—and these living arrangements explain why people tend to date and marry partners who are similar to them.

This form of sorting, called *demographic assortative mating*, is completely distinct from competitive matching based on physical attractiveness. Demographic sorting is based on who you meet; mate-value matching is based on how well you compete. We separate these two forms of matching because people's living circumstances depend on their demographics, not their attractiveness. If you happen to live in an affluent neighborhood, your neighbors are likely similarly affluent, similarly educated, and they probably share your political and religious views. These folks also frequent the same bars, restaurants, and social spaces as you. This means that regardless of your attractiveness—whether you're a 3 or a 9—the potential partners you meet come pre-sorted on various demographic variables.

The entertainment industry is the one place where this distinction between demographic and competitive sorting is murky—it is a place where attractive people live and work alongside other attractive people. Critically, because the celebrity couples that emerge from this milieu are so visible and so memorable, they might be the largest contributor to our sense that hot people exclusively date and marry other hot people. But do not assume that their relationships have implications for the rest of us. If celebrities spent more time with us normies, I guarantee they'd marry more of us.*

Mate-Value Matching in Long-Term Relationships

In the film *High Fidelity*, Rob (played by John Cusack) recounts his breakup with Charlie (played by Catherine Zeta-Jones): "The thing I learned from the whole Charlie debacle is that you gotta punch your weight. See Charlie? She's out of my class. She's too pretty, too smart, too witty, too much." If Rob is right, then perhaps mate-value discrepancies cause challenges later in a relationship. If you're in a long-term relationship with someone with more mate value than you, it is reasonable to wonder if it will all lead to heartbreak in the end.

The EvoScript tells us that if an attractive person thinks they can do better than their current unattractive partner, they'll trade up. Recall the *Time* magazine infidelity thesis: If people are striving to get the best possible deal, then couples with a mate-value mismatch are

---

* My favorite example: Mark Hamill, at the height of his fame as Luke Skywalker, married his dental hygienist, Marilou York.

less likely to last. Researchers used to think there was evidence for this intuition based on a famous study published back in 1980 showing that dating couples who stayed together were more similar in their attractiveness than couples who broke up. This study received considerable attention over subsequent years, and prominent evolutionary psychologists continue to advise people to pick partners who match their mate value.[23]

Later, however, another researcher conducted a meta-analysis of *all* the relevant data, and the evidence for this idea turned out to be pretty weak. Across all the existing studies, mismatched couples didn't seem to break up any sooner (or later) than matched couples. Not to mention, the mismatch-as-liability finding only emerged in a *subsample* of the original 1980 study; that full study showed no effect, too. In the meantime, plenty of other studies have emerged showing that the effects of attractiveness similarity on relationship satisfaction are tiny and insignificant in long-term relationships.[24]

Today, scientists call this idea the "attractiveness-exchange script," which is academic-speak for "unfounded stereotype." Now, you may not enjoy watching your attractive partner get attention from prospective suitors—if your partner is more attractive than you, it is possible that strangers will hit on your partner more than they hit on you. But there is no evidence that an attractiveness mismatch spells doom for your relationship. In fact, it does not even seem to be a meaningful risk factor.[25]

The reason why attractive partners don't commonly trade up is the compatibility factor: the extent to which I think you are especially desirable, above and beyond the consensus and selectivity factors. The compatibility factor tends to be a large component of initial attraction, and it gets even larger as people get to know each other over time. In other words, few of us get to date partners who are conventionally considered to be a 10, but many of us get to date partners *who we think are a 10*. People tend to create their own subjective reality in their relationships, and that's where most of their happiness (or lack thereof) comes from. How hot you are is mostly irrelevant—we experience our own perceptions as truth, and so many people have the luxury of thinking there's no room to trade up.[26]

SO HOW DO WE make sense of these findings in evolutionary terms? The EvoScript tells us that some people are catches and some people are not, and that when we meet strangers we use mate value to assess whether they are worth our time and effort, and if they're likely to give us a second look. But recall that in our ancestral past, humans were looking for mates within small networks; meeting strangers was fairly uncommon. The extent to which mate value mattered as humans evolved is probably captured by the rather small to inconsequential shaded portions of the "weeks" and "long-term acquaintance" cocktails of figure 1.3—that is, not very much. The attractive, highly desirable folks with their perfect figures would have done all right back then, but their advantage was modest—certainly not large enough to dominate a mating market. The process of finding and accepting your place in a mating hierarchy is only salient today because we live in large cities and towns, and spend so much time meeting strangers and swiping dating-app profiles.

By focusing too intently on these individual differences in desirability, we've ignored what truly matters—the idiosyncratic, relationship-by-relationship differences that cause you to genuinely believe that your crush is the hottest guy on the planet, even if no one else agrees. The math is crystal clear: Romantic feelings flow mostly from compatibility, especially as relationships evolve. If we want to explain why some romantic connections work and some do not, we need to understand the way that two people discover or create compatibility. Tired ideas about competitive markets can't get us very far.

Anna, One Year Later

That January evening in Anna's room—the one that ended with her hooking up with another guy—certainly seemed like the end of something at the time. I disengaged from her for a few weeks. A few new crushes materialized and then disintegrated. Thinking back, that wasn't my favorite winter in Ithaca.

But in reality, it was more like the end of the beginning. Anna and I stayed friends, and as far as my social life was generally concerned, she was a rejuvenating force. Within a few months, many of her social connections became my social connections; I learned to hack it in her world. What began as "learning my place" in the vertical, hierarchical sense became "learning my place" in the horizontal, democratic sense: I found new niches and new groups of people who shared my interests. The feeling of an expanding social circle is exhilarating all by itself, and I had Anna to thank for much of that.

At the same time, I had stopped pining for Anna. She was still as attractive as ever. But her attractiveness had become a fact I knew about her; it didn't make me dizzy anymore. She was still worldly and ambitious. But now when she talked about her goal of making it to every corner of the world, I thought it sounded exhausting.

A year later, my drives between Boston and Ithaca with Anna had become a ritual. It was liberating to talk about our romantic lives without any jealousy or sexual tension. On one memorable trip, as she and I were debating proper "make-out" techniques, she politely insisted that I pull over the car and kiss her. I obliged, out of pure curiosity and in deference to my former Anna-obsessed self.

It was the plot twist that I had desperately wanted a year earlier. But strangely, the kiss wasn't what I had imagined. It didn't trigger that head-over-heels, stomach-dropping sensation. There were no butterflies. We drove home and laughed about it. And that was it. Not a big deal.

In that one-year stretch, my perception of Anna had changed. Her sky-high mate value had worn off. As it often does.

· 2 ·

Real and Overblown Gender Differences

On gender, *A Star Is Born* is a rich text. The four versions of this film span nearly a century, and all four depict how a woman's rise to stardom coincides with—and indeed precipitates—a man's decline. Because the man and woman in the story are also romantic partners, we see the romantic appeal of success, as well as its mirror image. In the first half of each version of the film, his success makes him appealing, sexy, and inspiring. In the second half—especially in the 1954 version starring Judy Garland—her success emasculates him and (spoiler alert) becomes the death of him.[1]

You can read *A Star Is Born* as a conservative cautionary tale: It is not in a man's nature to step back and give his partner the limelight. Men are driven to provide, achieve, and win that bread. Women may be talented, too, but watch out: Her ambition is not exactly an aphrodisiac. Even today, women are advised to play down their salaries, their education, and their dreams for fear of upsetting prospective male partners. If she codes, she had better make it seem adorable and nonthreatening.

There is no shortage of research and public discussion about gender differences like these. The assumption that men and women *want* different things out of their sexual and romantic relationships is pervasive, and if true, it spells trouble for anyone with attributes that don't fit neatly into the traditional gendered boxes. This assumption feeds the pessimism of *A Star Is Born* and a thousand other gloomy takes on the challenges of heterosexual partnerships. This chapter is about how this assumption is mostly wrong: Our collective understanding of gender differences in the mating domain is a mess.

Why Is Gender Central in the EvoScript?

Evolution is all about the gametes.

In the 1800s, Charles Darwin observed that competition for mates could be a key driver of natural selection. He even gave this form of natural selection its own name: sexual selection. But Darwin could not explain why, in most species, it seemed to be the males that competed most intensely to be chosen by females. Male elephant seals beat the hell out of each other and risk serious injury. Male peacocks strut about with their attention-grabbing, unwieldy tails and risk becoming a snack for a predator. Meanwhile, the females kick back and watch the melees like *American Idol* judges. Why this pattern rather than the reverse?

The evolutionary biologist Dr. Robert Trivers came up with an answer over a century later. He pointed to differences in investment in offspring as the key force. This difference in investment starts with the egg and the sperm. Eggs are "expensive" compared to sperm—they take more energy to create in the first place—and so the simple act of fertilization involves more investment on the part of the female.[2]

This initial difference gets the ball rolling so that, in most species, the female ends up investing in offspring more than the male. In mammals, this difference is supercharged by internal gestation (with its accompanying deadly risks) and lactation: again, the female bears these exorbitant costs. These investment differences mean that a female needs to be choosy with the male that she selects. Her choices may also drive how the males behave: In animals as diverse as cichlids (a family of fish), dung beetles, red-winged blackbirds, and savanna baboons, females favor the males who demonstrate that they can provide access to territory or resources. She receives his caloric gifts; she does nonstop childcare.

One more note about gametes. In humans, men have a longer shelf life; geriatric sperm still have a little get-up-and-go. But for women, the odds of a given egg becoming fertilized start to drop around middle age. The EvoScript draws from this gender difference to suggest that men will be especially attuned to features like attractiveness and youth, which would have been cues to a woman's future fertility.

These observations have generated no shortage of predictions about how men and women approach attraction and relationships. Ancient selection pressures created man the provider and woman the child caretaker, and contemporary gender differences reflect this natural order. And lo and behold, "This is just how it is" commonly slides right into "This is what you should do to be desirable." Consider, for example, the oft-quoted statistic that for every 16-point increase in IQ, men are 35 percent *more* likely to get married, but women are 40 percent *less* likely to get married. The truth of this stat is that it comes from a study examining marriages that took place in the 1940s, when "marriage bars" forced women to choose between being married and having a high-status career. Today, when women do *not* have to drop out of the workforce to have a family, we see that intelligence, education level, income, and other associated features of high socioeconomic status positively predict the likelihood of getting (and staying) married. And critically, these effects are *the same* for men and women.[3]

So the IQ stat is about employment practices dating back eighty years, not evolution. But people like Jordan Peterson offer evolutionary-psychology-inspired advice based on it regardless, as he opines: "A woman who's very intelligent ... she's going to be a very intimidating target and fewer men in all likelihood are going to approach her."[4] If you're a twenty-first-century woman who wants a career and isn't willing to play dumb around the boys, you'll have to settle for being an intimidating spinster.

There is already one major problem with the narrative that prehistoric men, and not women, were desired for their ability to provision offspring. It implies that the human ancestral condition bore a striking resemblance to the contemporary nuclear family. In this anachronism, one man was the solo breadwinner of the household, and his wife served in a domestic role managing several children. But this vision comes from the minds of (male) academics of the mid-twentieth century who closed their eyes, leaned back, and imagined a natural state of the human condition that looked a lot like their own home life. In reality, women in hunter-gatherer contexts were responsible for bringing in half the calories, which meant that they had to be productive and industrious for the kids to survive. Not to mention that all adults—men and women—needed to hunt and gather more calories than they personally required, because the spoils were often shared well beyond any nuclear-family unit. Extended families worked together to raise children in cooperative networks; no woman was an island, and childcare was a shared endeavor. Nevertheless, the idea lives on that men have wooed young women with groceries and picket fences since time immemorial, and your desires are the natural and logical extension of the strengths and limitations of your genitals.[5]

What Do Men and Women Want in a Partner?

If you're going to share your life with someone, you'll probably want some assurances that you're making a good choice. For many people, these assurances come in the form of traits: They imagine finding a partner who is trustworthy, a partner who is kind and thoughtful, and a partner who is a good parent. Research shows that people tend to rate these traits quite highly.

Men and women reliably give different ratings for some traits. Ask people how much they want a partner who is wealthy and ambitious, and women's ratings will be notably higher than men's ratings. She thinks "Sign me up"; he thinks "Sure, but also downsides." Ask people how much they want a partner who is attractive, and men's ratings will be notably higher than women's ratings. She thinks "Sure, I guess"; he thinks "Essential."

The single biggest success story in the early days of evolutionary psychology was that these gender differences in stated preferences seemed to emerge worldwide. In 1989, Dr. David Buss published a now-famous study that found evidence for these gender differences across several different countries. In that era, conducting a study in two countries would have been a big deal; Dr. Buss collected data across thirty-seven of them. By documenting consistent gender differences across countries as distinct as Brazil, China, Germany, Iran, Israel, Nigeria, and Yugoslavia, this study catapulted evolutionary psychology into the scientific conversation. From this point forward, no mainstream scientist could contest the fact that women say they want "good financial prospects" in a partner more than men, and men say they want "good looks" in a partner more than women.[6]

These two medium-size gender differences in stated preferences became central to the EvoScript. Women's seemingly greater desire for an ambitious partner with good earning potential reflects the parental investment logic: More wealth means he can invest in her and her offspring. Men's seemingly greater desire for attractiveness reflects the fact that, in ancestral contexts, attractiveness was more closely linked to women's, rather than men's, fertility.[7]

These two gendered preferences *appear* to be reflected in the classic pairing of the wealthy man and the attractive woman. I vividly recall the photograph of model Anna Nicole Smith (aged twenty-three) and her husband, billionaire J. Howard Marshall (aged eighty-six), a tableau which graced textbook pages and lecture slides intended to illustrate lingering ancestral mate preferences when I was in school. This pairing is also encouraged by the recent "tradwife" (short for "traditional wife") and "stay-at-home girlfriend" trends on TikTok. In these videos, glamorous women encourage young women (and men, too) to embrace the natural pairing of the attractive, traditional woman and the wealthy male provider. The two TikTok stars depicted in figure 2.1 have dolled themselves up for the camera—with full lips, exquisite eye makeup, perfectly coiffed hair, and white lacy clothing—to imply that the more a woman radiates femininity, the larger the bank account of the man she can land.[8]

These preferences echo throughout the online dating space, too. Attractive online daters earn more right swipes than unattractive daters, but this pattern is stronger for women than for men. Rich online daters do better than poor daters, and this pattern is stronger for men than for women.[9]

FIGURE 2.1
Gendered mate preferences, as seen on TikTok.

The caption in the first video reads "Marry a low quality man who lacks a providers mindset with no ambition you will have a low quality life." The caption in the second video reads "A woman's looks is equivalent to a man's net worth."

But if you care about our evolutionary heritage, you should be skeptical of the relevance of gender differences in the online dating studies. Once more, with feeling: Most relationships in ancestral contexts formed through live, face-to-face interactions in small social networks. Swiping through hundreds of photos is an unusual modern phenomenon. Researchers sometimes use the term *evolutionary mismatch* for modern conventions with no ancestral parallels, like online dating, as well as information overload and the stresses of the contemporary workplace. Online dating reveals how humans handle a deluge of glossy, high-production stimuli, but it can't illuminate how humans evolved to navigate sex and romance. If men and women truly desire different attributes in a partner, these gender differences would need to be reflected in how people think and feel about real-life partners whom they have actually met. From ancient times to the present day—even in our hyper online world—a face-to-face meeting is an essential step in the process.[10]

For a different reason, you should also be skeptical that the classic pairing of the wealthy man and the attractive woman reveals anything about what men and women prefer in real life. The average heterosexual pairing would take this form even if men's and women's preferences for these attributes were identical. The reason is simple: Men and women differ in the extent to which they *possess* these two attributes. With respect to wealth and earning potential: Women still earn only $0.83 for every $1.00 a man earns in the United States, globally women earn about 20 percent less than men, and women remain unrepresented in leadership and management positions. The reverse gender difference applies to attractiveness: Women are considered to be more attractive than men on average—regardless of whether men or women are making the attractiveness judgments—probably because women spend more time and energy on their appearance than men do on a daily basis. The "she is hotter/he is more successful" observation tells you that these two average differences between men and women exist; this arrangement does not require gender-differentiated preferences.[11]

When I was in graduate school, my colleague Dr. Eli Finkel and I set out to unpack these issues. We wanted to find a way to test whether there were gender differences in the extent to which men and women actually liked a trait, without relying on online dating or getting misled by average differences in the attributes of men and women.[12]

We turned to speed dating, which was relatively new at the time. At a heterosexual speed-dating event, all the mixed-gender pairs get a chance to meet each other face-to-face for a few minutes. Eli and I recognized that speed dating offered a far better reflection of real-world attraction than online dating. We even tried speed dating ourselves—we were both single back then—and each four-minute interaction felt profoundly real, remarkably rich, and surprisingly high stakes. Like the nerds that we are, our main takeaway from that evening was that speed dating offered an unmatched data-collection opportunity.

We reserved the on-campus art gallery, dressed it up to look like a cocktail lounge, and recruited some single folks on campus who were willing to go on dates for science. Eli was the emcee of the events, and I was the stage manager. The trove of real-life attraction data that we captured in that one weekend was larger than almost anything that had existed up to that point. Once we had collected all that data, we turned to address the "What do men and women actually want?" question with something called the *revealed preference*.

THE REVEALED PREFERENCE can be illustrated by a thought experiment. Imagine you are a heterosexual woman, and I send you on five dates with five guys who play racquetball and five dates with five guys who play ultimate frisbee. With the racquetball guys, you struggle to establish a rapport: you're fidgeting, looking at the clock, and trying not to roll your eyes too hard. With the ultimate frisbee guys, conversation flows; you're laughing, asking questions, and sharing interesting stories.

When asked afterward, you rate the five ultimate frisbee guys as more likable than the racquetball guys, on average. You may not know why you liked some of them more than others, but for the purposes of this exercise, it doesn't really matter. Your ratings across all your dates *revealed* the fact that you have a preference for ultimate frisbee over racquetball guys.

Scientists call this a "revealed preference" or an "experienced preference." The preference is revealed by your real experiences with, in this case, a set of specific dates. We could say that a stated preference is your *idea* about how much you like something, but a revealed preference is what you *actually* like when you're out in the real world.[13]

Usually, scientists calculate revealed preferences with traits that range from low to high, like a 0–10 scale. Let's start with earning potential: Figure 2.2 shows what you might see at a speed-dating event when women meet men.

These men vary in their earning potential (the horizontal axis), and the women vary in how much they like those men (the vertical axis). This graph is similar to what Eli and I found when we asked our speed-daters to evaluate each other after a four-minute date. There's

REAL AND OVERBLOWN GENDER DIFFERENCES 59

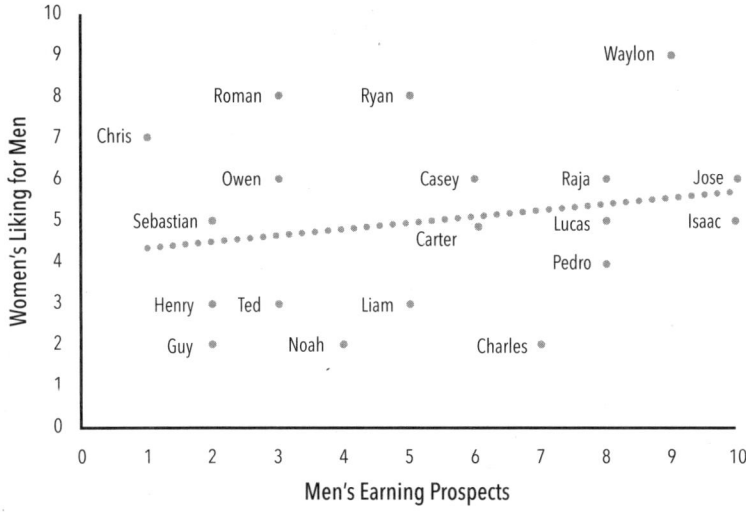

FIGURE 2.2
How much do women like "earning prospects"? (A bit)

a trend such that women tend to like men a little bit more when they rated them as ambitious, or when the men were on their way to promising majors or careers. (Major/career happened to be one of the more common topics of conversation at the events we hosted.) The trend is best illustrated by the slope of that line that runs through the middle of the chart. That line goes up and to the right; the steepness of that line tells you that women like earning prospects a little bit, *whether they can describe that preference or not.*

Then we flipped the genders, and we saw the same trend line (figure 2.3). The men liked the women a little bit more to the extent that those women seemed ambitious and were on their way to promising careers. Earning potential had the same modest effect as it did for the women evaluating men.[14]

The women in our study *thought* that they would value earning potential in a partner more than the men would. We asked them "If you were to go speed dating, how would you feel about earning potential?," and the standard difference emerged: The women were twice as likely to say they care about it as the men. But when you look at

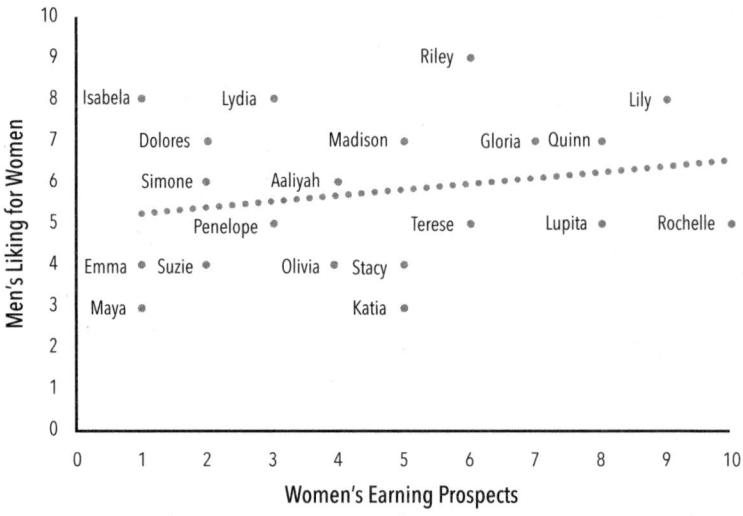

FIGURE 2.3
How much do men like "earning prospects"? (A bit)

who men and women *actually* liked, it just wasn't true; their preference was identical.[15*]

So why were people getting it wrong? One possibility is that the men on average *were higher on earning potential* than the women.[†] More of these men were likely to be engineers, or pre-law, or pre-med, for example—well on their way to earning that $1.00 for every $0.83 that women earn. Our participants—like many people—seemed to be mixing up two things: (1) their assumptions about what the other gender is like, and (2) the traits they want a romantic partner to have. In other words, when men and women say they want an attribute like earning potential in a partner, they don't access some personal truth about how much they prefer partners who do and do

---

* We also hosted one speed-dating event for gay men. I revisited the raw data, and their revealed preference for earning potential matched the revealed preferences of the heterosexual men and women. But crucially, to my knowledge, there are no published studies of revealed preferences in populations of gay men and lesbian women. It's an unfortunate gap in the literature, to put it mildly.

† This effect is reflected in the hypothetical data in the figures: Note how the data points shade just a bit higher on the horizontal 0–10 scale for figure 2.2 relative to figure 2.3.

not bring home the bacon. Instead, they regurgitate a simple gendered feature of the world, which in this case is: Men earn more than women.[16]

When it comes to physical attributes, men reliably say they care about attractiveness in an ideal partner more than women do. Men also say they'll care more about attractiveness if they were to go speed dating—the mirror image of what we saw for earning potential. But when these men and women actually went speed dating? Revealed preferences for attractiveness were identical for men and women. That is, the slope of attractiveness predicting liking was steep—about twice as steep as the earning potential slope, in fact. When you think someone is attractive on a speed date, you're highly likely to want that second date. But that slope is just as steep for men and women. Men think they prioritize attractiveness more than women. But the reality? Men and women prioritize it equally.[17]

There are two important implications here. First, men and women think they want different things in a partner, and when browsing photos online, their behavior shows (modest) gender differences. But when they meet face-to-face, these gender differences evaporate. What people say they want and what people actually want are two different things. Gender differences in stated preferences do not imply gender differences in revealed preferences. This distinction lurks throughout the online dating landscape: Dating apps cater to our *ideas* about what we like much better than they cater to what we actually like. This is why singles today feel like they're living a dual life—an online version and an offline version—and that they must construct the online version of themselves that caters to the imagined desires of members of their preferred gender. For anyone who struggles with that duality, or who doesn't fit the perfect airbrushed image of a gendered ideal, the solution is clear: Get offline as soon as possible and make face-to-face connections instead.

Second, people do some gendered things in heterosexual attraction contexts that seem pretty silly in light of these missing gender differences. For example, people assume that women will benefit more than men from enhancing their attractiveness. This assumption is based on the belief that men have a stronger preference for attractiveness than women, which the revealed preference data disputes. Enhancing attractiveness should work just as well for men![18*]

. . .

In the mid-2000s, evolutionary psychologists embraced speed dating as an exciting new arena to find support for gender-differentiated hypotheses. But by the time I was finishing up graduate school, everyone knew that in fact men and women did not differ in their preferences for earning potential or for attractiveness when meeting each other on short dates.[19]

But rather than see this moment as an exciting opportunity to revisit assumptions about the primacy of gender differences, the evolutionary psychological establishment began to treat speed dating as a uniquely strange context. I vividly recall chatting at a conference in 2011 with an evolutionary psychologist—one whose work I admire—as he shared his deep belief that speed dating was the odd factor here. He was certain that studies examining long-term relationships would show the gender differences that were missing in speed dating. Another declared to me, "No one understands what's going on with speed dating," implying that our approach was tapping into something unusual, with no real-world relevance.[20]

Scientists are supposed to be skeptical when something new comes along; that's their job. It was our job to see what happens if we probed beyond speed dating. This extension wasn't complicated, because it was straightforward to calculate revealed preferences for earning potential and attractiveness in ongoing relationships. Instead of predicting initial liking, we focused on predicting who was happy in their relationship, and who thought their relationship had a promising future. These two measures—*satisfaction* and *commitment*—are the gold standard in relationships research. Satisfied and committed couples

---

* Thankfully, Bravo understood this misperception, which is why they graciously gave us one hundred episodes of *Queer Eye for the Straight Guy*.

tend to stay together, and in evolutionary terms, relationship stability is key. If men and women differ in terms of how they weigh earning potential and attractiveness in a long-term mating situation, these measures should pick it up. Being with a higher earner should make women happier than men, and being with someone attractive should make men happier than women.[21]

My colleagues and I conducted a large meta-analysis, in which we analyzed around a hundred studies that examined the relationships of tens of thousands of people from fifteen different countries. The project canvassed every study we could possibly find that would allow us to calculate gender differences in revealed preferences for earning potential and attractiveness. It took years to compile. When the results finally came in, we found that these long-term relationship gender differences looked just like the speed-dating gender differences. When people felt that their partner was ambitious and had good earning prospects, they tended to be happier in their relationships—this was a medium-size effect; people who thought their partner was ambitious were more likely to feel like staying for the long term. But these revealed preferences were precisely the same for men and women. With attractiveness, the gender-differences story was similar. When people felt that their partner was attractive and sexy, they tended to be happier in their relationships, and this effect was quite large. But again, these revealed preferences were precisely the same for men and women. Finally, we considered alternative ways of measuring these attributes, such as annual income as a proxy for earning potential, and coder-ratings of the partner's attractiveness. Regardless of which measure we used, the supposed gender differences never emerged.[22]

This enormous project annihilated the conventional wisdom that earning potential and attractiveness have gendered consequences in established relationships, despite what people tend to believe. In reality, men and women are *both* likely to be happier in their relationships when they think they have an ambitious and successful partner, and when they think their partner is attractive. There are no gender differences.

This huge review came out in 2014, and since then nothing has come along that has offered a lasting, meaningful challenge to this conclusion. On the contrary, a 2025 study of more than ten thousand people across sixty different laboratories and forty-three countries found exactly the same thing: no gender differences in the appeal of earning potential and attractiveness. If you come across a version of the EvoScript that still talks about men and women differing in their desire for these attributes, you're reading an old draft. Recycle it.[23]

IF EARNING POTENTIAL and attractiveness do not predict outcomes like initial liking or relationship satisfaction differently for men and women, and stereotypical differences between men and women (men earn more, women are hotter) are creating the illusion that the genders are prioritizing these qualities differently, what can we make of the idea that women trade their attractiveness to land rich men? Indeed, TikTok tradwives are attempting to persuade young girls that the more attractive they make themselves, the easier it will be to land a good provider, a hypothesis that revolves around the *trade:* the hotter she is, the richer he is.

This pattern, too, is an illusion. First, consider the confounding variables. The matching phenomenon (see chapter 1) means that attractive women marry attractive men, and demographic assortative mating means that rich men marry rich women. Furthermore, being attractive and rich tend to go together. So if you choose to focus on only her attractiveness and only his income, yes you'll see a correlation, but many other forces are operating behind the scenes that have nothing to do with the trade-off between her looks and his money. One of the great sexist assumptions of mid-twentieth-century research on this topic is that studies proclaiming this particular gender difference *did not even measure* men's attractiveness or women's earning potential.[24]

To make the case that there is a trade-off, there would need to be evidence that women's attractiveness predicts men's earning potential, after accounting for the fact that attractive men marry attractive women, that rich women marry rich men, and that attractiveness and wealth are correlated. The studies that do account for these issues find no gender difference in the trade-off whatsoever. Some people do use their looks to attract a rich partner, but men and women are equally likely to do so.[25]

These same sorts of confusions apply to another pattern: women on average seem to earn just a little bit less than their husbands. That is, couples where he earns a little bit more than she does are far more common than couples in which she earns a little bit more than he does. This pattern might seem to validate the lesson from *A Star Is Born*, that partnerships are unstable if she is more successful than he is, so best to create an arrangement where he is a bit better off. This pattern is called the *gender cliff* in income, and you can see it in figure 2.4: There are more couples where he earns a bit more (in the range of 35–49 percent on the x-axis) than couples where she earns a bit more (in the range of 51–65 percent on the x-axis). But the explanation for this pattern is fairly straightforward, and it has nothing to do with women valuing earning potential more than men. Both genders would rather that their partners make more money, but because men earn more than women, women have a slightly easier time fulfilling this preference. Those are all the assumptions you need to produce a gender cliff; no preferences need to be gender-differentiated. If women were earning $1.00 for every $1.00 a man earned, there wouldn't be a cliff.[26]

If that idea sounds fanciful to you, consider education instead. Women may lag behind men in terms of income, but they have surpassed men in terms of level of education in the United States and Europe. Nevertheless, outdated ideas about gendered mate preferences live on. Public intellectual Scott Galloway warns of a looming mating crisis: "The bottom line is, we on the left like to think that men and women are exactly the same ... They aren't. They're different, including in their mating preferences. And the reality is, college graduate women aren't interested in mating with men who don't have college degrees." This statement simply isn't true. In newly married couples that have different levels of education, the wife is now generally more

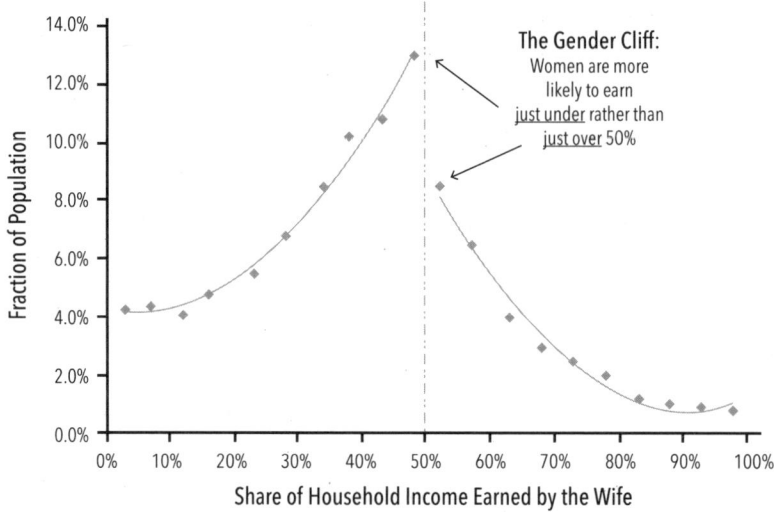

FIGURE 2.4

The "gender cliff" in relative household income

Note: Figure adapted from data in Bertrand et al.[27]

educated than her husband. Furthermore, now that women earn the majority of college degrees, highly educated women are *more* likely than highly educated men to marry partners without bachelor's degrees. We should be concerned about the growing number of disaffected young men in the contemporary West, but those concerns do not need to resort to imaginary primordial gendered preferences.[28]

Even if illusory gender differences pervade the domains of earning potential and attractiveness preferences, one meaningful gendered preference would remain intact: the timeless adage that she wants an older man and he wants a younger woman. Most men and women articulate this preference, and marriage pairings tend to reflect it. People also seem to construct their pools of mating options—the people they will actually consider dating—to fit within a certain age range, and these ranges trend younger for men than for women. In online dating, you can see these trends clearly: When men create their age filters on the dating apps, they construct a pool that ranges from a little bit older to far younger than they are (e.g., a 27-year-old man might set a range of 18–30). In contrast, women will construct pools that are somewhat older to a little bit younger (e.g., a 27-year-old woman might set a range of 25–35).[29]

But within each of these pools, once people meet face-to-face, something strange tends to happen. Basically, youth wins. Professional speed-dating events are already age-stratified; they are set up such that the men and women are roughly similar in age (events might be for heterosexual 35–45-year-old men and women, for example). Within a given event, we find that the young men do better than the older men, and the young women do better than the older women. And there is no gender difference: According to a study of ten thousand speed daters in their twenties, thirties, and forties, the appeal of youth—though not huge—is the same for both men and women. Similarly, in a recent study of over six thousand people on blind dates, men *and women* tended to like their dates more when the dates were younger.[30]

So the gender difference in age preference manifests in the way couples form, but it may derive mostly from a failure of imagination in the way people conceptualize their typical dating pool. Women are often drawn to dating younger men, provided that those younger men are open-minded enough to consider them in the first place.[31*]

Who Wants Sex, and When?

The EvoScript would have you believe that sexual desire is one of the single biggest sources of conflict for straight men and women. When relationships are casual, conflict is through the roof. And in ongoing relationships, her tendency to be sexually withholding will make him furious, as if the forces of natural selection forever grind men's and women's interests against each other.[32] The reality is far more nuanced and not nearly so stark.

---

* The OkCupid blog made the case (with data) that thirtysomething men's reluctance to date older women is grounded in straight-up ignorance: They don't realize that older women tend to be more interested in sex than younger women, and older women tend to be loving life more, on average.

There is one truly substantive gender difference in what men and women want: Men are more interested in having casual sex than women are. Survey data abound on this topic. One large study asked several thousand men and women worldwide how much they agree with statements like "Sex without love is okay" and "I can imagine myself being comfortable and enjoying casual sex with different partners"—a construct called *sociosexuality*. There was a consistent medium-to-large effect such that men agreed with these statements more than women did, and the gender difference showed up in nearly every country that they sampled.[33]

If we care about ancestral contexts, we should focus primarily on whether this difference shows up when people are meeting each other face-to-face. Some studies ask heterosexuals to think back on a time in their life when someone had propositioned them for casual sex—maybe a friend, an acquaintance, or even a stranger. In these real-life cases, about 40 percent of the women consented to casual sex with a man, but about 75 percent of the men consented to casual sex with a woman. That gender difference is also in the medium-to-large range.[34]

But why exactly do we see this gender difference? There are three major contributing factors. All three are consistent with gendered parental investment logic, and all three are consistent with "women are responding rationally to contemporary benefits and costs" logic. For this reason, most scholars have gravitated away from debates about whether these gender differences are due to biology or socialization—both must play a role—and into questions about where the difference is bigger vs. smaller, and why.

THE FIRST CONTRIBUTING factor is that men have lower thresholds for sex. Assume for a moment that a man and woman are *equally, but only somewhat*, attracted to each other. Does that mean they both want to have sex? To address this question, some studies ask men and women to map specific sexual behaviors onto their level of romantic attraction. For example, if people think about how much they would need to be romantically interested in someone in order to want to kiss them, you get 60 (on a scale of 1–100) for both men and women. For sex, the threshold is still 60 for men, but women's thresholds go up to 80. That's a decent-size jump.[35]

This threshold difference might be the source of the common misimpression that men want commitment less than women do. To be clear, there is not a shred of evidence for such a gender difference. When asked, men and women do not differ in their abstract desire for a long-term relationship, and once they get involved in a relationship, they are equally committed on average. But if men are more willing to have sex with someone that they only like "a little"—someone they don't want to commit to—then men will seem less interested in commitment than women in the subset of potential partners who exceed the "sex" threshold. But the reality is that men's and women's desire for commitment is the same; the difference is that men are more willing to have sex with women who they aren't all that into.

The second contributing factor is that women assume that men who proposition them for casual sex are bad lovers. Men, on the other hand, presume that women seeking casual sex know what they're doing in the bedroom.

A fascinating feature of this (medium-to-large-size) effect is that it flips the casual-sex gender difference on its head. That is, the heteronormative way I originally framed this issue was men are more interested in casual sex than women. But this isn't the only framing. We could have framed the issue like this: Do people prefer to have casual sex with women or men? This is a case where we can let the bisexual women arbitrate, and they are clear: All else equal, bisexual women would much rather have casual sex with a woman than a man. And they're onto something, because women report more satisfying oral sex (giving and receiving), more clitoral stimulation, more (and longer) foreplay, and more sessions with multiple orgasms when they're having sex with women rather than men. In other words, women tend to be more generous lovers on average, a difference that contributes to the infamous "orgasm gap" such that men are more likely than women to have an orgasm in a heterosexual encounter.

Bisexual women appear to be well aware of this trend, and hence they tend to prefer women for casual sex.[36]

The third contributing factor is that women think stranger = danger. A large part of the casual-sex difference emerges because, in some contexts, the people seeking casual sex are strangers. And in these cases, women are rightly freaked the f—— out.

In one famous example, researchers recruited fairly attractive men and women to help conduct a psychological study. These men and women had an important job to do: Approach people of the other gender randomly in a public place and ask them—and, yes, this is a direct quote—"I am sorry to disturb you like this, but I have been noticing you around and find you very attractive. Would you go to bed with me?" This question inspired some shock, and maybe a few laughs. But many people did say yes. And the ones who said yes tended to be men. The most comprehensive version of this study found that approximately 38 percent of men said yes to this request, but only 2 percent of women said yes.[37]

But notice the difference with the study described earlier. When women remembered being propositioned for casual sex in their daily lives—often someone they already knew—they said yes 40 percent of the time. When it was some random guy on the sidewalk, just 2 percent of women say yes. We can conclude that much of the casual-sex gender difference derives from women's wariness of consenting to have sex with a stranger.[38]

. . .

The pursuit of casual sex shows a meaningful gender difference: women are more wary of sex with men outside of a committed relationship, especially if he is a total stranger. In the environment in which we evolved, were she to become pregnant, she would have little certainty that he would invest in any subsequent offspring, or that he could be trusted as a safe and reliable group member. But recall that meeting tons of strangers is a modern oddity. Casual sex opportunities in our ancestral past were far more likely to involve people who knew each other—at least a little bit—and women are considerably more interested in casual sex in that context. Ironically, the abundance of strangers in our modern world appears to be exaggerating the gender difference in the desire for casual sex, relative to when we lived in small groups on the savanna. Also noteworthy is the fact that gender differences dissipate when the sex comes closer to matching women's rather than men's preferences: When sex lasts longer, involves more foreplay, and takes place between two people who know each other, women are far more interested in sex.[39]

This trend continues if we consider ongoing relationships. Believe it or not, humans mostly have sex in the context of committed rather than casual relationships, so if men and women do want different things, this should be the setting where most of the sexual conflict happens.[40]

The main gendered stereotype here is that he is perpetually in the mood, and she isn't. This difference supposedly creates conflict because—on an average night—she finds him pushy, and he thinks she is withholding. The cultural cornerstone *Annie Hall* highlights the challenges that couples face in the bedroom, and if you count the sexual-desire mismatches in the film, the woman resists the man's advances in 80 percent of the examples.[41]

In real life, the data are not nearly so stark. The gender difference in sexual desire for a romantic partner is small. The gender difference is not zero, as we saw with revealed preferences for earning prospects and attractiveness, but it's quite modest. If you had a random heterosexual couple in front of you and you tried to guess who was more likely to agree with the statement "I felt a great deal of sexual desire for my partner today," selecting the man would be correct a mere 57 percent of the time. That beats a 50/50 coin flip, but not by much, and it's a hell of a lot less than 80 percent. Similarly, in heterosexual relationships, about one-third of women and about half of men wish they were having more sex in their current relationship than they currently are. That's a gender difference, but not a dramatic one.[42]

So the gendered stereotype "Not tonight, darling, I've got a headache" is exaggerated.[43] Furthermore, part of the gap in the amount of sex that men are currently having vs. wish they were having can be explained by the fact that men reliably *underestimate* how much their partners are interested in having sex with them. In studies like these, researchers ask couples to answer two questions on a daily basis: How much sexual desire did you feel today, and how much sexual desire did your partner feel today? These couples are sternly advised not to peer at each other's answers, lest that knowledge change their responses. What emerges from these data is that men are missing the real-life signals. That is, the real problem is that she is in the mood, and *he* is rolling over and turning out the light. The size of this effect is hefty, too; generally speaking, men underestimate their partner's desire about 50 percent of the time. (They're accurate about 25 percent of the time, and they overestimate their partner's desire about 25 percent of the time.) In other words, they are about *twice as likely* to underestimate as they are to overestimate their partner's sexual desire. These numbers reflect a meaningful miscommunication—an effect that is indisputably larger than the "he wants sex and she doesn't" trope.[44]

MANY EVOLUTIONARY PSYCHOLOGISTS find my conclusion—that gender differences in romantic and sexual contexts are mostly overblown—quite shocking. Talk to a researcher who studies ongoing close relationships, though, and everything I have described so far sounds quite intuitive, or even mundane.

In the relationships-research corner of the scientific world, scholars have long assumed that the features that make people happy with their relationships were very similar for men and women. Nevertheless, this assumption was largely untested until a few years ago, when my colleague Dr. Samantha Joel looked into this possibility with cold hard data. Dr. Joel conducted a study that captured the best predictors of relationship satisfaction and commitment across more than eleven thousand couples using machine learning, which is an approach that can analyze tons of different measures all at once. Her approach examined how the difference between being a man or a woman compared to a variety of other personality and trait factors that people use to describe themselves. In her models, the measures that matter for predicting relationship satisfaction and commitment emerge routinely as winners; the ones that don't are kicked out. If men and women need different things to feel happy and committed in their relationships, then a binary measure of gender should be selected consistently by these models.[45]

But instead, gender was one of the worst contenders. In other words, to explain who was happy or unhappy in their relationships, the machine learning models repeatedly told Dr. Joel: "Don't bother looking at whether someone is a man or a woman—focus on the other traits that vary from person to person instead." It proved far more useful to look at other measures that describe what a person is like, such as age, self-esteem, neuroticism, and family history. If you want to know what factors have a major impact on relationship satisfaction and commitment, Dr. Joel's study suggests that gender is one of the worst places to look.[46]

The Desire Is There, So Change the Expectations

Men and women want the same things in a partner, initially and as relationships form. They *say* they have different preferences for earning potential and attractiveness, but these differences don't apply to what people *actually* like. Once men and women meet face-to-face, there are no gender differences in people's true "revealed" preferences. There is one central gender difference—men spend more time thinking about and pursuing casual sex, especially with strangers. But once people get into a relationship, the difference in sex drive becomes quite small and, if anything, men generally underappreciate their partner's interest in having sex on any given day.

Gender will always be an important consideration in our collective understanding of human sexual and romantic relationships. After all, some of the worst things that people do to each other in the sexual domain are gendered: sexual assault, sexual harassment, and sex trafficking are crimes that are committed almost solely by men. Furthermore, even though both men and women can behave violently in a relationship, women are far more likely to get hurt or killed by their partners in these altercations. Scientists should be in the business of documenting and explaining gender differences like these.

Nevertheless, there is a catch-22. As scientists come up with compelling academic arguments for the *biological* underpinnings of gender differences, the average person becomes more pessimistic about whether changing these societal ills is even possible in the first place. Chapter 9 will revisit this problem in more detail. For now, the key point is simply that clarity is essential. Some gender differences are real and will require the best minds to design interventions, and others are overblown yet live on in the public consciousness in the form of obsolete scripts and bad assumptions about how relationships work.[47]

One of the worst lingering assumptions is that women were passive in ancestral contexts. In reality, women were astoundingly productive, generating an equal share of the calories that kept the next generation alive. They didn't sit around idly, awaiting the return of the men and their meat. Throughout most of human history, male solo breadwinning was risky, inefficient, and rare: a weird idea that arose with industrialization and an increasingly stark split between men's public work-role and women's private homemaker-role. But it was not always this way, and there is every reason to assume that ambitious, productive women were desirable partners in the environment in which humans evolved. Based on the data I reviewed earlier, it seems that men desire women for their ambition in contemporary contexts, too, even if their stated preferences don't always reflect it.[48]

The fact that women were historically responsible for half the calories does not mean that the nature of men's and women's work was the same. Roles were commonly gender-differentiated. But these roles were highly variable from culture to culture: sometimes women hunted, sometimes men engaged in childcare. Humans can adapt to a wide array of work roles, living arrangements, and sexual norms as they pursue the most demanding task of all: raising the next generation of kin to reproductive age.[49]

I find that my pessimism evaporates when I keep these facts about heterosexual relationships front and center. We aren't asking anything unusual of men when we expect them to support, and frankly lust after, industrious and ambitious women. The problems are in the perceptions: Men *think* they desire ambition less than they actually do, and women *think* they desire ambition more than they actually do. Together, we collectively expect men to be more successful than their partners, but this stereotype cannot be explained by some deep, lingering romantic preference.[50]

If gender equality is the goal, this situation is encouraging. Changing what people truly desire is hard; it's much easier to be in the position of changing people's ideas and expectations about gender. Of course men (and women, too) are capable of making this mental shift. And in this light, *A Star Is Born* reads not as a conservative cautionary tale but rather as a progressive prophecy: Men who bind themselves to traditional masculine norms and fail to appreciate and support their romantic partner's successes will find themselves swept out to sea.

· 3 ·

Marriage Material?

Rachel is flying to Chicago again to spend the weekend with Zach. She'd been imagining their meeting at the airport all week: the way he'd raise one eyebrow at her before letting a smile spread across his face. But she also wonders if she's making a mistake.

They met over the summer while he was working briefly on the West Coast, and this is the third time she's flown east to see him. Whatever this undefined "thing" is that she and Zach have—a textbook "situationship," a term a friend had just introduced into her vocabulary—it's pretty confusing. And also thrilling. That evening, they go to a Cubs game with his friends, his fingers running across the back of her hand every so often; they stay out dancing so late that she has to check her phone to see if it's one a.m. or four a.m. He spends money on her, at both fancy spots and dive bars. The sex is revelatory.

Nevertheless, Zach is clear about monogamy not being his thing. While driving Rachel back to the airport at the end of the weekend, Zach tells her he can't wait until they get to spend a few days together again. Although he doesn't mention when or where.

In the language of evolutionary psychology, Zach is a master of *short-term mating strategies*. This approach is not something that every man can pull off, but Zach oozes charm. He has great hair—wavy, a little glossy, and swept to the side—and light stubble that says, "I can grow a beard and I can shave, I just don't do either." His humor is quick and infectious. He is sexy as hell. All these qualities mean that he has a major advantage when it comes to attracting women for brief liaisons without offering much by way of commitment. He might have taken a class on pickup artistry; hell, he could probably teach one. Zach is the quintessential cad, or—in the EvoScript—the alpha male.

After that Chicago trip, Zach and Rachel kept the momentum going over text for the next few weeks. But that next meeting (date? hookup?) never happened. Later that month, Zach applied his many charms to a woman named Laura. But with her, Zach quickly became exclusive. Apparently monogamy *was* now his thing. In fact, Zach would end up marrying Laura, and he would become a devoted parent. Zach was an alpha male using cad strategies . . . until he turned into a perfectly good dad.

And how did Rachel feel about this plot twist? Not particularly great. It's one thing to knowingly put a guy in a mental box stamped NOT BOYFRIEND MATERIAL. It's another thing when some other woman reels him in with relative ease. In the words of Sally Albright (played by Meg Ryan) in *When Harry Met Sally* . . . : "All this time I've been saying that he didn't want to get married. But the truth is he didn't want to marry *me*."

For Rachel, for Sally, for anyone in this position, it's unnerving when a partner makes the overnight transition from your friend-with-benefits to someone else's devoted long-term partner. The EvoScript whispers quietly in your ear, "You messed up somewhere." They were a catch all along, and you missed it. Or maybe you just weren't an appealing enough option. Either way, sucks for you.

But, once again, the EvoScript has led us all astray.

. . .

We see articles like: "Should I Choose the Steady Good Guy or Exciting Bad Boy?" "16 Signs She's Playing Games with You," "Why Nice Guys Finish Last: New Research Suggests a Biological Reason for Why Bad Boys Get All the Girls."[1]

Clickbait headlines aside, the pervasive assumption that some people have "short-term" dating potential while others have "long-term" appeal runs deep, undergirding our snap judgments, conversations with friends pre- and post-date, and the dating advice columns and books we lap up. This distinction forms the entire premise of the reality show *FBoy Island*, in which the women need to accurately distinguish between the male contestants who are "nice guys" and "FBoys" if they hope to go home with the final cash prize. If he's too charming, or too good a kisser, he may have a hidden agenda; send him packing. One study found that 25 percent of young women and 15 percent of young men have been misled into having sex with a prospective partner who deliberately exaggerated their feelings. To avoid feeling like an easy target, people spend an enormous amount of time and energy trying to weed out players.[2]

Take Avery, for example, who meets Aaron at a Super Bowl party. They immediately hit it off. But the next day, when Avery's co-workers point out that Aaron was chatting up other girls at the party, too, they write him off as a player. Avery ignores four texts from Aaron, assuming he must not be serious about her.

Or Sienna, who has been seeing Brandon for a few months after meeting on a dating app where both of them claimed to be looking for something casual. Brandon's friends worry he's wasting his time on someone who is clearly not wired for commitment, and Brandon interprets every unreturned text as indicating her lack of interest.

Or Jon, who goes on three fun dates with Evan followed by a stretch where Evan doesn't text for a couple days. Jon convinces himself that Evan must be talking to other men since "guys that attractive always keep their options open," and he abruptly ends things before he has the chance to be disappointed.

"I'm just looking for something casual" is a common refrain—and sometimes a sincere one. Some people genuinely believe that they aren't in the right headspace to start a serious relationship, and these beliefs can have meaningful, if modest, consequences. One study asked single people if they were "ready for a relationship" or not and then checked in with them a few months later. As it turned out, 22 percent of the "ready" folks and 14 percent of the "not ready" folks entered a relationship in the meantime.[3]

That difference—22 percent vs. 14 percent—is a real one; you shouldn't completely disregard what someone says they're in the market for. However, there lurks an additional assumption that we can peer beyond someone's *interest* in settling down, and instead assess their *ability* to have a healthy, long-term relationship. We try to count up the red flags: If he's too hot, too charming, then he is not capable of loyalty; if she's too independent and has had too many prior partners then she's not out for love. This archetype of the player—who has no ability to commit—has captured the cultural imagination far more deeply than it deserves to. As it turns out, discerning who is boyfriend or girlfriend material in any enduring sense of the term is exceptionally challenging, because relationship aptitude is surprisingly unstable and highly sensitive to the contours of a particular relationship.

Trade-offs in the EvoScript Narrative

The idea that some people are suited to long-term, monogamous relationships whereas others aren't predates the EvoScript; we have centuries of literature with "dark heroes" (think: sexy pirates, Casanova, or Don Juan) and "proper heroes" (think: sensitive nerds, or the male leads we root for in Jane Austen novels). But what does the science say about this distinction, and how strong is the evidence?[4]

The EvoScript explains short-term and long-term mating appeal by building off of a biological principle that no one would dispute: Animals need to be efficient with the way they spend calories. Ancestral hominids who exerted energy frivolously are not our ancestors because such a strategy was likely to be an evolutionary dead end. Reproducing successfully isn't easy, though. To do so, early humans would have had to navigate a tricky balance between spending energy on *mating effort*—landing a mate in the first place—and *parenting effort*—raising offspring.

Unsurprisingly, it's hard to spend energy on mating and parenting at the same time; attracting a partner and caring for children simultaneously is tough. This trade-off explains why humans tend to balance their efforts differently across time—a "life-stage trade-off." For most people, mating effort gradually gives way to parenting effort. When people are young, they spend a lot of time and energy enhancing their own mating appeal, attempting to attract a partner, and evaluating their romantic options. Eventually, they age and form a committed relationship. Prior to the advent of birth control, mixed-gender couples in committed relationships would likely then have had children. At this point, humans tend to shift their efforts toward parenting and raising children, which is a massively time-consuming (and exhausting) endeavor in any millennium.

So far, these observations are uncontroversial. But the EvoScript goes further, arguing that within humans, some people are more talented in the mating game and others more talented in the parenting game (known as the "individual differences" trade-off). Some people excel at flings, and some deserve rings. Some men are alpha cads, others are beta dads. There are the women you sleep with, and the women you marry.[5]

Let's begin with men. Evolutionary psychologists have argued that this individual-differences trade-off would have been prominent in ancestral, hunter-gatherer contexts. Within this setting you supposedly could spot the short-term-oriented men because they were charming and hedonistic. These men would pursue sexual opportunities yet only invest a relatively small amount of energy into each of the resulting offspring. The long-term-oriented men, meanwhile, were gentle and altruistic, sticking with one long-term mate. These betas likely had fewer children than the philandering alphas, but their familial devotion would give their offspring a better shot of surviving until reproductive maturity.

This trade-off is indeed common in the male birds of some species. For example, zebra finches tend to form pair-bonds, although they are not perfectly monogamous—the males and the females will stray under some circumstances. Furthermore, zebra finch males vary in their "quality," in the sense that some are more popular with the ladies than others. Studies show that the popular, high-quality males tend to engage in a more cad-like strategy: they show higher mating effort by attempting to mate with multiple females, but they show fewer caring activities directed toward their pair-bonded partner. Technically, this strategy works for these males, because they get more mating opportunities, and the females pick up the slack in their absence.[6]

Turning to hunter-gatherer women, evolutionary psychologists argue that similar trade-offs could have applied. When life was exceptionally dangerous—when predators or other deadly risks were abundant, for example—women might have experienced puberty at a younger age. This shift in "life history strategy" would have helped them to reproduce early and often, perhaps through casual encounters. Having many children relatively early in life could be reproductively advantageous for these women, especially in unstable conditions where long-term, investing partners were few and far between. Alternatively, the concept of partible paternity—the idea that one child can have more than one biological father, with each sexual act contributing to the pregnancy—has historically existed in some hunter-gatherer societies. In these contexts, a series of short-term relationships would be a good strategy for some women, especially if they needed to secure a bit of investment from many men. After all, if a man thinks that a woman's child is *partially* his offspring, why not send an extra slice of wild hare or honeycomb her way?[7]

The key assumption here is that dating and relationship patterns arise from people doing what they're good at and avoiding what they're bad at. But there are at least two ways these patterns could play out in the specifics.

MODEL 1: ZERO-SUM

The Zero-Sum model says that short-term appeal comes at the expense of long-term appeal, as if people reside on a slider between a "one-night thing" pole and a "put a ring on it" pole. Zero-Sum is a sanitized way of talking about the cruel dichotomies that have proliferated online in recent years, like the idea that a man is either a masculine, arrogant "Chad" or a nebbishy, provisioning "Beta"; a woman is either a popular, superficial "Stacy" or a bookish, desperate "Becky." The Zero-Sum model drives toward the conclusion that attractive men are bound to stray, as if—like zebra finches—we can't expect them to be devoted husbands when women are throwing themselves at them. On the flipside, when women tell their boyfriends, "You're the marrying type," men hear something demeaning because they assumes she means: "I'll take security from you while I fantasize about other, more attractive men."[8]

Women encounter these assumptions, too. In countless classic (*The Scarlet Letter*, *Dangerous Liaisons*) and modern (*Chasing Amy*, *American Pie*) tales, women lose their virtue if they indulge their sexual desires. The Zero-Sum model is also the reason that some straight men feel uncomfortable with women's previous sexual adventures—as if it's some biological reality that she's not marriage material because she had some fun hookups in the past.[9]

One evolutionary psychologist sums it up as follows: "Cads and dads are different human morphs, just as workers and queens are different morphs of ants."[10] Typologies this colorful are rare, though. More common is the assumption that the preference for monogamy vs. promiscuity exists on a spectrum, and it applies to both men and women. That is, some people "tend toward promiscuity, are quick to have sex, and experience lower levels of romantic relationship closeness." Other people, the gentle and devoted partners, "tend toward monogamy, prolonged courtship, and heavy emotional investment in long-term relationships." Most people fall somewhere in between.[11]

The Zero-Sum model does get one (and only one) thing right: people differ in their ability to attract sex partners. Evolutionary scholars point to certain attributes that would have made someone especially good at landing short-term relationships in our ancestral pasts because they signaled an ability to resist disease and infection. At the top of the list of health-signaling attributes are physical attractiveness, bodily symmetry, and social confidence. A partner with these features would presumably have offspring that are tough and hearty, too. And, if you're just having sex, those genetic contributions might be all your offspring get.[12]

As expected, people with these traits seem like they might fit the description of "Chad" or "Stacy." Physical attractiveness and confidence are strongly related to popularity at speed-dating events; people with these traits make positive first impressions.[13] Physically attractive and symmetrical people also tend to have more sex partners, hookup partners, and short-term relationship partners.[14] And even though our stereotype of the hot, charismatic player is probably a guy, the effects apply equally to men and women; that is, hot, symmetrical, and confident women are popular and land more sex partners, too.

Also, recall *sociosexuality* from chapter 2 (the belief that "sex without love is okay"). Both men and women who are higher in sociosexuality beliefs tend to be flirty and desirable, and they have more sex partners across their lifetime. In other words, when people have positive feelings about casual sex, they tend to have it more frequently.[15]

But Zero-Sum is a terrible model for the way human mating works. If the model is correct—if people devote effort to short-term mating *at the expense* of long-term effort—then these same people who have short-term success should have shortcomings in the long-term desirability department. It's true that these people who approve of casual relationships often *say* they're not looking for something long-term. However, Zero-Sum predicts three additional things. First, we should see that people with these sexy attributes *avoid* long-term entanglements. Second, we would also expect to see that, in cases where they do end up in a long-term relationship, they make their partner unhappy on average—they're selfish, likely to stray, or otherwise not great at being a decent partner. Third, we would also expect to see that the dependable, devoted, long-term-oriented folks do a worse job of landing short-term partners.[16]

All three predictions fail. First, with respect to avoiding long-term relationships, the actual pattern of data is exactly the opposite of the Zero-Sum prediction. That is, people who are physically attractive, confident, and high in sociosexuality are likely to have *more* long-term relationships in their history. What likely happens is this: People who are very appealing as short-term partners end up catching feelings for their hookup partners from time to time, and long-term relationships ensue. Also, if Zero-Sum were an accurate model, you'd also assume that someone's approval of casual sex would be a harbinger of their future long-term relationship avoidance—but it isn't. If you know that someone is single, their sociosexual attitudes have precisely zero ability to predict whether they will still be living that bachelor/bachelorette life a year later or settled into an official relationship.[17]

The second prediction is that if people with short-term appeal get into long-term relationships, they'll make their partners miserable with their casual orientation. Again, no. *None* of the features that make someone desirable in the short term make them less desirable in the long term. The effects of one person's physical attractiveness (again, as measured by independent raters) on a long-term partner's relationship satisfaction is essentially zilch. Same thing for the effects of symmetry and for sociosexuality. Attributes like social confidence show results that are (if anything) the opposite of the predicted pattern: These folks are desirable in the short term and (a little) desirable in the long term, too. In total, there is remarkably little evidence that the attributes that inspire short-term desirability have long-term costs. In most cases, these attributes are just irrelevant.[18]

Relatedly, people often assume that attractive people are a flight risk. If attractive men (or women, for that matter) have their eyes out for something on the side, that might be a strike against their long-term value. But when you look at the real-world data, it just isn't true: Attractive people are no more or less likely than unattractive people to cheat on their partners, or to be lured away from their partners. Men and women are not always faithful, of course: Infidelity is predictable from *other* factors. The biggest factors reside in the relationship itself (i.e., one or both partners are uncommitted or unfulfilled), although some could derive from individual factors, like problem drinking, or having lots of opportunities to meet alternative partners. The key point here is that short-term desirability is a pretty useless indicator for predicting what people will eventually do in a long-term relationship.[19]

Third and finally, if Zero-Sum were true, people suited to long-term relationships should do poorly in the short-term realm. Wrong again. In reality, being a gentle, kind person is irrelevant to your short-term prowess. For example, the extent to which people generally think you are friendly, responsive, and trustworthy has no bearing on the number of sex partners, hookup partners, and short-term relationship partners notched on your bedpost.[20]

Some defenders of the EvoScript might point to testosterone as an exception to everything I've laid out here. In other words, they might suggest that high-testosterone men have high short-term value but make bad long-term partners, and they're especially likely to cheat.

The causal logic here is actually backward, because testosterone is highly flexible and dynamic. Relative to the factors we described above (e.g., attractiveness, confidence), testosterone is less like a trait and more like a mood. The point of testosterone is that it helps men to compete for a partner in the first place. But it's costly for the body to keep producing all that testosterone if you don't need it, and so testosterone levels are very sensitive to someone's social context. When men are single, their testosterone is high. When they become involved in a *committed* relationship, their bodies don't need to spend energy making testosterone, so it drops. I emphasize "committed" because, if a man isn't super into his current relationship, his testosterone might stay elevated. Elevated testosterone is not great for his relationship, and he might be more likely to stray. But the conclusion is not that high-testosterone men make bad partners; the conclusion is that men's testosterone doesn't fully decrease when they are in unsatisfying relationships.[21*]

Okay so the Zero-Sum model is basically toast. There is remarkably limited evidence that short-term desirability comes at the expense of long-term desirability. Some people show off their sexy attributes to land short-term partners, but these attributes are either irrelevant to—or even boost—their long-term relationship prospects.

---

* People have long assumed that testosterone primarily matters in men. But recently, studies are bothering to examine women, too. And, what do you know? It turns out that all of these dynamics play out the same for women. Yes, men have higher chronic levels of testosterone, but that's the primary gender difference.

When you think about it, it starts to seem obvious: Being sexy and loyal are two independent things, and you could be both or neither. To me, this is reassuring; the idea that some people are by their nature good for a quickie but not for a commitment is demoralizing.[22]

But there is a second way a short-term vs. long-term trade-off model could work, in principle.

MODEL 2: INDEPENDENT STRATEGIES

Promiscuity vs. monogamy does not need to be an either-or choice. You could be high on both short-term and long-term desirability, or low on both, as in figure 3.1. For example, being more physically attractive might enhance someone's short-term desirability without affecting their long-term desirability (a person would move "up" in figure 3.1 without moving "left" or "right"). Generally being a jerk to everyone would likely decrease someone's short-term appeal as well as their long-term appeal (a person would move "down" and "left" in the figure). Many evolutionary psychologists implicitly or explicitly endorse an Independent Strategies model like this one.[23]

The Independent Strategies model has its advantages. In this model, short-term and long-term approaches are not opposites, so it can explain why our archetype of the ideal short-term partner partially overlaps with our archetype of the ideal long-term partner. When people dream up their ideal partners, they imagine that both short-term and long-term partners are exciting and fun, while the first one is especially hot and the second is especially kind and intelligent. You can see why evolutionary psychologists are fond of talking about people's "short-term and long-term mating strategies within their menu of mating" in this framework; people in the market for a long-term partner should show off how sweet and considerate they are, but people in the market for a short-term partner should find an excuse to unveil their sexy beach photos.[24] Select your appetizer from the front of the menu and your entrée from the back.[25]

But as a way of describing how relationships actually take shape, this model misses the mark. Remember, we ultimately want to ex-

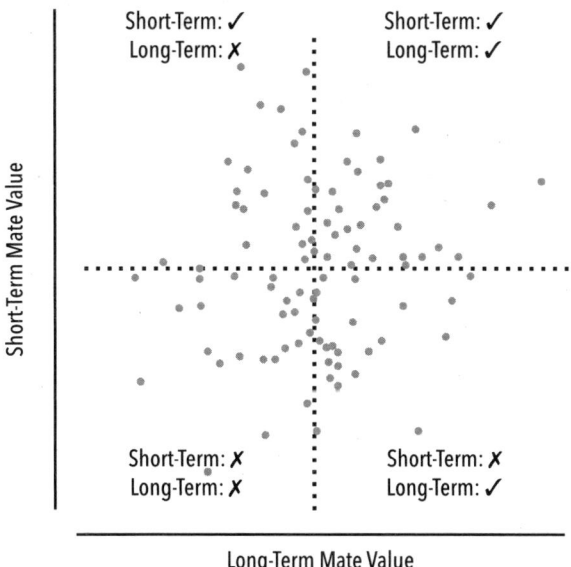

FIGURE 3.1
The Independent Strategies model

Note: In the Independent Strategies model, you could be a good or bad short-term partner, and you could be a good or bad long-term partner. The correlation between short-term and long-term mate value in this figure is $r = .12$, which means that about **56 percent of people** would be in the "good at both" or "bad at both" quadrants, and **44 percent of people** are in the "good at one, bad at the other" quadrants.[26]

plain how people pursue relationships—and how those relationships unfold over the short or long term. In that respect, Independent Strategies can't handle two lingering but essential issues.

The first issue is that it is harder to predict who is boyfriend/girlfriend material than who is hookup material. At first, many people find this fact to be counterintuitive, but it starts to become obvious when you dig into the data. Imagine that you have a ton of information about someone's *stable attributes and traits*—defined as whatever is generally true about that person across time and place—like how extroverted they are, how attractive they are, how witty they are, how personable they are, and so on. With all this information about a person, it is much easier to predict if they are initially appealing than it is to predict whether they are a good partner in their current relationship. Put differently, short-term mate value is more predictable than long-term mate value.

Earlier, I noted that factors like attractiveness, sociosexuality, and symmetry are irrelevant to whether people make their long-term relationship partners happy. This observation was a small part of a larger trend. On average, your stable traits and attributes say more about your short-term desirability than your long-term desirability. The Independent Strategies model cannot explain this fact, and a reasonable model of sexual and romantic relationships should at least try.

We already encountered echoes of this idea when we witnessed the ephemerality of mate value in chapter 1. There, we reviewed research in attraction contexts showing that people achieve less and less consensus about who is desirable as they get to know each other. Now we find something similar in long-term, ongoing relationships: Your stable traits and attributes can make you initially appealing (or not), but they can't really indicate if you're a good partner (or not). If people have a hard time agreeing about whether you're a catch, it makes sense that your stable traits don't provide many clues about what it would be like to be in a relationship with you.[27]

This phenomenon is dramatic, and it is best illustrated by a pair of studies I conducted with Dr. Samantha Joel and several of our colleagues. In one study, Samantha predicted the initial desirability of hundreds of speed-daters on first dates using a huge database of stable traits, like personality, sociosexuality, mate value, preferences, and more. Using machine learning, she was able to explain who generally conveyed a desirable first impression. In fact, these were the most impressive models that she ran; it's easy to find the popular people at the party.[28]

Then, Samantha used the same approach with several thousand committed couples. In this case, she used a huge database of stable traits in an attempt to predict who was desirable *to their romantic partner*. Again using machine learning, she now tried to explain who generally conveyed a desirable thousandth—rather than a first—impression. Now, the models performed terribly. In other words, only a tiny fraction (in Samantha's models, it was 5 percent on average) of someone's feelings about their romantic partner were due to the stable traits and attributes of that partner. The contrast between these two findings is depicted in figure 3.2.[29]

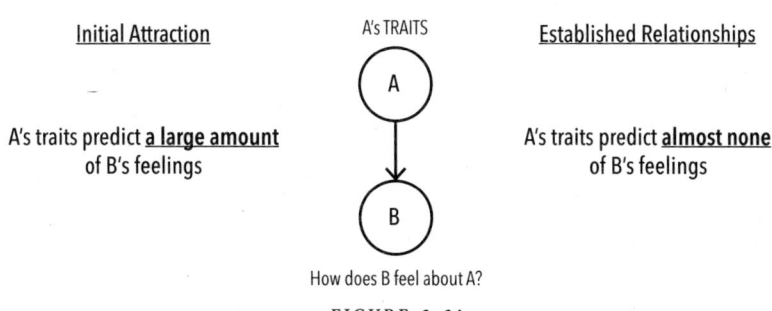

FIGURE 3.2:
How predictable are your feelings about me?

Note: In initial attraction settings, machine learning approaches could account for a large amount of B's feelings about A from A's stable attributes and traits (e.g., personality, preferences, etc.).[30] In ongoing, established couples, machine learning approaches could account for a very tiny proportion (about 5 percent) of B's feelings about A using the identical analysis.[31]

This difference—it is far easier to identify who is initially desirable than it is to identify who is desirable in the long term—is crucial for understanding human relationships. At a basic level, it means that it is much easier to answer the question "What makes you desirable?" in an initial-impression setting than in the context of a relationship. A truckload of information about "who you are" can explain how other people initially feel about you, but it barely explains how your romantic partner feels about you. Somewhere along the way, "who you are" got replaced by something else.[32]*

To be clear: Some people are bad relationship partners. They might be cruel, or disengaged, or difficult in a thousand different ways. They make their romantic partners miserable, and if you could whisk them away into a different relationship, they'd make those new partners miserable, too. The point of Dr. Joel's 5 percent value is that such

---

* The answer is compatibility—"who you are with me"—as we'll explain in detail in chapters 6 and 7.

cases are relatively rare. Five percent is not zero percent, of course; some people are bona fide psychopaths and should be avoided at all costs. But the most common pattern is that the things that were true about your personality or your traits before your relationship began do a pretty poor job of explaining how your partner feels about you. Many people with "good" traits—people who are generally kind, generous, or funny—have unhappy partners. Many people with "bad" traits—people who are generally arrogant, dull, or awkward—have happy partners.[33*]

The second issue is that in real life, it's pretty hard to pursue one (and only one) type of partner. Let's imagine you had the goal of finding a hookup—and only a hookup. I guess you could head to the club, show off your dance moves, and try to land the hottest partner you can. Presumably, you would not go to church, or to grandma's cookout. We all have stereotypes about where fling-worthy and ring-worthy partners tend to congregate, and I fully resonate with the intuition that the girls and guys at the club don't seem like girlfriend/boyfriend material. But critically, there is not a shred of actual evidence that where you meet someone affects whether you will land a long-term (rather than a short-term) partner: eharmony is responsible for a lot of casual sex, and Tinder is responsible for a lot of marriages. The manner in which you meet someone has very little, if any, bearing on how things turn out.[34]

"No big deal," you say. "Once I meet someone, I'll size up whether they're more appealing short term or long term, and then I'll know whether they're good for a hookup or something serious." Is it this straightforward? Figure 3.1 certainly suggests that plenty of people are high in one and low in the other. But figure 3.1 is based on what the people say about *their own* short-term and long-term desirability.

---

* Here's a thought experiment that should be clarifying: Imagine all your exes, at whatever age they were while they were dating you. Now, I beam two of them into the astral plane to have a conversation about what it is like to be in a relationship with you. If I could do this, it would be nearly a coin flip whether they would agree at all about how happy you make them. It would be very common that you make one romantic partner miserable, and you make the other one deliriously happy.

If you've just met someone, how desirable they seem for a short-term relationship vs. a long-term relationship can't really be pulled apart—often, we're open to neither or both, not one or the other. Check out the data in figure 3.3, which come from people's reports about whether someone they've just met is desirable short term or long term. These two judgments go together so often that in 86 percent of cases, this distinction doesn't matter—you either don't want anything romantic, or both short term and long term are perfectly okay. Put differently, only 14 percent of the people you meet have meaningfully distinct short-term and long-term value such that it would even matter what you were looking for. On date number one, if he is rude to the waiter, or he talks shit about his exes, or he monologues about himself nonstop—you're not weighing boyfriend vs. hookup material, you're just thinking "no."

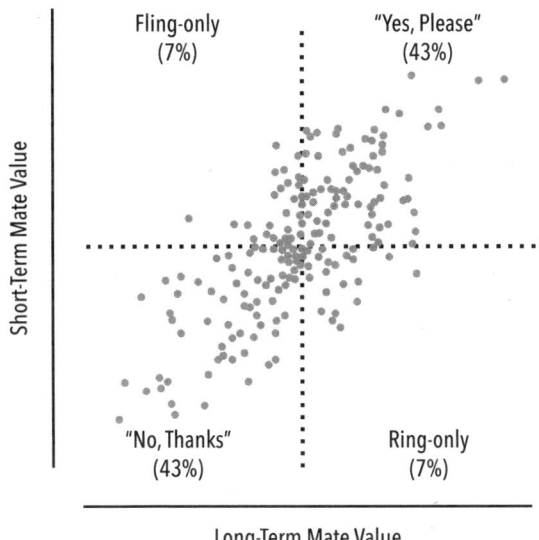

FIGURE 3.3:
How *you* experience the Independent Strategies model

Note: This is what happens when *you* attempt to evaluate someone's long-term and short-term value. Here, **86 percent of people** would be in the "good at both" or "bad at both" quadrants (43 percent each), and **14 percent of people** are in the "good at one, bad at the other" quadrants (7 percent each).[35]

No "menu of strategies" is going to do you any good in real life. Seeking out long-term and short-term partners based on where they're likely to congregate is a low-yield strategy, and to the extent that ring-only and fling-only are even separate kinds of people, good luck identifying who is who based on a first impression. It would be a lot simpler to use a generalist "if we're into each other, let's see where this thing goes" approach, at least as a relationship is forming. This approach makes a lot of evolutionary sense, too. In ancestral contexts, meeting new people was rare, and when you did, you probably had some time to keep gathering information until you figured out whether you clicked long term, short term, or not at all. But "let's see where this goes" is not the same as "order your flings on the front of the menu, and your boyfriend material on the back".[36]

Relationships—Even Hookups— Unfold over Time

Let's reboot and come at this issue a different way by grounding our models in people's *real-life* short-term and long-term romantic experiences. We start with the quintessential short-term relationship: the one-night stand. But first, what is a one-night stand, anyway? The answer shouldn't be hard; the definition is right there in the name! And yet when people reflect on the actual one-night stands they have had, the answer is often a bit more complicated. What follows is a set of real-life case studies, with names and other tiny details changed.

ADAM AND TABITHA

Adam is helping Charles move into his new apartment. While doing so, he meets Charles's new housemates, including a bold free spirit named Tabitha. Over the next few weeks, Adam periodically hangs out with Charles and his housemates, including Tabitha.

On one Friday night, they all go to a bar to watch some friends play in a band, and Adam and Tabitha get a little flirty. On Saturday, they play a drinking game at a party, and the flirting escalates. Afterward, Tabitha invites Adam back to her place; they have sex, and Adam spends the night.

A week ago, Adam had thought there was maybe potential with Tabitha. But the day after they hook up, they grab something to eat, and it goes badly. He's starting to wonder what he found interesting about her. He doesn't get the sense that Tabitha is especially into him, either; she mostly seems to want to end the whole interaction. A case of mutual "meh."

Adam and Tabitha hang out nine or ten more times, usually in a group, over the course of the next several months. They never have sex again; they flirt only once or twice. Tabitha even talks to Adam occasionally about an ex she is clearly not over. He listens politely and starts to realize how bad it would have been had he and Tabitha actually dated. Eventually, Charles gets a new apartment, and Adam and Tabitha don't see each other again.

Most people would say that Adam and Tabitha had a one-night stand that Saturday night when she invited him back to her place. After all, they only had sex one time; isn't that the definition? But note the key complexity: They did not meet on the night they hooked up, and they interacted several times afterward because they had overlapping social circles. A relationship that can be described as a one-night stand can also span weeks or months or even years. Let that observation sink in for a second. Because believe it or not, this is the most common pattern: Casual hookups are usually with people you've known for a little while and whom you will probably see again.[37]

Figure 3.4 plots out what happened with Adam and Tabitha from Adam's perspective, in a way that spotlights both the passage of time and his feelings for her. His interest rises, they hook up, their connection sputters, and his interest declines. Sometimes, that's how it goes. But Adam had other things going for him that year.

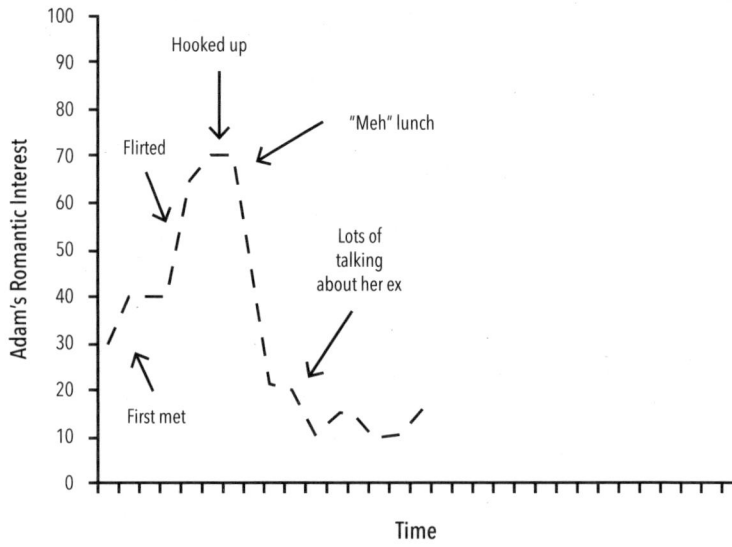

FIGURE 3.4:
How did Adam feel about Tabitha (one-night stand)?

Note: Adam's feelings about Tabitha = black dashed line.

ADAM AND JULIE

Several months later, Adam is traveling in Europe with a tour group of about twenty-five people. He knows some of them well, and others not at all. Julie is one of the new people he meets in this group. He doesn't make a good first impression. She is from Indiana, and he is from Boston, and all he knows about Indiana is that it's where Larry Bird is from. She is not impressed.[*]

But things start to turn around. They stay up late and trade tales with the other members of their group in a bonding session that lasts for hours. Julie's infectious laugh and animated storytelling captivates Adam in a way he didn't expect. The next night—the last night of

---

[*] Note for other Bostonians: Try to learn at least two non–Larry Bird–related facts about Indiana. For example, Indiana is the birthplace of all members of the Jackson 5, and no one knows to this day what a Hoosier is! (Larry Bird is a very famous basketball player who played for the Boston Celtics throughout the 1980s, and knowing about him is mandatory if you grew up there.)

their travels—their hands seemed to graze especially frequently as they sit side by side. Adam retires early, Julie confidently follows him upstairs, and they share a passionate night that marks the best imaginable ending to their trip.

Back in the United States, despite the fact that they are separated by hundreds of miles, they make plans to see each other again. And they follow through. After a few visits, they even make it "Facebook official." For several months, traveling back and forth between their respective cities feels like an invigorating expansion of their worlds.

But as the months progress, their differences start to become more and more apparent. They have a lot of trouble connecting with each other's social circles; they simply do not like each other's friends, which complicates their in-person visits. The logistics of dating long-distance start to overshadow the exhilaration of being together. They end up mutually breaking up about four months after they started dating.

Adam and Julie had something that approximated a standard dating relationship. They were genuinely into each other for a while. But then incompatibilities started to emerge, they had a hard time integrating themselves into each other's lives, and the barriers became too great. Figure 3.5 shows what their plot might look like, superimposed on Adam's with Tabitha.

Adam had a one-night stand with Tabitha and a dating relationship with Julie. Despite the obvious differences, we can spot a few interesting similarities if we look at the two trajectories together. First, try to imagine what Adam might have been thinking around the third or fourth time he hung out with these women (the "time marks" along the horizontal axis of figure 3.5). At this early stage, it wouldn't have been clear which trajectory Adam was on; he found them similarly (moderately) appealing. They were growing on him bit by bit, as the days and weeks passed.

Then, at about the time that things first got sexual, we hit a major inflection point. The trajectory stalls out for Tabitha, but it continues to rise for Julie. The hookup was a promising indicator of chemistry in the case of Julie, but not Tabitha. The Julie relationship certainly

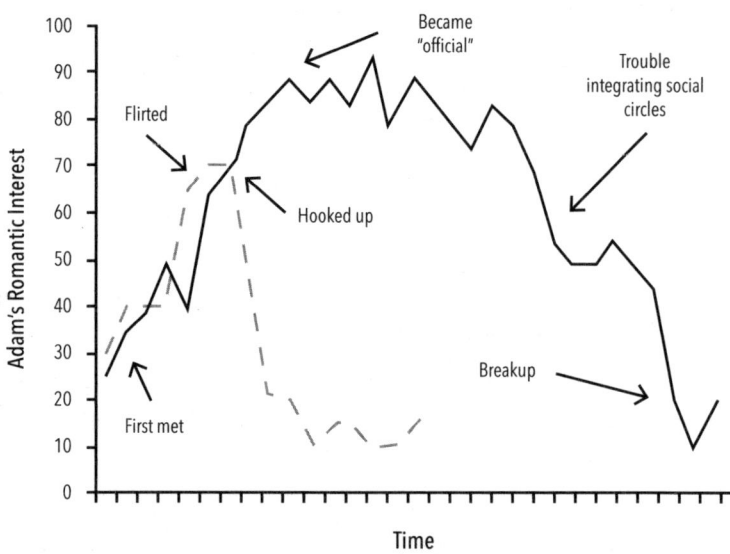

FIGURE 3.5
How did Adam feel about Julie (dating relationship)?

Note: Adam's feelings about Julie = black solid line. Adam's feelings about Tabitha = gray dashed line.

didn't last forever, but it looks in the figure as if that initial period of infatuation gave it more propulsive energy, until the compatibility challenges took over and brought them back down to earth.

A Trajectory Model of Short-Term and Long-Term Relationships

Relationships like Adam's have rising and falling trajectories. Yes, some relationships are short term, and some are long term, and many fall somewhere in between, but the growth of any relationship is a gradually unfolding, dynamic process, with a lot of uncertainty baked in.

Building a model of Relationship Trajectories requires only two assumptions, both of which are backed up by plenty of evidence. First, compared to short-term relationships, long-term relationships have more component parts—more ingredients. To have a short-term relationship, mutual sexual attraction is probably sufficient. Mutual sexual attraction *on just one occasion* is probably sufficient. For something long term, more challenges need to be overcome. Yes, you likely need mutual sexual attraction, but there are also questions about whether you enjoy spending time together, whether you help rather than hinder each other in daily life, and whether you can endure the hard stuff. Some pasta recipes have three ingredients and take a few minutes; some have fifteen, take hours, and can go wrong at innumerable points along the way.

Second, soon after you meet someone, compatibility is more like "compatibility potential." You can know that a new acquaintance is hot or socially skilled, sure, but it's hard to know whether you click until you've interacted a few times at a minimum. It's not easy to gauge what it's like to kiss or have sex with someone until, well, you get to kiss or have sex with them. And even when the physical elements are thrilling, two people can have real trouble integrating their lives as things get more serious.

So with these two (not terribly controversial) assumptions in mind, my colleagues and I constructed a model for relationships that looks something like figure 3.6. In this model, romantic interest (i.e., how much I am "into you") rises and then falls—dramatically so in relationships that end. Relationships where interest reaches greater "heights" tend to last longer. When things were at their peak, Adam spent many nights thinking about Julie, he stayed within constant reach of his phone to see if she'd texted, and he talked about her to his friends nonstop. ("She's great. Did I mention she's into horror movies? Did I mention we watched *Night of the Living Dead* and *28 Days Later* back-to-back? Yeah, she's great.") He never achieved anything close to this level of delirium with Tabitha, not even once.[38]

We can also observe that there are two overlapping phases. There is an initial sexy phase, where attraction and passion are central; in this phase, sexiness and charisma will make someone quite alluring. There is also a subsequent attaching phase where people see if they form an emotional connection to each other; if this happens, long-term-relationship mode takes over. Relationships can lose steam anywhere

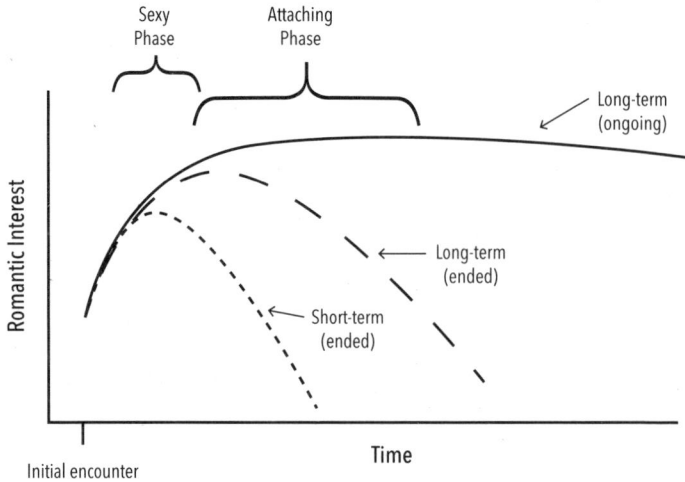

FIGURE 3.6:
Short-term and long-term relationships as arc-shaped trajectories

Note: The Relationship Trajectories model.[39] In the beginning (i.e., the left side of the graph), some people are more desirable than others. Later on (i.e., the right side), it's harder to predict who is generally desirable.

along this path. Some relationships make it into the sexy phase but don't have the kinetic energy to get much further, like Adam and Tabitha. Some make it through the sexy phase into the attaching phase but then start to fall apart, like Adam and Julie. And of course, some relationships navigate both and stay stable over the long haul.

In this framework, short-term and long-term relationships are two kinds of relationships that differ in how far they make it along this typical sequence. Short-term relationships are mostly about sexual attraction, and initially popular people have an advantage here. Long-term relationships are about sex, and deeper connection, too; it's very hard to identify who has an advantage or disadvantage out here.

The Relationship Trajectories model fixes the problems with the Independent Strategies model. First, it explains the asymmetry we saw regarding predictability in figure 3.2. When you first meet someone and are just forming a connection with them, your impressions are limited—you know what they look like, and how they generally come across to other people but little else. You can zero in on someone's traits to get a sense of "who they are" in general; grading compatibility ("who they are *with you*") at this point is only a little better than a coin flip. Once you spend time with them, compatibility will start to matter more, and how they come across to the rest of the world should start to matter less. Having value as a romantic partner will be about how the two of you click when you're together, not about them having, or not having, the right traits. There could be fifty or a hundred or more decision points as a relationship progresses—not because these moments illuminate a person's true nature ("weekends away expose how neurotic he is") but because you're learning where you do or don't fit together, and whether you want the relationship enough to work through the trouble spots ("he gets massively stressed out when sightseeing, but we both prefer beach vacations with no agendas anyway").

Second, the short-term and long-term distinction is now about outcomes—the length of time the relationship lasted—that reflect how much the relationship had going for it along the way. It's not about your intentions, where you met, or what strategy you used to reel someone in. The connection that started in a club and that was charged with sexual energy might lead to a brief hookup, or it might lead to a Saturday together strolling through IKEA. The generalist "let's see where this goes" approach can lead to both outcomes.

Critically, when you ask people to chart the trajectories of their real-life short-term and long-term relationships, the average trajectories look exactly like what you see in figure 3.6. On average, the trajectories break away from each other at approximately the point that the relationship starts to become sexual, as if that moment is key for assessing whether the chemistry is strong or weak. This pattern inverts the logic of separate short-term and long-term strategies. Short-term relationships aren't "for" sex; rather, good sex *propels* short term into long term. When Adam and Tabitha had a sexual experience that was underwhelming, they might have considered doing so a second or third time, but their enthusiasm waned quickly. But Adam and Julie's first hookup was electric, and so they thought: "Yes, let's definitely do that again, and maybe stay for breakfast."[40]

In this light, a short-term relationship is better understood as a euphemism for "I was a little into you," to paraphrase the *Sex and the City* mantra. That is, you were attracted to them enough to want to have sex with them—maybe just one or two times—but that's pretty much it. A long-term relationship is reserved for someone you were super into.

And you can't always tell the difference right away. There is an early period of uncertainty about where any given relationship is headed, and whether an emotional connection is plausible. There are twin risks in this strange phase: Overconfidence, on the one hand ("I can just tell we're meant to be") and risk-aversion on the other ("Any hint that he's a player and I'm going to bail"). It can be uncomfortable to linger in this liminal space, but nevertheless, try not to rush it. Eventually, two people can figure out what they want something to be, but it may take a while to know what kind of relationship will be the best fit.[41]

How Do Sexy—and Unsexy—People Form Relationships?

The EvoScript is grounded in the assumption that there are stable, trait-like differences in who has value as a short-term mate and as a long-term mate. Deep down, we are all zebra finches, balancing our investing strategies against our philandering strategies. This assumption turns out to be deeply misleading.

The Relationship Trajectories model is a more useful way of thinking of how relationships—both sexual and intimate—take shape. And critically, this idea captures the genuine will-they-or-won't-they experiences that people commonly have. Let's say you meet someone, and you think that maybe you're into him. When you get drinks the next day, does he seem into you, or not? At the party, do the two of you act as though you are connected by an invisible tether? When you kiss, is it breathtaking or forgettable? Anywhere along the way, whatever you have with him could continue to escalate, or come crashing back to earth.

Nevertheless, models of rising and failing arcs are not all warm fuzzies. First, uncertainty is the name of the game, even after we shed bad ideas about dichotomies that separate one-night-stand material and marriage material. The uncertainty comes not from being duped but rather by not knowing what you really think, not knowing what he really thinks, and not knowing if a relationship has legs. It's a persistent uncertainty that can turn the cool and collected into a desperate puddle of intrusive thoughts and text-checking mania. And the only way out is through.

Second, there is a paradox. Nearly anyone can be a good or a bad long-term-relationship partner, depending on the context and circumstances. But to get that far, people have to navigate an early relationship initiation phase where there are, to some extent, winners and losers. People who seem unappealing as short-term partners have fewer opportunities to get relationships off the ground. Even though they might be a great relationship partner for someone, they only rarely get the chance to try. Meanwhile, Zach gets to fool around with woman after woman, something clicks with one of them, and suddenly he's married.

Nevertheless, in an environment when most prospective romantic partners get to know each other over time, this design probably works well enough. As humans evolved, choices were limited, and most people would get opportunities to form mating relationships. Landing the "best" mate was overrated. Compatibility was paramount; you just needed some time to find and cultivate it.

Cultivate compatibility . . . in the service of what, exactly? Why do we humans so often find ourselves on trajectories that lead to long-term relationships anyway? Why does it feel awful to struggle to find a long-term partner—and certainly to lose one—and what does this signal about our ancestral past? This is where the attachment bond comes in, and we need to shift to a different branch of the science to understand how these bonds work and what they do for us.

· PART 2 ·

The Science of Close Relationships

· 4 ·

Attachment Part 1: Bonds of Support

You can tell that human close relationships are important by focusing on what happens when they end.

Austin went through a breakup that put him in a tailspin for about a year. Sleeping for more than a few hours at a time became rare. He was moody and unreliable, and his performance at work suffered. He drank to make the evenings less painful, only to wake up feeling worse than the day before. He thought about his ex-girlfriend all the time, ruminating about what had gone wrong.

But he spent almost no time lamenting the end of their sex life. The sex had been lackluster for a while anyway. If he tried to recall the early passionate days, his memories felt disembodied and strange.

No, the breakup was hard because he felt a deep urge to keep spending time with his ex. It felt like he had misplaced pieces of himself; being around her made him feel whole again. She felt similarly, and so they continued to have dinner several times a week. They would cook the same recipes that defined their life together: veggie chili, Basque chicken, Boboli pizza. Afterward, they would watch an episode or two of a show, just like always.

No sex. Sex was not the point.

The ordinary routines were the hardest to give up. They kept these going for months, even after they stopped living together. Extricating himself from these daily comforts was the most excruciating part of the whole ordeal. For so long, she was the person he leaned on—providing a sympathetic ear and reassuring words after the most draining days and basking in the reflected glory of his hard-earned victories. The occasional evening together could still make the setbacks feel small and the successes feel large. But the many evenings apart made the setbacks feel immense and the successes feel pointless.

The situation became a mess six months later, once a new relationship was on the horizon for him. His potential new girlfriend wondered why Austin would even want to spend time with his ex—unless, of course, the sexual attraction was still there. So then Austin found himself sneaking around to see his ex-girlfriend, just so they could complain about their bosses while catching up on the most recent season of *Abbott Elementary*. Needless to say, his new relationship had an inauspicious start.

Losing a relationship is stressful, even if some aspects of it are broken and unfulfilling. And losing a relationship is exceptionally difficult—and exceptionally confusing—if you have nowhere else to turn. In this way, breakups are a double whammy of stress: a traumatic event *and* the loss of the person who would have helped you cope with that event. Austin and his ex-girlfriend still wanted to be around each other to alleviate as much of the distress as they could, without actually getting back together.

Would it have been healthier in the long run if they had made a cleaner break? Sure. But such advice is sometimes harder to follow than it is to give. Letting go of a relationship can feel unnatural and dangerous because breakups implicitly ask people to imagine surviving alone, without someone else nearby for support, or aid, or encouragement. And since "going it alone" would have been the number one way to bite the dust on the African savanna, attaching is what humans evolved to do.[1]

. . .

Nonhuman animal mating partners bid adieu to one another all the time, with little melodrama. Among our mammalian cousins, only about 3 to 5 percent show evidence of pair-bonding between adult mating partners. And within this small handful of species, many of them engage in seasonal pair-bonding—the animal equivalent of summer camp. Humans are quite rare in our ability to bond with a mating partner for the time it takes to rear *multiple* offspring. Sometimes, we even bond until death do us part.[2]

This chapter and the next are about the nature of attachment bonds: what they are, how they work, and why they emerged during the peculiar evolutionary lineage of *Homo sapiens*. Bizarrely, these questions that are so central to the evolved psychology of human mating are barely acknowledged in the EvoScript. Luckily, there exists an entirely separate scholarly discipline on the psychology of human mating that revolves around attachment bonding rather than gender differences and mating markets. This alternative—called the science of close relationships—provides a new, rich way to think about why humans are the way that they are.

In the science of close relationships, support is central to what makes a bond strong and what bonds do to help us survive and thrive. Support comes in two forms: In one form, two people help each other recover from adversity (called "safe haven" support). In the other form, two people help each other rise to meet new challenges ("secure base"). And, to bring these twin forms of support to life, couples need to learn how to be a rock for each other when times are tough, and how to celebrate each other when times are good.

Attachment Bonds in Humans

When we're talking about humans, the term *attachment* refers to two related but distinct things. One of them is very much in the zeitgeist: the three different "styles" of relating to close-relationship partners (secure, avoidant, and anxious). We will delve into the styles in the next chapter, but first we need to unpack a second but nevertheless foundational meaning of the term *attachment:* the nature of caregiving bonds between two people.

In the mid-twentieth century, Dr. John Bowlby and Dr. Mary Ainsworth studied what happens to infants and young children when they are separated from their caregivers for long periods of time (what was then called *maternal deprivation*). In those days, popular parenting advice in the West cautioned against overindulging children's emotional needs; too much affection was tantamount to spoiling. To Bowlby and Ainsworth, this advice was deeply misguided, and their studies led to a series of influential books and articles proposing that children need a close, ongoing relationship with a caregiver in order to grow and develop in psychologically healthy ways.³

Their approach was evolutionary at its core. Consider that babies are blobs (or, when swaddled, burritos) for the first several months of life. They can't do all that much, and they aren't too particular about who is taking care of them. But things get interesting once babies start to become mobile. As any new parent knows, this is when the babyproofing must begin in earnest.

Natural selection installed a mechanism to mitigate the danger. As infants become little explorers, they also start to seek out specific, known others who are responsive, engage them in play, and comfort them when they are distressed. These "attachment" behaviors were important because they enhanced the infant's likelihood of survival in dangerous hunter-gatherer environments. Think about it: Around the same time they could crawl into the path of a woolly mammoth, babies become internally motivated to stay close to caregivers—who are vigilant for mammoths.* This early developmental stage also means that infant humans are accustomed to being dependent on others. A child comes to learn that she is safe because she has someone who is looking out for her, and with time, she'll internalize this sense of safety and venture further out into the world.

Sometime during the last few million years, natural selection repurposed the attachment system to apply beyond our early childhood relationships. Specifically, evolution applied the attachment system to adult mating relationships, too. Of course, sexuality and sexual desire remained central to mating relationships; those elements didn't go

---

* It also helps that caregivers find babies—especially their own—to be exceptionally adorable, as if babies were specifically engineered by natural selection to charm adults into taking care of them.

anywhere, and they commonly kickstart the whole process. But mating wasn't *just* about sex anymore. It was also about an emotional bond, or "pair-bond" in the language of evolutionary biologists.

The most intuitive evidence for this shift can be found in the similarities between parent-child and romantic partner attachments. Try to figure out whether the missing person in these statements is a **lover** or a **caregiver.**

1. Tatum doesn't like to be separated from _____ for long periods of time, or she starts to feel sad and lonely.

2. Amit feels confident and strong when he feels like _____ is there for him.

3. Maria feels anxious and preoccupied when she feels like _____ is *not* there for her.

4. Jordan feels safer just holding onto _____'s hand.

5. Chandra likes it when she and _____ caress and kiss one another and engage in prolonged face-to-face contact.

6. Chang feels ecstatic whenever she is reunited with _____.

7. Rowan feels like _____ can do no wrong.

8. Emerson is delighted whenever _____ uses private nicknames for him.

9. Marlowe constantly wants to share his experiences with _____.

10. When Uzoma is afraid or sick or threatened or distressed, she wants to be around _____.

Give up? It's impossible to tell; caregivers and romantic partners are equally applicable in all ten cases. That is, these examples all depict how the attachment system works in humans, regardless of whether the relationship is parental or romantic. You rarely *see* other couples acting this way, sure, but rest assured, this is what they're doing when you're not around.[4]

Attachment bonds remain a fixture in our lives, because we gradually transfer these behaviors—and the underlying emotional bonds from which they derive—from our caregivers to our romantic partners. As an example: When Austin was young, his father supported him in confronting the neighborhood kid who was terrorizing his friends, and the bullying stopped. Similarly, when Austin was an adult, his girlfriend inspired him to ditch his self-centered boss and transfer to a new department, where he found that his talents were appreciated. The two contexts are very different, but Austin had the same psychological experience in both. That is, when we have a person who is responsive to our needs and who is looking out for our well-being and security, we feel like we can take on the world.[5*]

But of course, these bonds don't necessarily last forever, and this brings us back to breakup. A breakup is the loss of a bond, and there is a common sequence to it. Breakups commonly begin with frantic texts and desperate bargaining, followed by depression and pints of ice cream, and finally the ability to detach and move on. This very same progression closely mimics the distress-depression-detachment sequence that young children experience when they lose an attachment figure.

The distress of a broken bond is baked deep into our biology, too. During a breakup, stress hormones are sky high. It's impossible to sleep or concentrate. We might even feel surges of adrenaline; our bodies know that something is dangerous and scary, but our hormonal systems (incorrectly) act like it's something we can run from. Again, children go through a similar experience when they lose a caregiver. The emotional bond is the same, and the devastation and confusion of losing it is the same.[6]

---

* There is a major difference in the nature of the attachment bond as it appears in caregiver-child relationships and adult romantic relationships. In most healthy adult romantic relationships, adults can flip who is in the caregiving and who is in the care-receiving role. In most healthy child-caregiver relationships, when the child is young, caregiving flows one way: parent to child.

Finally, note that throughout this whole discussion of attachment and bonding, I haven't used the word *monogamy*. Monogamy and attachment are not the same thing. Monogamy (in humans) refers to sex: specifically, the system or custom whereby two people have sex exclusively with each other. Sex is an important ingredient in building and maintaining attachments, of course, and we'll revisit this important fact repeatedly throughout this book. Nevertheless, very few relationship scientists would argue that monogamy is a defining evolved feature of human mating relationships, but virtually all of us would argue that humans evolved to form attachment bonds with romantic partners. As a case in point: A famous study of 166 cultures worldwide found that romantic bonding has been documented nearly everywhere, and as far back in history as we have written records. Not to mention, the practice of ethical non-monogamy illustrates how it's possible for people to have multiple attachment bonds and multiple sex partners during overlapping periods of time. For these reasons, the science is clear that the decision to maintain a monogamous sexual relationship is independent from whether two people have formed an attachment to each other, and the latter (rather than the former) is a critical feature of human mating relationships.[7]

Why Did We Evolve to Bond?

Pair-bonds between adult mating partners are not common in our neck of the evolutionary woods. Figure 4.1 is a phylogenetic tree that depicts the connections among different species of monkeys and apes, including humans. Evolutionary biologists use these trees to illustrate how species are related to one another, and they are based on information about how long ago various species shared a common ancestor. For example, about 25 million years ago (at the circle), there lived a species who would become the common ancestor of both the old-world monkeys (like mandrills, baboons, and rhesus monkeys) and the apes (gibbons, orangutans, gorillas, chimpanzees, and humans). At around that point, these two lineages begin to develop and evolve separately.

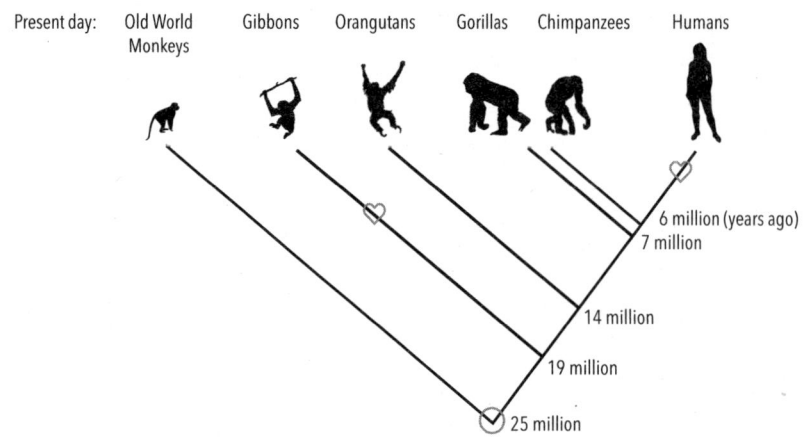

FIGURE 4.1
Pair-bonding on our branch of the phylogenetic tree

Note: The heart symbol indicates when pair-bonding emerged in a given evolutionary lineage. Timing estimates from Locke, et al.[8] Tree adapted from Fraley, et al.[9] The circle indicates the most recent common ancestor of the old-world monkeys and the apes.

With timescales like these—millions of years—natural selection can do plenty to reshape the way animals think and behave, and so it shouldn't be too surprising that primates differ considerably in the way they go about acquiring mates, even if we stick only to the species who are closely related to us. Gibbons are pair-bonding animals, and they commonly live in small family groups in territories that they vigorously defend against other families. Male and female orangutans maintain their own separate territories, and they only occasionally meet up for a sexual rendezvous. In gorillas, one male—the silverback—can control sexual access to a group of females, until he is dethroned by a younger, stronger male. Chimpanzees have a "promiscuous" system (yes, that's really what it's called) in which many males and females live in the same group and mate with pretty much everyone. For bonobos (who occupy the same branch as the chimpanzees), sex is sometimes a useful tool for getting everyone to chill out and relax.

Within this milieu, humans are probably most similar to the pair-bonding gibbons: Mating pairs in gibbons and humans (but not other apes) choose to mate with each other preferentially for an extended period of time, and they tend to form social units with these preferred partners. Gibbons, however, tend to live in single-family units, but humans have traditionally lived in groups that are much larger.

With the tree in figure 4.1, we can home in on the date when we humans began pair-bonding. Gibbons evolved their pair-bonding pattern sometime after their split from the human lineage (19 million years ago), which means we didn't get our tendency to pair-bond from the ancestor of the gibbons. Neither orangutans nor gorillas have a system in which a male and female choose to mate with each other preferentially; that is, no pair-bonding for them. Chimpanzees are our closest living relative, and they also don't pair-bond, so there's no reason to think that our shared ancestor was the bonding type. We humans must have evolved pair-bonding on our own, at some point in the last 6 million years.[10]

In order to understand when humans started pair-bonding, we need to begin with some educated guesses about *why* our ancestors evolved to pair-bond, and then it will be possible to estimate the moment in time when early humans made this shift.[11]

The primary purpose of pair-bonding in the animal kingdom is that it encourages males to invest in offspring. If a male feels a sense of attachment to his mate, he is going to be more eager to do what he can for her: food-sharing, a little extra grooming, or carrying an infant to help her conserve her strength. Not to mention, if he and his mate spend a lot of time together, he can feel more certain that the offspring are his, so his efforts are likely contributing to his own reproductive success.

Archaeological and anthropological tools can help us to date the point in our lineage when males would have stepped up their game as pair-bonding partners. About 1–2 million years ago—coinciding with the emergence of the humanlike-but-not-quite-human species *Homo erectus*—we see an intriguing series of events. Skulls were becoming much larger, which implies that brains were growing dramatically. This new development required a calorie-rich diet, including meat and cooked food, and indeed, evidence for coordinated hunting and the use of fire starts to appear in the fossil record around this time, too.

Large brains also necessitated an extended period of infancy. The birth canal and hip structure place a limit on how large an infant's head can be when it is born. To accommodate this constraint, babies started to be born early—before they were "fully cooked"—so that additional brain growth could take place outside the womb. As a result, the *Homo erectus* life cycle included a longer period of time where babies were helpless and needy.

How do these two developments impact pair-bonding? Together, these pressures—the need for more calories to support brain development, and extended infancy—meant that infants of the species *Homo erectus* required more food and protection than ever before. Even after weaning, humans still need massive amounts of care before they can reproduce themselves; in hunter-gatherer societies, children don't start bringing in more calories than they consume until they are well into their teenage years. So it is a good bet that *Homo erectus*, who emerged approximately 1–2 million years ago, was the early human ancestor who first evolved pair-bonding and high levels of investment. And much of this new investment would have been coming from the males.[12]

One more key piece of evidence in the fossil record suggests that natural selection was pushing *Homo erectus* males to become more dad-like. If you look at the species that precede *Homo erectus*, the males were considerably larger than the females—about 50 percent larger, to be exact. This is the sort of dramatic *sexual dimorphism* you tend to see in species where males acquire mates by fighting and dominating other males, as in gorillas. That is, male gorillas are also about one and a half times the size of female gorillas, because the pressures of their harem-style system means that the larger, stronger, dominant males will tend to be more successful in the mating game. But when *Homo erectus* appeared on the scene around 1–2 million years ago, this dramatic size difference evaporated. These males were only about 10 percent larger than the females. It's likely that the smaller males began sharing food with the mothers of their children, and they occasionally managed to solve conflicts with diplomacy rather than brute force. These males became more desirable to females—not in spite of their gentleness, but because of it—and their children were more likely to survive to adulthood and reproduce themselves. And so, with each generation, the difference between the size of males and females became smaller and smaller, eventually reaching the fairly low levels of dimorphism that you see in other pair-bonding species—and that we see in modern humans today (where men are about 10 percent larger than women).

Together, these shifts imply that, at around the same time that early human infants began to require more investment, male reproductive success no longer hinged on being an intimidating jerk. Instead, a male could be a helpful, caring, and generous cave-dwelling guy, and—lo and behold—the females would compete for his love and affection.[13]

HUMANS, THEN, evolved to form attachments to romantic partners. This evolutionary history of human mating does not require that we carve out a central role for mate value, or assert that males and females are dramatically different, or posit that people fall somewhere on a continuum from short-term to long-term specialist. It does not require the EvoScript.[14]

Instead, all we need is the assumption that survival among early humans hinged on intense investments in offspring, and that fathers' contributions—in addition to mothers'—were crucial. This assumption is clearly borne out in the anthropological record. In hunter-gatherer societies, fathers are vital providers of calorie-rich food, like meat from large-game hunting. But that isn't all. Fathers also protect their children from danger, especially threats from other men. They teach their children life skills: how to make tools, how to find natural resources, how to hunt, and how to follow social norms and rules. These efforts free up mothers to spend their energies elsewhere, thereby benefitting mothers' health and well-being in the long run.[15]

Ironically, these facts fit rather well with the parental investment logic and the powerful evidence of gender similarities in relationships that we reviewed in chapter 2. If natural selection shaped the behavior of men and women to coincide with humans' typical, extraordinarily high, levels of investment in offspring, then the genders *should* have evolved similar preferences. Specifically, men and women should desire each other for their ability and willingness to invest in offspring and to contribute to the larger group that sustains them. If you wanted to reproduce in the epoch of Pleistocene hunter-gatherers, the most reliable strategy for mothers *and fathers* was simple: Put in the effort.[16]

Safe Haven and Secure Base

Attachment bonds between adults help to coordinate their efforts to take care of helpless offspring. But that isn't all. Even if there are no young children in the vicinity, feeling bonded to someone carries benefits for one's own health and well-being. In part, these benefits accrue because bonds inspire people to support each other, and humans need support throughout life.

. . .

Sara and Emma's friendship revolved around friendly competition and their shared passion for art and literature. They pushed each other. Sara encouraged Emma to submit her essays to literary magazines, while Emma encouraged Sara to showcase her paintings at local exhibitions. But any dash of rivalry was overshadowed by their desire to share in each other's successes: Sara's wins always meant bragging rights for Emma, and vice versa.

Then, Emma's world fell to pieces when her mother received a cancer diagnosis. Her mother had always been her primary confidant; now Emma felt lost. She'd been dating a man for about a year, but she broke it off because his presence paradoxically made her feel even more alienated and alone. Emma felt compelled to push Sara away, too; their relationship had been constructed around challenge and celebration, not fear and vulnerability. But Sara wasn't having it. She accompanied Emma to doctor's appointments, researched treatment options late into the night, and provided a steady shoulder to cry on. For Emma's mother's final six months, Sara was by her side the whole time.

Their relationship began to deepen in ways neither had anticipated. They became steadily more aware of how much they relied on each other's presence, and they started daydreaming about a future together that resembled a partnership more than a friendship. Sara expressed jealousy when Emma joked about getting back out on the dating market, and Emma was shocked at how this confession made her feel nervous and excited; since both had only ever been sexually attracted to men, the jealousy was unexpected.

On a cold weekend in late January, Sara had the idea to visit a hidden gem of a bookstore/café across town. Emma had been feeling too exhausted and scattered to focus on writing since the diagnosis, but something about that evening reanimated Emma's passion for her work. They returned to Sara's apartment and collapsed in a heap, and with an energy both giddy and sexy, they finally acknowledged what they wanted from each other. From then on, they were officially a couple.

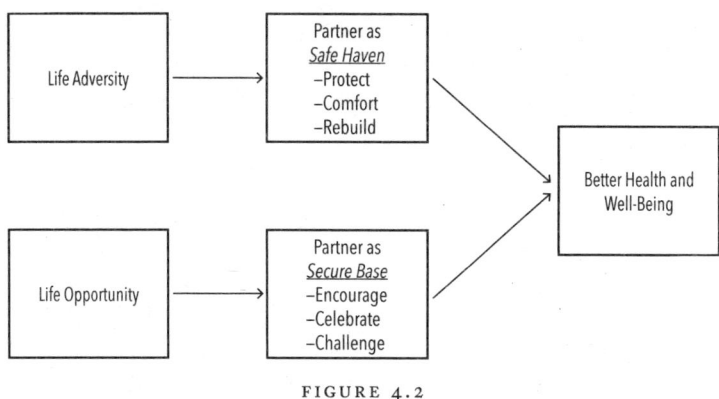

FIGURE 4.2
Safe haven and secure base

Note: Adapted from Feeney and Collins.[17]

Figure 4.2 illustrates two forms of support, both of which were central to Sara and Emma's relationship as they formed a bond and fell in love. The first is the *safe haven* function, which is captured by the top pathway. When we encounter adversity, we treat our partners as a safe haven by going to them for practical or emotional support. In childhood, we go to attachment figures when we're sad or hurt in order to feel comforted and safe. Similarly, in adulthood, we go to attachment figures when we encounter setbacks, to receive aid, to help us cope, or to feel understood and validated.

The second is the *secure base* function, which is captured by the bottom pathway. When we encounter opportunities, we treat our partners as a secure base by using them as a springboard to learn, discover, and create. In childhood, our attachment figures watch over us and give us confidence as we explore the world. Then, in adulthood, our attachment figures help us to set and pursue goals, encourage our ambitions, and bask in the reflected glory of our successes. Safe haven and secure base behaviors differ slightly between childhood and adulthood, but they're flowing from the same underlying biological system.[18]

Safe haven and secure base are like the yin and yang of relationship support. We need a partner to be a safe haven when we have to recuperate and regroup. Emma could have endured her mother's illness without Sara, but it would have taken a larger toll on her, and she would have had less bandwidth to be present with her mother. At other times, we need a partner to be a secure base when we gather ourselves to make excursions back out into the world. Emma might eventually have found her way back to writing if Sara hadn't been by her side, but it would have been a slower and less complete rediscovery of that joy.

The two forms of support can ebb and flow like seasons, too: For Emma, Sara was a secure base at first, followed by the emergence of a safe haven, followed again by the reemergence of a secure base. But there are no hard and fast rules. Sometimes, safe haven comes first; sometimes they grow in tandem.

Then there is the question of how sexual desire enters the picture.

In principle, two close friends—same- or mixed-gender—can offer safe haven and secure base support for each other without a hint of sexual desire. But the possibility is always there. Scientists often talk about sexual desire and safe haven/secure base as "mutually reinforcing systems," which means that one system might kick the other system into gear at a moment's notice. This is why two people like Emma and Sara—who did not previously identify as lesbian or bisexual—might find that safe haven and secure base *precede* sexual desire and passion for each other.[19]

TABLE 4.1
Safe Haven and Secure Base Quiz

Are you wondering if you use your partner as a safe haven and a secure base? If you have a romantic partner or close significant other, go ahead and rate these statements on a scale from 1 (strongly disagree) to 7 (strongly agree):

_____ 1. My partner is the person that I would want to go to, to help me feel better when something bad happens to me or I feel upset.

_____ 2. My partner is the first person that I would turn to when I have a problem.

_____ 3. My partner is my primary source of emotional support.

_____ 4. My partner is the person that I would want to go to, to be proud of me when something good happens to me or I want to celebrate.

_____ 5. If I achieved something good, my partner is the person that I would tell first.

_____ 6. My partner is a person whom I count on for advice.

Scoring key: Sum up #1, #2, and #3 to get your "safe haven" score. A total of 19–21 is considered high, 15–18 is medium, and anything 14 or below is low. Sum up #4, #5, and #6 to get your secure base score. Again, a total of 19–21 is high, 15–18 is medium, and 14 or below is low.[20]

People feel that their relationships are stronger if they think of their partner as a safe haven and a secure base. In surveys, they are likely to report more satisfaction (on statements like "My relationship is close to ideal"), commitment ("I want my relationship to last a very long time"), and even passion ("I feel a great deal of sexual desire for my partner"). These effects are extremely large; in a way, safe haven and secure base are fundamentally intertwined with the feeling that "My relationship is irreplaceable."[21]

The powers of safe haven and secure base are evident even sooner than you might imagine. In developing relationships—as two people are getting to know each other but before a relationship has even formed—safe haven and secure base are key indicators of romantic interest. That is, high scores on the statements in table 4.1 are a very promising sign that the relationship is worth pursuing in the first place.[22]

Furthermore, if you ask people whom they are *most* likely to seek out for safe haven and secure base support—among all the people in their lives—it only takes a few months of dating before "my romantic partner" becomes the most common response. After a few months together, the typical couple is approaching the "attaching phase" of that arc-shaped trajectory from back in figure 3.6.[23]

Some people feel that this attachment perspective glorifies the idea that people should want to be involved with one—and only one—other person. And it's true that attachment theory places a lot of weight on the idea that romantic partners form strong pair-bonds to each other, and it suggests that these bonds should be functional for keeping two partners together over time. For many people, a strong attachment to one partner renders them uninterested in romantic or sexual relationships with anyone else. There is a mononormative, "find your one and only" vibe to these findings and ideas.[24]

But attachment theory can also account for a variety of relational configurations beyond the prototypical romantic dyad. Children regularly bond to more than one caregiver, after all, and the science of attachment has long acknowledged that people can have multiple strong attachment figures. Therefore, the fact that some people can love and support multiple romantic partners at the same time—as evidenced by cultures that allow polygyny, or the contemporary polyamorous community in the United States—is perfectly consistent with attachment theory.[25]

Also, an attachment framework does not require that bonds be romantic or sexual. When people are single—over the long term, or in the interstitial period between one relationship and the next—they commonly form attachments to close friends or siblings, and they find secure base and safe haven support through those avenues. And to the extent that single people have meaningful, bonded, and supportive relationships with these close others, they experience less loneliness and greater life satisfaction. So yes, attachment bonds in adulthood are often romantic, but they can provide the same health and well-being benefits in platonic relationships.[26]

A related objection to the attachment perspective on human mating is that there is something deeply unsexy about the attachment, safe haven, and secure base concepts. After all, attachments both require and generate stability. Bonded couples naturally strive to make life predictable, and they craft routines that maintain their sanity. These impulses are good for healthy daily living, but they tend to squash the uncertainty and spontaneity that spark passion and desire. It is reasonable to wonder: If bonding drains sexual desire—the basic engine of reproduction—how can it be that humans evolved to form attachments to their mating partners? In this light, sexual desire seems incompatible with bonding.

There are two issues here that we need to untangle. First, this supposed fling vs. bond trade-off illustrates why the trajectory perspectives on the short-term vs. long-term distinction were so critical back in chapter 3. Early on, as two people are getting to know each other and romantic desire is increasing, there is no sexual desire vs. intimacy trade-off, period. On the contrary, sex can initiate the process of bonding (and vice versa, as with Emma and Sara), and people are commonly striving for both passion and intimacy. Of course, people can have sex with each other in the absence of any desire for bonding or intimacy, but having sex always entails the "risk" of infatuation, catching feelings, and forming an attachment. Sex and bonding are quite closely tied to each other as people initiate relationships.[27]

Second, many couples do experience something akin to a fling vs. bond trade-off *within the same relationship* over time, as passion and sexual desire gradually decline. This shift is real, but blaming it on the emergence of an attachment bond is probably incorrect. Consider the advice from famed sex therapist Esther Perel: Couples can keep their sex lives alive not by eschewing intimate bonding but rather by fostering a sense of mystery and curiosity about each other. Mystery and curiosity come for free at the start of a relationship. We forget about our daily stresses and focus all our energies on getting to know this new person; how many of us have happily let our work life slide after meeting somebody who sweeps us off our feet?[28]

Eventually, real life sets in again and competes with mystery and curiosity; responsibilities, demands on our time and attention, and exhaustion are hardly aphrodisiacs. The solution, then, is twofold. First, remember to be separate people, with independent goals and interests. Growth outside the relationship can rekindle the mystery; some degree of separation will mean that there will be new things to be shared and discovered. Second, spend time together in a way that subverts or avoids the daily grind and routines. There is great wisdom in the observation that middle-aged couples need to get away from work and the kids for a few days, spend time together doing something novel, and they'll soon be having sex again like they're teenagers.

Humans Need Humans

When we receive safe haven and secure base support from our partners, we are more likely to thrive. We believe that our lives have purpose and meaning, we feel a sense of connection to others, we give our time and energy generously, and we become optimistic and resilient. And all this support makes us literally healthier: We become calm and centered, we sleep better, and our immune systems run more smoothly. Safe haven and secure base offer a vivid illustration of why attachment bonding—yes, even in adulthood—is a central part of the way we navigate our social world.[29]

If you want a relationship to have real potential, try to cultivate safe haven and secure base support from the start. On the safe haven side, that cultivation looks something like this:

- **Create a sense of security** for your partner. There is commonly an early period of uncertainty as a relationship is getting off the ground; feelings can be murky and unstable and hard to pin down. But once you know this is someone you want to be with, say it, even if it makes you feel vulnerable. To be a safe haven, you have to show that you can be a rock for someone when they feel sad or defeated. No one wants to open up if they're afraid their partner might bolt at the first sign of real emotion.

- **Practice being a good listener.** Honest, meaningful, personal disclosures are rare. When your partner offers you one, it means that they trust you. But the onus is then on you to reflect care and sensitivity back to your partner. This reflection sounds easy in the abstract, but listening well is shockingly challenging if your partner's concerns don't seem like a big deal to you, or if you might have handled things differently. Most people find that becoming a good listener for their partner takes some practice—practice in the context of your particular relationship. It's okay to ask later: "Did I offer you the support you were looking for in that moment?" If the answer is "Sorta, kinda" or "Not really," accept the feedback and try again.

On the secure base side, that cultivation looks something like this:

- **Make a point of basking in each other's successes.** Bask even for the daily victories that seem small: You survived yet another grueling day of work and family demands? A toast is in order! Of course, the big wins require celebrations, too, and sometimes those can be especially tricky, because properly appreciating your partner requires putting yourself on the back burner temporarily. Ask for details! Show pride! Describe in your own words why your partner *deserves* to be excited.[30]

- Encouraging your partner will often require that you **accept your partner for who they are** and who they want to be. Sometimes, your partner may have goals and aspirations that seem strange to you, or that you would not pick yourself. Proper encouragement requires an ability to distinguish between what you might *imagine* wanting in their shoes and what your partner *actually* wants for themselves.[31]

HUMANS SURVIVE AND thrive when we have close others we can rely on. This fact reflects a fundamental human need—the *need to belong*—and this need evolved because our ancestors could only survive prehistoric dangers when someone had their back. Even today, bonds keep us alive, quite literally: Social connections provide the same life-extending benefits as exercise and quitting smoking. When I delve into these topics in my class, my students' faces tell a powerful story. I see relief if they currently have someone they can lean on, and profound sadness if they don't.[32]

The science of relationships is grounded in an evolutionary perspective on attachment and pair-bonding—it just happens to be a vastly different evolutionary perspective than the one we disassembled in the first part of this book. That is, attachment bonds offer a massive caveat to the EvoScript idea that relationship initiation is all about good genes and showing off. Yes, we sometimes find the hot jackasses appealing. But we also pursue partners who make us feel supported, who know how to encourage us when challenges arise, and who know how to celebrate our good news.

Pair-bonds are a small miracle, but they don't come free. The ingredients of strong attachments—commiserating, party-planning, and a willingness to set your own needs aside—require time and motivation. How fortuitous, then, that humans appear to possess several convenient psychological quirks that make these investments a whole lot easier. For example, romantic partners tend to see each other in the best possible light; aided by motivated reasoning, they exaggerate each other's strengths and compartmentalize any lingering flaws. When people are in committed relationships, they find alternative partners on the sidelines to be as appealing as gas station sushi. And finally, romantic partners commonly form communal relationships, which means that they try to meet each other's needs without worrying about whether their partner will pay them back at some point. The next chapter will explain how these pro-relationship biases and communal orientations form the core ingredients that explain the inner workings of highly functional romantic bonds.

· 5 ·

Attachment Part 2: The Biases That Bind

People tend not to be very objective about their relationships. Couples commonly come to see each other in the best possible light, and they develop a habit of devaluing any alternative partners who might be lurking on the sidelines. They do these things even if the relationship is still developing. And if the purpose of the pair-bond is to help couples withstand threats and challenges, these biases are downright essential.

The film *(500) Days of Summer* provides a vivid illustration of the biased way we look at our romantic partners. Tom, played by Joseph Gordon-Levitt, declares that he has fallen in love with Summer, played by Zooey Deschanel:

> I'm in love with Summer. I love her smile. I love her hair. I love her knees. I love this heart-shaped birthmark she has on her neck. I love the way she sometimes licks her lips before she talks. I love the sound of her laugh.

If you are a Zooey Deschanel fan, this speech may strike you as an objective assessment of Summer's positive qualities. Fair enough. But consider Tom's opinion later in the film, after he and Summer have broken up:

> I hate Summer. I hate her crooked teeth. I hate her 1960s haircut. I hate her knobby knees. I hate her cockroach-shaped splotch

on her neck. I hate the way she smacks her lips before she talks. And I hate the way she sounds when she laughs.

Romantic partners' attributes are subject to interpretation. When people are deeply in love and bonded to their romantic partners, those interpretations tend to be quite generous. After they break up? Not so much.

Biases Keep Your Relationship Going

It's tricky to demonstrate that something is a bias. Perhaps we could show that Tom is biased if we possessed some objective truth about the lovability of Summer's smile, hair, and knees. In real life, objective benchmarks are rare.

Instead, researchers usually look for psychological *shifts* that suggest an underlying bias. For example, imagine you discover that your new partner is less concerned about keeping a tidy apartment than you had realized. An objective person might think deeply about this troubling development and ponder whether it could be a red flag. A biased person, however, would react by minimizing the messiness and becoming more convinced that their partner is the greatest. "Okay, so she's a little messy. It's only because she's laid back and easy going, and that's why she's perfect for me in the first place. Plus, I get joy out of tidying up!" This statement isn't a lie; it might not even be wrong. But it is cognitive dissonance: The average person wants to believe their relationship is strong, so they reinterpret new information to suit that desired conclusion.

One classic study tested people's biases with compelling (but fake) *Psychology Today* articles arguing that conflict is good for a relationship. The average person likely finds this article concerning; very few people go around thinking their relationship is both happy and riddled with conflict. In response, people who read this article then believed that their relationships had more conflict than the people who did not read the article. "Good relationships have conflict, you say? Now that you mention it, I guess we do fight a lot!" In another study, some people read that relationships thrive when partners are different from each other. And then—surprise, surprise—these people tended to notice more differences between themselves and their partners. "She loves Bravo reality shows, I love Netflix reality shows. Look how dissimilar we are!"[1]

To an experimental psychologist, these are demonstrations of bias. They are shifts in people's thinking that make them feel better about their relationship in the face of new, potentially destabilizing information.

Here's another example: Tell a college-aged dating couple that their relationship is ultimately likely to break up; yeah, things seem good now, but the average couple like you eventually grows apart. When people hear discouraging messages like this, they react by bolstering their relationship in their minds. Specifically, they become more certain that their relationship is better than other people's relationships—a phenomenon called *perceived superiority*. To hell with your stereotypes about college couples; we're the exception![2]

Before you scoff at their defensiveness: People who engage in this line of reasoning are less, not more, likely to break up. In other words, being positively biased about your partner is a route to a lasting relationship. Experimenters in one study asked people to reflect on their romantic partner's greatest faults, and the relationships that ultimately lasted the longest were the ones where people engaged in more "yes, but" responses. Responses like "He can be withdrawn, but he shows me he cares in so many other ways" or "She is messy, but I wouldn't ask her to give up her free-spirited ways for anything." These statements might seem like silly excuses to outsiders, but the reality is that people maintain stable bonds by minimizing and compartmentalizing a partner's faults in this way.[3]

Researchers have documented so many biases like these that they have concluded that people go through their love lives with a "progression bias." That is, the typical relationship resides on a conveyor belt: People have the default impulse to invest in their relationships and make decisions that keep things moving forward. And it starts early. Recall the speed and ease with which we form attachment bonds: It takes mere months before people start using their new dating partners as a safe haven and as a secure base. Not to mention, the simple discovery that someone promising is into you is sufficient to kickstart the biased thoughts. ("Oh, she thinks I'm hot? You know, I never realized how funny she is!") Then, once we start making these investments in our relationships, it becomes easier and easier to keep the bond going and downplay any incompatibilities. And it's a good bet that we evolved to do it this way: What mattered was building a bond and setting the stage for investment, not finding the perfect partner.[4]

One massive caveat: Just because these biases sustain relationships on average does not mean that they are always a "good thing." In modern contexts, when choices are plentiful, it's possible that pro-relationship biases can cause people to stay committed to suboptimal partnerships. In other words, these biases can cause people to overlook "this will become toxic" flaws just as easily as they cause people to appropriately contextualize "we're all human" flaws. Sometimes, the red flags are worth taking seriously, and it sure would be wise to bail on a relationship sooner, before the investments become irrevocable.

Here, we encounter some limitations of the science to date: There is no manual for determining when the biases set people down a good or bad path. Most flaws are forgivable human flaws, and people would never form bonds at all if they couldn't spin them into something adorable, or at least tolerable. But some flaws are indefensible, and people with those flaws need to sort themselves out before bringing a romantic partner into their orbit. Sadly for relationship-seekers, there are very few objective, consistently applicable rules that can differentiate the forgivable from the indefensible flaws. For relationships that are currently going fine, it is nearly impossible to forecast whether things will or won't take a nasty turn in the future. Pro-relationship biases help couples endure the hard times, but they also explain why many couples end up riding out a bad relationship until it gets, well, *really* bad.[5]*

---

* We'll discuss more about what you *can* do to assess whether a troubled relationship should be fixed or ditched in chapter 7.

• • •

THE SAME BIOLOGICAL attachment system that sustains our pro-relationship biases and primes us to give and receive support was also designed by natural selection to tune itself to surrounding conditions. If you had positive experiences with your caregivers in childhood—if parents or other family members were reliably comforting and responsive, for example—you likely developed a *secure* "attachment style" with them. You would have internalized the belief that you were worthy of love, and you would have learned to rely on close others when you needed them.

There are two alternatives to the secure style. If you had experiences with caregivers who were unreliable, you likely developed an *avoidant* attachment style. You would have internalized the lesson that you can't really depend on anyone, and you would have learned to manage distress by yourself. Or, if you had experiences with caregivers who were sometimes present, sometimes absent, and sometimes intrusive, you likely developed an *anxious* attachment style. You would have internalized a sense that caregivers come to your aid only when you dramatically amp up the anguish, and you would worry a lot about whether others really loved you.[6]

The 2010 book *Attached* catapulted the science behind these three attachment styles into the public consciousness. These styles are a key part of the human pair-bond, too, and acquiring insight into one's own attachment style is potentially useful, because the styles can explain why people feel and behave the way that they do. If you are perpetually worried that your partner will leave you, you may have an anxious style, and there is perhaps a deeper origin for your fears of abandonment. If you find yourself needing more space than your partner naturally seems to give you, you may have an avoidant style, and you might want to interrogate why it is that you don't feel comfortable going to others for help.[7]

Nevertheless, pause for a moment before you get too deep into this self-diagnosis. Scientists' understanding of anxiety and avoidance has changed quite a bit over the last few decades. Critically, an attachment style does not appear to be a stable, immutable part of a person's identity. It is undeniably true that your relationship experiences are affected by your own personal qualities. You bring yourself with you—your baggage and your resources—wherever you go. It is also true that your relationship is likely to be an unhappy one if you feel anxiously or avoidantly attached to your partner. But it's also easy to overestimate the power of your attachment style by focusing too much on a single salient relationship, rather than the way that you behave across *multiple* relationships.

On this point, one particular study design has proven extremely illuminating. A select few research studies track how consistently satisfied or unsatisfied people are with their relationships *across different partnerships in their life*. Think about it: If relationship happiness flows from the stable aspects of your attachment style or personality, you should be similarly happy from one relationship to the next.

These studies have mostly documented *instability*. Specifically, if you're unhappy in one relationship, you have about a 60 percent chance of being unhappy in your next relationship and a 40 percent chance of being happy. Similarly, if you're happy in one relationship, you have a 60 percent chance of being happy and a 40 percent chance of being unhappy in your next relationship. While 60/40 is higher odds than a coin flip, it's not a certainty; people's experiences can differ quite a bit from one relationship to the next. For people who have the goal of moving from an unhappy relationship to a happy one, there is reason to be cautiously optimistic.[8]

It's possible to juice those odds further with some time off to work on yourself. Therapy generally helps with all things interpersonal. In experimental studies, psychotherapy causes people to feel happier in their relationships across the board, whether they're partnered or not, and regardless of who they're with. Also, a longer time lag in between relationships—a couple of years, rather than just a few months—predicts that a person will be considerably happier in their next relationship than in the one they left behind.[9]

Our attachment styles, too, can change as we grow and mature. The association between people's childhood experiences and their attachment style in adulthood is fairly small; many people who are anxious and/or avoidant children become secure adults, and vice versa. This carryover effect is weak because close others continually shape people's attachment styles throughout the entirety of their lives. When people have experiences with responsive partners later in adolescence or adulthood, they become more secure, in a permanent and enduring way.[10]

Critically, the path toward relationship security has little to do with the specific events that take place in our relationships. Rather, security follows from the way we interpret those experiences. For example, at an intuitive level, getting into a major fight or having to be physically apart from your partner sound like ingredients for attachment insecurity. On average, these are indeed unpleasant episodes in the moment. But the reality is, the long-term effects of these "bad events" dramatically differ from person to person and couple to couple: Many people find massive silver linings in these experiences, and subsequently, their avoidance and anxiety decline in a permanent and enduring way. People have considerable agency in the way that they allow major life events to impact their attachment style.[11]

Similarly, attachment styles are primarily shaped by current relationship experiences however responsive or rejecting those experiences happen to be. Consider that polyamorous folks—who are in multiple romantic relationships at the same time—form specific attachment styles *with each of their partners*. In other words, if you were polyamorous, you might be avoidant with partner one and not at all avoidant with partner two. To put specific numbers on it: Polyamorous individuals who are avoidant in one relationship have about a 58 percent chance of being avoidant in a second relationship. For anxiety, the story is similar. For people who are anxious in one relationship, there is about a 65 percent chance they'll be anxious in their second relationship.

These numbers are greater than 50/50, but they're certainly not determinative. You are not the same person as you were in prior relationships, and some degree of reinvention is nearly always possible. So yes, people have an attachment style, but those styles are more of a tendency than a destiny, and it's easy to underestimate how flexible your style can be.[12]

Biases Keep Interlopers at Bay

For weeks, Andre had been unable to shake a gnawing anxiety. His partner, Erica, was working on a major case, and the sheer volume of paperwork meant that she was staying late most nights. In and of itself, this development wouldn't be especially troubling. No, the real source of his worry was the new hire at Erica's law firm—a charismatic man named David with movie-star looks and a dazzling smile. Andre feared that David was the more appealing reason that Erica had been willing to spend so many hours at the office.

One evening, Erica arrived home, looking happy but exhausted and holding a stack of files. She kissed Andre hello and they sat down together. She gave him updates about the case, but Andre struggled to focus. His mind kept wandering to imagined scenarios of Erica and David sharing inside jokes, ordering takeout, and concocting more reasons to spend time together.

Andre tried to act casual. "So, how's it going with the new guy?"

"David? Yeah, I don't know about him. I mean, look, I'm glad to have an extra pair of hands on this one. But wow, is he full of himself. Telling people what to do even though he just got here; maybe listen before you start changing the whole strategy? Ugh."

Andre seemed relieved, but he wasn't ready to let go just yet. "He's pretty hot though, yeah?"

Only now did Erica identify Andre's anxiety. "Compared to you? Not close. Plus, what do I want with some maverick pain-in-the-ass? Exhausting."

A smile spread across both of their faces.

. . .

One of the greatest threats to any relationship is the possibility that another tempting partner will come along. To be sure, this threat was far less common in ancestral environments than in modern, highly populated ones. Nevertheless, had you lived back then, it's possible that a guy at the next campsite would have made eyes at you on occasion. How might ancestral-you have managed this temptation?

Again, biases come to the rescue. The bias in this case is called *derogation of alternatives,* and it refers to the fact that people who are involved in a committed relationship generally view alternative partners to be less desirable than they actually are. In other words, the fact that Erica was in a committed relationship caused her to believe that hot-but-overconfident David was less appealing than a single person would. This bias meant that Andre truly had little to worry about.[13]

This particular bias tends to emerge in all sorts of ways that aren't fully conscious. In one study, single and partnered people attempted to reconstruct an attractive opposite-gender face using a computer program that acted like a forensic sketch artist. When these sketches were done, the photograph that the partnered people recalled was less attractive than the photograph that single people recalled. The image that had lodged into partnered people's minds had degraded from hot to not.[14]

Partnered and single people behave differently, too, but in subtle ways. One series of studies recruited heterosexual men and women and found that partnered people used less inviting body language than single people when interacting with someone of the other gender. Committed people give off nonverbal signals that they aren't available, probably without even realizing it.[15]

This tendency to derogate alternatives seems to be amplified during moments when people feel especially in love with their partner. In other words, feeling bonded to a partner suppresses whether people even pay attention to attractive interlopers in the first place.[16]

Finally, assume for the sake of argument that a hottie does manage to break through someone's perceptual defenses. Okay, so Erica did notice that David's upper arms are particularly well defined. Paradoxically, that brief little fantasy about someone else is likely to make her feel *more* sexual desire for her partner Andre, not less. In other words, fantasies about other people have a way of rebounding back onto our current partners, as if the pair-bond compensates when we happen to notice alternative partners in our midst. These studies serve as helpful reminders that, despite the apparent power and ubiquity of the contemporary mating market, one of humans' most effective psychological tools for staying in a relationship is the ability to downplay or repurpose their feelings for alternative partners on said market.[17]

Of course, cheating and infidelity are real and profoundly destructive to relationships. Simply being partnered provides some protection from temptation, and the more committed you are to that relationship, the more protection you have. But that protection is far from foolproof, and courting temptation is risky: Maybe don't have that third drink with next-door campsite guy unless you're eager to play with fire.[18]

But in a broader evolutionary context, the cheating heart of *Homo sapiens* looks rather tame. Scientists have developed brand-new methods to estimate how often the woman in a married couple has a child who was not fathered by her husband. These researchers study time periods on the order of centuries, so they can assess the tendency to cheat as it existed before the advent of modern birth control methods. According to these studies, approximately 1 percent of children have historically been sired by someone who was not their purported father. As far as pair-bonding animals go, that is the low end of the scale—by a lot. In pair-bonding birds, the average number of offspring with an extra-pair father is around 10 percent. In nonhuman, pair-bonding mammals, it's closer to 40 percent.[19]

So yes, cheating happens, and it often tears relationships apart. Even that 1 percent estimate is hundreds of millions of people, historically speaking—many of whom experienced anger and heartbreak. But natural selection appears to have given humans an ability to bond with romantic partners, and avoid alternative ones, that outperforms many other pair-bonding species.

Recall the cover of the *Time* magazine article from my introduction, which asked whether infidelity was in our genes? The answer, as it turned out, is "Hardly at all."

• • •

COUPLES HAVE THE mental tools to see the best in each other and an instinct to dodge temptation, and the ones who perform these feats well are likely to stand the test of time. These facts are hard to reconcile with the "we're all looking to trade up" pessimism of the EvoScript. However, the ever-powerful market metaphor lives on in subtler forms. Consider a 2023 episode of *The Ezra Klein Show*, where LGBTQ-rights pioneer Dan Savage made the following observation:

> I think all relationships, if you really peel the layers back far enough, are, at some point, transactional. I pay for it with my husband. I don't pay for it with cash money. I pay for it with time, attention, affection, concern, making sure he goes to see the doctor when he needs to go see the doctor.

Many people will find this sentiment unobjectionable, and perhaps even obvious. Of course there is reciprocity between romantic partners, and you have to give something in order to get something.[20]

Nevertheless, calling this dynamic "transactional" is fundamentally misguided. And I only pick on Dan Savage to illustrate how deeply the market metaphor has infected our view of relationships: Even thinkers at the progressive vanguard can be tempted by the economic model of human mating. But the model is not correct, because most close romantic relationships do not use the same exchange norms that characterize contemporary market-based economies, as Savage implies. Instead, most relationships operate via communal norms, such that romantic partners regularly do things for each other in response to each other's *needs*, without any obligation to be "paid back." What's more: well-functioning relationships—those with a strong base of understanding, respect, and attunement—tend to be *especially* communal.[21]

The reason why relationships work this way harkens back, once more, to some psychological abilities that evolved among our early ancestors.

Two Abilities, Together in One Great Ape

As nonhuman animals go, chimpanzees are decent mind readers. If Rocky is staring at something, Bobo is likely to surmise that Rocky is staring at something interesting, even if Bobo himself can't see it. Similarly, if Bobo has a delicious fig in his possession, he's likely to be attuned to whether Rocky can see the fig, for fear that Rocky might try to steal it. Finally, Bobo can figure out if Rocky did something on purpose or by accident. And if Rocky seems unwilling (rather than simply unable) to share, Bobo is likely to go hang out with someone else.[22]

These are useful and rare cognitive skills in the animal kingdom. But here's an interesting wrinkle: Chimpanzees seem to deploy these exceptional mind-reading skills for competitive purposes, and competitive purposes only. That is, chimpanzees use mind reading to obtain rewards for themselves; they're paying attention to others' minds for their own personal gain.

You won't be surprised to learn that humans inherited these mind-reading skills, probably from our most recent common ancestor with chimpanzees. But the difference is that we deploy them beyond competitive settings. If you are staring at something valuable in my possession, I might correctly infer that you want some and spontaneously offer to share it with you. That's because humans have a separate skill that the other great apes lack: an extreme form of prosociality.[23]

Chimpanzees and the other great apes aren't terribly prosocial. They might share things with each other, sure, but only after a few rounds of intimidation or begging. When chimpanzee parents share food with their offspring, you might call it "tolerated theft." It certainly isn't "You've got to try this delicious mango."

If we hop over to a different part of the tree of life, we can find primates who are extremely prosocial, like humans. These primates, like marmosets and tamarins, are called *cooperative breeders*, which means that these animals live in groups and spread out the caretaking responsibilities. The adaptive logic is similar to pair-bonding, but cooperative breeding goes even further. For these animals, the motivation to be prosocial—to share food or offer protection—even extends to unrelated offspring.

Critically, humans are the only animals that have *both* outstanding mind-reading abilities and the extreme prosociality that comes with cooperative breeding. The combination of these two abilities yields behaviors that don't appear anywhere else in the animal kingdom. Because humans are extremely prosocial, we are motivated to share with other members of our group, just like marmosets and tamarins do. But combine this skill with mind reading, and humans want to share more than "stuff"—they also want to share the contents of their minds. In other words, we are motivated to share reality with our close others: I want to share my perceptions and my worldview with you, as if I want you to experience what I'm experiencing. This is why it feels terrible to show a hilarious YouTube video to a loved one if they don't even crack a smile. This is why a good meal tastes even more amazing if you are sharing it.[24]

Relatedly, humans have a uniquely powerful desire to teach. If I have some beneficial knowledge or skill, and I care about you, I should want you to have this knowledge or skill, too. Humans can also work together on joint problems: I know you understand this challenge in the same way that I do, and I want us to work collaboratively to find a solution.[25]

Humans—and probably only humans—want to share reality with our close others. We derive joy out of doing things for each other and building new things together. If the relationship is important enough, the only thing that we want in return is to feel valued and appreciated.

These ideas are much harder to reconcile with the economic model of human mating.

Well-Functioning Relationships Are Communal, Not Transactional

In season 2 of *The Bear*, chef Carmy is troubled by a looming appointment at his restaurant with fire inspectors, and his new girlfriend

Claire assures him that he has it under control. As a part of this conversation, she lets him in on one of the best-kept relational secrets:

CARMY: I'm really sorry, I just, like, um [tears up]

CLAIRE: Never, ever apologize.

CARMY: I just want you to know that this is really nice. So nice that I, uh . . .

CLAIRE: You're waiting for the other shoe.

CARMY: That's it.

CLAIRE: You wanna know a secret?

CARMY: Yes.

CLAIRE: Nobody's keeping track of shoes.

CARMY: Woah.

CLAIRE: I know!

In the universe of ongoing relationships—whether they are between close romantic partners, friends with benefits, platonic friends, acquaintances, parents and children, clients and customers, or you name it—there is a key distinction between exchange norms and communal norms. With exchange norms, two people do things to benefit each other, and there is a mutual understanding that those benefits should even out. If Jess covers for her co-worker Angelo's shift, Jess can expect that Angelo will do something comparably nice for her, and vice versa. Critically, the two of them must keep track of benefits given and received, so that over time, their professional relationship remains balanced. Exchange norms like these are useful because they create stable, predictable rules that give people confidence that they won't get taken for a ride.

Communal norms function quite differently. With communal norms, two people respond to each other's needs as best they can, without worrying about who has done what for whom. If Carmy needs something—be it a favor, a shoulder to cry on, or cheers of encouragement—Claire offers support if she can. It is neither necessary nor desirable for two people in a communal relationship to track the balance of benefits given and received; there is no ledger that records who contributes more. In the long run, if Claire happens to need less support than Carmy does, that's fine. Being in a communal relationship doesn't mean that Claire neglects herself; sometimes, she'll need favors, shoulders, and cheers, too. She *should* be paying attention to whether the relationship is meeting her needs. But in a communal relationship, she would be ignoring whether she is getting more or less than Carmy.

Putting yourself in a position to give more than you get perhaps sounds like a recipe for disappointment and frustration. "I do the grocery shopping so you can have fun with your friends, or make extra progress at work, or kick back and watch a show. And I'm not supposed to care whether you do the same thing for me?" Many people feel a powerful and understandable self-protective impulse that causes them to say "Hell, no" to this arrangement, at least in the abstract. Nevertheless, as long as your grocery shopping is not a broader symptom of how a relationship is failing to meet your own needs, then this arrangement is absolutely the right way to achieve a satisfying and lasting relationship.

The goal in a communal relationship is to drop the self-protective impulse. Too much self-protection hinders intimacy, which reduces trust, which smothers the major upside of being in a close relationship in the first place. Communal norms are essential because they make it possible for two people to rely on each other as a resource. That is, if a couple can trust each other and lose the vigilance, then risks and costs become distributed across two people rather than one. When two people have each other's backs, they look out for each other's welfare, and they set higher ambitions.

People unambiguously prefer to operate by communal rather than exchange norms in their romantic relationships. Specifically, people are far more likely to say that the ideal relationship is characterized by two people doing things for each other based on needs, and not because they expect to be paid back. In fact, the power of people's preference for communal over exchange norms dwarfs pretty much all other research findings on attraction and relationships: People resoundingly disagree that good close relationships involve the exchange of favors. Another key, nearly-as-gigantic effect comes from the same study: Married couples say that their relationship actually *does* function by communal rather than exchange norms.[26]

Couples are right to think this way because people who say that they place a high priority on meeting the needs of their partner and people who do nice things for their partner on a regular basis without expecting to be paid back—tend to be happier with life and happier in their relationships. On the flipside, people who keep track of the favors they give and receive tend to be somewhat less happy in their relationships.[27]

In some contexts, exchange relationships make sense. Markets have their place. Nevertheless, people want their romantic relationships to be communal, and they tend to be happiest when they can make it work that way.

To be clear, "communal" does not mean "selfless." People derive a lot of joy and meaning out of doing helpful things for their partners: It's highly rewarding to receive appreciation and gratitude, or to share a delicious mango and a funny YouTube video with a partner who responds with the appropriate level of appreciation and enthusiasm. Plus, people commonly take on their partner's needs as their own. Then, grocery shopping doesn't feel like a sacrifice, because you want your partner to have fun with their friends, or to kick ass on that work project, or to enjoy some time off. You genuinely want to see them thrive, succeed, and relax.

Of course, people will walk away from communal relationships if their own needs aren't being met. In fact, if you don't want to see your partner thrive, succeed, and relax, you might want to question whether *your* needs are being met. Being communal doesn't require you to drop all rationality. It simply means you dropped the market-based assumption that benefits should match contributions.

Building and Breaking Communal Patterns

Strong communal relationships do not emerge out of nowhere. First and foremost, if couples are going to make a communal relationship work, they need to have a solid sense of their collective needs. Naturally, that means being aware of your own stable, personal needs, and being aware of how your needs change as time passes and goals come and go. Consider two parents working full-time jobs with young kids: Both parents will feel the need to spend time with their kids, to spend time on work, and to spend time recuperating and staring into space. How will each partner experience these needs? And how will the relative power of these needs change when the kids are one, or five, or nine; when work responsibilities ramp up or cool down; when grandparents are eager to help out or need help themselves? The answers are challenging to forecast, and that's why a near-constant open-minded dialogue is essential for making a communal relationship work.

As this process unfolds, many couples end up building complex webs of goals and activities in which everything is connected to everything else. Here's an average Monday for Andre and Erica: Andre graciously takes Erica's laptop in to get repaired, but Andre needs the car to do so, and that requires Erica to shift the timing of her daily marathon training. Later, Erica's colleagues spontaneously take her out for drinks to celebrate a promotion, so Andre leaves work early to cook dinner so they can have a relaxing evening when she gets home. These multilayered edifices of mutual goals, needs, and preferences are unique to each relationship, and it takes considerable trial and error to figure out how to make sharing your life with someone delightful rather than stressful.[28]

As long as the relationship seems to be meeting both partner's needs, couples prefer to ignore who is doing more to keep this structure upright. If your partner generally seems to be there when you need them, it's all good. You get to take on faith that your partner is looking out for you, and you're perfectly happy to donate some of your time and energy to them. In fact, couples whose goals and needs are intertwined—they agree with statements like "What we do in day-to-day life is affected not only by our goals, but also by each other's goals"—tend to be happier in their relationships.[29]

However, people's attention tends to shift once their needs aren't being met anymore. People begin to notice how existing relational grooves that once worked well now feel terribly uneven and unfair. Only then do they start keeping track of who is contributing more. Not only is Erica training for a marathon, but she also decides to join a pickleball league that meets twice a week. The next time she stays late at work, Andre begins to count how many nights over the past month he has sidelined his own plans to pick up the slack for her. Naturally, he recalls making many sacrifices, but he has only vague, fuzzy memories of the things Erica did for him. It is remarkably easy for him—or anyone, for that matter—to feel aggrieved when privately calculating these costs and benefits. Not surprisingly, then, Andre arrives at the conclusion that he is doing far more than his fair share in this relationship. Distance and isolation follow.[30]

The impulse to keep track of who does more is usually a warning sign that the communal strength of the relationship is breaking down. This breakdown can happen for various reasons. Sometimes the wounds are self-inflicted, such as when modern couples take on too many professional and personal responsibilities and forget to build in daily time to reconnect with each other. But often, the source comes from outside the relationship itself.

Like stress. Stress is rough on relationships for two reasons. First, when couples are stressed, it generally means that they aren't spending time together; instead, they're off trying to manage the extra work nonsense, or family responsibilities, or financial crises, or health issues. Second, stress causes the (now limited) time that couples spend together to become the opposite of quality time. Instead, they're arguing or anxious about whatever unpleasantness is causing the stress in the first place.

The negative effects of stress play out on a daily level, such that people become more impatient and critical of their partners on days when they're especially stressed. The negative effects of stress also extend over time; people who experience more financial insecurity, or health problems, or any other kind of hardship outside of the relationship are less likely to be happy in their relationships over the long term.[31]

A recent study illustrates how communal systems can be put to the test under stress. During the early weeks of the Covid-19 pandemic, the government of New Zealand (like many other governments around the world) closed schools and childcare facilities to slow the spread of the virus. This was an extremely challenging time for parents of young children, who now had to find a way to balance childcare and work within the confines of their own homes. In a study of approximately three hundred parents who were enduring this stress, the researchers found that people became much more dissatisfied with their relationships if they were doing more than half of the household tasks and enjoying less than half of the leisure time. Furthermore, any imbalances in the division of housework and leisure time didn't seem to be related to how happy couples were before the school and childcare closures began. Rather, when the stressful times hit, couples started to feel mistreated if they were putting in more than their fair share.[32]

When things get sticky, it can be hard to maintain the faith and goodwill that enables someone to keep taking on their partner's needs as their own. Being willing and open to change existing patterns is key during these moments, especially if someone feels the urge to start tracking who gets to spend more time playing with their phone. Many couples wisely broke with their existing, unequal patterns of housework and childcare when the pandemic hit, such that fathers started to take on a relatively larger share of the responsibilities. In other words, mindlessly adhering to an imbalanced pattern may be a poor strategy when stressors make their appearance.[33]

Communal relationships tend to be the happier ones, and this fact is part of our bonded heritage, too. Attachments don't require market-like trading patterns; bonded partners don't pay costs to receive benefits of equal measure. The idea that romantic partners perform acts of kindness and generosity for each other as a form of payment is a residue from the flawed market metaphor. In fact, market-like patterns are commonly a warning sign that a communal relationship is fraying and reverting to something that doesn't resemble an attachment bond at all.

· · ·

Evolutionary psychologists are fond of a quote from evolutionary anthropologist Dr. Irven DeVore: "Males are a vast breeding experiment run by females." The idea illustrated by this quip is that female mating choices over the generations have shaped men to behave in a particular way. This comment is often invoked as an explanation for why men are aggressive and violent, or why they are enamored with boosting their power and status. "Ladies, you made us this way, because you actually love us for these qualities. You're welcome for the patriarchy."[34]

But when you look at the full evolutionary trajectory of *Homo sapiens*—and you start with the fact that we are first and foremost a pair-bonding creature—the implication completely changes. "Males are a vast breeding experiment run by females" implies that women shaped men into a creature that attaches and loves and cares for offspring. Women, through their choices over the last several million years, fostered these qualities in lieu of dominance and aggression. Women chose the men who had larger brains and who were similar to them in size and stature: the gentler, smarter men who were good parents and good partners.[35]

The remarkable thing about *Homo sapiens* is just how far we have traveled along this path since we diverged from our most recent common ancestor: The capacity to bond—to love and be loved—is universal across cultures and across time. These bonds are inextricably linked to our physiology, mental health, and physical health. The fact that women's choices did not eradicate bad male traits is important, but this observation misses the central defining feature of human evolution. The evolutionary story of our species is that men became nurturing protectors of their loved ones.

Finally, the "vast breeding experiment" comment implies a gender difference that is false in humans; it is equally true that females are a vast breeding experiment run by males. Men selected women to be intelligent, conscientious, resourceful, and once again, good partners and parents. Pair-bonding became adaptive, and partners of both genders selected each other to have the qualities that are conducive to it.

The evolved nature of human mating is that we have the capacity to love and bond, under the right circumstances. But the right circumstances can be elusive. After all, we aren't attracted to everyone we meet. Some relationships work out wonderfully, others do not. It's hard to develop the trust and intimacy that facilitates a true communal relationship. And as we have seen, relationship success doesn't hinge on finding the universally good partner. Success hinges on compatibility: finding the right partner *for you*.

How do we figure out if we're compatible with someone in the first place? That's the tricky part. Many laypeople—and many scientists, too—believe that compatibility derives from the fit between two people's attributes, traits, and preferences. In other words, if my personality matches your personality, we should make beautiful (e)harmony together. As we'll discover in the next chapter, the last decade of relationship science has found that this idea is deeply misguided: As intuitive as it may seem, we can't create good relationships by issuing questionnaires and creating matches from whatever makes sense on paper.

Compatibility will not be pinned down so easily.

· 6 ·

Compatibility, Fickle Beast

When I was in my twenties, I was the recipient of a truly profound romantic rejection. Not profound in the "I was sad and heartbroken" sense—although that part was true—nor in the "I became jealous and sulky" sense, although I did that, too. It was profound in the "I have deeply misunderstood what makes two people compatible" sense.

Lauren, the woman at the heart of this story, had begun drifting into my social orbit. She had an undeniable magnetism—she was charismatic, talented, intelligent. But what made Lauren truly remarkable was her ability to make those qualities contagious to those around her. Whenever I was in her presence, she had a knack for making me feel just as charismatic, talented, and brilliant. She could command the spotlight with grace, then effortlessly reel me into that radiant center alongside her. Being around her was downright intoxicating.

As long as I'd known Lauren, she'd always had a boyfriend. Then, suddenly, she didn't. One day we were chatting, and she declared that she was into me. It was a matter-of-fact aside—tossed out under the (correct) assumption that I would be reciprocating. She *was* confidence, purified and distilled into a physical form. But before I got ahead of myself, she warned me: There was another. We would just have to see how things evolved.

I was now in a competition, whether I liked it or not. Over the next few weeks, every word I spoke and every message I sent felt like it could be the decisive winning move. Or the losing one. I had to be attentive, but not desperate; charming, but not cocky. I had only met my rival a handful of times. He seemed personable, but with an edge to him. Despite my best intentions, I constantly obsessed about what he was up to. In fact, doing so sometimes made me feel better, because the two of them did not seem to be a good fit. Lauren and I enjoyed the same things, we had similar senses of humor, and we saw the world in the same way. But Lauren and this other guy? Weird fit. She was an incredible musician; he wasn't remotely musical. She was independent and driven; I'm pretty sure he still lived at home. My confidence rose.

That month was a stressful blur. But I remember the last night of this episode clearly. She suggested we meet at a bar—a place that my competitor was unlikely to be. This development seemed promising.

"I've made up my mind," she said.

My heart jumped.

"You're exactly what I've been looking for. You're smart; you're accomplished. We have pretty much everything in common."

There was a "but" coming, wasn't there?

"But I'm not feeling it. So I'm choosing him."

My stomach dropped.

It felt catastrophically unfair. The fit was there, we both agreed! We were perfect for each other. She was "Not feeling it"? I was being docked on a technicality. Nevertheless, any protests were pointless; it had been decided. I stood second on the podium.

Lauren and I had a ton in common, and I matched what Lauren was looking for in an ideal romantic partner. That much was indisputably true; we really were a perfect match . . . if we wrote it all out on paper. But the fact that I was similar to her—or that I matched her ideals—didn't cause her to feel anything for me. You'd think we would have been compatible, but unfortunately for me, we were not. In contrast, she and my rival were a massive mismatch on paper, and yet they ended up moving across the country together en route to a long and meaningful relationship.

. . .

How could this have happened? I had simply assumed that compatibility comes from the right mix of two people's interests, personality, preferences, and other personal attributes. After all, this assumption guides the stewards of the holy algorithms. Listen to Helen Fisher in her TED Talk: "They've never found the way two personalities fit together to make a good relationship. So it began to occur to me that maybe your biology pulls you towards some people rather than another." She argued that people evolved four personality types associated with the ratios of the chemicals dopamine, serotonin, estrogen, and testosterone in the brain. In an attempt to assess these chemically-driven personalities, she devised a set of questions for the website Chemistry.com like "I am very empathetic" (purportedly assessing estrogen) and "I pursue intellectual topics thoroughly and regularly" (purportedly assessing testosterone). A few years later, she claimed in another TED Talk to have cracked the code: People driven by dopamine and serotonin desire partners like themselves, and people driven by estrogen and testosterone desire their opposites.[1]

If you feel suspicious of these claims, you are right to be. Dr. Fisher correctly intuited that compatibility is important, but there's no scientific evidence that she could explain it by matching people using this questionnaire. And the problem isn't just the pseudo-biological scales. The problem is far deeper. The problem is that the *concept* of matching—similarity matching, preference matching, love-language matching, or any other kind of matching—doesn't really explain where compatibility comes from. Cultivating similarities in a relationship is fantastic. Harnessing positive biases to reframe your partner's attributes in the best possible light is wise. But drawing from a checklist of attributes to predict why we click with one partner and not another? It sounds nice, but compatibility just doesn't work that way.

Compatibility Is Vital

Compatibility is the central, essential ingredient in human mating relationships, regardless of whether we're talking about sexual attraction, relationship initiation, or long-term bonds. Compatibility is more important than mate value, and gender—and any other individual difference, for that matter. Compatibility explains why some pairs of people are especially into each other, some pairs never get things off the ground, and some pairs never let the idea cross their minds.

I've been at this idea relentlessly, but humor me as I lay out the full scope of the evidence. In chapter 1, we learned that the compatibility factor is the largest ingredient in the cocktail that makes up attraction. That is, people's romantic feelings about another person primarily derive from the way the two of them do or don't click. In initial-impression settings, the consensus factor—the engine of mate value—is certainly present, but the compatibility factor is larger. In other words, when you first meet someone, that sense of fit you have with them is more central than the extent to which they are generally desirable.[2]

Second, we also learned how the consensus factor gets smaller as people get to know each other. I also hinted at the fact that the compatibility factor begins to take over with time. In other words, people originally agree—at least a bit—about who is desirable and who is not, but that agreement gradually fades and is replaced by uniqueness. With time, people's impressions of one another are dominated by compatibility, as shown in figure 6.1.[3]

Third, we learned in chapter 3 that there are very few reliable ways to predict who will be a good long-term relationship partner: That is, it is remarkably hard to explain why you are (or are not) happy in a relationship using only information about your partner's personality and traits. This observation means that long-term relationship quality requires compatibility, not finding a "good man" or a "good woman" as a long-term partner.[4]

Fourth, there are key adaptive benefits to being in a close relationship, as we discussed in chapters 4 and 5. Central among these is that

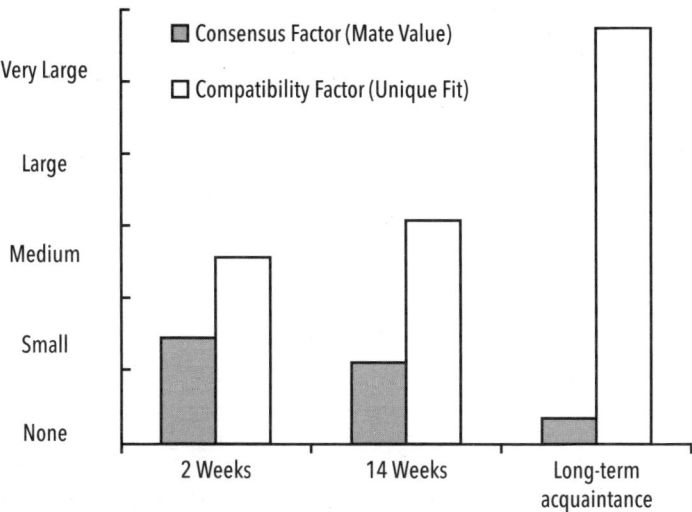

FIGURE 6.1
How large is the share of mate value vs. compatibility in the attraction cocktail?

Note: Estimates of the importance of the consensus and relationship factors are averages of all measures in study 2 (2 weeks and 14 weeks) and study 3 (long-term acquaintance) in Eastwick and Hunt.[5]

romantic partners serve as a supportive safe haven and a celebratory secure base for each other. These central features of our attachment bonds primarily flow from compatibility. Ask people whom they generally find supportive, and once again, their answers mostly reflect that unique-fit component. In families, for example, no one agrees about who the "supportive people" are; some pairs in a family are good at supporting each other, and some pairs are not. Support is all compatibility.[6]

Fifth and finally, in studies that simply ask people, "What does it mean to say that someone is a valuable mate for you?" the most popular answers revolve around "compatibility." We intuitively get that compatibility is central, despite the misleading messages of the EvoScript and the market metaphor.[7]

If compatibility is indisputably vital, then the next task is clear: predicting it. We want to use information about two people's personalities and preferences—things that are knowable even before a relationship forms—in a way that explains which couples will fit together beautifully and which couples will be a match made in hell.

Similarity is one intuitive starting place. If it were true that similar couples were more likely to work it out than dissimilar couples, we'd have an explanation for where compatibility comes from.

If only compatibility were so simple.

Similarity, Proximity, and Familiarity

Partners tend to be similar to each other on pretty much anything you could think to measure. Married couples, dating couples, or even couples who are just hooking up; there's a good bet that these two people have similar demographic and socioeconomic backgrounds, similar personalities, and similar levels of religiosity. They probably enjoy similar things in their spare time: Some couples are all about parties and concerts, while others prefer hiking and biking. They have similar politics and similar values; they even use similar words and phrases on their Facebook status updates. If you know the attributes of one partner, you can usually predict the attributes of the other partner quite well.[8]

The million-dollar question is, can these couple-level similarities explain why some people are compatible and others are not? Many people, including many researchers, look at this matchy mush and surmise that people prefer similar partners. In other words, it seems natural that people pair up this way because they direct their affections toward partners who share their values and their traits, and they eschew partners if they discover a large number of dissimilarities. This idea is called the *similarity-attraction* hypothesis.[9]

The similarity-attraction hypothesis feels compelling. When you see couples who are similar to each other, you might assume that these folks chose each other at some prior point *because* they were similar. But the existence of clusters of similar couples does not logically imply that people actively chose to date and marry similar partners. The reason is simple: It's very easy for couples to end up being similar to each other through an unrelated route. When it comes to who we date, structural forces—that is, situational constraints that have nothing to do with a preference for similar partners—can be massive. In other words, to date someone, you need to meet them, and structural forces mean that you will only get to meet a tiny fraction of the universe of possible romantic partners. And this tiny fraction is already a lot like you.

Most of the time, meeting someone is an act of chance, facilitated by the fact that the two of you just happened to be in the same place at the same time. In many parts of the world and at most times throughout history, people didn't venture too far from where they grew up. And so, no surprise, they ended up marrying someone who grew up just down the street. Even in our hyper-online age, people tend to marry someone from their zip code about two-thirds of the time. Online dating could have changed the game, but it really didn't, because the algorithms feed users similar partners who already live nearby, and there's a limit to people's willingness to travel for a first date.[10]

Psychological research studies routinely illustrate the pull of proximity, and the effect sizes are very large. In one classroom-based study with randomly assigned seating, students who were assigned to sit next to one another liked each other more (nearly twenty *times* more) on day one, and they were more likely to be friends by the end of the year. This process is analogous to the way people commonly meet each other because of where they live, work, or go to school. Relationships typically form because people are induced to interact by happenstance; very few people chat up complete strangers with whom they have no history.[11]

The primary reason why proximity has these effects is that we tend to like people more if we encounter them more. That is, on average, familiarity breeds liking, not contempt. With laboratory demonstrations, this trend is clear: Randomly assign people to spend time chatting with each other, and they'll start to like each other more with each interaction.[12]

So classically, we tend to meet people who are nearby, and the more times we run into them, the chances increase that we're going to like them. And because life is not remotely randomly assigned—

we decide to take some classes rather than others, or we participate in some activities and not others, or we take this job but not that job—we tend to meet and spend time with like-minded folks who share our preferences and values. Combine this tendency with the fact that we already live in neighborhoods and towns that are socially stratified, and people are primed to fall in love with their doppelgangers.

Does that mean that *all* the similarity we observe in real-world couples can be boiled down to the fact that similar people tend to meet each other more frequently? It's hard to say for sure. But if similarity-attraction were playing a meaningful role, there is one clear sign that would emerge: Among the people you meet, you would tend to be more attracted to similar rather than dissimilar partners.

Similarity-Attraction Is a Bust

Let's say you were a member of the marching band. In the typical course of your everyday life, you would interact primarily with the other band geeks, and you might end up dating one of them. It's a tale as old as time—or at least as old as band camp. If circumstances were to arise that allowed you to meet a few soccer players, or drama folks, or science-club members, the similarity-attraction hypothesis states that you would still gravitate toward your fellow musicians.

Many studies test this idea by introducing people to a set of partners that is more heterogeneous than their typical milieu, like in a speed-dating format. Across every single one of these studies, the extent to which two people are similar fails to predict their romantic attraction for each other. In other words, despite your existing tendency to pursue the musicians, you'd be just as likely to pursue the soccer, drama, or science enthusiasts, assuming that you had the opportunity to meet them in the first place.[13]

Other studies come at this idea through a back door by calculating how similar people's *exes* tend to be. Think about it: If similarity-attraction was a powerful force, then the people that you have chosen to date in the past should be especially similar to each other. In fact, similarity-attraction should create a world in which your exes are more similar to each other than they are to *the rest of the people in your social network*. In other words, the people who at one point earned a "Sure, let's try this" from you should look different from the people who received a hard pass.

My colleagues and I examined this question using the extensive dating histories of more than five hundred young adults. At first, it seemed like people's exes showed high levels of similarity—until we looked deeper at the choices available in their networks. For example, across the entire dataset, people's exes were similarly religious: If you dated a religious person when you were seventeen, you were likely to date a religious person again at nineteen.

But religiosity is concentrated in particular locations: Americans who live in the South tend to be more religious than those who live in the Northeast, for example. Fortunately, we can use statistical techniques to determine how much of the similarity among exes on religiosity was due to where people lived. The answer was: all of it. Even though people's exes were similarly religious, the people they *didn't* date within their local dating pool had the same level of religiosity. That is, these young adults seemed to be dating similarly religious partners only because of where they lived; they didn't have a personal preference for a similarly religious partner. This same pattern emerged for all the other factors we examined, too, like intelligence and educational aspirations. In other words, just as with the speed-dating studies, there was remarkably little evidence that people were actively choosing to date more similar partners, given their available choices.[14]

Okay, so people don't seem to be selecting similar partners in the first place. But imagine a relationship is underway already. Perhaps similar partners are especially likely to be happy with each other—or perhaps their relationships are more likely to last? Wrong again. Across the dozens of studies that have examined whether similarity predicts relationship satisfaction, no form of similarity reliably does much of anything: traits, demographic variables, interests, attachment styles, even political views. Dissimilar couples are just as likely to make it work as similar couples.[15]

The funny thing is, most people are deeply convinced that they want to be with a partner who is similar to them. But their intuition about the causal order is probably backward. It's not that people perceive similarities, and then they experience attraction; rather, they experience attraction, and *then* they start to perceive similarities. It's not that similar couples become happier with their relationships over time; rather, happy couples tend to emphasize and grow their similarities.

In other words, when you fall for someone, you begin a similarity hunt. He likes rock climbing? You've been meaning to try that! She's a foodie? You're basically a foodie-in-training! The 2015 film *The Lobster* depicts this process with exquisite black humor. In the film, single people who take too long to find a partner are sentenced to be transformed into nonhuman animals. As a result, the singles become desperate to find something in common with a prospective partner before their time runs out. One couple bonds over their propensity for nosebleeds; for others, it's loving to ski, or having studied the social sciences. Any unique feature will do: Find a similarity, and build a relationship around it, quick!

In real life, this similarity hunt is not a matter of life and transmutation. But it is important, in the same way that the relationship biases (see chapter 5) are important for sustaining relationships in the long run. With a common interest or two to focus on, we feel a sense of validation, like our worldview is fundamentally correct. That feeling then generates a sense of perceived similarity—together we are birds of a feather—and it becomes easier to imagine that we can cooperate and coordinate to do great things, and that disagreements will be minimal and manageable.[16]

The kicker is that, not unlike in *The Lobster*, a sense of perceived similarity can come from almost anywhere: a hobby that we enjoy, a belief we share, the people we like, the people we dislike, the work we do, an outdoor activity, an indoor activity, our love of a specific form of art, film, food, music, or anything else that might inspire fandom. From there, motivated reasoning will cause us to overestimate the extent to which we agree on most other things, and if we encounter something we genuinely do disagree about, we'll minimize the importance of that topic.* In the meantime, we'll start to discover new things that we both value and enjoy, and we'll generate a new sense of shared meaning around them—a "sharing is believing" effect. Altogether, this motivated-reasoning smorgasbord explains why it doesn't really matter how much two people are similar across the full catalog of their interests and personalities. There are so many different things in the world that people can bond over, and it is a complete gamble whether you will or won't discover the one or two bits of shared-reality gold with a given person.

The broad failure of the similarity-attraction effect also explains why the unyielding pursuit of someone who is similar to you on some particular dimension ("I need to meet another Buffalo Bills fan" or "I'm only willing to date other people like me who work hard and play hard") is yet another example of the way that people needlessly impose constraints on their own search for a partner. The smaller you set the pool of eligibles based on a handful of similarities, the more likely you are to be baselessly ruling out potentially good matches. Perhaps even worse, by setting a small pool, you may be focusing too intensely on a small set of partners for relatively superficial reasons, and you're perpetually going to be disappointed. Instead, recognize that your personality and your interests—and your partner's personality and interests—will shift and grow as an acquaintanceship or a relationship evolves. If you're willing to chill out on the similarities-as-dealbreakers, you'll likely feel your dating world expand and breathe a bit. There are plenty of people in the world with whom you could find common ground—if you felt like finding it.[17]

What Do You Want in a Partner? Does It Matter?

Similarity doesn't explain where compatibility comes from in the first place, but there are perhaps other forms of matching that are more promising. After all, people have no shortage of answers when you

---

* If you wonder how politically mismatched couples make it work—and there are plenty out there—this minimization process is a big part of it.

ask them, "What do you want in a romantic partner?" Sure, some of their answers are just repackaged ideas about similarity: Gamers will want to date other gamers, and adventurous types will imagine a thrill-seeking ideal partner. But it doesn't have to be that way. Someone might happen to find confidence or a sense of humor particularly desirable in an ideal partner, even if they don't fancy themselves as particularly confident or funny.[18]

This form of matching is commonly called *preference matching*. Similarity is about whether a potential partner matches what you yourself have; preference matching refers to whether someone matches *what you think you want* in a partner. The critical questions are therefore: To the extent that someone matches your ideals, are you more attracted to them and are you happier in your relationship with them?

Here's an illustration: Some time ago, I had a housemate who passionately believed that he could only be happy with an easygoing, laid-back romantic partner. As for me, it's not that I wanted someone high-maintenance. Rather, *easygoing* was simply not a trait I would have prioritized. In other words, we had different ideal partner preferences for the trait *easygoing*: My housemate claimed that he placed a lot more weight on it than I did. So, if preference matching were a source of compatibility, we can make a clear prediction about his and my attraction patterns. Specifically, if he and I met a variety of single women, he should be especially attracted to the easygoing women and turned off by the high-maintenance women; in contrast, this dimension should be irrelevant to my level of attraction. This logic should feel familiar (it's the same as the revealed preferences we encountered back in chapter 2). Now, we're interested in whether revealed preferences differ depending not on gender, but on differences in what my housemate and I say we want in a partner.[19]

The actual studies themselves don't always capture the preference-matching hypothesis so cleanly. A few years ago, I became frustrated with the state of the science on this topic. Many studies were reporting sloppy analyses that failed to precisely capture preference matching. A frequent error: It is very common that people who say they want a religious partner end up with a religious partner. This finding has little to do with preference matching, however, because people who say they want a religious partner already tend to be surrounded by religious partners. The cause is, once again, proximity: If you knew who these folks could have dated—but didn't—they would have been religious, too. Mistakes like these turned the whole literature into a choose-your-own-adventure exercise, where researchers could claim whatever they wanted to claim about preference matching. This is not ideal because researchers just talk past each other, and there's basically no progress.

To address this situation, some colleagues and I initiated a large, international project in collaboration with a huge consortium of researchers. It was a type of project called a "registered report," which means that the entire plan is peer-reviewed by a journal before anyone even collects data in the first place. Registered reports ensure that we can all trust the results however they turn out because we committed to the methods and analysis plan before knowing what would happen.

We assessed the partner preferences of over ten thousand people from forty-three countries across all six populated continents of the world; from Canada to Chile, from Germany to Ghana, from the UK to the UAE. We asked people to rate how much they desired thirty-five different traits in an ideal romantic partner: sexy, honest, sensitive, fun, financially secure, supportive, extroverted, smells good, and pretty much everything in between. Finally, we also captured how people felt about their actual romantic partners, if they had one; if they were single, we captured how they felt about someone that they were currently interested in romantically. Using this enormous database, we put ourselves in a position to address decisively whether preference matching can account for compatibility.

What we found was a mixed bag. People did experience more attraction to partners who matched, rather than mismatched, their preferences, but there were two caveats. One is that the effects were fairly modest in size. The second is that these modest effects only emerged when aggregating across the full set of thirty-five traits. In other words, the extent to which a given partner matched a person's preference for "sexy" made an infinitesimal contribution to that person's attraction. Same thing for honest, sensitive, fun, financially secure, supportive, extroverted, smells good, etc. My housemate's preference for easygoingness in isolation would not have had a meaningful or detectable effect. Only the aggregate mattered, and even then, only if you squint.[20]

According to this study, it is possible to explain a small portion of where compatibility comes from: Matching across a wide variety of traits will predict attraction, for single and partnered folks alike. The problem is that people might find it challenging to do this kind of mental math, and thirty-five traits require a lot of investigative work if you're pondering whether to go on a second date. The temptation, then, is to focus on a few "must haves" in a partner—your three key traits that are nonnegotiable. Maybe you say you must have a partner who is extroverted, adventurous, and exciting; my housemate said he must have a partner who is easygoing, intelligent, and successful. One could imagine focusing on the top-line must-haves and then not worrying about the rest.

This simplified approach sure does sound appealing. The problem is, it doesn't work at all. Or at least, it can't explain who you are more or less compatible with. Yes, you'd likely be happier with a partner when they are extroverted, adventurous, and exciting—your three must-haves. But the kicker is that you would be just as happy with a partner who is easygoing, intelligent, and successful—the three must-haves listed by my housemate. Those three must-haves are good, but someone else's three must-haves would have been just as good. So focusing on a few nonnegotiable items can't isolate compatibility.[21]

Once again, motivated reasoning partly explains this pattern. It's tempting to believe that traits like "exciting" or "successful" are objective, independently verifiable facts about a person. But traits have a great deal of subjectivity to them. If you happen to think that "exciting" is an important quality in an ideal romantic partner, that belief all by itself is enough to cause you to think that your current partner is exceptionally exciting. Not to mention, we all have different ideas about what counts as part of a trait, and the same trait can have positive or negative connotations, depending on how you want to interpret it. If you like someone, "exciting" means "energizing," and "successful" means "thriving." If you don't like someone, "exciting" means "reckless," and "successful" means "workaholic."[22]

Traits are useful as a shorthand: a sketch of a stranger, or an abstract summary to describe someone who isn't in the room. But traits can be so abstract and so flexible that when it comes to attraction and relationships, it's more useful to focus on the way a person's behaviors make you *feel*. You tell your friends you're attracted to someone because they're "exciting," which is fair enough. But the reason that a particular person inspires us romantically is usually more in the micro: Your partner could be exciting because they'll spontaneously take you to two new password-protected speakeasies on a random Saturday night, or because they'll pull you away from your daily grind for an impromptu hike up a newly discovered trail, or because you can never predict what scheme they'll concoct for your anniversary this year. Any of these behaviors could conceivably fit in the category "exciting," and you get to define "exciting" however you see fit. What ultimately matters are the feelings their behaviors elicit in you, rather than whether they match some dusty old checklist of must-haves.

IN THE END, finding someone who fits your preferences across a large set of traits can explain a portion of where compatibility comes from. Optimistically, all possible partner preferences across all traits perhaps account for 3 to 4 percent of the compatibility factor. That's not nothing, but it's pretty small on the whole.

In the end, was my housemate right when he claimed that he wanted an easygoing romantic partner more than anything? Yes, in the sense that he genuinely believed it, and he was convinced that he could not handle high-maintenance women. But no, in the sense that he didn't tend to pursue or desire exceptionally easygoing women; traits like "easygoing" appealed to him in the same way it appealed to the rest of us. And when he got into a relationship, their compatibility had nothing to do with what he said he was looking for before he met her.

His story is pretty standard. And so we keep digging for the source of compatibility.

Other Mythical Methods for Explaining Compatibility

There are three other intuitive ways of accounting for compatibility that use related, attribute-matching types of approaches: love languages, opposites attract, and—more recently—algorithmic matching. Let's consider each of them.

LOVE LANGUAGES

Okay, it's time. Love languages. Let's do this.

Love languages are probably the single most popular relationship-y topic to permeate popular culture in the last several decades. The concept was concocted by Gary Chapman, a pastor and counselor, as a way of describing how romantic partners express love for one another. He described five love languages: quality time ("I tend to express my feelings for my partner by . . . spending my free time with him/her"), words of affirmation ("complimenting my partner"), gifts ("giving him/her a thoughtful birthday gift"), physical touch ("holding my partner's hand"), and acts of service ("running errands for him/her"). He leveraged these languages into a very lucrative business, with his books selling millions of copies worldwide.[23]

For what it's worth, Gary Chapman more or less made these up. Love languages weren't informed by the existing treasure trove of work on communication in couples, so not unexpectedly, they aren't comprehensive. Notably absent is the way that people offer assurances and commitment when their partners feel insecure, or the way that people express understanding and care when navigating conflict.[24]

But there's no need to be precious about this. Let's just take the five love languages at face value and ask a basic scientific question: Is it possible to measure all five and use them to predict sensible things, like relationship satisfaction? On this front, love languages check out just fine: They're all lovely things that partners do for each other. People tend to be happier in their relationships when their partners spend quality time with them and use words of affirmation. Gifts, physical touch, and acts of service are nice, too, although not quite as relationship-enhancing.[25]

However, the fact that the five love languages are nice does not necessarily mean that it matters whether romantic partners engage in behaviors that match each other's preferred love language—that's the central claim that gets repeated ad nauseam. This is a compatibility hypothesis: People should be happier in relationships if their partner uses their preferred love language rather than some other love language.

Once again, the matching idea doesn't work out. A recent study was the first to capture what love languages people supposedly preferred and what love languages their partners actually used. Specifically, the researchers asked one hundred couples to respond to twenty statements about their preferred love languages (e.g., "I feel especially loved when my partner spends his/her free time with me"), and twenty statements about what love languages they themselves tend to use (e.g., "I tend to express my feelings to my partner by spending my free time with him/her"). Across all of these love-language questions, we'd want to know whether the match between what one person *preferred* and what their partner *expressed* predicted relationship satisfaction. When you do the statistics properly, it turned out that love-language matching didn't make a difference; the match between a person's preferred love language and their partner's expressed love language had no meaningful effect on satisfaction.[26]

Just to be clear: Love languages are fine![27]* It's a really good idea to tell your partner that you appreciate them, and they'll be much happier if you spend quality time with them. If they ask you to take out the trash, it's kind if you do it. But there is no matching component here. Just because a partner uses your preferred love language doesn't make the two of you more compatible.

---

* But beware the early editions of Chapman's *The Five Love Languages* book: The examples and advice were deeply sexist and wedded to traditional gender roles and heteronormative assumptions.

OPPOSITES ATTRACT?

It's possible that the similarity-attraction hypothesis has the story exactly backward. Instead, perhaps the opposites-attract phenomenon explains where compatibility comes from. If extroverts were uniquely attracted to introverts, if practical hard-workers were uniquely attracted to free spirits, or if especially feminine women were uniquely attracted to especially masculine men, then we'd perhaps have new insights into the source of compatibility. As I noted at the start of this chapter, several online dating companies claimed in the mid-2000s to have developed algorithms that could match people based on their personal qualities. Although the exact matching formula was always a proprietary secret sauce, these companies claimed that romantic compatibility could be derived from a blend of similarity in certain life domains and opposites attracting in others.[28]

None of these ideas have borne out in the actual data: Like we saw with similarity, there is no evidence that opposites are more attracted to each other. This conclusion applies regardless of the trait or attribute. Shockingly, it is even true for traits like gender stereotypicality, which is classically captured by both a feminine "communal" set of traits (like gentle and sympathetic) and a masculine "agentic" set of traits (like assertive and dominant). One might naturally assume—as did Dr. Helen Fisher at the start of this chapter—that a woman who possesses the feminine traits would be a good fit with a man who possesses the masculine ones. They aren't; on average, relationships are better off when both men and women adopt a more feminine, communal orientation.[29]

One reason it's tempting to think that opposites make for good relationships is that couples often take on complementary roles when they divide up chores and responsibilities. As we'll see in the next chapter, the extent to which two people effectively mesh their lives in this way is something that happens in the moment, and it's nearly impossible to predict how that blending is going to turn out from people's personalities or other factors that are knowable ahead of time. Finding someone with the opposite of your chore preferences isn't a shortcut to compatibility.

In the end, the opposites-attract hypothesis also doesn't provide any insights into compatibility.

ALGORITHMIC MATCHING

If both the similarity-attraction and opposites-attract phenomena fail, is the algorithmic secret sauce from online dating companies like eharmony and Chemistry.com just (gasp!) an unscientific sales tactic?

An easy answer to this question is: Of course it is an unscientific sales tactic! These companies have never published their algorithms in a way that would be open to other scientists, nor do they share their data with the scientific community in order to allow scientists to reproduce and verify their analyses. So by definition, yes, their claims are unscientific.[30]

A more nuanced answer is that the secret sauce could be both a sales tactic and *true*, even if the process remained opaque and unscientific. In other words, maybe it's possible to combine the traits and attributes of two people, feed them into an algorithm, and figure out whether they're going to hit it off. There could be counterintuitive forms of matching that do, in fact, work—forms of matching that don't fit into the similarity, ideal-matching, or opposites-attract buckets. Perhaps athletic folks work well with introverts, or hot men work well with bookish women, or anxiously attached people work well with dominant ones. Maybe the algorithm can concoct the recipe if we humans can't divine it ourselves.

A few years ago, my colleague Dr. Samantha Joel took on this challenge. By using the most up-to-date machine learning techniques with existing data, Samantha was able to investigate whether algorithmic matching is possible in principle. First, she looked at thousands of dates between heterosexual speed-daters and isolated the compatibility component specifically. We already reviewed in chapter 3 how she was able to predict who was initially desirable, using a ton of information about people's personality, attributes, values, and more. But Samantha also tried to use this same set of traits to predict which *pairs* of people were uniquely compatible at the speed-dating event. If any intuitive or counterintuitive forms of matching could predict compatibility from traits, this procedure would find them.[31]

What she discovered was shocking: The machine learning algorithms completely bombed. They couldn't remotely predict which pairs worked well together. Nada. Zip. Zero percent success. Popularity is predictable, yes. But compatibility, no—it is not discernible from the traits and attributes of the two people, assessed before they actually meet.[32]

Samantha didn't stop there; she went on to examine what happened in existing couples, too. Once again, she tested whether it was possible to take people's personality, attributes, and values and use that information to explain which existing couples were especially compatible. The same results emerged: The combination of two people's traits and attributes explained (at most) 2 percent of why some couples were compatible and some couples were not.[33]

These findings force us to entertain the notion that compatibility just doesn't work this way; that is, compatibility does not arise from the combination of "who you are" and "who they are." Love and attraction are not about the proper mixing of personality, traits, and other attributes, regardless of what the online salespeople say. In other words, you can't learn very much by assessing who fits well together on paper.[34]

Compatibility Is Mysterious, but Not Mystical

In the *Black Mirror* episode "Hang the DJ," a popular matchmaking algorithm called Coach can supposedly match people (with near-perfect accuracy) to a lifelong, compatible romantic partner. By the end of the episode, we discover that Coach works by iteratively simulating how a couple's relationship will ultimately turn out, using whatever information was available before the two people ever met in the first place. In other words, in this fictional universe, a realistic and compelling narrative arc can be constructed from two people's traits and attributes: Wind people up, put them together, and watch the predictable outcomes unfold.

This idea—that someone's traits and attributes make them compatible with some people and not others—makes for delightful science fiction. But it makes for fairly weak science, not to mention a healthy dose of dashed expectations. When I received my silver medal from Lauren, her rejection was bewildering because it seemed obvious that the two of us were the best fit, and we were destined for great things together. But instead, she was destined for great things with someone who, initially at least, seemed like a disastrous fit.

The broader lesson is that matching on similarities and dissimilarities doesn't predict attraction or relationship satisfaction in any meaningful or consistent way. Hunting for similarities with your partner is a wonderful way to build shared reality, but documenting two people's similarities and differences from batteries of questionnaires and trying to predict whether they'll live happily ever after is pointless. Ideal-partner preference matching works, but the overall effects are pretty small, and they only emerge if you aggregate across many, many traits. Love languages are nice, but there's no matching element to them.

If you are single and searching, or if you are ambivalently partnered and trying to ascertain whether your relationship has a future, these lessons can be frustrating. As someone who spends day and night studying this topic, I agree. It sometimes feels like a cruel prank that compatibility—the central defining feature of attraction and close relationships—is so scientifically elusive.

But consider the possibility that we're still handcuffed by the market metaphor, even by this point in the book. Yes, we have embraced the importance of compatibility over the idea that mating is all about winners and losers. Yes, we have recognized that strong relationships are characterized by communal bonds rather than a gender-differentiated exchange of goods and services. But all of the attempts to predict compatibility in this chapter required lining up the benefits and the costs of dating this person vs. that person, as if desire lurks within a shopping list of attributes. Even after we acknowledged the enormous idiosyncrasy in who people consider to be a "valuable" mate, the matching approaches continued to focus on the value that two people brought with them into the relationship. To find love, land the best possible deal.

These ideas have been popular for a very long time: the dominance of the economic model of human worth, and the must-haves that people strive to fulfill as they order up their ideal partner. I get it—these ideas are seductive. But the matching and market-orientated explanations fail to explain how human mating relationships work. What they miss is that relationships are *created* from thousands of tiny decisions as two people construct a shared history that transcends and even subsumes their traits and preferences. And like any other complex structure that grows without a blueprint—piece by precarious piece—the outcome is remarkably challenging to predict until construction gets underway.

· 7 ·

Relationships as Creative Chaos

"I should probably tell you something now, just to get it out of the way. I hate jazz."

Sebastian freezes.

Mia asks, "Are you okay?"

"What do you mean you hate jazz?"

"It just means that when I listen to it, I don't like it."

In this scene from *La La Land*, Sebastian (played by Ryan Gosling) and Mia (Emma Stone) have just uncovered what could be a massive stumbling block in their evolving situationship: She does not think highly of his life's passion. Sebastian is a musician with ambitions of opening his own jazz club. Had Mia's feelings about jazz been apparent from a Tinder profile, there is not the remotest chance that he would have matched with her. (Not to mention, he doesn't care for LA actress types.)

"Yeah, but it's such a blanket statement, you don't like jazz." He takes a beat and looks around, then asks: "What are you doing right now?"

He takes her to a midday performance at the Lighthouse Cafe, giving an enthusiastic sermon about why jazz is such a unique yet underappreciated craft. Mia listens with interest while gently poking fun at him, pretending to have a sincere appreciation for Kenny G. She receives an unexpected callback for an audition, and his enthusiasm on her behalf is infectious: He graciously pretends that "*Dangerous Minds* meets *The O.C.*" sounds like a good premise for a show.

(Even she knows that it isn't.) He offers to take her to see *Rebel Without a Cause* to research the part.

These moments launch Mia's relationship with Sebastian, and they construct it around two joint goals. The first is for Sebastian to make enough of a living as a musician that he will eventually be able to open his own club, and the second is for Mia to become a successful writer and actress. Despite her original skepticism, Mia comes to love jazz—or at least, she comes to love it when she sees it through Sebastian's eyes. Similarly, Sebastian serves as the primary audience and fanboy for Mia's writing and performance. Their relationship takes shape around their pursuit of these dreams, as if their career aspirations and having someone to share in those aspirations have become one and the same.

Compatibility is not about two people matching up their traits and attributes. If it were, Mia and Sebastian would never have gotten off the ground, given their dim initial opinions of each other's central defining life goals. What the film illustrates instead is how compatibility is largely constructed, in small cumulative ways over time. Finding one thing—anything—you like about someone can be a springboard to a second thing, and then a third, and through this cascade, with luck and time, two people just might manage to shape and mold their lives around each other. This gradual process of relationship formation, in which two people change who they are along the way, explains why relationships are so idiosyncratic, and why the reasons that you are compatible with one person will typically be distinct from the reasons that you are compatible with someone else.

Returning to the Social Relations Model

In the opening chapter, we encountered the Social Relations model: the three-ingredient cocktail that makes up every feeling that one person has about another person. Those three ingredients were the consensus factor, which is akin to popularity, the selectivity factor, which is about how much you desire people in general, and the compatibility factor, which is about the unique relationship between two people.

That discussion was mostly about initial attraction. But there is nothing inherent in the model that limits these three factors to attraction; we could ask the same questions about emerging or established relationships. The meanings of the three factors change a little bit, but the same principles hold.

Before getting into the actual research, consider this thought experiment. Imagine that you are currently involved in multiple romantic relationships—with Andrew, Darius, Diego, and Rafael, all at once. And these men are all involved in multiple relationships, too. In this polyamorous scenario, we could isolate the three ingredients of the cocktail once more. The consensus factor would represent how satisfied Andrew's romantic partners are with him, on average. Is he the kind of person who generally makes all his partners (including but not limited to you) satisfied or unsatisfied? The selectivity factor would represent how happy you are on average, across your relationships with Andrew, Darius, Diego, and Rafael. The compatibility factor would be the extent to which you are particularly happy with a given partner, above and beyond the other two components; maybe you happen to be exceptionally happy when you're with Diego specifically, and you're exceptionally unhappy with Rafael.

The research I'm describing here remains hypothetical; it hasn't yet been conducted in actual polyamorous communities.* Nevertheless, even in monogamous couples, the three factors are still part of the cocktail, making people feel the way that they do. From the limited data we have about these factors in ongoing relationships—usually gathered by collecting information from people's exes—here's what we know. The consensus factor is very small; there is little consensus about who is a good or bad partner. Some of your exes thought you

---

* This is one of many reasons that research on polyamorous relationships—which is still getting off the ground—has the potential to reveal significant insights that we simply cannot get from studies of monogamous couples.

were great, some of them thought you were terrible. The selectivity factor is medium; some people are generally happy or generally miserable in relationships, regardless of who they're with. And the compatibility factor? It's huge.[1]

As we learned in the last chapter, the compatibility factor can't really be boiled down to matching. Compatibility doesn't arise from the right fit between the personalities and preferences that two people bring to the table. It isn't helpful to think about dating as the search for a missing puzzle piece.

Instead, the vanguard of the research right now is this: Relationships are good or bad because they have a history to them. These histories contain stories that make each relationship distinct from all the other relationships in a person's life. Relationships consist of a thousand layered decisions that slowly and gradually blend two people's interests and goals, like with Sebastian and Mia. Relationships develop patterns—rituals and routines that often only make sense to the two people involved—and these patterns cannot (easily) be unwound. In short, couples achieve success or misfortune in relationships because of how they create their joint story, how they blend themselves and their lives together, and how they construct patterns and habits.

The Long, Chaotic Process of Human "Mate Choice"

You could imagine a pair-bonding species that engaged in "mate choice" by doing the following: Males and females meet each other and size each other up, and some mates pair off and copulate. Then, fertilization happens quickly, offspring are born, and bi-parental caretaking begins. In fact, many pair-bonding and monogamous species work this way: Choice is fast, and conception is easy-breezy. If compatibility mattered in such a species, mating partners would need to assess it quickly, probably using a courtship ritual that allowed prospective partners to assess whether their attributes match in the right ways.

In contrast to this version of a pair-bonding process, human mating is slow and luxurious. For our species, the process of deciding to form a relationship usually requires a lengthy series of interactions. Some interactions might be one-on-one, some might involve the presence of peers, and some might require input from family members. Some of these interactions might be casual, some might be emotionally meaningful, some might have sexual overtones. Each occasion is an opportunity to learn whether an interaction with a prospective partner is enjoyable, rewarding, and supported by a broader community. The uncertainty of this period follows from the fact that prospective partners can tap out at any time: Sebastian could have bailed at Mia's Kenny G joke, or Mia could have found Sebastian's speechifying insufferable. A step forward is almost always revocable, backtracking is common, and progression is rarely linear.

In this light, "mate choice" is a particularly misleading concept when it comes to human mating; most of the time, it's very hard to point to a single moment in time when two people chose each other. More commonly, feelings ebb and flow as two people slowly ramp up the intimacy.[2]

Furthermore, as biologist Dr. Richard Prum points out, this insight applies to sexual intercourse itself. That is, due to a few species-specific oddities, even sex is not a true "mate choice" event in humans. For one, humans have concealed ovulation, which means that there are no obvious, visible signs that a woman is ovulating and likely to conceive. Even when ovulation is imminent, conception is far from assured. And women are able to have—and interested in having—sex throughout their cycles; in contrast, ovulating females in many species are physically unable to have intercourse outside of a specific window of fertility.[3]

Therefore, men and women who are considering each other as partners commonly have sexual intercourse several times as part of this lengthy mate-choice process. Bad sexual chemistry? Best to let this one go. Good sexual chemistry? A keeper.

Other aspects of our history are consistent with the idea that extended sexual courtship played a key role in human mating evolution. For example, the human penis is very different in form and function from the penises of the other great apes, and these differences can reveal insights into adaptive evolutionary pressures that our ancestors faced over the last several million years. Gorillas and chimpanzees have rather small penises, and copulation typically lasts only seconds. There's certainly no evidence that these animals would like sex to last longer because the act itself is pleasurable.

Not so in humans. As Dr. Prum argues, many aspects of human sexuality seem especially well designed to provide a cornucopia of pleasurable sensations. For one, the human penis evolved to take on a unique shape with a bulbous tip, which can in principle be pleasurable for women during intercourse. Also, the human penis is considerably larger than the penis of our great-ape relatives. A larger penis provides not only pleasure during sex, but also enables a wide variety of sexual positions. Critically, one of these positions is face-to-face copulation, which facilitates bonding and potentially stimulates the woman's clitoris. Because humans find sex pleasurable, they are creative in their sexual experimentations with each other, and they are especially enthusiastic about having sex as part of the courtship process. Again, other primates don't seem motivated by sexual pleasure in the way that humans are.[4]

In this formulation, humans evolved to use sex—from kissing to intercourse, and all the culturally normative forms of heavy petting in between—to decide whether to have *more* sex with a person. Women's orgasms are not designed to pick out the sperm of "quality men," as some EvoScript enthusiasts suggest. Nor are women's orgasms a happy evolutionary accident arising from the fact that the penis and the clitoris are formed from the same tissue during development. Rather, a woman's orgasm is one cue among many that a relationship may be viable with a specific person; sexual pleasure is motivating in and of itself. As humans were evolving, it seems quite likely that a man who was motivated to provide a woman with pleasurable sex was especially likely to be chosen *by that woman* for sex again. In essence, what makes humans special are our *re-mating* preferences, and these preferences derive directly from prior experiences with a particular prospective partner. When two people have a good experience together—sexual or otherwise—they will try to replicate it a second, or a third, or a fourth time. Like the progression bias from chapter 5, one promising experience makes people eager to search for more.

"That was good; let's do this again." That's what human mate preferences look like. Not a set of disembodied, abstract attributes; not a checklist of activities and interests. Humans don't find mates by carefully selecting which suitor most closely fits an ideal romantic partner template. Rather, our preferences are bound to particular people, as we repeatedly test and retest the waters with them. And compatibility is all about how this testing and retesting process unfolds.[5]

The trick, of course, is that sequences of interactions are chaotic, in the "chaos theory" sense of the term. In other words, there is a lot of randomness inherent to all that testing and retesting, and any given pair could get very lucky or very unlucky. Jeff Goldblum has several memorable moments as Dr. Ian Malcolm in the original *Jurassic Park*, but he is at his swaggering best when he illustrates chaos theory for Dr. Ellie Sattler (played by Laura Dern) while flirting with her at the same time. He seductively places a drop of water on her hand and asks her to predict which direction the water will roll off. When two seemingly identical drops placed in the seemingly identical spot roll in different directions, he describes what makes complex systems unpredictable: "Tiny variations . . . [that] never repeat and vastly affect the outcome."

Social interactions are also complex systems, and tiny variations in the goals, moods, thoughts, and desires of two people can make it very challenging to control or predict how interactions will unfold. Two people who are getting to know each other might get lucky by discovering that they share a mutual friend, or they might hit a wall by discovering that they have vastly different tastes in movies. Chance dictates whether that initial conversation winds its way to the mutual friend (which is a cue to continue testing the waters) or to the different movie tastes (which is a cue to bail). To make matters more complicated: Having different movie tastes can be a death blow if it's the first thing you learn about someone, but it can easily be swept aside after establishing your similar views on food, travel, and the best way to spend a Sunday outdoors. The cardinal rule of relationship initiation is that feelings can change—for the better or the worse—suddenly and unpredictably. Surges of "yes, please" and "no, ick" behave as chaotically as Dr. Malcolm's drops of water.[6]

. . .

Julian and Lloyd are both single, and mutual friends have just introduced them to each other at a bar after work. Julian sits down with his drink across from Lloyd and says, "I can't believe they're playing this song. My dog literally howls every time it comes on. Which is too bad because I rather like it."

Here are three different ways that Lloyd can respond:

1. "Oh, sad, what does your dog have against Adele?"

2. "When I was a kid, our dog would run and hide when my dad put basketball games on. Maybe the squeaking shoes?"

3. "I worked in a place like this one summer, and anything that was on the radio at that time stresses me out to this day."

All three replies are decent; they play off some component of what Julian had said using "yes, and . . ." logic. They could conceivably progress in a variety of directions. But let's see what happens if we play out the scenarios.

Assume Lloyd picks the first response. What happens next is that he and Julian get into a conversation about Adele. They both like Adele, but they aren't superfans or anything. Especially unfortunate is that Lloyd is generally not much of a pop music guy to begin with. He feigns interest as Julian shifts to talking about what he saw at Coachella last year, but this route is mostly a dead end for the two of them.

If Lloyd picks the second response, he and Julian begin a conversation about how dogs howl at the strangest things. But this ends up being a bust, too. Lloyd doesn't have a dog currently, so he and Julian can't connect over the joys and challenges of contemporary dog-parenting. Lloyd tries bringing up basketball again—he still regularly attends Lakers games with his dad—but Julian doesn't bite.

If Lloyd picks the third response, Julian asks him about that miserable summer job. This line of inquiry is a winner. As it turns out, both Julian and Lloyd had worked as waiters during that same summer, and they reminisce about the insatiable demands of tourists and how they had both been turned off by the service industry forever. The conversation drifts to other earlier jobs they worked for long hours and little pay, culminating in a discussion about what they love about their current careers. Spark ignited.

Critically, there was no reliable way for Lloyd to know which reply was going to set the conversation with Julian on the path to a nugget of conversational gold. This example illuminates how most free-flowing conversations work: They roll along chaotically as two people search for something—anything—that fosters a connection. Of course, with sufficient time and motivation, two people can backtrack from a dead-end topic and try again. But in the modern era of fifteen-minute Tinder coffees and high expectations, people often aren't willing to grant many restarts before they bail.

The takeaway lesson: Whenever two people meet for the first time, it is challenging even for the most socially skilled people to find an animating topic that generates mutual interest and connection. But most pairs do have something to bond over—it just takes a little (or a lot of) luck to find it.

Relationships as Tiny Cultures

Of course, relationships don't stop after a few pleasant interactions. As couples start interleaving their daily lives, the grooves and patterns that they establish become even more meaningful. Ask any marriage therapist, and they'll likely tell you that entrenched patterns present considerable obstacles for couples who need to turn things around.

Other patterns—from idiosyncratic sexual overtures that only your partner understands, to the way you begin and end your day together—are the details that give each relationship life.

In one of her most popular videos, TikTok creator Sam Showalter reflected on the "weird, shared culture" of her relationship that she could never replicate with anyone else. For example, she and her boyfriend have a shared language, including a hand gesture called "hurt paw" which they use to mean that someone is feeling sad, sick, or in pain. She also describes specific dyadic habits: When she absentmindedly bites her nails, he'll yell "Rat! Rat!" and pretend to spray her with rat poison to get her to stop—a practice that she apparently adores. They have unique customs, like a "collective birthday" that sits at the midway point of their two birthdays, and an earlobe-rubbing ritual that they find comforting while watching TV. Finally, there are nicknames: "He calls me Bucket—that's my nickname—and I don't know where that came from. But I know that if no one ever called me Bucket for the rest of my life it would bring me to my knees."[7]

These behaviors may sound odd to you, but researchers who study couples often describe relationships as tiny, two-person cultures. Just like a culture, couples develop their own shared language, like Sam's "hurt paw," "Bucket," and "Rat!" shorthand. Customs like these—even the silly ones—promote attachment because they foster the feeling that two people are building something unique and irreplaceable. To quote Greta Gerwig in her role as the titular character in the film *Frances Ha*: "It's this secret world that exists right there in public, unnoticed, that no one else knows about."[8]

The tiny culture of a couple grows increasingly complex with time, and it becomes opaque to outsiders. If you've ever spent time as a third-party observer of someone else's relationship, it can be as bewildering as being dropped into an unfamiliar civilization. Why did he get upset when she asked if he was really going to buy that? Why did she seem so deliriously relieved when he offered to take charge of the weekend plans? What was the significance of that lengthy story featuring lots of people you didn't know? Other couples' relationships don't come with a guidebook, but it would be handy if they did.

Tiny cultures also illustrate why the reasons you are compatible with one person may have nothing to do with the reasons you are compatible with someone else. Sam's boyfriend would surely have less luck with the "Rat!" routine with a new girlfriend. Indeed, he would be unwise to assume that any new girlfriend would even appreciate having attention drawn to her bad habits in the first place. Sam clearly interprets his attentiveness as a sign of caring and affection; another girlfriend might interpret those same gestures as nagging or paternalistic.

Also, if the tiny culture of a relationship somehow gets disrupted, expect trouble. From the outside, the customs and idioms of other couples might seem arbitrary or unnecessary to you. But to the couple members themselves, these norms are often practically and emotionally significant. I knew a couple who would read to each other any texts they received from exes. They developed this custom because their relationship began in a cloud of uncertainty as they slowly weaned themselves off their most recent ex-partners. Opening up their text lives to each other helped them to reduce anxiety, establish trust, and commit more fully. For some couples, this custom might have had the opposite effect, but for this couple, it worked.

The best way to foster a strong relationship is to build a culture around the things that you and your partner appreciate about each other in light of your own specific history together. I'll illustrate with the story of Alex and Marco.

. . .

Alex and Marco's relationship began with food and an accompanying "let's try everything" spirit. For their first date, Alex suggested that they go to a restaurant that had just opened in midtown. Her former partner had not been an adventurous eater, so her bucket list had become extensive. Marco was a neophyte and up for anything.

Course after course introduced them to flavors and combinations they had never encountered before. From the broccoli with pomegranate and candied pecans to the roasted duck drizzled with apricot glaze, every bite was a revelation. They discussed each dish for hours, long after they had left the restaurant to grab a beer at a dive bar near Alex's apartment. They wondered if they could remember the risotto and crispy prosciutto recipe well enough to make a facsimile of it. That first night, they stayed up until two a.m. trying to make it themselves (and not quite succeeding).

In those early days, their relationship thrived in Alex's modest apartment kitchen. Alex excelled at improvising dishes and balancing flavors; Marco was responsible for acquiring whatever gear and ingredients they needed to expand into new cuisines and styles. As their relationship matured, their evening routine revolved around those meals. Work responsibilities eventually intruded on their lives, of course, but mealtimes together were sacred: No phone scrolling, no TV, no distractions. If something about the relationship made them feel sad or frustrated or anxious, dinner would provide the opportunity to work it out. In their first year, they laughed and cried together many times while sitting at that small apartment table.

Their approach to food dovetailed with the mantras that defined their relationship. Be open and creative; try things that might not work; don't yuck someone else's yum. And most central of all: Make the time to be present with each other.

The opening act of Alex and Marco's relationship illustrates three critical components of the way that couples build a culture together.

1. **The story of us:** Alex and Marco co-created the story of who they were as a couple. The story was grounded in the activities they loved doing together in the beginning—cooking and eating—but it also incorporated their broader values of openness and togetherness. This narrative made their relationship feel unique and wholly their own. There is considerable wisdom in forging a lucid narrative like this one because having a vivid and coherent origin story as a couple is associated with relationship satisfaction.[9]

2. **Self-expansion:** Alex's interest in food became their joint interest in food. A cardinal rule of close relationships is that romantic partners adopt each other's interests, attributes, and values. In other words, people tend to incorporate their partners into themselves; they happily blur the line between self and partner, especially when they are falling in love. Furthermore, including the partner in the self is an unambiguously good sign: self-partner overlap is associated with greater satisfaction, a lower likelihood of infidelity, and a lower likelihood of breakup.[10]

3. **Pattern creation:** Alex and Marco established customs in their relationship around cooking and meals that helped them to maintain a sense of connectedness and shared reality. Couples commonly build habits like these by drawing upon the same "that was good, let's do this again" spirit I mentioned prior. The patterns that stick become the grooves that spread across the landscape of couples' daily lives. When those patterns are set up well, they steer partners toward joy and away from conflict.[11]

All three components reinforce the key lesson from chapter 6: It is remarkably challenging to predict how compatible two people are going to be until they start building the relationship. First, very few narratives in real life are set in stone before they unfold; people have agency and choice along the way to shape the story into what they want it to be. Had that initial dinner been uninspiring, Alex and Marco might have written a very different script for their relationship—if they had formed one at all.

Second, there are no hard and fast rules about how partners trade and shape each other's values and interests, and the number of possible permutations for the way two people self-expand together is nearly limitless. Alex and Marco began with an interest of Alex's (contemporary restaurants) and morphed it into a related but not identical joint interest (a love of cooking together). Meanwhile, they had other interests—like Marco's love of trail running in the morning, and Alex's love of riding her stationary bike at night—that remained solely their own. No metric of similarity matching could possibly have divined that they would bond over certain activities but not others.

Third, their pattern of cooking and sharing meals together would eventually support other key parts of their relationship. Dinner became a distraction-free zone—as they focused first on the food, and then on each other. In this way, that meal came to serve as the key time and place for the two of them to take stock of whatever was happening with their relationship. Food brought them together originally, and by deciding day after day to maintain the centrality of that part of their relationship, they built a strong resource that helped them to remain connected.

. . .

Tiny cultures work, but that doesn't mean they can remain forever frozen in amber. Over time, patterns can cause problems, and sometimes, routines get stale. The sexual fantasy that you two enacted when you first got together was hot, but on the twentieth rerun, it's not nearly as thrilling. Any activity that is initially exhilarating will eventually become comfortable, and sometimes couples get so contented with comfortable that they forget to rekindle the excitement. Family-systems therapists spend an inordinate amount of time helping couples to recognize the patterns they have created and how those patterns are harming the relationship or limiting each other's ability to grow.[12]

In some cases, outside factors force existing patterns to change, and couples may not be fully aware of how the pattern had been serving them. Alex and Marco continued their regular routine of connecting over cooking for many years, through the early months of raising a child together. But with time, meals started to revolve around their kid and her tastes, and it became harder to keep the elaborate cooking and dinner routine alive. This shift to a new evening pattern meant that Alex and Marco lost the time that they had come to rely on for reconnection without realizing it, and soon a distance crept in between the two of them.

A good family-systems therapist would point out to Alex and Marco they would need to alter some of their other routines to build the time for connection and joint creativity that had been lost. For example, their pattern of working out separately was worth interrogating. Yes, it had worked fine for a long time for Marco to run in the morning and Alex to cycle at night. But if they could find a way to enjoy working out together, it might provide a regular opportunity to reconnect. Yes, their love of cooking elaborate dinners together might be a relative rarity now that they were parents. But if they could establish a habit of making lunch together, they could keep their sense of creative togetherness alive, even though a midday meal offers less time to linger. To fix a broken pattern, couples must identify what is implicit, make it explicit, and be willing to rearrange the pieces for the sake of the relationship.

Tiny cultures—the patterns, practices, and pet names that comprise couples' day-to-day lives—are the main source of what works and what doesn't work in a relationship. And these tiny cultures are staggeringly idiosyncratic, even if you were to observe the same person in different relationships over the course of their life. Marco loves Alex for her culinary creativity, and he loved his prior girlfriend for being so funny in a crowd. But he derives no pleasure from imagining Alex as a performer, nor from imagining his old girlfriend as a dynamite chef. We like different people for different reasons, and these reasons usually do not translate from partner to partner. Similarly, inside jokes and callbacks can foster connection by providing a bridge between a relationship's past and present, but they only work in the relational context that spawned them—by definition.[13]

That's not to say that people are wholly inconsistent across relationships: Someone who provides support well in one relationship will probably be at least a decent support provider in their next relationship.

But critically, the patterns that make two relationship partners compatible or incompatible emerge organically within the context of each relationship. Relationships are what two people build together over time, and there's not a good way to know what two people will create until construction is underway.[14]

・ ・ ・

People commonly feel that they must adhere to one of two seemingly oppositional sets of beliefs about relationships. One set is called *growth beliefs:* The idea that some couples have the determination and grit to build something fabulous and other couples don't. The other is called *destiny beliefs:* The idea that some couples are meant to be together and other couples are not. People love to argue about which beliefs are the "correct" ones: growth (e.g., "a successful relationship is mostly a matter of learning to resolve conflicts with a partner") or destiny (e.g., "relationships that do not start off well inevitably fail").[15]

The idea that relationships are chaotic co-constructions illustrates how both the growth and destiny concepts are simultaneously true. Growth beliefs are about how good things are constructed over time. Close, caring relationships don't emerge instantaneously, and they have to be maintained, monitored, and nurtured. But destiny beliefs remind us that relationships sometimes go badly because of unfortunate circumstances and ossified patterns that were set back in the early days when the future was unknown. So if you happen to have a happy relationship, whatever miracle brought you and your partner together and granted you the patterns you enjoy to this day, it's appropriate to have some humility about how you got here.

The Challenges of Creating Compatibility in the Modern Dating Landscape

Dating is often a slog, to put it mildly. People endure countless coffee dates, ghostings, letdowns, and breakups. Dating is a numbers game, sure, but it seems like there are more ways for "getting to know someone" to go wrong than right. If compatibility just materializes from the ether, chaotically and organically, then why does it feel so rare?

It would be Pollyannaish for me to imply that people can fall head over heels for *anyone* if they just get sufficiently lucky with their initial conversation topics. But compatibility can indeed emerge for many pairs under the right circumstances. Troves of research studies encourage two unacquainted people to engage in small escalations of intimacy disclosures over an hour or so, and these studies are remarkably effective at boosting positive feelings (more on these "fast friends" approaches in chapter 10). So compatibility can certainly be grown in short order, when two people take the opportunity to genuinely open up to each other. Personal confessions don't automatically lead to marriage, of course, but they do enhance the likelihood that both people will consider a second date.[16]*

The spontaneous emergence of compatibility also feels rare because people tend to overestimate the extent to which conversations with new acquaintances will be awkward, and underestimate the extent to which they will enjoy them. These findings again illustrate the ubiquitous difference between what people think they will like and what they will actually like: People may avoid starting up a conversation with someone new because they fear it will go badly, but these fears are unfounded on average.[17]

A lackluster love life is oftentimes a structural problem. Let's say you seem to keep dating the same losers over and over again, like the contestant on the fictitious *Saturday Night Live* dating show "What's Your Type?" who is drawn only to corny, insufferable men in their forties. Perhaps you need to listen to your friends and become more discerning in your tastes. But my bet would be that this consistency comes from where and how you're meeting these people in the first place, rather than something about who you're choosing to date

---

* *The New York Times* carried an article with the questions developed by researchers in these studies to boost positive feelings: Daniel Jones, "The 36 Questions that Lead to Love," January 9, 2015, https://www.nytimes.com/2015/01/09/style/no-37-big-wedding-or-small.html?smid=url-share.

within your pool. In this sense, successful "open casting" beyond your type may require a change of scenery.[18]

In fact, because compatibility can emerge with a modicum of fortune, the decision about who fits within your field of eligibles is your *primary* avenue for exerting control over how your romantic life will unfold. Recall the progression bias from chapter 5: Once people get involved in a relationship, they tend to make decisions that maintain good feelings and harmony, which reinforce the stability and longevity of the relationship. So if you want someone who will treat your career as equal to their own, don't surround yourself with med school students who are expecting to marry a "doctor's wife." If you are certain you don't want kids, don't surround yourself with people who are certain they do. If you're routinely meeting people who have mismatching life goals and preferences—and if you're meeting enough of them—I can virtually guarantee that you will end up discovering and creating compatibility with one of them. The only reliable way of dodging such a major lifestyle trade-off is to craft your pool accordingly.[19]

As relationships evolve, a new challenge can emerge: Some people generally don't appear to be relationship material. After all, many of the markers of strong relationships seem like qualities that some people have more than others: compassion, communication skills, resilience, patience, empathy, humility, and impulse control, just to name a few. If you have these traits, it is true that your relationships will be more satisfying and more communal. If you don't have these traits, you should cultivate them.

Having said that: In my experience, people overestimate the importance of stable attributes in relationships. Remember that people's satisfaction across two different relationships matches 60 percent of the time and mismatches 40 percent of the time, and you can conceptualize this 60/40 split as the consequence of the *sum total* of all of people's stable attributes pushing them in a happy or unhappy direction. A 60/40 split is higher than 50/50, so having all the right interpersonal skills will put you in a slightly better position to have a successful and satisfying relationship. But most of the reasons why a relationship is satisfying or unsatisfying flow from the construction of the relationship itself.[20]

This observation explains why, once a relationship exists, it is surprisingly hard to intervene effectively by targeting the skills and abilities of the two partners. Most attempts to teach relationship skills at scale—with large programs that show couples how to communicate or handle conflict—have been big disappointments. These seminars don't really work, and it's not because people can't understand how to "fight fairly." The problem is that conflict management and good communication have to be cultivated within the context of a particular relationship, and each couple has their own logic, patterns, and origin story. You can show people videos of couples displaying nasty tactics, like contempt or stonewalling or diffusing responsibility, but the abstract knowledge that "these behaviors are bad" is a far cry from putting that knowledge into practice when the conflict is real and the stakes are high.[21]

Indeed, effective couples therapy—the kind of therapy that actually works—requires a third-party coach who digs in and gets to know that couple's logic, patterns, and origin story, encouraging them to identify their unspoken rules and assumptions and change the ones that aren't working. Relationships can be fixed, but improvement requires a recognition that two people built that relationship to work in a particular way for a complex set of reasons, and those reasons may need to be deconstructed and scrutinized before any reconstruction can begin.

So don't get too bogged down by concerns about whether someone is or is not relationship material. If you're in a state of ambivalence about a potential or current romantic partner, a more useful question is this: Do they have two or three qualities that you would want to build a relationship around? Rather than worrying about whether someone has red flags, focus on whether their green flags are a draw. Maybe he isn't the most attractive man you've ever dated, but no one has ever made you laugh so hard. Maybe she is considerably to the right of you politically, but she makes you feel supported and listened to. People are complicated, no partner checks all the boxes, and the key question is whether you want (and I do mean *want*) to construct a relationship around what works and compartmentalize the parts that don't.

I won't apologize for my optimism, because it is bound to the data: Nearly anyone can have a satisfying relationship under the right circumstances. But critically, there is one kind of person who isn't capable of being relationship material: A person who engages in *proactive* aggression. Proactive aggression is a systematic and sustained strategy to intimidate someone, threaten them, make them feel afraid, humiliate them, possess and control them, or destroy their belongings. When a relationship partner does these things repeatedly and deliberately, it's time to go, even if you know the contrition is coming. The proactive piece is important because many people are hot-headed in relationships in a *reactive* way; if they feel insulted or disrespected, they might fly off the handle. A reactive pattern can be addressed with therapy. But proactive aggression—the cold, calculating, make-your-partner-fear-for-their-safety-and-doubt-their-sanity type of aggression—is a hard "no." This attribute is the *one* major empirically validated red flag to watch out for because these people should not be in relationships, and you need them out of your life.[22]

Relationships Are Sandboxes, Not Adjacent Cubicles

Humans evolved in a context where extreme prosociality became adaptive for group living, and natural selection layered this ability on top of a psychological system that was already highly attuned to others' thoughts and feelings. So we became creatures who feel good when we share what's on our mind; we genuinely want our close others to experience the same joy we get from a song, a joke, an idea, a vista, or a meal. Building and sharing a joint worldview with another person feels terrific—but not because we're trying to "get stuff" from them. It feels terrific because these behaviors are the main way that people foster the closeness and security that have long been central to human attachment bonds. Happy relationships have more in common with kids playing together in a sandbox than co-workers putting in a productive day at the office.[23]

There is a challenge in being a species who mates this way: The construction of any relationship, good or bad, is inherently unpredictable. Some sandcastles seem initially promising and crumble unexpectedly; some look strange until the light hits them just so, and you wonder how you had missed the grandeur. Magnificent things emerge when two people find themselves in the right sandbox at the right time, induced to interact by serendipity, and compelled to continue because each interaction was a bit more enjoyable than the last.

And of course, sometimes two wonderful people bring out the worst in each other, and after they drive their relationship into a ditch, they call it quits and tell everyone who will listen that their former partner was an awful person. But that's rarely the full story. Relationships are built, and despite everyone's good initial intentions, some of those constructions are shoddy. After the collapse, we dust ourselves off and move on, and the ability to do so is part of the human mating condition, too.

If this is how humans form and maintain relationships, you know what would be a bad idea? It would be a bad idea to give people the sense that there are a *ton* of romantic choices for them waiting just around the corner—that a middling first impression is a cue to check out the next sandbox. It would be a bad idea to create a market that caters to the strengths of the ultra-attractive, reproduces the experience of playing a video game, and convinces people that good relationships come from landing the partner with all the best attributes. It would be a bad idea to convince people that the way you form relationships is by hitting on stranger after stranger and unplugging from your existing networks of friends and acquaintances. These bad ideas would stifle the initial ingredients of fortune and coincidence while making dating and relationships needlessly depressing for a lot of people.

Thanks, Internet.

· PART 3 ·

Finding Connection in the Real World

· 8 ·

Moving Online

In college, I dated someone for a while named Amanda. The story of how we got together says a lot about how people used to initiate relationships before the online dating era.

At first, I knew Amanda only by name—she was the kind of acquaintance you nod to and say, "Hey" as you pass by—but that was all. It requires an uncommon level of social confidence to launch a conversation with someone you don't know, and I didn't yet have it.

Nevertheless, I knew a friend of hers—Crystal—and Crystal was a pro at connecting people. So from time to time, Crystal would wave me over in the cafeteria, and I would find myself sitting with a group of eight to ten people, including Amanda. Mostly, we all interacted as part of a group; lengthy one-on-one conversations were uncommon. But Amanda certainly made an impression on me. She taught me how to combine milk, Froot Loops, and Sprite in the proper proportions to create a solid goo. Strangely, that lesson made her even more attractive to me. Love and goo are mysterious things.

After a while, I started timing my arrivals for when she and her friends would be there. At dinner one day, she threw an orange at me from point-blank range and then laughed uproariously as I deflected it back into her mashed potatoes. That seemed promising. I started to surmise that she didn't have a boyfriend, nor did she seem particularly smitten with the other guys who regularly ate with us. But was she actually into me? And even if she was, what was I supposed to do, exactly? We were always hanging out in a group, and it was very hard to steal away. I didn't even have some super smooth way of contacting her; I mainly had to hope that she showed up at the next gathering.

One night, we went to—I hesitate to call it a party—it was like a large hangout in someone's bedroom. Now the flirting between us was escalating, but we were trying to keep it contained. Someone had the idea to grab a bunch of blankets and pillows, watch a movie, and sleep over. Six people in one room.

So we did, and Amanda and I just happened to find spots close to each other. I clearly was supposed to make a move, but there were still so many people around! Darkness enveloped the room, and we slowly and deliberately turned to face each other, cocooned together under a mound of sleeping bags. We stifled any sound that might give us away as we inched closer. Our lips finally met, and our hands instinctively intertwined as we fell asleep. As first kisses go, it was pretty exhilarating.

The next day, as we left, we confessed that we were into each other. This moment was also, quite literally, the first moment that we had been alone together.

. . .

Today, this meet-cute feels quaint; a product of a bygone era with fewer electronic distractions and far more unplanned face-to-face interaction. If Amanda and I were single today, our paths to each other would have likely started on a dating app instead of winding through a network of friends-of-friends. We would have known the other person was "single and looking" from the very beginning—a pre-condition for even starting to communicate—instead of the possibility of a romantic connection emerging slowly from a pool of ambiguity. We would have formed first impressions of each other based on photographs and self-descriptions, not live, face-to-face interactions. ("You'll know I'm interested if I'm hurling citrus" comes across very differently on a dating profile than it does in real life.)

And critically, today we would date in a tiny two-person bubble: A first date at a coffee shop, a second date at a restaurant, and so on.

Back in the nineties, Amanda and I were nearly always surrounded by other friends as we were getting to know each other. Indeed, without these friends—Crystal, especially—we wouldn't have met in the first place. Today, there would be a love/life barrier.

A study by Dr. Michael Rosenfeld and colleagues illustrates this dramatic shift (figure 8.1). In the second half of the twentieth century, the most common way that heterosexual Americans met their romantic partners was through mutual friends. About 30 percent of couples formed this way, whereas online dating was virtually unknown until the mid-1990s. But then online methods began to increase, and they overtook meeting through friends around 2013. Ever since, online dating has continued to dominate, while the matchmaker-friend has drifted downward.[1]

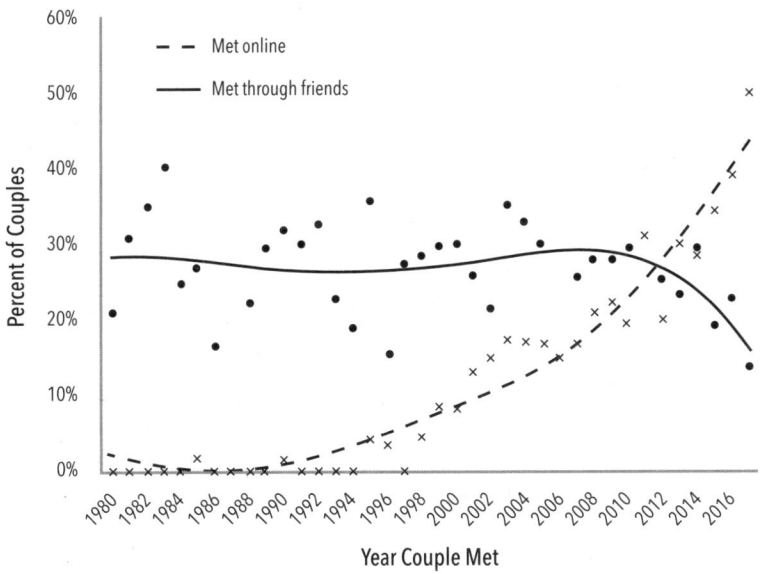

FIGURE 8.1
Disintermediating your friends

Note: Dots represent percentage of couples who met through friends in a given year; x's represent percentage of couples who met online in a given year. Data from Rosenfeld et al.[2]

Maybe this shift is an unmitigated good for our relationships. After all, the offline-network approach to meeting partners has some issues. Sure, this approach is great when your network contains plenty of single people of your preferred gender(s), but it's depressing when everyone is already paired up. It's exciting for your friends when they successfully set you up, but dividing up those same friends after a nasty breakup is painful. There have been countless times and places throughout history where seeking out partners could be anxiety-provoking or downright dangerous for LGBTQ folks.

Nevertheless, people seem to prefer doing it the old-fashioned way: One study found that 65 percent of respondents felt that "the best way" to form a relationship was to meet through friends or for a friendship to turn romantic. In stark contrast, only 1 percent said that online methods were best. Furthermore, people who identify as LGBTQ seem *especially* drawn to the friends-to-lovers pathway. And yet, here we are. Online dating is now central to the way that many younger and older adults navigate relationship initiation.[3]

If you have been single and looking at any point in the past twenty years, the odds are high that you have had a brush with online dating. It's possible your experience was positive; after all, online dating has created countless millions of relationships that never would have existed otherwise. But for all the good that online dating has done, it has changed the way we collectively think about attraction and dating, in subtle and not-so-subtle ways. For many, the apps have turned dating into a cross between a video game and a résumé exchange. It is often a solitary activity: you, your phone, and a list of dealbreakers for company. Not to mention, online dating can bring the worst parts of dating to the fore by exaggerating gender differences and making you feel like a clearance item at the bottom of the bin.

This chapter is about the shift from offline-network to online-dating methods of finding a partner and starting a relationship. Even though the contours of the way we date online have changed over the years, the basic pluses and minuses of online dating have proven to be fairly consistent. It's a good thing that online dating provides options for people with depleted social networks. But at least four features are worse than the classic offline approaches: Online dating offers too much choice, features an abundance of creeps, encourages counterproductive filtering, and exaggerates differences between men and women. As a user, there are things you can do to make the experience better and to reclaim the lost benefits of the offline approaches, especially once you recognize that the *apps* succeed when you spend your time swiping—and *you* succeed when you use the apps only as a springboard to communing out in the real world.

The Case for, and Against, Online Dating

The latter part of the twentieth century witnessed the rise of many consumer services that helped people to find relationships without going through friends, family members, and neighbors. There were several sociological reasons for these developments: In much of the Western world, young people started to delay marriage because they first sought to build a career or "find themselves." This delay often meant that once people were ready to marry they had a smaller pool of nearby singles. The average workplace boasts a meager number of similarly aged peers compared to the average school, and local ties to people's neighborhoods and interest groups atrophied. At the same time, consumer services were becoming a more central part of the economy, and so businesses found it lucrative to provide ways for singles to connect with each other. For example, newspapers sold space for personal ads, and video dating services would record prospective daters attempting to put their best foot forward and mail the tapes around to other users. In many ways, online dating was the next logical step in the evolution of these earlier services.[4]

Online dating has given us a few things that are truly new. First and foremost, online dating turns relationship formation into a less social, less collaborative process: The dominant way that humans have paired up for eons was through a matchmaking milieu of friends, acquaintances, and immediate and extended family, but with online dating, you're typically going it alone. Second, online dating presents users with a dizzying array of prospective partners, especially in modern urban and suburban environments. Third, with online dating, first impressions mostly come through photographs or written text (like information about your preferences in an "about me" section) rather than in-person interaction. Together, these features make online dating quite different from the dating and courtship approaches of decades past and wildly different from the network-mediated, limited-choice, face-to-face environments in which humans evolved. The question is, are these shifts ultimately helpful or unhelpful for the twenty-first-century dater?

Online dating would have died a long time ago if these new features lacked value. The reality is that many people do not want their romantic choices to be constrained by their existing networks. People want options, and few have the ability to hop to new social circles using charm alone.

Furthermore, consider the fact that there is great variability in the size of people's networks of prospective dating partners. Before the advent of the apps, meeting potential partners could be especially hard for some people, like people from the LGBTQ community, single parents, or older adults. Socially anxious people find it much easier to initiate relationships online rather than in person. For some folks, online dating has provided a set of prospective partners that could make the difference between dating someone or not dating anyone at all.[5]

In some cases, it might be good for a society to push people to look beyond their existing networks for romantic partners. In the 1860s, Queen Victoria briefly stopped holding balls for wealthy debutantes during "The Season." (Yes, this was the inspiration for the many episodes of *Bridgerton* we all binged.) With no balls, the aristocracy had to go out and meet more commoners. Not surprisingly, they then married many of those commoners. As a consequence, over the ensuing decades, political power and wealth became more evenly distributed throughout British society. Not a bad outcome of moving outside your courtship comfort zone![6]

Also, consider that throughout the late twentieth century, people commonly met romantic and sexual partners at work. But as #MeToo has highlighted, powerful people create hostile workplaces when they treat their employees like a personal dating pool. With online dating, there is no need for people to rely on their workplaces—and certainly not their subordinates—for romantic opportunities.

Finally, even if your friendship network does have a few single people in it, giving people the option to seek out new romantic horizons seems like a reasonable, humanistic thing to do. Recall that the way two people meet has no measurable impact on how their relationship unfolds; relationships that form through online dating are just as stable and satisfying as those that form through social networks. If modern technology allows people to choose their own romantic destiny, why stand in the way of progress?[7]

Online dating has given people more options. Options can be a very good thing. But not always. And online dating has also made relationship initiation harder in more ways than one.

The first problem with online dating is *choice overload*. Online dating doesn't just provide "more options." Often, it provides a deluge, even if you use filters to select people who are nearby, approximately your age, and so forth. Choice overload is a phenomenon that applies well beyond dating. In any sphere where choices are required, overabundance is bad news. Having too many options tends to make people more dissatisfied with their eventual selection, and they'll even try to defer committing to that selection. A classic paper in the consumer preferences realm found that people were less happy about the chocolate they selected—and less likely to buy one at all—when they encountered a display of thirty types of Godiva rather than six. In the many experimental studies that have examined this phenomenon, the negative effects of choice tend to be more pronounced when the options involved are complex, like when the advertised products differ on many attributes rather than just a few. Those findings don't bode well for online dating either; people differ on a countless number of attributes.[8]

The sequential manner in which people typically browse potential partners leads to complications, too. People are the most openminded at the moment they start swiping through profiles, eager to give each person a chance. But as they keep browsing, they adopt more and more of a rejection mindset. Once they find reasons to rule one partner out, they add that to the list of reasons to rule future partners out, and so it gets harder and harder to find partners who hit all the marks.[9]

The general sense of "blah" that eventually seizes most online daters derives from this seeming abundance of options. Touched-up perfection appears to pervade the Internet, and it's so easy to attend primarily to other people's flaws in real life. And if the rejection-mindset is your headspace—you're the consumer who deserves to be impressed—you'll find it hard to open up to someone or get genuinely excited about them. Dating feels like an exhausting exercise in "relationshopping."[10] A friend of mine who is a veteran online dater put it this way:

> If you don't have to work for it—to put yourself out there and risk embarrassment or heartbreak—the end result will always be boredom. You jump from one to another, never really embracing any individual beyond mild interest. The grass is always greener, there is always the "better" partner. You turn dating into a streamlined process, and in the end you lose all focus on what you're looking for.

When there is such a vast catalog to peruse, it can be hard to find something interesting in another person. Limited sets of choices heighten the stakes—both the risks and the rewards—by taking hypothetical perfection off the table and forcing people to take a second or third look at a person.

The second problem is that online dating is often demeaning, if not downright scary. Of course, you aren't the only one browsing. You are also being browsed, alongside thousands of other suitors. And the feeling of being evaluated is pervasive, especially if your inbox is empty.

Offline rejection can sting, too, but it's often covert. The hottie you were chatting up at a party moments ago might have taken off for a million different reasons; you don't need to assume that it was about you. When meeting potential partners in everyday life, it's easier to lean on a vast set of ego-protective explanations beyond "I'm undesirable." But with online dating, it's more tempting to interpret each ghosting and dead text thread as a rejection; the reasons that have nothing to do with you are less salient. This is perhaps why single men and women who use Tinder report elevated concerns about their appearance and feel greater shame about how they look, relative to single men and women who don't use Tinder. Few people feel great about themselves when they're perpetually compared to a photoshopped ideal.[11]

And if you do manage to attract attention, it may not be the attention you want, especially if you're a woman. Consider that your network of friends probably contains a number of people who are looking out for your best interests: They'll tell you not to date Ryan—he's trouble—and if you're going to date Jordan, watch out for his ex. With online dating, the people you meet don't come with referrals, and plenty of jackasses can create a seemingly decent dating profile.[12]

This lack of accountability is especially unnerving because some unappealing traits are overrepresented in populations of online daters. These traits include Machiavellianism (e.g., people who agree with statements like "Most people can be manipulated"), narcissism (e.g., "Group activities tend to be dull without me"), and psychopathy (e.g., "I'll say anything to get what I want"). Of course, you'll find these people offline, too. But if you ever suspected that these traits tended to be especially prominent in your Tinder dates, there is actual evidence that your suspicion is correct. For example, one survey of Tinder and non-Tinder users found that the Tinder users were more likely to have all these traits—especially (and alarmingly) psychopathy.[13]

It is easy to overlook the risks of online dating that arise from the lack of a meaningful pre-date vetting process on most apps and sites. A lack of safeguards and the relative anonymity of online dating create an opportunity for some men to completely misrepresent themselves. This is why so many women have harrowing stories about their experiences: According to a Pew Research Center survey, more than 50 percent of women have experienced harassment—or worse—from someone they met through an online dating site. Harassers and narcissists have always existed, of course. But in the past, your social network could have tipped you off before you made the decision to spend alone time with one. Even if you were meeting strangers in bars, your friends would have been beside you, ready to offer a speedy extraction.[14]

In principle, you could get around some of these problems by being really, really strict with the dates you consider. You want to limit your pool to thirty-two-year-old dog-lovers within a two-mile radius who have a graduate degree and are at least five foot eleven? Maybe that will quickly narrow the options to the small subset of partners who will be perfect for you. But here is the third problem: These kinds of filters are probably pointless.

Filtering will narrow the pool, but it is likely also raising your expectations—and therefore setting you up for disappointment—because you're in fact narrowing the pool arbitrarily. Your carefully curated set of matches aren't likely to be better dates for you than a set of matches drawn at random, because it is remarkably hard to discern compatibility from a profile.

A few years ago, my colleagues and I conducted a study that mimicked the typical online dating sequence, where people first form impressions of partners using an online written "profile" and then meet those partners face-to-face. Specifically, we wanted to understand what happens when people encounter prospective dates who match—or mismatch—what they think they want in a romantic partner.

Imagine that you're in this study. In part one, we ask you how you feel about a prospective romantic partner based only on a very simple dating profile. Unbeknownst to you, we have constructed this profile specifically for your eyes, and you have been randomly assigned to see one of two versions of it. If you were assigned to the "preference-matching" version, you would see a self-description supposedly written by your upcoming date, and this self-description would contain a set of traits that matches what you want in a partner. Let's say that two traits that truly define your ideal partner are "considerate" and "trustworthy." Lo and behold, your upcoming date described themselves that way! But if you were assigned to the "preference-mismatching" version, you'd see that upcoming date had jotted down a set of traits that are irrelevant to what you're looking for. Let's say that you personally don't put much stock in traits like "ambitious" and "adventurous." Well, for what it's worth, those are the traits on your date's self-description.

Sure enough, when we asked participants how they felt about this upcoming date, they were more excited in the preference-matching than the preference-mismatching group. The left side of figure 8.2 shows a meaningful difference between the two bars. In other words, if you said you wanted a partner who is considerate and trustworthy, you were more excited about the partner with the considerate and trustworthy profile (preference matching, white bar) than the partner with the ambitious and adventurous profile (preference mismatching, gray bar).

In the second part of the study, you actually have a five-minute, real-life mini-date with the supposed owner of this very simple dating profile. To cut down on the awkwardness, you and your date are given some artwork to discuss. Specifically, you are asked to describe a set of drawings to your partner that they cannot see, and they describe a set of drawings for you that you cannot see. In other words, you get to interact face-to-face with your date, but the task is constrained so you wouldn't be able to figure out that the profile you had seen was made up by us, the researchers. Then, you again tell us how excited you are about this person. Now, it no longer matters whether your date has the traits you were looking for in a partner. That is, your preferences have no effect on your liking ratings at all, as evidenced by the fact that the two "face-to-face" bars in figure 8.2 are statistically identical and differ only trivially.[15]

Here's a useful way of thinking about this study: When people say they're looking for certain traits in a romantic partner, they're making an educated guess about whether they'll click with someone. When all you have to go on is written, descriptive information, that guess makes a lot of sense.

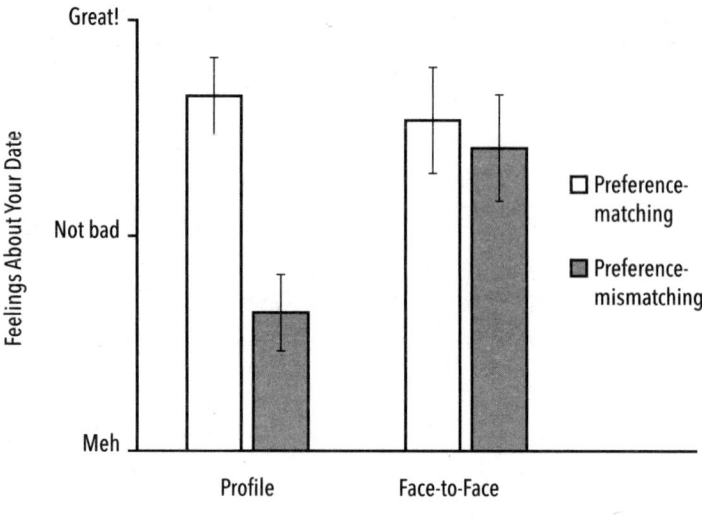

FIGURE 8.2
Your preferences matter when perusing a profile, not face-to-face.

Note: Data from studies 1 and 2 in Eastwick et al.[16] On the left side, the white bar is higher than the gray bar with a medium effect size. On the right side, the bars are the same height.

But once you meet the partners behind those profiles, you don't need that educated guess anymore. You have your gut reaction to the actual, real-life person instead. How did it feel to interact with them? If you *felt* something, you'll want to go on a second date—profile traits be damned. Also, recall that traits like "ambitious" or "adventurous" are not objective facts about a person; there are many ways that someone could embody these attributes. In one partner, ambitious means inspiring, and in another, it means appallingly cutthroat. One adventurous partner makes you feel alive; another adventurous partner makes you see your life flash before your eyes. It's quite easy to interpret the meaning of these traits to fit your gut reaction. "I said I didn't want someone ambitious, but he's the *good kind* of ambitious."

People commonly have strong opinions about their must-haves in a partner, and they want to reduce the deluge, so they're tempted to restrict their dating pools to potential partners who fit that vision. But the way they enact these preferences on the apps—through filters, or by quickly swiping left on anyone who deviates from their type even slightly—is probably one big expectation-raising waste of time. Once that face-to-face meeting happens, a partner's qualifications "on paper" go out the window.

Finally, there is the issue of how online dating amplifies differences between heterosexual men and women. In general, online dating sites and apps are designed to get you to focus on attributes that can be assessed quickly. Quantifiable information—like education level, income, or height—features prominently and can be compared easily across different partners. Attractiveness can be rapidly gleaned from photographs, of course. Responsiveness, communal orientation, or any of those other features that get your relationship off to a good start? Until you spend time with someone, those components are mostly guesswork.

It so happens that men and women *think* they have different preferences for the attributes that feature prominently on the apps: Women say they care about education, income, and height, and men say they care about attractiveness. And, just as people tend to gravitate toward their must-haves when looking at profiles (figure 8.2), men and women swipe right when they see the attributes that they think they want in a partner.[17] But as we discussed at length in chapter 2, these gender differences evaporate once people meet face-to-face. So the swiping action on the apps fosters the illusion that men and women have different desires, reinforcing stereotypes and forcing people to compete over a set of easy-to-assess attributes that ultimately won't matter very much.[18]

The most dramatic evidence that online dating exaggerates gender differences derives from data on heterosexuals' basic yay or nay decisions. In real life, if you introduce a random man to a random woman, there is a gender difference in who says yes to a second date, but it's a modest difference. At speed-dating events, men are 50/50 on whether they're sufficiently interested in a woman to want to see her again. Women are more likely to say no than yes at a rate of 65 to 35. This gender difference (50/50 vs. 65/35) is small.[19]

But on Tinder, something different happens. Men swipe right at about 50/50 again. For women, however, 95 percent of the time it's a no. These results are, of course, wildly different: a huge gender effect.[20]

Online dating takes a modest heterosexual gender difference from real life (i.e., men are 1.5 times more likely to say yes than women) and blows it way out of range (i.e., men are 10 times more likely to say yes than women). This difference is a giant red flag: Face-to-face impressions and online dating are two fundamentally different contexts with different sets of rules. And it goes without saying that humans evolved to consider prospective partners through face-to-face impressions, not five seconds of staring at a screen. For this reason, the mechanics of online dating don't support the fundamental truth espoused by proponents of the EvoScript, or any other perspective suggesting that we should submit to our fate as romantic consumer goods. Online dating can't tell us much about how men and women feel when they meet in real life, from the first face-to-face meeting onward.

How to Make Online Dating (a Little) Better

Online dating has survived despite its notable shortcomings. People are eager for ways to meet new partners, and online dating has produced a great many success stories. For these benefits, people are willing to bore themselves with choice, waste time filtering through troves of profiles, and run the gauntlet of unvetted creeps.

For many people, the shift to online dating means that romance is now something that they need to set out to find, usually by advertising the best version of themselves that they can convincingly sell. The time required to be a part of this market is no joke, with the average user spending nearly ninety minutes per day on the apps—even more if you really get into the "game" of it all. All that investment, just so prospective partners will spend a mere five to ten seconds looking at you (yes, that's all the average person spends!) before encountering one tiny underwhelming detail and left-swiping.[21]

We need to recognize online dating for what it is: a market-metaphor-reinforcing, evolutionarily novel approach that bypasses the first step of the in-person network. If online dating isn't for you, that's completely understandable; it often feels unnatural, and it caters to some people's strengths more than others. These days, the whole online dating industry seems to be struggling to stay profitable; troves of new pay-to-play options mean that you also have to fork over the extra cash or risk languishing at the bottom of people's feeds. We'll talk more about offline alternatives in chapter 10. But if you're going to give the apps a spin, there are some things you can do to improve the whole experience.[22]

LIMIT THE POOL, AND STAY FOR THE THIRD IMPRESSION

First, the hardest thing about online dating is balancing the tension between two forces. On the one hand, there is the overwhelming deluge of options. On the other hand, there is a temptation to use filters—provided by the app, or in your head—to limit the deluge to something more navigable. In the end, what happens is that people go out with too many people from a pool that they have filtered too heavily.

Instead, try dating fewer people within a more diverse pool. To manage this, you have to be willing to interrogate your own ideas of what you dislike: Is it really terrible that she's a consultant or that he's a yoga instructor? In many cases, you'll find that you've been artificially limiting your experiences based on your assumptions and stereotypes. Then, once you've practiced being more open-minded, try to keep the number of people you're actively dating to a minimum—say, three at a given time. Too many suitors in rotation makes the whole endeavor feel like a job, and it lowers the stakes for any one potential partner. To swap in someone new, you have to be willing to swap someone out. Dating coach Logan Ury sums up the strategy as follows: "If expanding your settings means a bigger menu, then dating fewer people at a time means savoring each dish."[23]

How long are you supposed to savor, exactly, before you know if you like the dish or not? This is a challenging question, but we can make an educated guess.

Imagine that dating is a game of prediction, and your strategy is to keep giving someone a try if there is a decent chance that you'll fall for them in the future. Conceptualized this way, the best strategy is to make a call after your *third* impression.

By impression, I mean: your physical attraction, how they make you feel, and how much you enjoy being around them. Your impression also includes whatever uncontrollable gut reaction you have when you see them or hear their voice or touch their hand. It includes how you feel about *yourself* when you're together: You want a partner whose positive qualities feel contagious—someone who makes you feel desirable—not someone who makes you feel small in comparison. There is no set length of time for how long it takes this impression to coalesce in your mind: It can happen in a matter of minutes, or it could take as long as a traditional multi-hour date.

We need to figure out how stable these impressions tend to be, and the thousand-crushes dataset that we covered back in chapter 2 offers some insights. This one-of-a-kind study charted how single folks felt about potential romantic partners over a period of several months. Because participants reported their romantic interest in the same prospective partners over and over again, we can chart how stable their impressions were at various points in time (figure 8.3).[24]

This figure shows that first impressions are not all that stable. In other words, your first impression does only a modest job of predicting how you'll feel about the person in the future; a bad first impression could be followed by a great one, and a great first impression could be followed by a bad one. Your second impression is a much better signal of how you'll eventually feel; notice the massive jump in stability. If you have the time and headspace, a third impression is better still. After this point, additional impressions offer diminishing returns for a while; if you don't like someone after a third impression, odds are, you're not going to like them going forward.

To be clear: Your third impression won't be perfect. Sometimes we

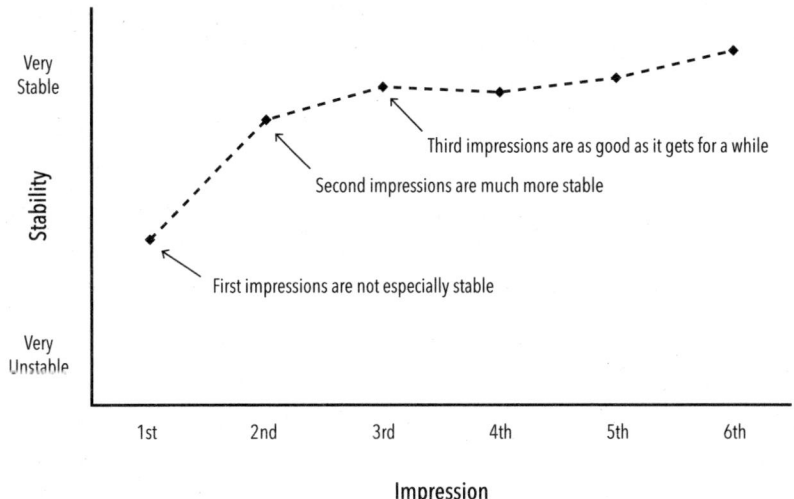

FIGURE 8.3
Impressions get more stable with (a little) time

Note: Data reanalyzed from Eastwick et al.[25]

come around on someone on the tenth or twentieth impression. But time is limited, and your third impression is a better predictor than pretty much anything else that has ever been documented. It's certainly better than a "date-'em-til-you-hate-'em" strategy, or a "I'll just keep dating 'my type'" strategy.

PUT THE PHONE DOWN AND GET OFFLINE

People put up with online dating for that larger pool, despite all the grief and aggravation. But the abundance of options wasn't the only reason that online dating became so dominant. We can also gain some insights by zeroing-in on trends in the way people socialize. Basically, the online dating explosion is a consequence of the way that in-person networks atrophied with the advent of the smartphone. We didn't just start dating on our phones; we started using our phones as a substitute for all socializing.

I recognize that the smartphone enjoys blame for many societal ills these days, and opinions differ on whether this reputation is deserved.

Nevertheless, one point about smartphones is completely uncontroversial: Socializing on phones has displaced socializing in person.[26]

First, let's compare teenagers in the mid-2010s—the first generation of teens who had limitless access to smartphones—to teenagers in prior decades. At about this time, high schoolers started "going out" less often. They socialized in person about one hour less *per day* than teens of earlier decades. They went to fewer parties, dropping from an average of five hours of partying per week in 2000 to two hours per week in 2015. This time adds up: Teens lost upward of forty in-person get-togethers with friends each year.[27]

The loss of in-person socializing was not limited to teens. Adults have been spending more time alone, too, and less time with people outside their households. This trend—which also accelerated in the middle of the 2010s—is evident for men and women, for younger and older adults, and for all levels of income and education. These are unfortunate trends, because it's also uncontroversial that loneliness is associated with a lack of in-person socializing.[28]

Now, recall figure 8.1, which depicted trends in the ways that people meet their romantic partners. In that figure, the matchmaker-friend approach dropped off in the mid-2010s, at exactly the same point that people started going out less often. Online dating coasted at a modest level of popularity for a very long time before it finally achieved exponential growth in the middle of the 2010s. So strictly speaking, it wasn't online dating that displaced the offline-network approaches. Rather, it was the rise of the apps: the bright colors and delightful pings that turned the smartphone into a dating video game. Indeed, dating app interfaces have been increasingly gamified, such that now the act of swiping and the accompanying sound effects are designed to be rewarding all by themselves. You're not supposed to make a choice and log off; you're supposed to keep playing.*

The better strategy, naturally, is to meet people offline as soon as

---

* Hinge at least boasts some awareness of the online dating downsides, given their "designed to be deleted" slogan and the fact that (as of this writing) basic users could only filter on a small subset of attributes.

you can do so safely. People are meant to be experienced, not ranked and charted using some grading rubric. Of course, an in-person meeting doesn't guarantee that your dates are truly experiences. It's very easy to turn dates into interviews—or small meetings that you need to fit in between other meetings. This is not a setup for success. Get to know each other as people, not as products, and not as candidates for a position.[29]

Activities are ideal, and if you're going to take my three-impression advice seriously, pick three very different activities. If one has to be a twenty-minute coffee date, okay, but then make sure the other two are longer and more interactive: Take a cooking class, take a dance class, go biking, go roller-skating, go ice-skating, go watch a sporting event, go chocolate/olive oil/wine/tequila tasting, or go to a karaoke bar and embarrass yourself. Your goal is to be playful and engaged. Don't schedule your app dates on Tuesdays—when nothing in town is open—and then wonder why your dates are boring.[30]

Remember also that dating can be a collective activity, even if you're relying on the apps. A friend of mine in graduate school matched with someone on a dating website, then met him in person and thought "not for me." But instead of blithely moving on to her next match, she introduced him to one of her single friends. Those two hit it off, and now they're married. Dating is not supposed to be something you do all by yourself with only your smartphone for company; it's supposed to be something that people do together. My favorite idea: Host "used date" parties built around this collective dating concept. Specifically, all the invitees bring a former online date where there was *no mutual* click. Make it your mission to introduce your Tinder plus-one to someone cool; your "meh" is surely someone else's "mm-hmm." What goes around comes around, and all.[31]

Online and Real Life Are Not the Same Thing

People would rather be socializing with friends and letting romantic possibilities fall out organically. Remember: 65 percent of folks would rather form a relationship through friendship, compared to

1 percent who prefer online methods. But our in-person networks are not what they used to be. We don't often get together with friends—sometimes in a pack under a pile of sleeping bags—and see where the night takes us.[32]

Given this reality, online dating has done wonders for millions of people. If I were single and looking, I'm sure I would be on the apps, too. Nevertheless, online dating is embedded in a larger trend in the way we socialize. Smartphones, social media, and the Internet in general have habituated us to a form of social interaction that is notably different from what we experience in person. For loved ones at a distance, technology works wonders for helping us to remain close and connected. But when it comes to forming an impression of someone new, the online medium encourages all the wrong things. Online impressions are all about sizing someone up, usually just based on a picture. Even worse, it fosters the impression that we're all disposable—that an initial, surface-level negative impression is sufficient to move on.

Live interactions inspire a different default. Most of the time, when we're face-to-face, we want interactions to be smooth and effortless. And so we strive to be pleasant, tolerant, and understanding, which then gives us a window to actually get to know someone.[33]

As we've seen in recent years, it's pretty hard to have pleasant, tolerant, and understanding interactions online. Which brings us to another problem.

· 9 ·

Disrupting the Manosphere

The last decade of the Internet has changed how I view the evolutionary psychological project.

In the beginning of this book, I described nineties-era evolutionary psychology as thrilling and wrong. I still find it thrilling, and I think that my fellow relationship scientists and I have built up an alternative to the EvoScript that is far less wrong. So far, so good.

But today, I also view evolutionary psychology as reckless. It is reckless because we know that evolutionary frames feed into laypeople's tendencies to rely on two particularly pernicious modes of thought: *essentialism* and *determinism*. Tradwives and men's rights advocates take evolutionary findings to mean that we can cure our societal ills by returning to the way things were done in the past, to a time when the spheres of men and women were well defined and separate. This is an essentialist claim. Alternatively, the incels and red pillers take evolutionary psychological findings to mean that our romantic fates are set in stone by our genetic gifts—a determinist claim. This chapter is about these trends, as well as the scientific studies and debates that illuminate this problem.

You likely don't subscribe to the tradwife or red pill worldviews yourself. Nevertheless, you may have endorsed a (far less pernicious) inversion of these ideas. You may, for example, have *resisted* the claims of evolutionary psychology because you feared that embracing them implied an essentialist or determinist logic. "If gender differences are evolved," you thought, "then are we to believe that men can't help their regressive preferences?" Therefore, you concluded: "Ev psych sucks."

These ideas are all part of the same tangled, philosophical mess. Even if every single evolutionary psychological claim had been true, there is not a shred of evidence in evolutionary psychology that supports an essentialist or deterministic worldview, and those who push the EvoScript to these extremes have become utterly untethered from the science. This chapter will interrogate how the ideas embedded in evolutionary psychology have been distorted by red pillers and the men's rights movement, and we'll see how "returning to our evolved roots" has little to do with their distorted, anti-feminist vision and more to do with rebooting our in-person social networks.

The Rise and Fall of Alana's Community for Involuntary Celibacy

A longstanding positive feature of the Internet is that it provides an easily accessible support forum for people experiencing any number of life challenges. This benefit is especially salient for those with stigmatized or marginalized identities. If you consider the way that the Internet has historically helped gay and lesbian teenagers find community online—especially if they have no in-person network where they live—it is hard to overstate how much good these online spaces have been able to do.[1]

But sometimes, an online space can go very bad, very quickly.

• • •

Alana's story is both inspiring and heartbreaking. In the nineties, Alana was a teenager who had never been in a romantic or sexual relationship. But it wasn't that she didn't want one. Rather, the whole romantic process seemed scary, the rules were inscrutable, and she wasn't sure that anyone actually wanted to be in a relationship with her.[2]

With access to the Internet in college, she spent time reading other people's moving, personal accounts about how they came to understand their own sexuality. She ended up having her first romantic relationship at age twenty-four, and with some new perspective, she looked back on her own teenage dating troubles and realized that she had a story to tell. As she wrote in 1997:

> This article is about people like me ... and maybe you too. People with a problem nobody talks about: I will call it "involuntary celibacy." It can happen whether you are outgoing (like me) or shy; whether you are gay (like me) or straight. It's not uncommon—you can probably think of a "maiden aunt," or an acquaintance who never mentions a boyfriend, girlfriend, husband or wife. Our society expects us to form couples and families, though, so I felt embarrassed for never having a significant other.
>
> I have written this article because I want people to start talking about this problem.... By sharing, we can learn that others are in the same situation. People can help each other accept themselves and solve any problems they might have. Each person who speaks up makes it easier for others to "come out of the closet" to themselves and the world. So I am speaking up about being involuntarily celibate.[3]

Inspired by the way that labels helped so many in the LGBTQ community to find identity and meaning, Alana chose the label "involuntarily celibate" to provide scaffolding for this common experience.

This article would kick off Alana's Involuntary Celibacy Project, a simple website that provided a space for several hundred people to support one another as they navigated frustration and rejection in the domains of dating and sex. Critical for Alana was that the group remained committed to personal growth through honesty and self-reflection: Repetitive complaining was discouraged, and misogynistic complaints were banned outright. The problem was not with "them," and the solution was all about "you." The community connected over their loneliness rather than their anger, and the narrative was humanistic: Own your role in your problems, have empathy for yourself and others, and take charge of your social and romantic life. A community like this one—which included people who had already made some progress through the challenges of dating—offered proof that hope was warranted.

Then, in the early 2000s, things began to change. Alana moved on to a new phase in her life and left the site behind. Many of the people who remained wanted to adhere to her original vision that encouraged self-reflection. But there were so many men who directed their anger beyond the specific women who had rejected them; they directed it at all women. When these men didn't like the moderated forum that Alana had created, they took their rage to unmoderated ones instead.*

Online communities about romantic rejection grew and splintered and grew some more. The (now mostly male) clientele cross-pollinated with other new online spaces, like the alt-right site 4Chan. These men were lonely, too, but they achieved a sense of connection through their trolling exploits on social media. They reveled in violent rhetoric; they referred to women as subhuman "femoids," as if women were machines who did not experience true emotion. At this intersection, the term *incel* came to be associated with a twisted mirror image of Alana's original vision: a form of male grievance that has since inspired several mass shootings and countless instances of "everyday" harassment and abuse.[4]

Today there are between sixty thousand and a hundred thousand active participants on incel websites and related online forums. Of course, in a group this large, not all participants are causing harm; many are simply lonely and searching for community. But the misogynist incel strain—and its gravitational pull on many young men—has ballooned into a massive societal problem.[5]

How exactly did we get such a dramatic shift from empathic humanism to misogyny? In brief, Alana's narrative lost the battle for

---

* The Reddit page r/ForeverAlone/—which is heavily moderated—is one modern instantiation of Alana's original vision.

hearts and minds. Her approach provided a healthy, positive solution for people's troubles, but embracing it required hard work. It's not easy to dismantle the mental biases and assumptions that feed one's loneliness. Instead, a competing narrative emerged, offering explanations that stoked men's outrage and feeding their desire to view modern feminism as the real nemesis. This new narrative sent Alana's humanistic approach to the margins. And this new narrative had the advantage of claiming that it was backed by science. The science of the EvoScript.[6]

ALANA DISCOVERED HOW the term *incel* had been appropriated by this misogynistic movement in the wake of a 2014 mass shooting by Elliot Rodger in Isla Vista, California. She was perplexed and distraught that the shooter had become an inspirational martyr-like figure for many men online, all of whom appeared to identify with the incel label she had created. Rodger would ultimately inspire other shooters, like Alek Minassian, who posted to Facebook "The Incel Rebellion has already begun! . . . All hail the Supreme Gentleman Elliot Rodger!" before murdering eleven people in Toronto in 2018. These are not isolated incidents: Against a backdrop of increasingly frequent mass shootings worldwide, the percentage of these shootings that are motivated by misogyny has quadrupled since 2014. Incel narratives are making young men very angry.[7]

This should never have been Alana's legacy. She had organized a community around a noble and compassionate idea, only to discover that people had taken that idea and used it for reprehensible ends. She described feeling like "the scientist who figured out nuclear fission and then discovers it's being used as a weapon for war."[8]

The EvoScript was similarly exploited. Despite evolutionary psychologists' best intentions, many of their bleaker ideas about the nature of human mating seeped out of the ivory tower and worked their way into every corner of the Internet, where they were appropriated by angry men to explain their romantic frustrations. If Alana discovered nuclear fission, the EvoScript showed how to enrich uranium.

Specifically, the three pillars of the EvoScript that we covered in chapters 1–3 are core to the incel worldview. That is, incels believe that there is a hierarchy of mate value, that mating is fundamentally about conflict between the evolved desires of men and women, and that there are certain types of people that are suited for certain types of relationships. Combine these assumptions with incels' personal experiences of being romantically rejected, and incels conclude that they have low—perhaps permanently low—mate value. They have internalized the idea that the EvoScript reflects the unalterable nature of men and women, and they believe that meaningful heterosexual relationships are a myth.[9]

It is not new that young men become susceptible to radicalization and aggression when they perceive themselves to be low status or when they are romantically frustrated. What is new is the way that incel rhetoric has been directly influenced by evolutionary psychology. In claiming a scientific foundation for their ideas, these men found a way to weaponize the EvoScript as a tool to recruit others to their cause.[10*]

There is a deeper reason why evolutionary psychology was particularly vulnerable to exploitation. Specifically, when people adopt an evolutionary lens, they become more likely to believe in essentialism and determinism. Essentialism refers to the idea that a person has a deep, underlying essence that places them in one category rather than another; for example, many people think that men and women differ because they possess distinct, underlying, fundamental essences. Determinism refers to the idea it is possible to predict a person's behavior or experience with a high degree of certainty; for example, many people think that a person's genetically endowed level of attractiveness powerfully determines their romantic fortunes.[11]

Essentialism and determinism are common: They pervade high school biology textbooks, for example. But critically, these beliefs are

---

* Those who have the fortitude should read Laura Bates's moving, personal account of the year she spent researching incels—and the graphic and violent threats to which they subjected her—in her book *Men Who Hate Women*.

not value-neutral; they have some nasty consequences, especially when aggrieved men on the Internet take them out for a spin.[12*]

Biological Essentialism and Men's Rights Activism

Essentialism refers to the idea that things have essences: some underlying, deep quality that explains what something "really is." Any time people use categories, they are likely using essentialist thinking to some extent. For example, you might have observed that bears have a stocky build, thick fur, sharp claws, and omnivorous appetites. Essentialism would lead you to conclude that these similarities flow from an underlying, deep "bear-like" essence that is shared by all members of the bear category. Furthermore, this essence differs from the essence that would be shared by all members of the "lizard" category, and there is no way for an animal to be both a bear and a lizard.[13]

Sometimes, people apply essentialism to categories of people, and the most commonly essentialized category is gender. The average person thinks that women share similarities that can be linked to an underlying female essence, and that men share similarities that can be linked to an underlying male essence. Surely, the average person does not believe that men and women are as different from each other as bears and lizards. But the same principles apply: People think that men are men because they have a man essence, and they are not women because they do not have a woman essence.[14]

These essences can have different origins. One theory of the case is *social essentialism*. If you believe in social essentialism, you think that essences come from social conditions or parenting practices: Women are kind and nurturing because they have been encouraged to take on those qualities as young girls, and men are ambitious and confident because they have been encouraged to take on those qualities as young

---

* The consequences of believing in essentialism and determinism are distinct from the (both psychological and philosophical) questions of whether essentialism and determinism are actually true. We'll consider these complex "But are they true?" issues toward the end of the chapter.

boys. Another theory of the case is *biological essentialism:* These different essences arise from an underlying, innate biological source.[15]

The tension between social and biological essentialist beliefs has real societal consequences, as illustrated by the history of men's rights activism. In the 1970s, the men's rights movement had a lot in common with the women's rights movement. There were plenty of "men's liberation activists" who, inspired by second-wave feminism, directed their ire toward the traditional male gender role and the patriarchal system that sustained it. According to this view, the mid-twentieth-century ideal of man—the rugged, unflappable, stoic provider—was a trap. A man who embraced this ideal had to work himself to the bone, his relationships with women were tense and unfulfilling, and he lived in fear of not being "man enough." Young boys were given no encouragement to be empathic or sensitive or aware of their feelings. Rather, the message was: "Don't be a wimp."

Like feminists, men's liberation activists identified patriarchy as the problem. They acknowledged that men have more power and resources in our society, but they saw that these privileges also confined men to a role that limits the full range of their potential and experience. The solution was for men to give up their claim to powerful roles and reject the system that enables the oppression of women. Then, your relationships with your wives and children would improve, you would be freed from the pressure of having to be the sole provider, and you wouldn't be bound to "masculine" experiences alone.[16]

Anyone familiar with the men's rights movement today is probably wondering what the hell happened.

In this century, men's rights activists glorify masculine things. They claim that men are at their best when they are dominating and showing their strength, and that the real enemy all along was feminism. According to these activists, feminism has encouraged women to step outside their natural roles as nurturers and child caretakers. Furthermore, because feminism inspired women to compete with men for provider roles, it has inhibited men's ability to harness their innate alpha potential, and it ignored women's own "hardwired" tendencies to sexually desire a small cadre of "high-quality" men and financially exploit the rest.[17]

Their anger congealed into an Internet-fueled movement that included incels, among other hypermasculine activist groups, and anti-feminist rhetoric proliferated through social media, memes, videos, and podcasts. One could argue that this backlash against feminism played a pivotal role in the 2024 U.S. elections, as young men were drawn to Donald Trump, and the energy of the manosphere seeped back into halls of power.[18]

The personalities in this space vary in the extent to which they appeal to general audiences. Among the most popular figures is the mystical culture warrior Jordan Peterson, who fights feminism with claims like "The idea that women were oppressed throughout history is an appalling theory."[19] Moving further extreme, we have NFL player Harrison Butker, who advises women to ignore the "diabolical lies" that their careers will be fulfilling and to embrace their innate desire to serve as mothers and homemakers.[20] Then, consider former kickboxer Andrew Tate—an Internet celebrity worshipped by teenage boys—proudly proclaiming that women "bear responsibility" if they are raped.[21*] Finally, you'll find Nick Fuentes, prominent white supremacist who Tweeted in response to Trump's 2024 election victory: "Your body, my choice. Forever." Channeling men's grievances into misogynist rage has become very popular and very lucrative.[22]

The influence of these men has become mainstream. For example, the number of teenage girls experiencing sexist comments online has more than doubled since 2018. Schools everywhere are struggling to contain Andrew Tate's misogynistic memes like the Andrew Tate Hand Gesture (which means "Shut up, woman") or MMAS ("make me a sandwich"), which have become pervasive among teenage boys. These boys often don't start by identifying as alt-right enthusiasts;

---

* As of this writing, Andrew Tate awaits trial for rape and sex trafficking charges in Romania, and he also faces related civil and criminal charges in the United Kingdom and the United States.

they may become interested in men like Tate because they're attracted to the edgy "Can you believe he said that!" ethos or the trinkets of manly success like cars and cash. For many, the misogyny grows slowly.[23]

The way men's rights activism turned from "feminists as allies" to "feminists as enemies" is complex. There were always going to be some men who were willing to help women smash the patriarchy, and other men who viewed men's rights and women's rights as a zero-sum game. But from today's vantage point, a critical difference between the men's liberation activists of the seventies and the contemporary manosphere can be found in the emphasis placed on social vs. biological essentialism.

Early men's liberation activists targeted gender roles and the patriarchal system that spawns them. Implicit in this social essentialist argument is that people can change their roles, either at an individual level (by choosing to be a stay-at-home dad, for example) or at a systemic level (by working to dismantle barriers that keep women out of the workforce). The popular scientific framework underlying these ideas is called *social role theory*.

If you want a society in which traits are not gendered, then social role theory explanations help you identify what to fix. For example, to boost women's participation in STEM (science, technology, engineering, and math), you might highlight accomplished women in science, or create spaces that help women feel that they belong when pursuing traditionally masculine careers, or fight the discriminatory practices that actively exclude women. The mirror image is true as well: If you want to increase men's participation in care work—like teaching, nursing, or social work—you could increase the visibility of relevant male role models and cultivate men's sense of belonging in those fields. The point is that a science that focuses on social role explanations inspires the insight that gender differences would be different if social conditions were different.[24]

As evolutionary psychology rose to prominence in the nineties, it clashed with social role theory. The evolutionary perspective posited that gender differences reflected something about the *evolved* nature of men and women, and role-based causes were not necessary to produce the difference. A reasonable, albeit heated, scientific debate ensued.[25]

But the way that evolutionary approaches addressed social problems was quite different from the social role approaches. Evolutionary psychologists were attuned to the possible mismatch between our modern environment and the environment in which we evolved. A popular example: We crave fatty foods because these foods were valuable and rare in our hunter-gatherer past. Tens of thousands of years ago, these cravings were adaptive, but we overindulge now that these foods are freely available. This is a novel insight that potentially informs our modern dietary woes.[26]

Nevertheless, in the domain of mating and gender, this approach proved regressive when filtered through our media ecosystem. People heard that our modern problems are a consequence of having drifted too far from our ancestral roots. As the EvoScript became more and more entrenched in our culture, the manosphere took this framework and ran with it. They claimed that roles are baked into our biology: Men evolved to be providers, women evolved to give birth and nurture children. The patriarchy arises from men's and women's fundamental nature; men pursue status and dominance because their forefathers used these attributes to attract women on the savanna. The manosphere personalities invite frustrated young men to imagine returning to a utopian primordial past in which men had dominion over women, and they insist that women will be perfectly content with this arrangement once they shed modern feminism. Even the tradwives of TikTok gleefully feed the right-wing male fever dream that "female submission is a woman's natural desire."[27]

Shaping the environment to match our evolved nature is sometimes a useful exercise. With modern diets, our digestive systems and metabolisms have evolved to consume a vastly different diet from the one most of us eat today, and our bodies have not caught up with the rapid pace of the food industrial complex. It is reasonable to posit that eating real food is healthier because that's what humans evolved to do. But in the mating domain, the suggestion that we could thrive by returning to our evolved past has proven disastrous. Add to this the incorrect EvoScript tenet that men and women have fundamentally different essences that were forged in the fires of a prehistoric "man-the-provider, woman-the-caretaker" patriarchy, and these ideas were begging to be hijacked by the regressive male grievance crowd.

Biological Determinism and the Black Pill

The second set of beliefs that causes problems at the intersection of angry young men and the EvoScript is determinism. An outcome is "determined" when a set of initial conditions reliably leads to that outcome. Stick the word *biological* in front of it, and now it's a set of initial biological conditions—something about someone's genes, or their evolved nature—that reliably leads to that outcome.

Biological essentialism and biological determinism are beliefs that often go together, but technically, they are two different things. Essentialism is about believing that an underlying quality makes one thing similar to another thing. Determinism is about believing that some outcomes are possible and others are not.[28*]

Determinism is a core component of the incel worldview. Some rudimentary googling about incels will lead you to the red pill, which (as described in the introduction) references the fictional pill in *The Matrix* that the character Neo (played by Keanu Reeves) ingests when he is ready to accept difficult, unvarnished truths about the world. In this case, the red pill concept is that women are hardwired to obtain the most attractive and highest status man that they can find, and therefore a man's options are determined by his desirable traits in conjunction with women's preferences and power. But peel back the misogyny, and the red pill is merely the mating market assumption from the EvoScript. As a man, you have a mate value that

---

* To paraphrase a helpful example from behavioral geneticist Dr. Paige Harden illustrating why these concepts are not the same: You might imagine that musical ability is biologically determined without thinking about the category of "musician" as sharing a natural essence, or you might imagine that people who are Catholics share a natural essence without believing that someone's religious behaviors are biologically determined.

is determined by your consensually desirable traits: your status, your attractiveness, or your charisma. If you want to successfully compete for women's affections, you need to boost those traits.

Many men first attempt to address this problem with red pill–inspired solutions, and again, these perspectives vary in their level of toxicity. Some of it is repackaged warrior-stoicism and self-discipline: Be tough, get ripped, don't cry, land a tradwife. Alternatively, some men adopt pickup artistry, which encourages them to prowl just as *The Game* did twenty years ago. What this advice misses is that many women would also like a man with emotional depth and range, and they would prefer not to get hit on by strangers when going about their day. And so, for many men, none of this advice actually changes their romantic fortunes.[29]

What do these struggling men then do? The common incel progression is that they turn from the red pill to the black pill. The black pill takes the mating market idea further to suggest that men's attributes are fixed: They cannot be learned, improved, or changed. Unattractive and socially awkward men are destined to a life alone. In other words, rather than questioning the mating market concept of the EvoScript, some men embrace biological determinism and conclude that the problem was in thinking that their traits could improve at all. When this happens, the romantic frustrations of the typical awkward adolescent now have an air of inevitability. Boys and men who think this way become extremely depressed and angry—or "blackpilled"—and they lose hope that their romantic lives will ever get better. For countless desperate and angry men, these ideas have become fodder for suicidal ideation, violent fantasies, and virulent misogyny.[30]

The black pill is a strict form of biological determinism. It plays on people's lay understanding of the way that certain uncommon genetic mutations work: For example, people with two copies of a particular mutation in the CFTR gene will develop cystic fibrosis, basically without exception. Incels who are blackpilled similarly feel that their poor romantic outcomes are inevitable, basically without exception. Very few people (and no practicing scientists) believe in such a strict one-to-one mapping of genes and romantic outcomes, but a looser form of determinism is everywhere in the idea that outcomes are *less changeable* if they arise from biological—rather than learned or cultural—causes.[31]

Pause for a moment before you feel confident that you are immune to this loose form of determinism. Imagine I were to tell you, as Dr. Daniel Nettle and colleagues did in a recent study, that a certain group of teenage women "... get pregnant because there is an evolutionary advantage to doing so." After learning this information, you probably think it is much harder for these teenagers to change their behavior, relative to cases where you were told that these teenage women become pregnant because it is part of their culture, or because it is a choice that they make. You made this inference because you, like most people, assume that biological, evolutionary, and genetic causes lead to outcomes that are more fixed and less changeable. These are deterministic beliefs that you harbor.[32]

Especially troubling are studies showing that simple descriptions of evolutionary psychological scientific findings, if presented without caveat, prey on laypeople's existing beliefs in biological determinism. In these studies, people read simple, textbook-like descriptions of evolutionary psychology and parental investment theory, alongside the basic EvoScript rationale for why men should be dominant and aggressive and women should be submissive and nurturing. In response to this information, the average person thinks that changing men's and women's behaviors will be especially hard, and gender differences might always be the way they are. In other words, because the typical person holds loose biological deterministic beliefs, they become pessimistic about change when they read about evolutionary psychology. These studies potentially explain why people who hold progressive values oftentimes resist evolutionary explanations.[33]

It's hard to blame people for their lurking deterministic beliefs, because the science itself often reinforces them. For example, evolutionary psychologists are fond of pointing out how certain features that seem suboptimal in modern contexts—like men's greater desire for sexual variety or for very young women—are highly resistant to historical and cultural attempts to change, and that this resistance implies an evolved basis. They'll note that "Men's stronger interest in casual sex and sexual novelty has survived society's best efforts to eradicate it" or "Human males appear to be so constituted that they resist learning *not* to desire variety" or "Telling men not to become aroused by signs of youth and health is like telling them not to experience sugar... as sweet."[34] Biological determinism lurks in these statements: Men have an evolved desire for sexual variety and youth, and that's why it's so hard to change.

The point, once again, is that beliefs in biological essentialism and determinism are not value-neutral: They have real-world consequences that make it harder to achieve progressive outcomes, and harder for people like Alana to help alleviate others' rejection-related anxieties. At the extremes, there are some who take these interpretations quite far, and so we end up with the misogyny of the manosphere and the defeatist logic of the black pill. But even the average person interprets evolutionary psychological findings about gender differences or mate value through their existing essentialist and deterministic lenses.

The Flimsiness of Biological Essentialism and Determinism

I want to be crystal clear: I am not here to advocate any kind of scientific censorship. Keeping research from the public is not remotely consistent with liberal or enlightened values, nor is it likely to engender trust in science or academic institutions. On the contrary, in this chapter, I am trying to help save evolutionary psychology from itself. Essentialism and determinism are not central to the goals of the science; they are accidental by-products. We didn't know that the men's rights movement would use evolutionary psychology to justify essentialist beliefs about men and women, and we didn't foresee that the incels would use evolutionary psychology to justify their bleak ethos of biological determinism. But today, we know the risks, and the only responsible course is to push back.[35*]

The point of leverage is this: In reality, essentialist and determinist beliefs are not justifiable in any coherent or consistent way. It's not that they're never true; they're just not true enough to be useful.

With respect to biological essentialism, the major error is the lay assumption that biological causes somehow negate the existence of developmental or learned ones. Nature and nurture are not mutually exclusive, and both forces work together to shape who people are. Nevertheless, when you tell people that differences between men and women follow from men's and women's evolved natures, they hear that social or learning explanations are not needed, and that the new evolutionary explanations replace the old, role-based ones. This is nonsense.[36]

A more accurate message follows from modern "biosocial" role perspectives that highlight how biology and social learning work *in tandem*. In this framework, biological differences between men and women constrain and shape the typical roles available to them. For example: Women can nurse infants, and men have more upper body strength. So in many cultures and historical periods, it was far more efficient for women to care for very young children and for men to serve in combat or to work heavy equipment. But within these constraints, norms and conventions shaped gender roles with considerable latitude: Under the right circumstances, men can care for young infants just as capably, and women can serve as equally badass soldiers.

This kind of flexibility is not new, either. As long as *Homo sapiens* has existed as a species, socialization has played a role; there is no original "natural" state that men and women can return to, untouched by norms and conventions and culture. So today, socialization perpetually remains a candidate for any attempts to address societal woes. If you want to imagine a future where men and women have

---

* Indeed, one of my academic heroes, Dr. Lisa Diamond, fought with gusto against regressive groups who manipulated her research findings to support their anti-LGBTQ conversion-therapy agenda.

different skills and interests than they do today, biosocial role perspectives point the way.[37]

As for determinism: People's lay beliefs about uncommon genetic mutations (like cystic fibrosis) have nothing to do with the way complex behavioral traits actually work. Genes *predict* outcomes like intelligence or educational attainment, but the same genetic propensity can generate a staggering range of downstream outcomes. Some people with all the "genetic promise" in the world don't finish high school; some people without it achieve advanced degrees. A given biological precondition can lead to a wide variety of behaviors, and a given behavior has many simultaneously operating causes.[38]

Furthermore, just because something is "biological" or "evolved" doesn't mean it is hard to change. Poor eyesight is largely genetic; it's also easy to fix by popping some glasses on your face. Humans evolved in a context where we slept in caves and moved long distances every few months; many of us are now partial to beds and pillows and staying put. It's biological to want to eat a steaming plate of food that's placed in front of you; depending on your culture, people nonetheless wait patiently until everyone has been served or until someone says a prayer. Human behaviors that have a strong biological or evolved component are still quite malleable.

The flipside is true, too. Some things that are purely learned can become very entrenched and hard to resist. The Stroop task, for one.* On a Stroop task, words like *red*, *green*, and *blue* are presented on a screen in fonts of varying colors, and your job is to resist reading the word and instead say the color of the font. "Learning" is the primary reason that your brain feels like it's grinding to a halt as you do the Stroop. Specifically, the Stroop task is hard because you learned to read. You practiced reading so much that it became nearly impossible for you to stop the habit of reading words that are in front of you.[39]

And just to bring the point home: The Stroop task is vastly *harder* than a commonly used evolutionary psychological task that requires

---

* If you haven't heard of the Stroop task before, flip to appendix B to do a quick Stroop task on yourself.

men to turn their gaze away from photographs of attractive women. Yes, a man can stop himself from gawking at women—the supposedly irresistible biological urge—much more easily than he can stop himself from reading.[40]

Biological essentialism and determinism are sticky ideas, but they are mostly a distraction, especially when it comes to sex and relationships. First, all complex human attributes are multidetermined, with many biological, learned, and cultural causes. Second, even when causes are partly biological, so what? Whether a cause is evolved, cultural, habitual, or otherwise is not a useful marker of whether you can change the outcome.

How to Talk to the Pill-Curious

You may have a person in your life—probably a young man—who is intrigued by the characters and ideas that pervade the manosphere. (Yes, even the tradwife content is largely for men.) Given the cultural dominance of the EvoScript, many of the concepts and studies I've described in this book remain underappreciated. Figure 9.1 contains

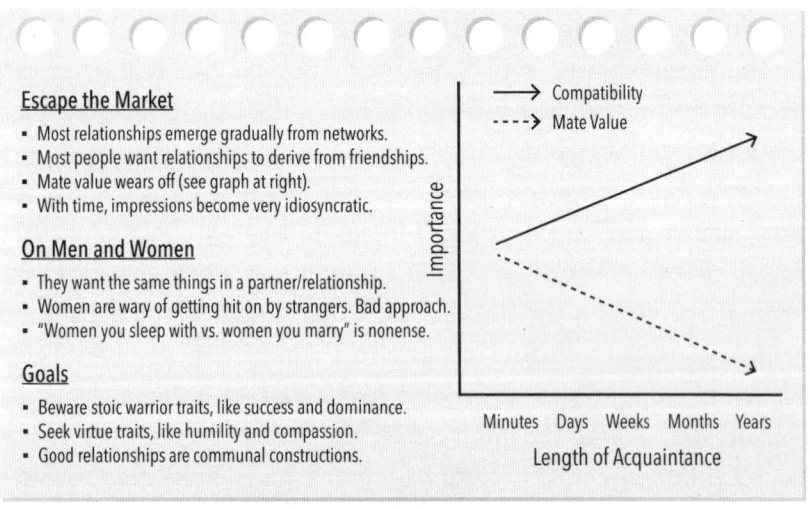

FIGURE 9.1:
A cheat sheet for productive conversation with a pill-curious young man

a cheat sheet with material that might help increase his resistance to those market-oriented, red/black pill messages.

Of course, whenever you're trying to persuade someone about anything controversial, listen and try to lead with empathy. And if this young man is suffering, remember that humans are bonding creatures who begin to fall apart if we feel like we don't belong.

For starters: Odds are that a young man who feels aggrieved about sex and romance implicitly has a "mating market" model of sex and relationship initiation in mind. If you ask him questions about how he imagines that relationships take shape, he will probably describe strangers meeting in bars and random hookups at clubs. He probably will not describe sexual relationships evolving slowly from social networks, which is how most casual and serious relationships form—and how most people want relationships to form.[41]

His experience may be that attractiveness, charisma, and other components of mate value are the end-all-be-all that explains why some men get to have sex and some don't. He may be surprised to learn that the long-term acquaintance contexts that spawn most relationships also happen to be the contexts where mate value matters the least and impressions become staggeringly idiosyncratic. You might encourage him to spend less time in settings that foster higher levels of consensus about traits like attractiveness: Chatting up strangers and online dating are probably less promising than cultivating in-person networks of friends and acquaintances. Hitting on strangers is a unique, strange modern skill that few people possess; in contrast, humans have formed relationships from networks for eons. Networks are not instant panaceas, because networks can become stale; if he hasn't been out socializing much, it can take a while to get reintegrated. But socializing with friends is for everyone, and it's typically enjoyable in and of itself.[42] (I'll have more advice along these lines in the next chapter.)

As I mentioned in chapter 7, people's decisions to hang out with some folks rather than others is the primary way they exert choice over the kinds of people they end up dating. So if he feels like he isn't meeting many women—even casually—he may need to expand the range of spaces he inhabits. Expanding may be a challenge for some men in light of the widening gap in political views among young people, as women have moved to the left over issues like #MeToo and the overturning of *Roe v. Wade* in the United States. Online tradwives may be thriving, but the real-life tradwives are vanishing! Therefore, if a young, socially conservative, heterosexual man were to assume that he'll only be comfortable around like-minded individuals, he might be restricting his prospects dramatically. But if he instead expanded his horizons, he might have more options. Of course, he can't just crash a slam-poetry reading; he'd have to go into those spaces respectfully with the assumption that everyone has something to learn from one another.[43]

He might believe that men and women have very different goals and preferences in the dating arena. Acknowledge that women are indeed wary of casual sex, especially with strange men they do not know. Advise him not to *be* one of those strange men. Beyond that, few differences remain: Men and women want partners who are smart, funny, attentive, supportive, and make them feel special. Men and women both enjoy sex and will be happiest in relationships that are communal and bonded. Most important of all, men and women do not experience perpetual relational conflict because of their differing evolved needs and preferences but rather have a whole host of mental biases that help them see the best in each other. Indeed, for all psychological qualities, any gender differences that do exist are likely to be tiny and swamped by individual variability.[44]

He may also think that some people's sexual histories make them unsuitable as relationship partners, but this is merely an old stereotype: Anyone can be a good or bad relationship partner depending on the relationship that they construct along the way. Dads and cads; alphas and betas, Madonnas and whores; all nonsense. A true "life's not fair" lesson is that attractive, charismatic people will get many opportunities to have sexual and romantic relationships; if he doesn't have those gifts, he'll get fewer at bats, so to speak. That reality is annoying—even distressing. Luckily, lasting relationship happiness has nothing to do with a person's lifetime stats of sexual and romantic conquests but rather hinges on building a relationship constructed around communal patterns, where partners look out for each other's needs.[45]

Finally, at the level of values, emphasize that the Internet warrior personalities don't have a monopoly on the qualities that make someone a good man. Resilience and courage, sure. Becoming emotionally distant and clawing your way to dominance? That ethos made a lot of mid-twentieth-century men—and the people around them—quite miserable. Buy him a copy of *Death of a Salesman*.

There are alternative traits and values worth striving for. Humility. Generosity. Justice. Compassion for others, especially those who are down on their luck. These are virtue ethics, rather than success ethics. Pursuing virtue ethics makes you feel like a part of something bigger; pursuing success ethics leaves you feeling empty. Look up to people like Keanu Reeves, a respectful king of a man who has given away much of his fortune to charity, founded a cancer research institute, and fights to free Tibet. You know him—he played Neo. The guy who actually took the red pill.[46]

Getting Our Networks Back

Regardless of your gender, dating troubles are normal. But if you are a man, dating troubles plus Internet misogyny plus the EvoScript means that you might view your dating troubles as women's fault because you are part of an underclass of men, in which case there probably isn't anything you can do about it except to rage against the feminists.[47]

Solutions to our online dating and online hating troubles exist—and none of them involve eschewing evolutionary explanations. Sexual education curricula for young people could spend more time on the "learning to date" struggles that Alana built her original community around. These programs could even add some EvoScript and biological essentialism/determinism myth-busting for flavor! Alternatively, sometimes distraction will be the answer because obsessing about a lack of sex makes the problem worse. For example, the U.S. military found success in reducing deployed troops' sexual frustrations by adding recreational and educational opportunities that kept them socially engaged.[48]

The time is perfect for social-engagement innovations, precisely because online dating is so dominant, and our real-life social networks have deteriorated. Consider a recent study that documented how many "close friends" adults possess (figure 9.2). At the high end, nearly 50 percent of adults surveyed in 1990 reported having 6 or more close friends; in 2024, that number was down to 25 percent (white bars). Most depressing of all, the number of adults reporting no close friends at all has risen from a mere 3 percent in 1990 to 17 percent in 2024 (gray bars). That is, nearly 2 out of every 10 adults today have no close friends.[49]

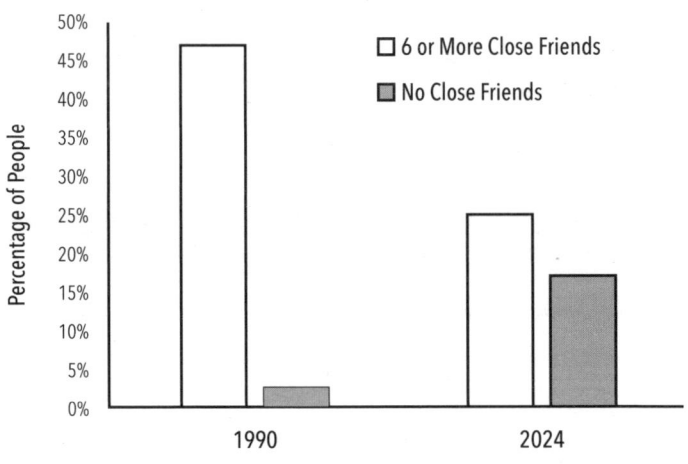

FIGURE 9.2
The shift from many to zero close friends

Note: Since 1990, fewer people have six or more close friends (white bars), and many more people have no close friends (gray bars). Data from Cox and Pressler.[50]

Of course, it's a good thing that the Internet can provide social connection for people. But just like we saw with online dating, it's a particular form of social connection that does some things well and other things poorly.

When it comes to loneliness, a stranger's personal story in an online forum can provide valuable inspiration. But the pervasive draw of our phones is sapping away our desire to interact in person—and perhaps our close friendships with it. Also, negativity and anger are exceptionally catchy, and if you haven't noticed, the Internet is pretty good at spreading catchy things. As a result, the men's rights movement has never been stronger, and its devotees are clear that men reclaim their true evolved greatness by defeating feminism.

To state the obvious: We evolved in a context where we expected to have real people around us. Friends and family who depended on us, and vice versa. And in that context, popularity mattered less—far less than the online universe of dating apps and incel propaganda would imply. This isn't to say that offline networks are a cure-all for loneliness or dating troubles. But if we're going to create a new framework for understanding the evolved nature of human romantic relationships, let's start with this: Our bonds were designed to be unique and idiosyncratic and bound to the people nearby that we could touch and see and hear.

· 10 ·

Real Relational Solutions

We are creatures who evolved to form sexual relationships and romantic attachments within small networks. Mate value and competitive markets have a limited influence on how these bonds form and take shape, and they likely had even less influence in the environments in which humans evolved. Instead, compatibility is the essential component that explains why we bond to some people rather than others. Compatibility itself belies market-based metaphors because it has little to do with how people's traits and attributes match up, and everything to do with the patterns that people build together, even from the first few moments.

Our modern dating innovations don't seem well suited to this new scientific vision of human connection. Online dating is structured in unhelpful ways, and we're drowning in an outdated pop evolutionary psychology that feeds essentialist and deterministic impulses. Nevertheless, here are three truly relational approaches that can help the twenty-first-century dater survive this landscape: (1) Build mixed-gender networks of friends and acquaintances; (2) address loneliness first, rather than the lack of a partner; and failing that, (3) hit the road.*

---

* In this chapter, I offer little advice about improving your mate value. Of course, it's generally wise to exercise, eat healthy food, and practice good personal hygiene. But advice in the category of "make yourself more appealing" quickly descends into patronizing and unhelpful. If you're reading this book, I'm going to assume you've got the basics covered, and you're ready for the truly relational ideas.

Build Mixed-Gender Networks

This is a story about how I learned to stop worrying and love the friendzone.

Angie and I had been friends since the first week of college. After we graduated, we lived together for two years. We both worked in New York City, bouncing around various forms of paid and unpaid work as we figured out what we wanted to do with our lives. More than once we woke up puzzling over the appearance of a new piece of furniture in the kitchen—a stool, or a set of shelves—usually the result of a late-night, tipsy impulse grab from a street-side pile on our way home. (We were not rich.)

Romantically, our lives ran along parallel tracks. We commiserated when crushes fizzled, or when we got ghosted. If Angie observed that a woman was just not into me, her insights made it easier for me to move on. I offered her a similar perspective on male ambiguity and ambivalence.

I know how this friendship appeared to others. After a few margaritas, our neighbors once asked us: "You two are going to get together eventually ... right?" That was the generous interpretation. The ungenerous one? The assumption that one of us—probably me—was desperately waiting in the wings. Surely, I had to be stuck in the *friendzone*.

The TV show *Friends* infused pop culture with countless terms and concepts over its ten-year run. One memorable example comes from a season 1 episode in which Joey admonishes Ross that he and Rachel are headed for the friendzone: a pathetic relationship status in which Ross secretly pines for Rachel while she only sees him as a friend. Ross (eventually) avoids this fate, but the friendzone is a common experience for the rest of us: Unrequited love is ubiquitous and often occurs in the context of friendships. Furthermore, most people feel attracted to a friend at some point in their lives, and in many mixed-gender straight friendships, there exists some sexual attraction on the part of one or both parties.[1]

No one enjoys being stuck in the friendzone. Many people find themselves investing heavily in something that they imagine to be a burgeoning relationship, only to have it become unmanageably imbalanced and too painful to sustain. Friendships with people of one's preferred gender carry this risk, and before Angie, I worried about it all the time.

The manosphere has seized upon this pervasive anxiety to transform the friendzone from an inoffensive reflection on the complications of mixed-gender heterosexual friendships into a misogynistic trope. To them, it's patently obvious that "men and women can't be friends." In fact, it's worse than that: Straight men who are friends with women have fallen into a trap for chumps. In their formulation, women use the friendzone as a manipulative tactic: She keeps him around as a plaything or to soothe her loneliness while she waits for the true alpha male to come along. The friendzoned man is given false hope by listening to her tales of wanting a "nice guy" before she runs off with someone who is definitively not so nice. For this online crowd, the friendzone is one more illustration of the many ways that women are devious and coldhearted in their quest to wield power over men.[2]

The friendzone concept deserves to be rehabilitated, especially in light of manosphere nonsense. For singles of all genders, in constructing your social world: If you don't have friends of your romantically preferred gender, you're doing it wrong. You should fix that.[3][*]

AS WE'VE DISCOVERED, forming relationships from friendships remains fairly common; chatting up strangers has never been a prerequisite for romantic success. Though meeting through friends has declined relative to online dating, the friends-to-lovers pathway remains a top-three approach. What's more, pretty much any approach

---

[*] The lessons in this section are most urgent for straight, cis men and women, largely because the overwhelming majority of LGBTQ folks *already have* networks that feature people with diverse genders and sexualities. Nevertheless, the horizon-broadening benefits of a mixed-gender friend network should apply widely, even if the dating-pool benefits apply mainly to straight folks.

to meeting someone (yes, even online dating) follows a friendship-then-romance sequence a *majority* of the time. Among folks under thirty and in LGBTQ relationships, friends-first initiation is exceptionally common, characterizing more than 80 percent of all romantic relationships. For these reasons, people will inevitably come across many real-life friendzone examples that "work out."[4]

There are two important wrinkles. First, the friends-first approach takes a while: If you consider the set of romantic relationships that has formed through friendships, the typical amount of time between becoming friends and the relationship turning romantic is about a year. So if it's going to happen, it probably isn't going to happen overnight. Second, *intentionally* traversing the friendzone to form a romantic relationship is a risky, low-likelihood strategy. If you again consider the set of relationships that form through friendships, it is about twice as likely that both parties develop feelings for each other gradually than it is that one party successfully woos the other out of the friendzone.[5]

Making matters more complicated: Romantic relationships are very rare events when you consider the full set of eligible potential partners that a typical person knows. Putting a precise number on this rarity is very challenging because people aren't great at keeping track of every single person they've met who could become a romantic partner. But a reasonable best guess for young heterosexual adults living in the contemporary Western world is that somewhere between 1 percent and 5 percent of cross-gender acquaintances will turn romantic at some point. In other words, the odds that the average single person will form a romantic relationship with a given acquaintance is somewhere in the single digits. That's not winning-the-lottery rare, but it won't happen too often for most people. Most acquaintances and friends remain acquaintances and friends.[6]

Let this all wash over you for a second. If you are single and lonely and hoping to form a relationship, you are hoping for a rare event. And if it's going to happen through friendship—which it certainly can—it's probably going to take some time, without you even realizing that it's happening.

The friendzone is not a magic shortcut to forming a relationship. Don't make a friend of your romantically preferred gender while harboring ulterior motives, or to buy time to show off what a nice person you are. If your attraction to someone is so profound that you can't fathom being just friends, you should probably set that possibility aside if the feelings are not immediately mutual.

But what about getting friendzoned by someone where your attraction isn't all that strong? Or getting friendzoned by someone who—in fairness—you aren't attracted to either?

These friendzones are magnificent.

My sibling-energy friendship with Angie makes the case. New York City is magnetic but daunting—especially if you don't have a lot of money—and it's hard to imagine how I would have managed it without Angie. As a young adult, not knowing how you're going to make an income next month can be terrifying. If you're jobless, it's tempting to pack it in and move back to your hometown. Angie and I confronted this financial insecurity side by side, and it seemed far more manageable. When I met someone I was especially into, Angie knew how to make me look good, either by teeing me up to tell a good story, or by telling one herself and letting me coolly bide my time. Finally (and hilariously), I had a doomed stint in a Coldplay–meets–Dave Matthews jam band playing clubs in New York City and North Jersey. It probably would have been an even shorter stint had Angie not come to every show, and I carry with me the stage-confidence that I earned to this day.

I also learned from watching the ways her experiences were different from mine. In a couple of ways, she had it easier. Strangers at bars took more of an interest in her than in me. I probably paid for more drinks and cover charges than she did.

But let's be real. Angie had to deal with stresses from which I was completely exempt. Take issues of safety. I enjoyed carefree shortcuts down dark, quiet streets; Angie would go well out of her way to stay in well-lit thoroughfares. A mutual female friend once ended up in a sketchy part of town because I gave her bad directions. When I acted insufficiently contrite, Angie laid into me, and with good reason: "You cannot fathom how scary that probably was for her!" At one point, Angie worked at a place where the sexual harassment was particularly intense; she endured it because she needed the job to keep affording the rent.

Much to the disappointment of our neighbors, Angie and I never remotely considered anything romantic. Instead, she was the most loyal and steadfast wingman I ever had.

People who fear the friendzone would tell you that embarking on this friendship was dangerous. The cult of "men and women can't be friends" would have you believe that genuine mixed-gender friendships are impossible, and the only reason to maintain them is that they might one day "pay off" in a romantic or sexual way. If I had bought into these ideas, I would have missed out on my friendship with Angie—the key person who helped me survive New York.

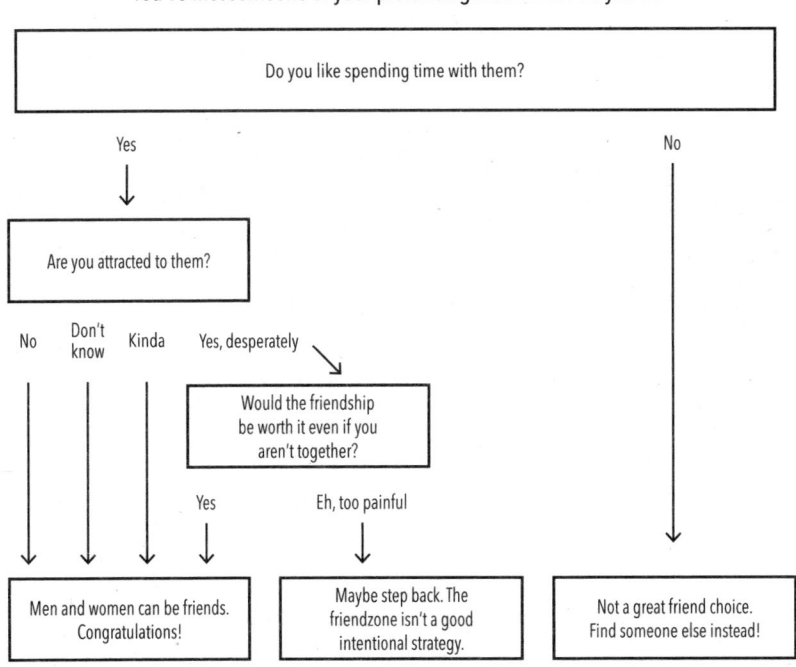

FIGURE 10.1
Can straight men and women be friends? A guide.

My male friendships were meaningful, too, of course. But in my experience, attitudes and beliefs congeal when straight guys only interface with other guys. Too much masculine same-ness cultivates and nourishes competitive us vs. them assumptions about the genders. For men, women begin to seem like strange and inscrutable creatures. Mixed-gender friendships are an easy solution, and the calculus isn't all that complicated.

The scientific record backs up my recommendations, too. When heterosexual men have more female friends (and fewer male friends), they tend to be less sexist in their beliefs, and they're less likely to objectify women. So straight men whose friendship circles contain a greater proportion of women are safer bets as boyfriend material than men who are only friends with other men.[7]

Lest you think that these men with lots of female friends are desperate losers: Heterosexual men who have larger other-gender networks of friends are *more* likely to find a romantic partner over time. Like I said, Angie was my number one wingman. In fact, this finding is true for all genders: Anyone with a more gender-diverse network is more likely to find a case of mutual attraction. Intriguingly, for straight folks, *same*-gender friends do not provide a romantic edge: The number of same-gender friends a person has is basically irrelevant to their relationship prospects.[8]

Naturally, living in a gender-diverse network can present challenges. When someone overinterprets your purely friendly signals, the vibe may become uneasy or downright depressing ("How on earth did my vanilla questions about his trip to California imply that I was attracted to him?!"). Also, breakups happen: If you're going to date friends or friends-of-friends, you'll need to be able to end things gracefully. Straight people should take more lessons from LGBTQ folks, who tend to be more successful at keeping cordial relations with exes than straight men and women. Of course, continuing to hold a torch for your ex generally bodes poorly for your well-being or your prospects with a new partner, but simply inhabiting the same social network as your ex is neither good nor bad on average.[9]

A mixed-gender network—built slowly and gradually over time, without ulterior motives—is an effective, low-tech dating intervention from a time before Tinder. The men's rights bros online would like to persuade straight men that platonic female companionship is unnatural and destructive to their romantic prospects. They couldn't be more wrong.

. . .

"You need to work on yourself before you get into a relationship." There are several reasons why this cliché has such resonance for people. Naturally, to find a maximally satisfying relationship, people need to work through their own trust, avoidance, or self-esteem issues. Those who have the tools to overcome these concerns tend to be happy across all their romantic relationships—present and future.[10]

The importance of mixed-gender networks highlights another, less obvious reason why this statement is true. When people are working on themselves, pursuing their hobbies, and figuring out what they need and want, they'll often expand their networks as a part of this process. They take a dance, pottery, cooking, acting, or martial arts class. They join a kickball, softball, pickleball, or some other kind of sports-ball league. They spend more time at the dog park or the skate park. They go back to church; they start volunteering. They find activities they enjoy, and they meet other people who enjoy them, too. Their networks morph and expand, and invisible tethers pull prospective romantic partners into each other's orbit.

We've always relied on this method of connection. From the emergence of *Homo sapiens* as a species through the mid-twentieth century, close and distant kin played a romantic-networking role in most contexts. An aunt chats with a cousin, a gathering is organized for Saturday, and Elissa meets Jacob for the first time. As extended family ties weakened in many parts of the world, "found families" of friends and acquaintances—especially mixed-gender found families—rose to fill the gap.

I wish I could deliver the following advice to the past version of myself who was single-and-not-loving it: "Stop thinking about where you go to meet women to date. Just be around people, period." Our brains need social connection—and not just romantic ones. I should have been meeting people in groups and other contexts that encouraged repeated interaction. I should have been capitalizing on the familiarity-breeds-liking effect and letting the romantic possibilities emerge organically.

But no, I was gripped by the historically improbable idea that relationships are born from one sparkling unicorn conversation with a stranger. Catch someone's eye; deliver the perfect line; reach for the same pair of gloves at the exact same moment. This idea has burrowed deep into our collective psyche: Like children of wealthy parents at an amusement park, we expect the express pass into couplehood. It happens, sure, but the aspiration is mainly a distraction. Even if you're on the apps, it's often going to take a while, and connections in networks are still going to play a role as things unfold.[11]

Relationships are much more likely to form as networks shift than by force of will. So when people tell you they found a relationship when they were least expecting it, it's not magic. It's probably because they were busy doing things with other people. Which is precisely how partners come together.

Treat the Loneliness First

Many people who are single and searching for a partner have happy and fulfilling social lives otherwise. For others, the search is a struggle, and the lack of a partner and a broader sense of loneliness go hand in hand. In fact, sometimes people have difficulty separating romantic longing from plain-old loneliness, and it can be easy to mistake the desire to be in a relationship for the desire to be around more people. Fortunately, the most effective ways of finding a romantic partner have a lot in common with the most effective ways of addressing loneliness, and tackling the loneliness first can make the partner-search more fun and less frantic.[12*]

---

* The sciences of how we build friendships and how we build romantic relationships often converge on the same lessons. Nevertheless, there is one major difference between

We may have yielded our modern dating woes to the capitalist machinations of the Match.com conglomerate and the rest of the apps, but we've treated loneliness like the genuine public health concern that it is. Governments have marshalled considerable resources in the service of addressing the contemporary epidemic of loneliness. For example, the United Kingdom funds a wide variety of community-based loneliness initiatives, spearheaded by an actual minister of loneliness. In 2023, the surgeon general of the United States released a major report on the epidemic of loneliness that rivaled the scope and gravity of earlier efforts to draw attention to the dangers of smoking. Nonprofits and community organizations have taken a considerable interest in reducing loneliness, too.[13]

One critical yet counterintuitive aspect of the experience of loneliness is that it doesn't always track a person's objective social resources. Some people with a great many close, nearby friends can still feel lonely; some people with just one or two close friends can feel sufficiently socially connected. Similarly, someone's intuitive sense that they have dating options may or may not objectively track the number of eligible singles in their vicinity. Loneliness and dating isolation are subjective experiences, and of course, that doesn't make them any less real.

In large part, loneliness is subjective because it's grounded in a thorny approach-avoidance conflict—so thorny that it's sometimes called the "porcupine problem." In the original nineteenth-century allegory, a group of prickly porcupines need to huddle together for warmth on a cold day, but their quills drive them apart. The porcupines oscillated between their desire to approach and their desire to avoid being hurt, ad infinitum. Lonely people experience this tension acutely: They are motivated to restore their sense of social connection, but they also become self-protective and vigilant for signs of

---

the platonic and romantic realms when it comes to initial-impression strategies: the benefits of being especially selective. Romantically, being unselective and hitting on person after person comes across as desperate and undesirable. But if your goal is to make friends, there's nothing wrong with being unselective and open to friendships with many people.

rejection. In contemporary settings, given that we are no longer literally dependent on our local small group for survival, it's easy for this protective instinct to become an isolationist one.[14]

Nevertheless, there are strong approaches that work at scale. Many of the government-supported solutions in the United States and the United Kingdom bring communities of people together around an event or in the service of others. Groups that meet consistently or events that take place regularly—again, capitalizing on the familiarity-breeds-liking effect—are likely to be particularly effective in this regard.[15]

There are psychological approaches that work on an individual level, too. Loneliness is usually a downstream consequence of people's thoughts and perceptions. Not surprisingly, then, some of the most reliable evidence-based treatments help people to change those thoughts and perceptions—specifically, the self-defeating impulses that constitute the prickly, avoidant half of the porcupine problem.[16]

Negative thought patterns are stubborn, and changing them requires considerable practice, as anyone familiar with cognitive behavioral therapy will tell you. You first need to notice the emergence of the negative thought ("She'll probably reject me" or "He wants nothing to do with me"). This meta-recognition is tricky all by itself because self-protective thoughts flash into our minds very rapidly and without intention. Only after catching the negative thought can you add a more positive, less guarded thought that reduces the avoidant impulse. ("Even if they reject me, attraction is mostly idiosyncratic, and it has absolutely no bearing on my value as a long-term partner.") Changing thought patterns is hard, but according to the best data that scientists have gathered, the most effective routes out of loneliness target people's thoughts in this way.

Sometimes, small tweaks in our style of interacting with the world are helpful, too. During a time when I was living on my own, my (then-long-distance) partner would periodically remind me to spend time with nearby friends face-to-face. The science has proven her right, as did my own experience: Spending time with other people in person is considerably better than texting or video chats for boosting well-being. But any form of mutual communication is better than passively scrolling social media, which seems to drag lonely people down further.[17]

In one-on-one interactions, the avoidant and self-protective impulses that accompany loneliness paradoxically lead people to do things that yield worse initial impressions. Especially on dates, people mistakenly believe their job is to self-promote: You have to be attractive, be funny, be charming, and make them fall for you. These performative instincts are misguided. Dates will go more smoothly if you can be curious and interested in the other person; wherever possible, ask questions to keep the conversation moving in the same direction, rather than shifting the focus back to yourself. Be an audience, and don't require an audience.[18]

And when you do disclose, offer up something a little deeper about yourself. A famous study by Dr. Art Aron found that a set of questions that escalated in the extent to which it elicited intimacy and vulnerability (table 10.1) produced more closeness than small talk. This is the "fast friends" procedure we encountered back in chapter 8.

TABLE 10.1

Examples of Dr. Aron's Escalating Intensity Questions

INTENSITY LEVEL	QUESTION
LEVEL 1 GETTING COMFORTABLE	For what in your life do you feel most grateful?
	Take 4 minutes and tell your partner your life story in as much detail as possible.
	If you could wake up tomorrow having gained any one quality or ability, what would it be?

INTENSITY LEVEL	QUESTION
LEVEL 2 GETTING REAL	If a crystal ball could tell you the truth about yourself, your life, the future, or anything else, what would you want to know?
	Is there something that you've dreamed of doing for a long time? Why haven't you done it?
	What does friendship mean to you?
LEVEL 3 GETTING VULNERABLE	Complete this sentence: "I wish I had someone with whom I could share . . ."
	Tell your partner what you like about them; be very honest, saying things that you might not say to someone you just met.
	If you were to die this evening with no opportunity to communicate with anyone, what would you most regret not having told someone, and why haven't you told them yet?

NOTE: Questions from Aron et al.[19]

Of course, within five minutes of meeting someone, you shouldn't jump to the intense, level 3 questions. In Dr. Aron's study, the questions scaled up slowly over the course of about an hour. By that point, people generally vibe on more self-disclosure than we assume, even during an initial one-on-one meeting.[20]

As I mentioned in chapter 2, when my collaborator Eli Finkel and I were both single—and before we began hosting our own speed-dating events to study initial attraction—we went to a speed-dating event in Chicago to get a sense of what it was like. Beforehand, Eli took the liberty of printing out Dr. Aron's questions on laminated cards, which made for a good bit on his speed dates. (I respect that the man makes no effort to hide his nerdiest impulses.) What's more, recent research has found that preplanning a few conversation topics is remarkably helpful for making conversations go smoothly. So if you're getting ready for a coffee date with someone you matched on the apps, maybe take five minutes to google something that stands out from their profile, just so you can arrive with an intelligent question or two. (Laminated cards not recommended.)[21]

Hit the Road

So your local friends are great, and you've become well practiced at challenging and transforming your own self-defeating thoughts. And yet, your networks really are stale, and another salsa class just isn't in the cards. In these cases, it's perhaps time for a change of scenery.

One more time, we can find wisdom in a branch of science that illuminates how ancestral humans faced mating-related challenges. Specifically, anthropological work on the behavior of contemporary hunter-gatherers illustrates our impressive flexibility when romantic options get *really* limited.

. . .

Early humans benefited from living in groups that ranged from thirty-five to eighty people, depending on the season and the circumstances. As nomadic hunter-gatherers, this was the Goldilocks-size range for us. On the one hand, groups any smaller than this would have had disadvantages. Fewer people meant fewer pairs of vigilant eyes, and some essential tasks like hunting large game are virtually impossible unless many people work together. On the other hand, you don't want a group to get too large. With a large group, it's hard to nimbly move to a new location when resources begin to dry up, and you're more likely to have slackers and free riders in your midst.

But there is one major disadvantage to life in a group of this modest size: Sometimes, randomly, the number of eligible young men and women gets out of balance. In a group of, say, fifty people, a five-year stretch might yield a low number of births, or all the babies are skewed toward one gender just due to the luck of the draw. A few years later, the group could be facing a situation in which there are six eligible bachelors and one eligible bachelorette, or six eligible bachelorettes and one eligible bachelor. What happens to the partnerless young people?

The solution is simple enough: The unpartnered folks take off for parts unknown, *Eat Pray Love*–style.

In humans, this dispersal process is not gendered as it is for many other animals. That is, both men and women have historically migrated as imbalances occur, depending on who is over- or underrepresented. In most other group-living animals, one sex evolves to be the dispersing type, and the other sex evolves the instinct to stay close to home. For example, you don't want to be a solo male chimpanzee roaming around, far from your group. If you encounter some rival males, there's a good chance that you'll be attacked. So in chimpanzees, the females are the ones who leave to find a mate once they are old enough; the males are homebodies. Other species, like gorillas, show the opposite pattern: Males migrate, and female family members stick together.[22]

Humans, however, can flexibly disperse, depending on the balance of romantic options. One study captured this process using twenty-five years of data on the Savannah Pumé hunter-gatherers. During this stretch of time, five groups of Pumé numbered approximately two hundred people in total (i.e., roughly forty people per group), and they lived in an area of west-central Venezuela that was about the size of the five boroughs of New York City. The researchers found that young people tended to shift back and forth among these groups, depending on where potential romantic partners were more numerous. If one group had an overabundance of women, young men came knocking; if one group had too many men, what do you know, a few eligible women arrived. The lesson is clear, for everyone: If you're not doing well close to home, seek your fortunes elsewhere.[23]

This flexible dispersal strategy has the additional benefit of bridging alliances between groups. The young people in this study were basically traversing the distance between Brooklyn and the Bronx to find mates, which is about a half-day hike. That's far enough to feel like a journey, for sure. But it's not so far that you'd never see your parents or siblings again; family reunions are still possible. Through this process, networks grew and expanded in ancestral contexts: Depending on young people's romantic needs, connections between different groups strengthened or weakened, and groups found trading partners and common allies.

There is an ancient wisdom in the instinct to head out of town when the romantic prospects dry up. At one time about twenty years ago, I found myself in this position. After a few years in New York City, many of my friends were scattering, and my networks were contracting rather than expanding. I was drawn to Chicago, a city where I knew just a few people.

Over those first few months, I went to a lot of happy hours and house parties with people I barely knew. Slowly, gradually, my circles grew. I became friends with people who were different from my friends back in New York. I was used to hanging out with engineers and computer scientists. My friends in Chicago were in theater, comedy, or academia.

I experienced two meaningful changes in the wake of this move. One change was that these new networks altered how I saw myself. For example, I had thought of myself as a person with reasonable cultural tastes. In fact, it turned out that my tastes were provincial: *These* people had taste, and they regularly referenced esoteric but unmistakably cool musicians and artists I had never heard of. More important, their sociality was contagious, and I grew to enjoy the simple act of introducing people to each other. They coaxed me into playing (semi) organized sports for the first time in ten years. They got me out of the house when it might have been my instinct to stay in and play video games. It turned out that I wasn't a brooding introvert after all! Or at least, not in this context—not with these friends.

People underestimate their own flexibility. Much of the way that we think about ourselves—what we're capable of, or what's good or bad about us—is shaped by the people nearby. Friends are mirrors that reflect a particular version of ourselves back at us, and new social circles provide an opportunity to try out a new set of roles and attributes.

The second change was that my dating life improved relative to what it had been just a few months earlier in New York. In Chicago, connections emerged organically from the fabric of everyday life. I met one woman named Jess through my Wednesday night kickball league. We were on different teams, but we all converged after the games at Carol's Pub, a windowless dive with perpetually sticky floors. Jess and I began by exchanging barbs across the table, and eventually our postgame recaps became a ritual. Until one night, we looked around to discover that we were the only two people left, and she declared with confidence: "I think this"—her index finger bouncing back and forth between us—"is bound to happen."

Or my friend Grace, who served with me on a joint project at work. At first, our relationship was defined by a gently competitive tension, until I lobbied her to accompany me to a Halloween party in Uptown. That invitation felt like a release valve. We danced; we joked; I introduced her to new people. Later, Grace and I spilled out onto the sidewalk, and as I walked her home, it became clear that something had finally clicked between us.

These casual relationships eventually faded, and without hard feelings. What remained was the sense that my expansive social circle was fostering possibilities. This shift didn't happen because my mate value had risen in any observable sense; if anything, I was poorer now that I was living on a meager graduate student stipend rather than a bona fide salary. My dating life improved because I had been rebooting and growing a brand-new network.

To be sure, moving is a privilege. People often have obligations, and it takes money to uproot oneself. Most people can't move on a whim. But when networks fossilize, moving is a decent option that has been a part of the *Homo sapiens* repertoire for a very long time.

· CONCLUSION ·

Gender, Love, and Evolution

Navigating dating and close relationships doesn't have to be demoralizing. We can first trash overblown claims about the hierarchy of mate value and the accompanying market metaphors. Also, rejection loses some of its sting when we recognize that the true evolutionary story of human bonding revolves around the search for compatibility in small groups.

Relationship science has provided countless insights into how we form and maintain bonds, not to mention plenty of actionable advice. Nevertheless, I worry about whether the science that I love will continue to be mangled by people who don't get it—people who don't recognize that humans are bonding creatures, and people who think there is something natural about sticking men and women into tiny, distinct boxes. In reality, the science of human mating is deeply compatible with a progressive and feminist worldview. We just need to fix our warped conceptions of masculinity.

The manosphere personalities champion a version of masculinity and relationships that conveniently fits old-fashioned narratives: It is right and good for men to be traditional, tough, macho, steroidal. To men, women are for sex or mothering, not both—and certainly not for friendship. They explain men's lagging performance at school and work by lamenting how men have become too effete to control and dominate the way they used to.

But, to paraphrase Hamlet, there are more ways to be a man than are dreamt of in that philosophy.

A reimagined version of masculinity revolves around protecting friends and loved ones; it centers camaraderie and loyalty; it engages in acts of bravery and grit and perseverance. It considers women as peers and equals. It has the self-assurance to embrace interests and ideas that earlier generations would deride as emasculating. (I love a crisp French rosé; come at me, bro.) It requires that men develop a sensitivity to others' vulnerabilities, not a callousness to suffering.

Men's wages are stagnating, it's true. But a progressive style of masculinity is oriented toward the jobs of the future—teachers, nurses, social workers, and counselors—jobs that are all about cultivating relationships and caring for others. We need to make sure that young men see themselves in these professions. Just as young women increasingly recognize that they can develop the skills and abilities for success in science and engineering, we need to promote the message to young men that they can develop the nurturance and generosity required for success in the health and education sectors.[1]

With this version of masculinity, young men will find that confidence and compassion are not mutually exclusive. As the journalist Caitlin Moran asserts: Feminism's key contribution was that it gave women a philosophy that licensed them to question gender. Women realized they could bend and shift the rules about gender to their own liking; maybe the rules fit, or maybe they didn't, but feminism encourages you to pick and choose. There was nothing about being a CEO, mechanical engineer, or computer programmer that inherently limited those experiences to men. For women who found their calling in caring for others—in the workplace, or at home, or both—that was fine, too. Men need a philosophy that gives them a similar freedom to pick from the pantheon of masculine and feminine "ways to be" in the world. Many will discover that they can be strong and caring at the same time.[2]

But there is an ingredient that is still missing in this popular conception of the new masculinity: How can we incorporate issues related to sex and attraction and relationships? It is tempting to believe that these particular topics inevitably feed into the narrow-minded vision of masculinity in two respects. First, the EvoScript has so completely captured our cultural conception of sex and attraction that even progressive thinkers hesitate before broaching the topic. It's common to hear "Men and women are so different in this sphere, you can't fight human nature!" from people who spend the rest of their free time smashing the patriarchy. Second, it can be awkward to be a modern liberal and extol the value of relationships. "You'll be happy and healthy in a long-term committed relationship" is reasonable advice that also has a cringey, old-fashioned ring to it.

But progressives can embrace the true story of human love and evolution. On gender, yes, there are real differences when it comes to interest in sex with strangers, and the fear that women experience when they are around a man they don't know well. But the rest of the long process of human mate choice unfolds very similarly, regardless of gender or sexual orientation. The same attributes are appealing in men and women, full stop; I hereby declare the forthcoming cavalcade of male teachers and nurses to be "husband material."

We can elevate the value and importance of long-term relationships without celebrating an old-timey conceptualization of marriage. Nothing about the centrality of relationships to humans' health and well-being reinforces the idea that a husband has dominion over his wife, or even that a relationship is about a piece of paper at city hall. Human relationships are fundamentally about attachment. This perspective centers not gender, but rather the way that close relationships provide safety and security, opportunities to support and celebrate, and a way to be a part of something communal. There's nothing inherently old-fashioned about that.

I am under no illusion that those of us who study attraction and relationships have it all figured out. My colleagues and I are tethered to the science, and the scientific consensus shifts and grows and changes all the time. I find it exciting to ponder what new things will be discovered in the next year, or in the next decade, and I feel lucky to participate in this process.

I didn't write this book because I think I have all the answers. I wrote this book because I saw a creeping and pernicious pessimism, supercharged by a handful of angry men online. It dawned on me that these men seemed to have an outdated understanding of human attraction and relationships. Their ideas reflected a science that had frozen in the mid-1990s—a science that was merely *one of many* evolutionary perspectives on human mating that somehow never managed to evolve its own way into the twenty-first century.[3]

I realized that people weren't aware of the new evolutionary science of human mating that I know and love. A science that has found that mate value wears off, that men and women don't meaningfully differ in what they want, that mate choice doesn't happen in a single moment, that being a good long-term partner is not about developing the right set of personal attributes. Instead, relationships are what two people build along the way. Relationships begin chaotically and unfold slowly and unpredictably over time. Relationships work best when they are communal, and when they help people grow beyond their own boundaries. Relationships are intimately connected to the solutions to our loneliness epidemic. And most important of all, relationships have always been about attachment and networks, about bonding and alliances, and about love and family—biological, blended, and found.

· ACKNOWLEDGMENTS ·

If this book had been a scientific paper, many other names would be listed alongside mine.

Dr. Alison Ledgerwood—my partner in all things—pored over the first draft of every chapter. She deserves credit for the funniest jokes and catchiest ideas, and she also ensured that the weakest jokes and worst ideas hit the cutting-room floor. Every time I hit a roadblock, she graciously listened to my complaints and guided me to the solution, even when it was a solution I didn't want to hear. On countless occasions, she reassembled and reconfigured our daily schedule to unearth precious pockets of time for me to write. Most critical of all: When I was pondering whether I should even attempt this book in the first place, I put together a (very) rough draft of the first chapter. She saw through the clunkiness and declared that this project was going to work. That moment was my green light, and the book would not have happened without it.[*]

The second person to read each chapter was my perennial collaborator, Dr. Eli Finkel. Eli knows these scientific literatures cold, and his ability to channel "the other side" in any debate is remarkable. I relied on him to tell me where I needed to shore up an argument, where I had neglected a relevant line of work, and where I hadn't been entirely fair. Finally—after I finished drafting this book but before its initial release—Eli and I launched our podcast, *Love Factually*, on a lark. Chatting on mic about relationship science in rom-coms turned

---

[*] A sharp-eyed reader will also notice that Alison has the photo credit, which she claims "is just evolutionarily what women do: We stake our claim on a man via copyright."

out to be the best thing I could have done with my professional time, and it deepened my desire to bring this incredible branch of research to the public.

Leah Trouwborst, my initial editor at Crown, was the third person to read this work in full. My original sketch of this book seems cringeworthy in retrospect, and this whole endeavor might have turned into an unmitigated disaster without Leah. From our very first meeting, she seemed to have a deeper vision for this book than I did. And for every meeting after that, I had the thrilling sense of being a student again—when you comprehend about 80 percent of what your advisor is saying, and you frantically take notes knowing that every tiny morsel of advice will lead to a decision that improves the final product. I am also extraordinarily grateful that Leah was willing to meet with me a *lot*, especially when I was having a (needless) freak-out, and I realize only now that this level of editorial attention is far from universal. Leah, this book reflects your influence from cover to cover.

Finally, I am deeply indebted to Kate Craigie, my editor at Cornerstone who responded to the bat signal and swooped in to get this manuscript over the finish line. By the time that Kate reviewed this book, some of the text had existed on the page for years, and I was no longer able to see the holes. She immediately spotted the parts that remained confusing and worked with me to find clean solutions. Kate was another generous soul who met with me extremely frequently, and this book benefited immensely from her guidance as it made the final transition from a splat of ideas to a coherent work of nonfiction.

I owe a great debt to all the researchers who conducted the studies that make an appearance in this book. Three of my collaborators deserve special mention: Dr. Samantha Joel, Dr. Lucy Hunt, and Dr. Elizabeth Keneski. This book required the foundation provided by Samantha's machine learning work, Lucy's mate-value studies, and Liz's innovative approach to capturing relationship trajectories. These three projects sparked fundamental shifts in the way I think about attraction and close relationships, and I feel very lucky that I got to conduct research alongside these remarkable scientists.

In addition, I have been fortunate to work with a talented array of students in the Attraction and Relationships Research Lab, including (in approximate chronological order): Natasha Tidwell, Brian Bishop-Wilkey, April Buck, Taylor Anne Peele, Jennifer Sanders, Leigh Smith, Sabrina Huang, Jehan Sparks, Andre Wang, Alexander Baxter, Aline da Silva Frost, Alexa Alcser-Isais, Eva Meza, Rose Bern, and Elina Moreno. I have also worked with several truly impressive senior colleagues over the years. I want to give a special thank-you to Dr. Alice Eagly, who advised me throughout graduate school and taught me the meaning of academic rigor, and Dr. Jeff Simpson, who demonstrated how someone could be an evolutionary scholar and a close relationships researcher at the same time.

I would never have embarked on this journey if I hadn't had the incredible fortune of being friends with Dr. Paige Harden. Paige walked me through every step of this process, including introducing me to my fabulous and supportive agents Melissa Flashman and Will Francis at Janklow & Nesbit. I am also grateful to the rest of my publishing team at Crown and Cornerstone, including Amy Li and Vanessa Phan for their detailed and perceptive editorial feedback, as well as Gillian Blake and Helen Conford for believing in this book in the first place. Finally, thank you to Elina Moreno and Christopher Lopez for posing for the CFD-style photos.

Thank you to my parents for the staggering number of opportunities they gave me as a kid and young adult, and to all the wonderful people who provided stories for this book. Last but not least, I don't know where I'd be without Los Dudes, The Kids, Gingerbread, Zin Bodie, and Fia Lina.

· APPENDIX A ·

Effect Sizes as "Guessing Game"

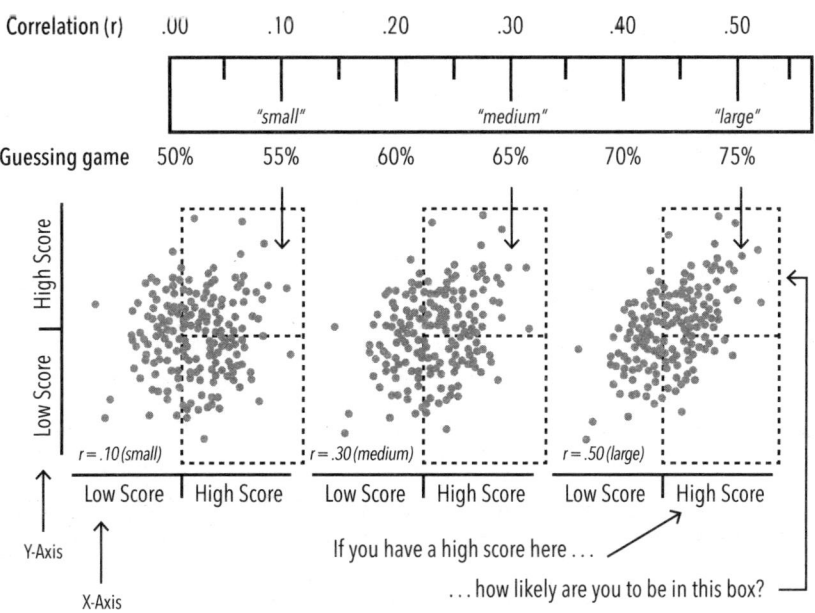

FIGURE A.I
Effect sizes as a "guessing game"

These pictures depict small ($r = .10$), medium ($r = .30$), and large ($r = .50$) correlations. To understand what a correlation means, we can turn it into a guessing game: If I know that you have a "high" rather than a "low" score on one measure (the x-axis that runs from left to right), the effect size tells me about the likelihood that you will have a "high" rather than a "low" score on the other measure (the y-axis that runs from top to bottom).

- If an effect size is small and you have a high score on the x-axis, there is a 55 percent chance you will score in the top half of the y-axis measure.

- If an effect size is medium and you have a high score on the x-axis, there is a 65 percent chance you will score in the top half of the y-axis measure.

- If an effect size is large and you have a high score on the x-axis, there is a 75 percent chance you will score in the top half of the y-axis measure.

If you look at the figure closely, you can see how for a large effect size, there are many more points in the upper right box rather than the lower right box. For the small effect size, there are more points in the upper right than lower right box, but this difference is much more subtle. This game works in reverse, too: If I know you have a low score on the x-axis and the effect size is large, there is a 75 percent chance you have a low score on the y-axis. For an effect size of zero, having a high score on the x-axis means that there is a 50 percent chance you will score in the top half of the measure on the y-axis; in other words, no better than flipping a coin. (Estimates from Rosenthal, R., and D. B. Rubin, "A Simple, General Purpose Display of Magnitude of Experimental Effect," *Journal of Educational Psychology* 74, no. 2 (1982): 166–169.)

· APPENDIX B ·

The Stroop Task

The Stroop task works in two parts. First, read the *colors* (black, white, or gray) of these words aloud. I mean it: Actually say the colors of the words out loud, to yourself. Yes, even if you're on the train:

WHITE (white)	**BLACK** (black)	GRAY (gray)
BLACK (black)	WHITE (white)	WHITE (white)
GRAY (gray)	**BLACK** (black)	GRAY (gray)

Easy, right? Here, do it again—remember, read the *colors* of the words:

WHITE	GRAY	BLACK
BLACK	GRAY	WHITE
WHITE	BLACK	GRAY

It's harder the second time. The difference in how long it takes you to do these two tasks is called a measure of "executive control." That is, it's a measure of how well you're able to inhibit an impulse (in this case, your impulse to read the text of the word) and do something else instead (in this case, to say the color aloud).

· NOTES ·

INTRODUCTION

1. Eastwick, P.W. and L.K. Smith, "Sex-Differentiated Effects of Physical Attractiveness on Romantic Desire: A Highly Powered, Preregistered Study in a Photograph Evaluation Context," *Comprehensive Results in Social Psychology* 3, no. 1 (2018): 1–27; Hinge, "What's the Biggest Challenge Men Face on Dating Apps?: A Q&A with Aviv Goldgeier, Junior Growth Engineer," Hinge Inside (blog), August 6, 2017, https://web.archive.org/web/20190719163307/; https://hingeirl.com/hinge-reports/whats-the-biggest-challenge-men-face-on-dating-apps-a-qa-with-aviv-goldgeier-junior-growth-engineer/; Jonason, P.K. and A.G. Thomas, "Being More Educated and Earning More Increases Romantic Interest: Data from 1.8 M Online Daters from 24 Nations," *Human Nature* 33, no. 2 (2022): 115–131; Lee, L., et al., "If I'm Not Hot, Are You Hot or Not? Physical-Attractiveness Evaluations and Dating Preferences as a Function of One's Own Attractiveness," *Psychological Science* 19, no. 7 (July 2008): 669–677; Rudder, C., *Dataclysm: Who We Are (When We Think No One's Looking)* (Toronto: Random House Canada, 2014); Tuckfield, B., "Attraction Inequality and the Dating Economy," *Quillette,* March 12, 2019.
2. Goñi, M., "Assortative Matching at the Top of the Distribution: Evidence from the World's Most Exclusive Marriage Market," *American Economic Journal: Applied Economics,* 14, no. 3 (July 2022): 445–487.
3. Wright, R., "Our Cheating Hearts," *Time,* August 15, 1994.
4. Fein, E. and S. Schneider, *The Rules: Time-Tested Secrets for Capturing the Heart of Mr. Right* (New York: Grand Central Publishing, 1995): 26, 127.
5. *Counsel Culture,* "The Matter of Monogamy Ft. Dr. Laura Berman," March 11, 2024, https://www.youtube.com/watch?v=oJNmeBe1o9k.
6. Fisher, H.E., "The Brain in Love," TED Talk, February 2008, https://www.ted.com/talks/helen_fisher_the_brain_in_love?language=en.
7. "Dating is just sales," Reddit, April 17, 2023, https://www.reddit.com/r/seduction/comments/12pp00g/dating_is_just_sales/.

8. "What does an upward trajectory in mate value look like in women?," Reddit, April 15, 2022, https://www.reddit.com/r/evopsych/comments/u4c8fp/what_does_an_upward_trajectory_in_mate_value_look/.
9. Williamson, C. (@ChrisWillx), "I got sent a quote this week . . ." Twitter, March 22, 2023, https://twitter.com/ChrisWillx/status/1638563151590334464?s=20.
10. *This Morning*, "The Woman Behind Controversial Dating Guide 'The Rules,'" April 24, 2023, https://www.youtube.com/watch?v=J22IsaaQhdQ.
11. Rogan, J., "#1959—David Buss," March 23, 2023, *The Joe Rogan Experience* (podcast), https://open.spotify.com/episode/3aYGkvFj8PZTzfHvGuYCTw.
12. Ellis, B.J. and H.H. Kelley, "The Pairing Game: A Classroom Demonstration of the Matching Phenomenon," *Teaching of Psychology* 26, no. 2 (March 1999): 118–121; Miller, G.F., "Mutual Mate Choice Models as the Red Pill in Evolutionary Psychology: Long Delayed, Much Needed, Ideologically Challenging, and Hard to Swallow," *Psychological Inquiry* 24, no. 3 (July 2013): 209.
13. Buss, D.M., *Evolutionary Psychology: The New Science of the Mind*, 6th ed. (New York: Routledge, 2019).
14. Gangestad, S.W. and J.A. Simpson, "The Evolution of Human Mating: Trade-offs and Strategic Pluralism," *Behavioral and Brain Sciences* 23, no. 4 (August 2000): 573–644; Goetz, C.D., et al., "Sexual Exploitability: Observable Cues and Their Link to Sexual Attraction," *Evolution and Human Behavior* 33, no. 4 (2012): 417–426.
15. Conroy-Beam, D., "How the Incels Warped My Research," *The Boston Globe*, May 16, 2024.
16. Beauchamp, Z., "Our Incel Problem," *Vox*, April 23, 2019; Hines, A., "How Many Bones Would You Break to Get Laid?," *New York Magazine*, May 28, 2019.
17. Bowles, N., "Jordan Peterson, Custodian of the Patriarchy," *The New York Times*, May 18, 2018.
18. Baxter, A., et al., "Initial Impressions of Compatibility and Mate Value Predict Later Dating and Romantic Interest," *Proceedings of the National Academy of Sciences* 119, no. 45 (November 2, 2022).
19. Dunbar, R.I.M., "The Social Brain: Psychological Underpinnings and Implications for the Structure of Organizations," *Current Directions in Psychological Science* 23, no. 2 (April 2014): 109–114; Goetz, C.D., et al., "Evolutionary Mismatch in Mating," *Frontiers in Psychology* 10 (December 2019); Hill, R.A. and R.I.M. Dunbar, "Social Network Size in Humans," *Human Nature* 14, no. 1 (March 2003): 53–72; Kramer, K.L., R. Schacht, and A. Bell, "Adult Sex Ratios and Partner Scarcity Among Hunter–Gatherers: Implications

for Dispersal Patterns and the Evolution of Human Sociality," *Philosophical Transactions of the Royal Society B: Biological Sciences* 372, no. 1729 (July 31, 2017); Marlowe, F.W., "Hunter-Gatherers and Human Evolution," *Evolutionary Anthropology* 14, no. 2 (2005): 54–67.

20. Stauder, J. and T. Kossow, "Opportunities and Constraints of the Partner Market and Educational Assortative Mating," *Journal of Family Issues* 42, no. 11 (2021): 2554–2588.
21. Eastwick, P.W., E.J. Finkel, and S. Joel, "Mate Evaluation Theory," *Psychological Review* 130, no. 1 (2023): 211–241.
22. Buss, D.M. and D.P. Schmitt, "Mate Preferences and Their Behavioral Manifestations," *Annual Review of Psychology* 70 (2019): 82.
23. The evidence that "mate-value matching" is irrelevant to initial attraction and relationship satisfaction is vast. Here is a sampler of that evidence with respect to several classic traits that are supposedly relevant to mate value: The average correlation between similarity in emotional stability and relationship satisfaction across both samples was $r = .01$ in Dyrenforth, P.S., et al., "Predicting Relationship and Life Satisfaction from Personality in Nationally Representative Samples from Three Countries: The Relative Importance of Actor, Partner, and Similarity Effects," *Journal of Personality and Social Psychology* 99, no. 4 (August 2010): 690–702. The average correlation between mate-value similarity (on classic mate-value measures) and attraction was $r = .00$ in Eastwick, P.W. and L.L. Hunt, "Relational Mate Value: Consensus and Uniqueness in Romantic Evaluations," *Journal of Personality and Social Psychology* 106, no. 5 (March 2014): 728–751. The average correlation between "attractiveness similarity" and relationship stability (i.e., not breaking up) was $r = .04$ in Feingold, A., "Matching for Attractiveness in Romantic Partners and Same-Sex Friends: A Meta-analysis and Theoretical Critique," *Psychological Bulletin* 104, no. 2 (September 1988): 226–235. The average correlation between similarity in (a) attractiveness, (b) emotional stability, (c) avoidance, (d) anxiety, and (e) self-esteem, and initial attraction was $r = .04$ in Luo, S. and G. Zhang, "What Leads to Romantic Attraction: Similarity, Reciprocity, Security, or Beauty? Evidence from a Speed-Dating Study," *Journal of Personality* 77, no. 4 (July 2009): 933–964. The average correlation between similarity in (a) vocabulary, (b) matrix reasoning, (c) IQ, (d) emotional stability, (e) anxiety, and (f) avoidance, and marital satisfaction was $r = .00$ in Watson, D., et al., "Match Makers and Deal Breakers: Analyses of Assortative Mating in Newlywed Couples," *Journal of Personality* 72, no. 5 (November 2004): 1029–1068. In the posted raw data, across 1,848 speed dates, the correlation between the similarity (i.e., absolute value of the difference) between two partners' "mate value" scores (as rated by

independent coders) and romantic attraction was $r = .06$ in Wurst, S.N., S. Humberg, and M.D. Back, "The Impact of Mate Value in First and Subsequent Real-Life Romantic Encounters" (preprint, submitted January 26, 2018), https://osf.io/adej3/. The average correlation between similarity in (a) 14 desirable attributes, and (b) emotional stability and romantic attraction was $r = -.01$ in Tidwell, N.D., P.W. Eastwick, and E.J. Finkel, "Perceived, Not Actual, Similarity Predicts Initial Attraction in a Live Romantic Context: Evidence from the Speed-Dating Paradigm," *Personal Relationships* 20, no. 2 (June 2013): 199–215. See also Weidmann, R., et al., "Trait and Facet Personality Similarity and Relationship and Life Satisfaction in Romantic Couples," *Journal of Research in Personality* 104 (June 2023).

24. Bolger, N., A. Davis, and E. Rafaeli, "Diary Methods: Capturing Life as It Is Lived," *Annual Review of Psychology* 54, no. 1 (February 2003): 579–616; Kenny, D.A., "PERSON: A General Model of Interpersonal Perception," *Personality and Social Psychology Review* 8, no. 3 (2004): 265–280.

25. Blair, K.L. and R.A. Hoskin, "Transgender Exclusion from the World of Dating: Patterns of Acceptance and Rejection of Hypothetical Trans Dating Partners as a Function of Sexual and Gender Identity," *Journal of Social and Personal Relationships* 36, no. 7 (July 2019): 2074–2095; Bradbury, T.N. and B.R. Karney, *Intimate Relationships*, 4th ed. (New York: Norton, 2024); Diamond, L.M. and K.L. Blair, "The Intimate Relationships of Sexual and Gender Minorities," in *The Cambridge Handbook of Personal Relationships*, ed. A.L. Vangelisti and D. Perlman (Cambridge: Cambridge University Press, 2018), 199–210; Doss, B.D. and G.K. Rhoades, "The Transition to Parenthood: Impact on Couples' Romantic Relationships," *Current Opinion in Psychology* 13 (February 2017): 25–28; Fingerhut, A.W. and L.A. Peplau, "Same-Sex Romantic Relationships," in *Handbook of Psychology and Sexual Orientation*, ed. C.J. Patterson and A.R. D'Augelli (New York: Oxford University Press, 2013), 165–178; Junkins, E.J., "Psychology Observed within Every Romantic Relationship Study: Testing Equality of Parameters across Diverse Gender and Sexual Identities" (PhD diss., University of Illinois at Urbana–Champaign, 2024), https://www.ideals.illinois.edu/items/132610.

26. Bailey, J.M., et al., "Sexual Orientation, Controversy, and Science," *Psychological Science in the Public Interest* 17, no. 2 (September 2016): 45–101; Camperio Ciani, A., et al., "Possible Balancing Selection in Human Female Homosexuality," *Human Nature* 29, no. 1 (2018): 14–32; Conley, T.D., "Perceived Proposer Personality Characteristics and Gender Differences in Acceptance of Casual Sex Offers," *Journal of Personality and Social Psychology* 100, no. 2 (February 2011): 309–329; West, T.V., D. Popp, and D.A. Kenny, "A Guide for the Estimation of Gender and Sexual Orientation Effects in Dyadic Data: An

Actor-Partner Interdependence Model Approach," *Personality and Social Psychology Bulletin* 34, no. 3 (March 2008): 321–336.

27. Cohen, J., "A Power Primer," *Psychological Bulletin* 112, no. 1 (July 1992): 155; Rosenthal, R. and D.B. Rubin, "A Simple, General Purpose Display of Magnitude of Experimental Effect," *Journal of Educational Psychology* 74, no. 2 (1982): 166–169.

28. Bleske-Rechek, A. and M.M. Gunseor, "Gendered Perspectives on Sharing the Load: Men's and Women's Attitudes toward Family Roles and Household and Childcare Tasks," *Evolutionary Behavioral Sciences* 16, no. 3 (2022): 201–219.

29. Fraley, R.C., O. Gillath, and P.R. Deboeck, "Do Life Events Lead to Enduring Changes in Adult Attachment Styles? A Naturalistic Longitudinal Investigation," *Journal of Personality and Social Psychology* 120, no. 6 (2021): 1567–1606; Park, M., et al., "The Effects of Psychotherapy for Adult Depression on Social Support: A Meta-analysis," *Cognitive Therapy and Research* 38, no. 6 (2014): 600–611.

CHAPTER 1

1. Cooley, C.H., *Human Nature and the Social Order* (New York: Charles Scribner's Sons, 1902); Leary, M.R., "Making Sense of Self-Esteem," *Current Directions in Psychological Science* 8, no. 1 (February 1999): 32–35.

2. People's sense of their own mate value (i.e., people who say, "In general, I tend to have many options for romantic partners") was closely linked to how they were rated by initial interaction partners on attractiveness and sexiness ($r = .37$), confidence ($r = .27$), fun/exciting traits ($r = .26$), and charisma ($r = .26$); these are medium-to-large effects. But self-ratings of mate value were essentially unrelated to whether they came across to initial interaction partners as friendly/nice ($r = .08$), intelligent and smart ($r = .07$), and dependable/trustworthy ($r = -.02$). Data reanalyzed from Eastwick, P.W. and E.J. Finkel, "Northwestern Speed-dating Study I" (2005), UNC Dataverse, V1, https://doi.org/10.15139/S3/HK7KZQ; Eastwick, P.W. and E.J. Finkel, "Northwestern Speed-Dating Study II" (2007), UNC Dataverse, V1, https://doi.org/10.15139/S3/52MIJO. See also Kavanagh, P.S., S.C. Robins, and B.J. Ellis, "The Mating Sociometer: A Regulatory Mechanism for Mating Aspirations," *Journal of Personality and Social Psychology* 99, no. 1 (2010): 120–132.

3. Back, M.D., et al., "Why Mate Choices Are Not as Reciprocal as We Assume: The Role of Personality, Flirting and Physical Attractiveness," *European Journal of Personality* 25, no. 2 (March 2011): 120–132.

4. Kirsner, B.R., A.J. Figueredo, and W.J. Jacobs, "Self, Friends, and Lovers: Structural Relations among Beck Depression Inventory Scores and Perceived

Mate Values," *Journal of Affective Disorders* 75, vol. 2 (August 2003): 131–148; Kirsner, B.R., A.J. Figueredo, and W.J. Jacobs, "Structural Relations among Negative Affect, Mate Value, and Mating Effort," *Evolutionary Psychology* 7, no. 3 (July 2009): 374–397.

5. Ellis, B.J. and H.H. Kelley, "The Pairing Game: A Classroom Demonstration of the Matching Phenomenon," *Teaching of Psychology* 26, no. 2 (March 1999): 118–121.

6. Matching on physical attractiveness was $r = .39$, averaged across 27 studies and 1,299 participants, in this meta-analysis: Feingold, A., "Matching for Attractiveness in Romantic Partners and Same-Sex Friends: A Meta-analysis and Theoretical Critique," *Psychological Bulletin* 104, no. 2 (September 1988): 226–235.

7. Kenny, D.A. and L. La Voie, "The Social Relations Model," in *Advances in Experimental Social Psychology,* ed. L. Berkowitz, vol. 18 (Orlando, FL: Academic Press, 1984), 141–182.

8. To get these values, researchers need to have many raters and many targets. These folks all evaluate each other in a big milieu, sometimes called a "round-robin" design. Only then can you calculate: Within this group of people, how much does consensus matter, how much does selectivity matter, and how much does compatibility matter? Most studies on human mating don't go through all this work. Kenny and La Voie, "The Social Relations Model," 141–182.

9. Hehman, E., et al., "The Unique Contributions of Perceiver and Target Characteristics in Person Perception," *Journal of Personality and Social Psychology* 113, no. 4 (2017): 513–529; Xie, S.Y., J.K. Flake, and E. Hehman, "Perceiver and Target Characteristics Contribute to Impression Formation Differently Across Race and Gender," *Journal of Personality and Social Psychology* 117, no. 2 (August 2019): 364–385.

10. Ma, D.S., J. Correll, and B. Wittenbrink, "The Chicago Face Database: A Free Stimulus Set of Faces and Norming Data," *Behavior Research Methods* 47, no. 4 (January 2015): 1122–1135.

11. In SRM studies, the values for consensus are commonly expressed as a percentage of the full attraction cocktail. The average values depicted in figure 1.3 are as follows. Photographs: 25.0 percent. Initial interactions: 25.1 percent. Weeks: 14.8 percent. Long-term acquaintance: 6.3 percent. 30 percent is considered large; 20 percent is considered medium, 10 percent is considered small, and anything below 10 percent is considered inconsequential. Values derived from seventeen studies from the following articles: Asendorpf, J.B., L. Penke, and M.D. Back, "From Dating to Mating and Relating: Predictors of

Initial and Long-Term Outcomes of Speed-Dating in a Community Sample," *European Journal of Personality* 25, no. 1 (January 2011): 16–30; Eastwick, P.W., et al., "Consistency and Inconsistency among Romantic Partners over Time," *Journal of Personality and Social Psychology* 112, no. 6 (March 2017): 838–859; Eastwick, P.W. and L.L. Hunt, "Relational Mate Value: Consensus and Uniqueness in Romantic Evaluations," *Journal of Personality and Social Psychology*, 106, no. 5 (March 2014): 728–751; Hehman, E., et al., "The Unique Contributions of Perceiver and Target Characteristics in Person Perception," 513–529; Hönekopp, J., "Once More: Is Beauty in the Eye of the Beholder? Relative Contributions of Private and Shared Taste to Judgments of Facial Attractiveness," *Journal of Experimental Psychology: Human Perception and Performance* 32, no. 2 (April 2006): 199–209; Jauk, E., et al., "How Alluring Are Dark Personalities? The Dark Triad and Attractiveness in Speed Dating," *European Journal of Personality* 30, no. 2 (March 2016): 125–138; Joel, S., P.W. Eastwick, and E.J. Finkel, "Is Romantic Desire Predictable? Machine Learning Applied to Initial Romantic Attraction," *Psychological Science* 28, no. 10 (October 2017): 1478–1489; Luo, S. and G. Zhang, "What Leads to Romantic Attraction: Similarity, Reciprocity, Security, or Beauty? Evidence from a Speed-Dating Study," *Journal of Personality* 77, no. 4 (July 2009): 933–964; Marcus, D.K. and R.S. Miller, "Sex Differences in Judgments of Physical Attractiveness: A Social Relations Analysis," *Personality and Social Psychology Bulletin* 29, no. 3 (March 2003): 325–335; Payne, K.T., "Does Psychopathy Predict Desirability in Speed Dating Situations? A Social Relations Analysis" (PhD diss., The University of Southern Mississippi, 2011), https://aquila.usm.edu/cgi/viewcontent.cgi?article=1621&context=dissertations; Xie, S.Y., et al., "Perceiver and Target Characteristics Contribute to Impression Formation Differently across Race and Gender," 364–385.

12. Hönekopp, "Once More: Is Beauty in the Eye of the Beholder?," 199–209.
13. Eastwick, P.W., et al., "What Do Short-Term and Long-Term Relationships Look Like? Building the Relationship Coordination and Strategic Timing (ReCAST) Model," *Journal of Experimental Psychology: General* 147, no. 5 (May 2018): 747–781; Rosenfeld, M.J., R.J. Thomas, and S. Hausen, "Disintermediating Your Friends: How Online Dating in the United States Displaces Other Ways of Meeting," *Proceedings of the National Academy of Sciences* 116, no. 36 (August 2019): 17753–17758; Stinson, D.A., J.J. Cameron, and L.B. Hoplock, "The Friends-to-Lovers Pathway to Romance: Prevalent, Preferred, and Overlooked by Science," *Social Psychological and Personality Science* 13, no. 2 (March 2022): 562–571. The statistics in the footnote derive from Rosenfeld, M.J., R.J. Thomas, and S. Hausen, "How Couples Meet and Stay

Together 2017 v1.1 " (computer files, Stanford University Libraries, 2019), https://data.stanford.edu/hcmst2017.
14. Eastwick and Hunt, "Relational Mate Value," 728–751.
15. Kenny, D.A., et al., "Consensus in Interpersonal Perception: Acquaintance and the Big Five," *Psychological Bulletin* 116, no. 2 (September 1994): 245–258; Rosenthal, R. and D.B. Rubin, "A Simple, General Purpose Display of Magnitude of Experimental Effect," *Journal of Educational Psychology* 74, no. 2 (April 1982):166–169.
16. Generally speaking, selectivity effects are in the range of 20–40 percent. Intriguingly, research by Dr. Eric Hehman and his colleagues has shown that the prominence of selectivity effects tends to vary depending on the *trait* that perceivers are considering. For example, people differ quite a bit in the extent to which they think others are generally "creative." So this would be a common situation: You think people are inventive and inspired, whereas I think that people are unimaginative and bland. But there's not much evidence that these perceptions change over time the way consensus does. Hehman, E., et al., "Unique Contributions of Perceiver and Target Characteristics in Person Perception," 513–529. See also Kenny, D.A., *Interpersonal Perception: The Foundation of Social Relationships,* 2nd ed. (New York: Guilford Press, 2019).
17. Back, M.D., et al., "Personality and Social Relationships: What Do We Know and Where Do We Go?," *Personality Science* 4, no. 1 (2023); Eastwick et al., "Consistency and Inconsistency among Romantic Partners over Time," 838–859; Eastwick and Hunt, "Relational Mate Value," 728–751; Kenny, *Interpersonal Perception.*
18. Stinson et al., "The Friends-to-Lovers Pathway to Romance," 562–571.
19. The size of the attractiveness-matching effects were: $r = .60$ (matching for couples getting together within a month of meeting); $r = .10$ (matching for couples getting together a year after meeting); $r = .60$ (matching for couples who were not "friends first"); $r = .30$ (matching for couples who were "friends first"). Values from Hunt, L.L., P.W. Eastwick, and E.J. Finkel, "Leveling the Playing Field: Longer Acquaintance Predicts Reduced Assortative Mating on Attractiveness," *Psychological Science* 26, no. 7 (July 2015): 1046–1053.
20. The association of coder-rated attractiveness on speed-dating popularity was $r = .49$ for men and $r = .52$ for women; both effects are large. Values from Asendorpf et al., "From Dating to Mating and Relating," 16–30.
21. The effect of coder-rated physical attractiveness on participants' romantic interest in potential partners ("crushes") was a meager $r = .03$ in Eastwick, P.W., et al., "Predicting Romantic Interest during Early Relationship Development: A Preregistered Investigation Using Machine Learning," *European Journal of Personality* 37, no. 3 (May/June 2023): 276–312.

22. Maestripieri, D., A. Henry, and N. Nickels, "Explaining Financial and Prosocial Biases in Favor of Attractive People: Interdisciplinary Perspectives from Economics, Social Psychology, and Evolutionary Psychology," *Behavioral and Brain Sciences* 40 (2017).
23. Levy, A., "David Buss: Pick a Partner with a Similar Value in the Mating Market," January 4, 2022, *Through Conversations Podcast* (podcast), https://www.youtube.com/watch?v=XLS5snBioAs; White, G.L., "Physical Attractiveness and Courtship Progress," *Journal of Personality and Social Psychology* 39, no. 4 (1980): 660–668.
24. The average correlation between "attractiveness similarity" and relationship stability (staying together rather than breaking up) across all three studies that measured these variables was $r = .04$, which is basically no effect at all. Values from Feingold, A., "Matching for Attractiveness in Romantic Partners and Same-Sex Friends," 226–235. See also George, D., et al., "Couple Similarity on Stimulus Characteristics and Marital Satisfaction," *Personality and Individual Differences* 86 (November 2015): 126–131; McNulty, J.K., L.A. Neff, and B.R. Karney, "Beyond Initial Attraction: Physical Attractiveness in Newlywed Marriage," *Journal of Family Psychology* 22, no. 1 (February 2008): 135–143.
25. Hoplock, L.B., D.A. Stinson, and C.T. Joordens, "'Is She Really Going Out with Him?': Attractiveness Exchange and Commitment Scripts for Romantic Relationships," *Personality and Individual Differences* 139 (2019): 181–190.
26. At a broader level, a psychologist like me wants to know about a person's own subjective judgments of their partner's attractiveness. That is, if I want to know how healthy a relationship is likely to be, I want people's "insider" judgments of that relationship; I don't care as much about what the rest of the perceiving community thinks. For example, in established ongoing relationships, other people's judgments of your partner's attractiveness (as rated from a photograph) are likely to have no effect at all on your relationship satisfaction. But your own judgment of your partner's attractiveness affects your own satisfaction a great deal. Eastwick, P.W., et al., "Is a Meta-analysis a Foundation or Just Another Brick? Comment on Meltzer, McNulty, Jackson, & Karney (2014)," *Journal of Personality and Social Psychology* 106, no. 3 (2014): 429–434.

CHAPTER 2

1. Dargis, M., "In 'A Star Is Born,' Equality Is Deadly," *The New York Times*, October 24, 2018.
2. Darwin, C., *The Descent of Man* (New York: D. Appleton, 1871); Trivers, R.L., "Parental Investment and Sexual Selection," in *Sexual Selection and the Descent of Man, 1871–1971*, ed. B. G. Campbell (Chicago: Aldine, 1972), 136–179.

3. Gentile, G., "Will a High IQ Make You Less Likely to Marry?," *Forbes*, October 19, 2022; Taylor, M.D., et al., "Childhood IQ and Marriage by Midlife: The Scottish Mental Survey 1932 and the Midspan Studies," *Personality and Individual Differences* 38, no. 7 (May 2005): 1621–1630; Van Bavel, J., C.R. Schwartz, and A. Esteve, "The Reversal of the Gender Gap in Education and Its Consequences for Family Life," *Annual Review of Sociology* 44 (2018): 341–360.
4. Peterson, M., "How IQ Could Affect You Getting Married," June 17, 2022, https://www.youtube.com/watch?v=NPUWpc_fRNU.
5. Sear, R., "The Male Breadwinner Nuclear Family Is Not the 'Traditional' Human Family, and Promotion of This Myth May Have Adverse Health Consequences," *Philosophical Transactions of the Royal Society B: Biological Sciences* 376, no. 1827 (June 2021).
6. Buss, D.M., "Sex Differences in Human Mate Preferences: Evolutionary Hypotheses Tested in 37 Cultures," *Behavioral and Brain Sciences* 12, no. 1 (March 1989); Buss, D.M., "Sexual Strategies: A Journey into Controversy," *Psychological Inquiry* 14, no. 3 & 4 (2003): 219–226.
7. The gender difference in the stated preference for physical attractiveness is $r = .26$ in Feingold, A., "Gender Differences in Effects of Physical Attractiveness on Romantic Attraction: A Comparison across Five Research Paradigms," *Journal of Personality and Social Psychology* 59, no. 5 (1990): 981–993. The gender difference in the stated preference for earning potential is $r = .32$ in Feingold, A., "Gender Differences in Mate Selection Preferences: A Test of the Parental Investment Model," *Psychological Bulletin* 112, no. 1 (July 1992): 125–139.
8. Marcotte, A., "The Insidious Rise of 'Tradwives': A Right-Wing Fantasy Is Rotting Young Men's Minds," *Salon,* November 27, 2023.
9. Jonason, P.K. and A.G. Thomas, "Being More Educated and Earning More Increases Romantic Interest: Data from 1.8 M Online Daters from 24 Nations," *Human Nature* 33, no. 2 (2022): 115–131; Lee, L., et al., "If I'm Not Hot, Are You Hot or Not? Physical-Attractiveness Evaluations and Dating Preferences as a Function of One's Own Attractiveness," *Psychological Science* 19, no. 7 (July 2008): 669–677.
10. Goetz, C.D., et al., "Evolutionary Mismatch in Mating," *Frontiers in Psychology* 10 (December 2019).
11. The gender difference in the extent to which women are rated as more attractive than men was $r = .24$ in Eastwick, P.W. and L.K. Smith, "Sex-Differentiated Effects of Physical Attractiveness on Romantic Desire: A Highly Powered, Preregistered Study in a Photograph Evaluation Context," *Comprehensive Results in Social Psychology* 3, no. 1 (2018): 1–27. See also Heilman, M.E., "Description and Prescription: How Gender Stereotypes Prevent Women's Ascent up the Organizational Ladder," *Journal of Social Issues* 57, no. 4 (Winter 2001): 657–

674; Kowal, M., et al., "Predictors of Enhancing Human Physical Attractiveness: Data from 93 Countries," *Evolution and Human Behavior* 43, no. 6 (November 2022): 455–474; Shrider, E.A., et al., *Income and Poverty in the United States: 2020* (U.S. Census Bureau, Current Population Reports, 2021), report number P60-273.

12. One quick note about these differences before we move on to what men and women actually want. First, men and women show these differences in stated preferences regardless of whether they are thinking about someone they'd want to marry or someone they'd just want to hook up with. The size of the difference is reduced a little bit in the hookup realm relative to the long-term realm, but the difference remains. So these stated preference gender differences are robust, regardless of how you ask the question, see Eastwick, P.W., et al., "The Predictive Validity of Ideal Partner Preferences: A Review and Meta-analysis," *Psychological Bulletin* 140, no. 3 (2014): 623–665.

13. Ledgerwood, A., P.W. Eastwick, and L.K. Smith, "Toward an Integrative Framework for Studying Human Evaluation: Attitudes Toward Objects and Attributes," *Personality and Social Psychology Review* 22, no. 4 (November 2018): 378–398.

14. The gender difference in the extent to which women vs. men actually preferred earning potential was $r = -.01$. Specifically, these effects were $r = .18$ for men and $r = .17$ for women in Eastwick, P.W. and E.J. Finkel, "Sex Differences in Mate Preferences Revisited: Do People Know What They Initially Desire in a Romantic Partner?," *Journal of Personality and Social Psychology* 94, no. 2 (2008): 245–264.

15. The gender difference in the extent to which women vs. men said they preferred earning potential, averaged across four different measures was $r = .17$. When converted to an odds ratio, this value is 1.89; that is, women were about twice as likely to rate earning potential important as men in Eastwick and Finkel, "Sex Differences in Mate Preferences Revisited": 245–264.

16. Eastwick, P.W., L.K. Smith, and A. Ledgerwood, "How Do People Translate Their Experiences into Abstract Attribute Preferences?," *Journal of Experimental Social Psychology* 85 (November 2019).

17. The gender difference in the extent to which men vs. women actually preferred physical attractiveness was $r = -.04$. Specifically, these effects were $r = .35$ for men and $r = .39$ for women in Eastwick and Finkel, "Sex Differences in Mate Preferences Revisited," 245–264.

18. Schmitt, D.P. and D.M. Buss, "Strategic Self-Promotion and Competitor Derogation: Sex and Context Effects on the Perceived Effectiveness of Mate Attraction Tactics," *Journal of Personality and Social Psychology* 70, no. 6 (June 1996): 1185–1204.

19. In 2015, a famous initiative called the Reproducibility Project attempted to quantify whether 100 studies published in prestigious psychological journals could be replicated by independent research teams, and our 2008 study of gender differences in speed dating was one of the 100 studies (i.e., Eastwick and Finkel, "Sex Differences in Mate Preferences Revisited"). The independent team led by Dr. Dylan Selterman carried out a precise replication of our study and found results that nearly perfectly matched what we originally found: no gender differences in revealed preferences for earning potential and attractiveness. Selterman, D.F., E. Chagnon, and S.P. Mackinnon, "Do Men and Women Exhibit Different Preferences for Mates? A Replication of Eastwick and Finkel (2008)," *SAGE Open* 5, no. 3 (September 2015).
20. Li, N.P. and A.L. Meltzer, "The Validity of Sex-Differentiated Mate Preferences: Reconciling the Seemingly Conflicting Evidence," *Evolutionary Behavioral Sciences* 9, no. 2 (2015): 89–106.
21. Le, B., et al., "Predicting Nonmarital Romantic Relationship Dissolution: A Meta-analytic Synthesis," *Personal Relationships* 17, no. 3 (September 2010): 377–390; Robles, T.F., et al., "Marital Quality and Health: A Meta-Analytic Review," *Psychological Bulletin* 140, no. 1 (2014): 140–187.
22. The gender difference in the effect of a partner's earning prospects on one's own relationship satisfaction was $r = .02$. Specifically, these effects were $r = .28$ for men and $r = .30$ for women. We also looked at "real" measures of earning potential, like a partner's actual income levels. This measure was irrelevant to relationship satisfaction, and it was equally irrelevant for men and women: $r = .02$ for men and $r = .04$ for women. The gender difference in the effect of a partner's attractiveness on one's own relationship satisfaction was $r = .08$. Specifically, these effects were $r = .48$ for men and $r = .42$ for women. These values are reanalyzed meta-analytic data (using only partnered participants) from Eastwick et al., "The Predictive Validity of Ideal Partner Preferences," 623–665. We also looked at all the studies that used separate samples of third-party, "objective" raters to determine the attractiveness of both members of the couple. Like with income, this measure was irrelevant to relationship satisfaction for both men and women: $r = .08$ for men, $r = .03$ for women. Data from Eastwick, P.W., et al., "Is a Meta-analysis a Foundation or Just Another Brick? Comment on Meltzer, McNulty, Jackson, & Karney (2014)," *Journal of Personality and Social Psychology* 106, no. 3 (2014): 429–434.
23. The gender difference in the effect of a partner's earning prospects on one's own relationship satisfaction was $r = .00$. Specifically, these effects were $r = .27$ for men and $r = .28$ for women. Also, the gender difference in the effect of a partner's attractiveness on one's own relationship satisfaction was $r = .02$.

Specifically, these effects were $r = .46$ for men and $r = .45$ for women in Eastwick, P.W., et al., "A Worldwide Test of the Predictive Validity of Ideal Partner Preference-Matching," *Journal of Personality and Social Psychology* 128, no. 1 (2025), 123–146.

24. Elder, G.H., "Appearance and Education in Marriage Mobility," *American Sociological Review* 34, no. 4 (August 1969): 519–533.
25. McClintock, E.A., "Beauty and Status: The Illusion of Exchange in Partner Selection?," *American Sociological Review* 79, no. 4 (August 2014): 575–604.
26. Grow, A. and J. Van Bavel, "The Gender Cliff in the Relative Contribution to the Household Income: Insights from Modelling Marriage Markets in 27 European Countries," *European Journal of Population* 36 (January 2020): 1–23. Also, the extent to which wives earn more than their husbands is unrelated to the likelihood of divorce. In the middle of the last century, this trend was true (although small) and touted heavily by commentators who lamented that women's career prospects boded poorly for the survival of the nuclear family. But once we look at couples who were getting married in the nineties (the couples for which we have the most recent good data), any effect of the wife's relative earnings on divorce has evaporated, see Schwartz, C.R. and P. Gonalons-Pons, "Trends in Relative Earnings and Marital Dissolution: Are Wives Who Outearn Their Husbands Still More Likely to Divorce?," *RSF: The Russell Sage Foundation Journal of the Social Sciences* 2, no. 4 (August 2016): 218–236.
27. Bertrand, M., E. Kamenica, and J. Pan, "Gender Identity and Relative Income within Households," *The Quarterly Journal of Economics* 130, no. 2 (May 2015): 571–614.
28. De Hauw, Y., A. Grow, and J. Van Bavel, "The Reversed Gender Gap in Education and Assortative Mating in Europe," *European Journal of Population* 33 (2017): 445–474; Kilander, G., "Professor Warns of a 'Mating' Crisis in US as Fewer Men Go to College," *The Independent,* September 27, 2021; Van Bavel, Schwartz, and Esteve, "The Reversal of the Gender Gap in Education" 341–360.
29. Rudder, C., *Dataclysm: Who We Are (When We Think No One's Looking)* (Toronto: Random House Canada, 2014).
30. The gender difference in the extent to which women vs. men actually preferred age in a blind date partner was $r = .04$. Specifically, these effects were $r = -.07$ for men and $r = -.03$ for women (i.e., both sexes had a tiny preference for *younger* partners on blind dates) in Eastwick, P.W., et al., "No Gender Differences in Attraction to Young Partners: A Study of 4,500 Blind Dates," *Proceedings of the National Academy of Sciences* 122, no. 5 (February 2025). The gender difference in the extent to which women vs. men actually prefer age in a speed dating partner was $r = .00$. Specifically, these effects were $r = -.19$ for men and $r = -.19$

for women (i.e., both sexes prefer younger partners at speed dating) in Kurzban, R. and J. Weeden, "HurryDate: Mate Preferences in Action," *Evolution and Human Behavior* 26, no. 3 (May 2005): 227–244.

Another strange finding emerges when we look at how relationship satisfaction changes in couples as they age. If youth were more important to men than to women, then the advancing age of one's romantic partner should be more depressing for men's rather than women's relationship satisfaction. But there is not a shred of evidence that this is true: Both genders sour on their relationships as they enter midlife (work-family balance is rough) and then rebound somewhat in old age. There is no gender difference in this pattern, see Bühler, J.L., S. Krauss, and U. Orth, "Development of Relationship Satisfaction across the Life Span: A Systematic Review and Meta-analysis," *Psychological Bulletin* 147, no. 10 (October 2021): 1012–1053.

31. OkCupid, "The Case for an Older Woman: How Dating Preferences Change with Age," Medium, February 16, 2010, https://medium.com/@okcupid/the-case-for-an-older-woman-99d8cabacdf5.

32. Buss, D.M., "Sexual Strategies Theory: Historical Origins and Current Status," *The Journal of Sex Research* 35, no. 1 (1998): 19–31.

33. The gender difference in endorsing positive attitudes toward casual sex was $r = .34$ in Schmitt, D.P., et al., "Sociosexuality from Argentina to Zimbabwe: A 48-Nation Study of Sex, Culture, and the Strategies of Human Mating," *Behavioral and Brain Sciences* 28, no. 2 (April 2005): 247–311. If you had a random man and woman in front of you and you had to pick who had more positive attitudes about casual sex, selecting the man would be correct 67 percent of the time.

34. The gender difference when people recall consenting to casual sex in the past was $r = .31$ in Conley, T.D., "Perceived Proposer Personality Characteristics and Gender Differences in Acceptance of Casual Sex Offers," *Journal of Personality and Social Psychology* 100, no. 2 (2011): 309–329.

35. The gender difference in the threshold for having sex with someone was $r = .27$ in Eastwick, P.W., E.J. Finkel, and J.A. Simpson, "Relationship Trajectories: A Meta-Theoretical Framework and Theoretical Applications," *Psychological Inquiry* 30, no. 1 (2019): 1–28.

36. The average effect size in satisfaction with both giving and receiving oral sex for women in same-gender vs. mixed-gender relationships was $r = .25$, and the effect size for "Orgasm experienced more than once during a single sexual experience" for women in same-gender vs. mixed-gender relationships was $r = .20$ in Blair, K.L., J. Cappell, and C.F. Pukall, "Not All Orgasms Were Created Equal: Differences in Frequency and Satisfaction of Orgasm Experiences by Sexual Activity in Same-Sex versus Mixed-Sex Relationships," *The Journal of Sex Research*

55, no. 6 (2018): 719–733. The effect size for the belief that men vs. women are bad lovers was $r = .33$, and bisexual women's preference for having casual sex with women vs. men was $r = .41$ in Conley, "Perceived Proposer Personality Characteristics and Gender Differences in Acceptance of Casual Sex Offers," 309–329. See also Conley, T.D. and V. Klein, "Women Get Worse Sex: A Confound in the Explanation of Gender Differences in Sexuality," *Perspectives on Psychological Science* 17, no. 4 (July 2022): 960–978; Dickman, K., G.M. Wetzel, and D.T. Sanchez, "The Role of Partner Gender: How Sexual Expectations Shape the Pursuit of an Orgasm Goal for Heterosexual, Lesbian, and Bisexual Women," *Social Psychological and Personality Science* 16, no. 5 (July 2025): 495–506.

37. The gender difference when people actually consent to casual sex with an other-gender *stranger* was $r = .49$ in Hald, G.M. and H. Høgh-Olesen, "Receptivity to Sexual Invitations from Strangers of the Opposite Gender," *Evolution and Human Behavior* 31, no. 6 (November 2010): 453–458. See also Clark, R.D. and E. Hatfield, "Gender Differences in Receptivity to Sexual Offers," *Journal of Psychology & Human Sexuality* 2, no. 1 (1989): 39–55.

38. The effect size for the belief that men vs. women strangers looking for casual sex are dangerous was $r = .41$ in Conley, "Perceived Proposer Personality Characteristics and Gender Differences in Acceptance of Casual Sex Offers," 309–329.

39. Consider that women have a stronger preference for foreplay than men ($r = .26$) and women *get* more foreplay in same- vs. mixed-gender sexual encounters ($r = .30$ across a variety of non-intercourse activities) in Dickman, Wetzel, and Sanchez, "The Role of Partner Gender," 495–506. See also Purnine, D.M. and M.P. Carey, "Age and Gender Differences in Sexual Behavior Preferences: A Follow-up Report," *Journal of Sex & Marital Therapy* 24, no. 2 (1998): 93–102.

40. Twenge, J.M., R.A. Sherman, and B.E. Wells, "Declines in Sexual Frequency among American Adults, 1989–2014," *Archives of Sexual Behavior* 46, no. 8 (2017): 2389–2401. In defiance of their bacchanalian stereotype, college students were about four times more likely to have a sexual experience in the context of an ongoing romantic relationship than in the context of a casual relationship in Walsh, J.L., et al., "Do Alcohol and Marijuana Use Decrease the Probability of Condom Use for College Women?," *The Journal of Sex Research* 51, no. 2 (2014): 145–158.

41. Sanchez, D.T., J.C. Fetterolf, and L.A. Rudman, "Eroticizing Inequality in the United States: The Consequences and Determinants of Traditional Gender Role Adherence in Intimate Relationships," *The Journal of Sex Research* 49, no. 2–3 (2012): 168–183.

42. Smith, A., et al., "Sexual and Relationship Satisfaction among Heterosexual Men and Women: The Importance of Desired Frequency of Sex," *Journal of Sex*

& *Marital Therapy* 37, no. 2 (2011): 104–115. The gender difference in sexual desire for a romantic partner was $r = .13$ in Frankenbach, J., et al., "Sex Drive: Theoretical Conceptualization and Meta-Analytic Review of Gender Differences," *Psychological Bulletin* 148, no. 9–10 (2022): 621–661.

43. Cox, T., "Not Tonight, Darling, I've Got a Headache," *The Daily Mail*, May 11, 2016.

44. Across three studies, the overall effect size for men's tendency to underestimate their partner's sexual desire was $r = .40$ ($r = .53$, study 1; $r = .26$, study 2; $r = .41$, study 3). Although not reported in the paper itself, these values were (on average across the studies in this paper): 45.5 percent underestimation, 26.5 percent accurate, and 27.5 percent overestimation in Muise, A., et al., "Not in the Mood? Men Under- (Not Over-) Perceive Their Partner's Sexual Desire in Established Intimate Relationships," *Journal of Personality and Social Psychology* 110, no. 5 (2016): 725–742; Muise, A., personal communication, February 24, 2024.

45. Joel, S., et al., "Machine Learning Uncovers the Most Robust Self-Report Predictors of Relationship Quality across 43 Longitudinal Couples Studies," *Proceedings of the National Academy of Sciences* 117, no. 32 (August 2020): 19061–19071.

46. A gender difference that you might think would be quite large but is actually quite modest concerns whether men and women are more concerned about the sexual aspects of an infidelity. Naturally, infidelity is often devastating to couples, whether that infidelity is sexual, emotional, or (as is commonly the case) both. Nevertheless, a lot of ink has been spilled over whether the sexual (vs. emotional) aspects of the infidelity are more upsetting and jealousy-inducing for men. This is another case where, when people are pondering imaginary scenarios, the gender difference is quite large. But when people reflect on what was distressing about actual infidelity experiences, the men tended to focus on the sexual aspects of the infidelity only slightly more than women did—a small effect, $r = .12$ in Sagarin, B.J., et al., "Sex Differences in Jealousy: A Meta-analytic Examination," *Evolution and Human Behavior* 33, no. 6 (2012): 595–614. So this is yet another case where a hypothetical context greatly exaggerates the size of the gender difference.

47. Conley and Klein, "Women Get Worse Sex," 960–978; Morton, T.A., et al., "Theorizing Gender in the Face of Social Change: Is There Anything Essential about Essentialism?," *Journal of Personality and Social Psychology* 96, no. 3 (March 2009): 653–664.

48. Hewlett, B.S., "Culture, History, and Sex: Anthropological Contributions to Conceptualizing Father Involvement," *Marriage & Family Review* 29, no. 2–3 (2000): 59–73; Sear, "The Male Breadwinner Nuclear Family."

49. Wood, W. and A.H. Eagly, "A Cross-Cultural Analysis of the Behavior of Women and Men: Implications for the Origins of Sex Differences," *Psychological Bulletin* 128, no. 5 (2002): 699–727.
50. Eastwick et al., "A Worldwide Test of the Predictive Validity of Ideal Partner Preference-Matching,"123–146.

CHAPTER 3

1. Grayson, A., "Why Nice Guys Finish Last: New Research Suggests a Biological reason for Why Bad Boys Get All the Girls," June 19, 2008, https://abcnews.go.com/Health/story?id=5197531&page=1; Jean, E., "Ask E. Jean: Should I Choose the Steady Good Guy or Exciting Bad Boy?," *Elle*, November 1, 2017, Shepherd, T., "16 Signs She's Playing Games with You (It's Clear as Day If You Spot These)," A Conscious Rethink, May 4, 2022.
2. This gender difference is significant, albeit a small effect size of $r = .13$, in Haselton, M.G., et al., "Sex, Lies, and Strategic Interference: The Psychology of Deception between the Sexes," *Personality & Social Psychology Bulletin* 31, no. 1 (January 2005): 3–23.
3. In this study, about 18 percent of single people went on to form a relationship over a 3–7 month period. Within this group, folks who agreed with statements like "I feel that this is the 'right time' for me to be in a committed relationship" were more likely to end up in a relationship by an odds ratio factor of 1.46, which is akin to a small effect size of $r = .10$, or the difference between 22 people and 14 people out of 100; Hadden, B.W., C.R. Agnew, and K. Tan, "Commitment Readiness and Relationship Formation," *Personality and Social Psychology Bulletin* 44, no. 8 (August 2018): 1242–1257. Effect sizes converted at https://www.psychometrica.de/effect_size.html.
4. Kruger, D.J., M. Fisher, and I. Jobling, "Proper and Dark Heroes as Dads and Cads: Alternative Mating Strategies in British Romantic Literature," *Human Nature* 14, no. 3 (September 2003): 305–317.
5. Aitken, S.J., M. Lyons, and P.K. Jonason, "Dads or Cads? Women's Strategic Decisions in the Mating Game," *Personality and Individual Differences* 55, no. 2 (July 2013): 118–122; Figueredo, A.J., et al., "The K-factor: Individual Differences in Life History Strategy," *Personality and Individual Differences* 39, no. 8 (December 2005): 1349–1360.
6. Burley, N., "Sexual Selection for Aesthetic Traits in Species with Biparental Care," *The American Naturalist* 127, no. 4 (April 1986): 415–445; Burley, N., "The Differential-Allocation Hypothesis: An Experimental Test," *The American Naturalist* 132, no. 5 (November 1988): 611–628; Gangestad, S.W. and J.A.

Simpson, "The Evolution of Human Mating: Trade-offs and Strategic Pluralism," *Behavioral and Brain Sciences* 23, no. 4 (August 2000): 573–644.

7. Del Giudice, M., "Sex, Attachment, and the Development of Reproductive Strategies," *Behavioral and Brain Sciences* 32, no. 1 (2009): 1–21; Hrdy, S.B., *Mother Nature: A History of Mothers, Infants, and Natural Selection* (New York: Pantheon Books, 1999).

8. "I think I destroyed our relationship trying to compliment my boyfriend," Reddit, August 7, 2024, https://www.reddit.com/r/TrueOffMyChest/comments/1em5x6t/i_think_i_destroyed_our_relationship_trying_to/?rdt=55330.

9. Endendijk, J.J., A.L. van Baar, and M. Deković, "He Is a Stud, She Is a Slut! A Meta-analysis on the Continued Existence of Sexual Double Standards," *Personality and Social Psychology Review* 24, no. 2 (May 2020): 163–190; Marks, M.J., T.M. Young, and Y. Zaikman, "The Sexual Double Standard in the Real World," *Social Psychology* 50, no. 2 (2019).

10. Kruger, Fisher, Jobling, "Proper and Dark Heroes as Dads and Cads," 308.

11. Schmitt, D.P., et al., "Sociosexuality from Argentina to Zimbabwe: A 48-Nation Study of Sex, Culture, and the Strategies of Human Mating," *Behavioral and Brain Sciences* 28, no. 2 (April 2005): 247; see also Fletcher, G.J.O., et al., *The Science of Intimate Relationships*, 2nd ed. (Malden, MA: Wiley-Blackwell, 2019); Hertler, S., M. Perñaherrera-Aguirre, and A.J. Figueredo, "An Evolutionary Explanation of the Madonna-Whore Complex," *Evolutionary Psychological Science* 9, no. 3 (May 2023): 372–384.

12. Gangestad, S.W., et al., "Changes in Women's Mate Preferences across the Ovulatory Cycle," *Journal of Personality and Social Psychology* 92, no. 1 (January 2007): 151–163; Rhodes, G., "The Evolutionary Psychology of Facial Beauty," *Annual Review of Psychology* 57 (2006): 199–226.

13. The effect of physical attractiveness (as coded by independent raters) on popularity at speed-dating events was a large effect of $r = .51$ ($r = .49$ for men and $r = .52$ for women in table 3) in Asendorpf, J.B., L. Penke, and M.D. Back, "From Dating to Mating and Relating: Predictors of Initial and Long-Term Outcomes of Speed-Dating in a Community Sample," *European Journal of Personality* 25, no. 1 (January 2011): 16–30. Also, across two datasets, both men and women were perceived to be much more desirable at speed-dating events to the extent that they were rated as "confident" ($r = .60$ for men and $r = .59$ for women), effect sizes analyzed from Eastwick, P.W. and E.J. Finkel, "Northwestern Speed-dating Study I" (2005) UNC Dataverse, V1, https://doi.org/10.15139/S3/HK7KZQ; Eastwick, P.W. and E.J. Finkel, "Northwestern Speed-Dating Study II," (2007) UNC Dataverse, V1, https://doi.org/10.15139/S3/52MIJO.

14. Across three datasets, the average correlation of someone's physical attractiveness (as coded by independent raters) with three different measures of short-term desirability—their reported number of sex partners, reported number of short-term partners, and reported number of "hookup" partners—was a small effect of $r = .14$ ($r = .15$ for men and $r = .12$ for women, which is basically the same) in Eastwick, P.W. and E.J. Finkel, "Northwestern Speed-dating Study I" (2005) UNC Dataverse, V1, https://doi.org/10.15139/S3/HK7KZQ; Eastwick, P.W. and E.J. Finkel, "Northwestern Speed-Dating Study II" (2007) UNC Dataverse, V1, https://doi.org/10.15139/S3/52MIJO; Rhodes, G., L.W. Simmons, and M. Peters, "Attractiveness and Sexual Behavior: Does Attractiveness Enhance Mating Success?," *Evolution and Human Behavior* 26, no. 2 (March 2005): 186–201. Also, the association of fluctuating asymmetry with people's total number of sex partners was a small effect of $r = .15$ ($r = .17$ for men and $r = .13$ for women in table 5) in this meta-analysis: Van Dongen, S. and S.W. Gangestad, "Human Fluctuating Asymmetry in Relation to Health and Quality: A Meta-analysis," *Evolution and Human Behavior* 32, no. 6 (November 2011): 380–398.
15. The correlation between sociosexual attitudes and number of lifetime sex partners was a medium-to-large effect of $r = .40$ ($r = .38$ for men in table 3 and $r = .42$ for women in table 4) in Penke, L. and J.B. Asendorpf, "Beyond Global Sociosexual Orientations: A More Differentiated Look at Sociosexuality and Its Effects on Courtship and Romantic Relationships," *Journal of Personality and Social Psychology* 95, no. 5 (November 2008): 1113–1135. Relatedly, among people who are currently in a relationship, there is a correlation between the extent to which people believe that "sex without love is okay" and relationship dissatisfaction, although this effect is fairly small: The correlation between one's own sociosexual attitudes and satisfaction/commitment with a current partner is the small effect of $r = -.15$ ($r = -.16$ for men in table 3 and $r = -.13$ for women in table 4).
16. The correlation between sociosexuality and wanting a long-term relationship is about $r = -.31$ on average, a medium effect size. That is, people who are comfortable with casual sex tend to *disagree* with statements like "I am interested in maintaining a long-term romantic relationship with someone special," see Jackson, J.J. and L.A. Kirkpatrick, "The Structure and Measurement of Human Mating Strategies: Toward a Multidimensional Model of Sociosexuality," *Evolution and Human Behavior* 28, no. 6 (November 2007): 382–391.
17. Coder-ratings of physical attractiveness predict having *more* prior romantic relationships (longer than 3 months) with a small effect size, $r = .16$. Ratings of confidence provided by fellow speed-daters predict having *more* prior relationships (longer than 3 months) with a medium effect size, $r = .28$. Both

effects are the opposite of the direction predicted by the Zero-Sum model. Effect sizes analyzed from Eastwick, P.W. and E.J. Finkel, "Northwestern Speed-dating Study I" (2005) UNC Dataverse, V1, https://doi.org/10.15139/S3/HK7KZQ; Eastwick, P.W. and E.J. Finkel, "Northwestern Speed-Dating Study II" (2007) UNC Dataverse, V1, https://doi.org/10.15139/S3/52MIJO. The correlation between sociosexual attitudes and number of lifetime *romantic* partners is a small-to-medium effect of $r = .23$, which is in the opposite of the direction predicted by the Zero-Sum model ($r = .25$ for men in table 3 and $r = .20$ for women in table 4) in Penke and Asendorpf, "Beyond Global Sociosexual Orientations," 1113–1135.

18. The effect of a partner's "objective" (independent coder-rated) attractiveness on one's own relationship satisfaction is a less-than-small effect of $r = .06$ ($r = .08$ for men and $r = .03$ for women in table 2) in Eastwick, P.W., et al., "Is a Meta-analysis a Foundation or Just Another Brick? Comment on Meltzer, McNulty, Jackson, & Karney (2014)," *Journal of Personality and Social Psychology* 106, no. 3 (2014): 429–434. In some (unpublished) data described in Gangestad and Simpson, "Evolution of Human Mating," the association of men's fluctuating asymmetry with women's "emotional support/nurturance" and "commitment" was $r = -.09$ (i.e., a small effect that is the opposite of the direction predicted by the Zero-Sum model; Steven Gangestad, personal communication, September 9, 2022). (Only men were tested in that study.) Also, the average effect of a partner's sociosexuality on one's own relationship satisfaction/sexual satisfaction/commitment was the less-than-small effect of $r = -.05$ across two articles: French, J.E., E.E. Altgelt, and A.L. Meltzer, "The Implications of Sociosexuality for Marital Satisfaction and Dissolution," *Psychological Science* 30, no. 10 (October 2019): 1460–1472; Webster, G.D., et al., "An Investment Model of Sociosexuality, Relationship Satisfaction, and Commitment: Evidence from Dating, Engaged, and Newlywed Couples," *Journal of Research in Personality* 55 (2015): 112–126.

    Social confidence makes the story especially grim for the Zero-Sum model. Confidence is part of a broader personality trait called *emotional stability*. There are many studies on emotional stability in close relationships—covering thousands and thousands of couples. If anything, these effects are the opposite of what would be predicted by the Zero-Sum model: People tend to be happier with more confident, emotionally stable partners. This effect is rather small ($r = .17$ in the Esplin meta-analysis), but nevertheless, it is not remotely consistent with the idea that confident people end up being bad long-term relationship partners, see Esplin, C.R., et al., "Neuroticism and Relationship Quality: A Meta-analytic Review," *Journal of Personality and Social Psychology* 128, no. 3 (2025): 594–610; John, O.P. and S. Srivastava, "The Big-Five Trait Taxonomy: History, Measurement, and Theoretical Perspectives," in *Handbook of*

Personality: Theory and Research, ed. L.A. Pervin and O.P. John, 2nd ed. (New York: Guilford Press: 1999), 102–138.

19. The average correlation of one's own attractiveness with infidelity was $r = .01$ for men and $r = -.08$ for women—which are very small effect sizes—across the following four articles: Gangestad, S.W. and R. Thornhill, "The Evolutionary Psychology of Extrapair Sex: The Role of Fluctuating Asymmetry," *Evolution and Human Behavior* 18, no. 2 (March 1997): 69–88; McNulty, J.K., et al., "Attentional and Evaluative Biases Help People Maintain Relationships by Avoiding Infidelity," *Journal of Personality and Social Psychology* 115, no. 1 (2018): 76–95; Rhodes, Simmons, and Peters, "Attractiveness and Sexual Behavior," 186–201; Rhodes, G., G. Morley, and L.W. Simmons, "Women Can Judge Sexual Unfaithfulness from Unfamiliar Men's Faces," *Biology Letters* 9, no. 1 (February 2013). Nevertheless, it is true that people with more positive attitudes toward casual sex (i.e., higher sociosexuality) are more likely to cheat in a current, long-term relationship; these effect sizes in one very large study were $r = .18$ for men and $r = .24$ for women in Penke and Asendorpf, "Beyond Global Sociosexual Orientations," 1113–1135. However, a major caveat is in order: These data can't tell us anything about the causal order of events. Because in studies like this one, people report their sociosexuality well after their relationship is underway—even after they have already cheated! So it is equally (if not more) likely that some people find themselves in flailing relationships, they cheat, and *then* they develop more positive attitudes toward casual sex. And even if a study were to measure sociosexuality when people are single, follow them over time as they form a relationship, and then see if they cheat, the (at best) small effect size that could emerge would certainly not be enough to rescue the Zero-Sum model.

    In terms of how features of the relationship itself predict infidelity: The average correlation of commitment on infidelity was the large effect size of $r = -.50$ in two studies in Drigotas, S.M., C.A. Safstrom, and T. Gentilia, "An Investment Model Prediction of Dating Infidelity," *Journal of Personality and Social Psychology* 77, no. 3 (1999): 509–524; the effect of problem drinking on infidelity was $r = .22$ in Graham, S.M., et al., "Problem Drinking and Extradyadic Sex in Young Adult Romantic Relationships," *Journal of Social and Clinical Psychology* 35, no. 2 (February 2016): 152–170. For more information on predictors of infidelity, see Previti, D. and P.R. Amato, "Is Infidelity a Cause or a Consequence of Poor Marital Quality?," *Journal of Social and Personal Relationships* 21, no. 2 (April 2004): 217–230.

20. Across two datasets, the average correlation between someone's (a) "responsive," "dependable/trustworthy," and "friendly/nice" qualities (as rated by strangers on a first impression) and (b) their reported number of sex partners, short-term partners, and "hookup" partners was essentially zero, $r = -.01$ (and separately, it

was basically zero for both men, r = .06, and women, r = -.07). Effect sizes analyzed from Eastwick, P.W. and E.J. Finkel, "Northwestern Speed-dating Study I" (2005) UNC Dataverse, V1, https://doi.org/10.15139/S3/HK7KZQ.

21. Edelstein, R.S., "Testosterone Tradeoffs in Close Relationships," in *Advances in Experimental Social Psychology*, ed. B. Gawronski, vol. 65 (Cambridge, MA: Academic Press, 2022), 235–280; Roney, J.R. and L.T. Gettler, "The Role of Testosterone in Human Romantic Relationships," *Current Opinion in Psychology* 1 (February 2015): 81–86.

22. Sometimes, you see handwringing over the "risky" casual sexual behavior of young people. There might indeed be good reasons to reduce risky adolescent sexual behavior (e.g., preventing unwanted pregnancies or the spread of STDs). Nevertheless, there is often an additional finger-wagging assumption that adolescents who have casual sex are doomed to have poor long-term relationship outcomes. There is no evidence to support this assumption: Having sex early in life is basically totally unrelated to the satisfaction of one's later long-term relationships or the long-term likelihood of getting married, see Harden, K.P., "True Love Waits? A Sibling-Comparison Study of Age at First Sexual Intercourse and Romantic Relationships in Young Adulthood," *Psychological Science* 23, no. 11 (November 2012): 1324–1336; Wolfinger, N.H. and S.L. Perry, "Does a Longer Sexual Resume Affect Marriage Rates?," *Social Science Research* 113 (July 2023). Furthermore, the correlation between having premarital sex and divorce was a measly r = .05, which is less than small, in Heaton, T.B., "Factors Contributing to Increasing Marital Stability in the United States," *Journal of Family Issues* 23, no. 3 (April 2002): 392–409.

23. In addition, this model can also account for data suggesting that women who are paired with good dads (i.e., men in the bottom right quadrant) will find themselves drawn to sexy cads (i.e., men in the top left quadrant) specifically when they are at the most fertile point in their ovulatory cycle. Research on such "ovulatory shifts" is undergoing massive re-examination with larger samples in recent years, so the jury remains out on what exactly is robust in this research area. Suffice to say, if the key findings hold together—that women trade off their interest in good dads vs. sexy cads as a function of where they are in their cycle—the Independent Strategies model could account for this finding; see Arslan, R.C., et al., "Using 26,000 Diary Entries to Show Ovulatory Changes in Sexual Desire and Behavior," *Journal of Personality and Social Psychology* 121, no. 2 (2021): 410–431; Gangestad, S.W. and T. Dinh, "Robust Evidence for Moderation of Ovulatory Shifts by Partner Attractiveness in Arslan et al.'s (2020) Data," *Journal of Personality and Social Psychology* 121, no. 2 (2021): 432–440.

24. Buss, D.M., "Desires in human mating," *Annals of the New York Academy of Sciences* 907, no. 1 (2000): 48.

25. Buss, D.M. and D.P. Schmitt, "Sexual Strategies Theory: An Evolutionary Perspective on Human Mating," *Psychological Review* 100, no. 2 (April 1993): 204–232; Buss, D.M. and D.P. Schmitt, "Mate Preferences and Their Behavioral Manifestations," *Annual Review of Psychology* 70 (2019): 77–110; Li, N.P. and D.T. Kenrick, "Sex Similarities and Differences in Preferences for Short-Term Mates: What, Whether, and Why," *Journal of Personality and Social Psychology* 90, no. 3 (2006): 468–489.
26. People who felt they were desirable to other peers of their preferred sex as "a short-term mate or casual sex partner" were just a bit more likely to think they were desirable as a "long-term mate or marriage partner," $r = .12$, see study 1, in Ko, A., et al., "Functionally Calibrating Life Satisfaction: The Case of Mating Motives and Self-Perceived Mate Value," *Journal of Happiness Studies* 24, no. 2 (2023): 651–675.
27. Once again, the strongest trait-level predictor of long-term mate value is emotional stability, and this effect was a modest $r = .17$ meta-analytically in Esplin, "Neuroticism and Relationship Quality," 594–610. As we'll discover in part 2 of this book, being a good partner comes from something that isn't so trait-like.
28. Joel, S., P.W. Eastwick, and E.J. Finkel, "Is Romantic Desire Predictable? Machine Learning Applied to Initial Romantic Attraction," *Psychological Science* 28, no. 10 (October 2017): 1478–1489.
29. Your personality explains how *you* feel about your partners, of course; this value was about 20 percent (as opposed to the meager 5 percent capturing how well your personality explains how *your partner* feels about you) in Joel, S., et al., "Machine Learning Uncovers the Most Robust Self-Report Predictors of Relationship Quality across 43 Longitudinal Couples Studies," *Proceedings of the National Academy of Sciences* 117, no. 32 (August 2020): 19061–19071.
30. Joel, Eastwick, and Finkel, "Is Romantic Desire Predictable?," 1478–1489.
31. Joel et al., "Machine Learning Uncovers the Most Robust Self-Report Predictors of Relationship Quality," 19061–19071.
32. Eastwick, P.W., E.J. Finkel, and S. Joel, "Mate Evaluation Theory," *Psychological Review* 130, no. 1 (2023): 211–241.
33. Eastwick, P.W., et al., "Consistency and Inconsistency among Romantic Partners over Time," *Journal of Personality and Social Psychology* 112, no. 6 (March 2017): 838–859.
34. In one set of studies, short-term and long-term relationships were most likely to originate through: friends (21 percent), at school (19 percent), at work (15 percent), at a social gathering (13 percent), online dating (12 percent), at a bar/club (6 percent). But critically, the venue did not have any impact on whether it spawned a short-term or long-term relationship, see Eastwick, P.W., et al.,

"What Do Short-Term and Long-Term Relationships Look Like? Building the Relationship Coordination and Strategic Timing (ReCAST) Model," *Journal of Experimental Psychology: General* 147, no. 5 (May 2018): 747–781. Another study found that the venue where people met their partner (online vs. offline) affected (a) future likelihood of breaking up with an effect size of $r = .02$, and (b) future satisfaction in the relationship with an effect size of $r = .05$. These tiny effect sizes tell us that it does not really matter how you meet your partner (despite the title of the paper): Cacioppo, J.T., et al., "Marital Satisfaction and Break-ups Differ across On-line and Off-line Meeting Venues," *Proceedings of the National Academy of Sciences* 110, no. 25 (June 2013): 10135–10140.

35. The correlation between "I would like to have a long-term, committed romantic relationship with [name]" and "I would like to have a short-term romantic relationship (e.g., a one-night sexual encounter or brief affair) with [name]" across $N = 2,184$ first impressions was $r = .72$, in Eastwick, P.W. and E.J. Finkel, "Northwestern Speed-Dating Study II" (2007) UNC Dataverse, V1, https://doi.org/10.15139/S3/52MIJO.

36. Here's more evidence that this challenge is pervasive: Let's say you're super into someone, and you would really like to form a dating relationship with them. On average, what is the likelihood that in the coming weeks and months you're going to succeed? It's about 15 percent, according to one study that tracked people over time: Eastwick, P.W., et al., "Predicting Romantic Interest during Early Relationship Development: A Preregistered Investigation Using Machine Learning," *European Journal of Personality* 37, no. 3 (May/June 2023): 276–312. Now, let's say you are actively in a friends-with-benefits relationship with someone, and you fully intend for this to be a short-term thing. Now, what is the likelihood that in the coming weeks and months you're going to form a dating relationship with them anyway? Again, it's about 15 percent in Machia, L.V., et al., "A Longitudinal Study of Friends with Benefits Relationships," *Personal Relationships* 27, no. 1 (March 2020): 47–60. Whether you're trying to (the first case) or not (the second case), the odds of both of you catching feelings are about the same.

37. Eastwick et al., "What Do Short-Term and Long-Term Relationships Look Like?," 747–781; Wade, L., *American Hookup: The New Culture of Sex on Campus* (New York: W. W. Norton, 2017); Walsh, J.L., et al., "Do Alcohol and Marijuana Use Decrease the Probability of Condom Use for College Women?," *The Journal of Sex Research* 51, no. 2 (2014): 145–158.

38. Eastwick et al., "What Do Short-Term and Long-Term Relationships Look Like?," 747–781; Eastwick, P.W., E.J. Finkel, and J.A. Simpson, "Relationship Trajectories: A Meta-Theoretical Framework and Theoretical Applications," *Psychological Inquiry* 30, no. 1 (2019): 1–28.

39. Eastwick et al., "What Do Short-Term and Long-Term Relationships Look Like?," 747–781; Eastwick et al., "Relationship Trajectories," 1–28.
40. There is evidence in support of these ideas: People give high ratings to statements like "I would like to have a short-term relationship with this person" for people they like "a little." Ratings for statements like "I would like to have a long-term relationship with this person" are high only for people they like a lot. Also, when people are thinking about a potential romantic partner (prior to any hookup), and they are asked whether what they have is a short-term relationship, a long-term relationship, or an "I don't know *what* this is yet" relationship, a full 82 percent of people select the "I don't know" option in Eastwick et al., "Relationship Trajectories," 1–28.
41. You might be tempted to assume that sex work is an example that deserves to be its own "type" of mating behavior—because it's about sex and only sex. In most cases, however, this assumption would be completely wrong. The majority—perhaps even the vast majority—of *paid* sex takes place between people who have had sex with each other previously. For men who frequent escorts and brothels, an ongoing relationship is often the whole point: These johns want to have repeated experiences with sex workers they genuinely like, and often real intimacy is involved. Even streetwalkers—the most dangerous and marginalized form of sex work—have regular clientele. This is not to say that all forms of paying for sex can fit into a model like figure 3.6, but the fact that men pay for sex does not in and of itself provide evidence for a separate type of sexual relationship; these men are often paying for the intimacy that comes with the prototypical romantic relationship, see Freund, M., T.L. Leonard, and N. Lee, "Sexual Behavior of Resident Street Prostitutes with their Clients in Camden, New Jersey," *The Journal of Sex Research* 26, no. 4 (1989): 460–478; Sanders, T., "Male Sexual Scripts: Intimacy, Sexuality and Pleasure in the Purchase of Commercial Sex," *Sociology* 42, no. 3 (June 2008): 400–417; Weitzer, R., "Sociology of Sex Work," *Annual Review of Sociology* 35 (2009): 213–234; Westerhoff, N., "Why Do Men Buy Sex?," *Scientific American*, October 1, 2012.

CHAPTER 4

1. Baumeister, R.F. and M.R. Leary, "The Need to Belong: Desire for Interpersonal Attachments as a Fundamental Human Motivation," *Psychological Bulletin* 117, vol. 3, (May 1995): 497–529; LeRoy, A.S., et al., "Implications for Reward Processing in Differential Responses to Loss: Impacts on Attachment Hierarchy Reorganization," *Personality and Social Psychology Review* 23, no. 4 (November 2019): 391–405.

2. Kleiman, D.G., "Monogamy in Mammals," *The Quarterly Review of Biology* 52, no. 1 (March 1977): 39–69.
3. Bretherton, I., "The Origins of Attachment Theory: John Bowlby and Mary Ainsworth," *Developmental Psychology* 28, no. 5 (1992): 759–775.
4. Hazan, C. and L.M. Diamond, "The Place of Attachment in Human Mating," *Review of General Psychology* 4, no. 2 (June 2000): 186–204; Shaver, P., C. Hazan, and D. Bradshaw, "Love as Attachment: The Integration of Three Behavioral Systems," in *The Psychology of Love*, ed. R.J. Sternberg and M.L. Barnes, (New Haven, CT: Yale University Press, 1988): 68–99.
5. Coan, J.A. and D.A. Sbarra, "Social Baseline Theory: The Social Regulation of Risk and Effort," *Current Opinion in Psychology* 1 (February 2015): 87–91; Hazan, C. and P.R. Shaver, "Attachment as an Organizational Framework for Research on Close Relationships," *Psychological Inquiry* 5, no. 1 (1994): 1–22.
6. Sbarra, D.A. and C. Hazan, "Coregulation, Dysregulation, Self-Regulation: An Integrative Analysis and Empirical Agenda for Understanding Adult Attachment, Separation, Loss, and Recovery," *Personality and Social Psychology Review* 12, no. 2 (2008): 141–167.
7. Scholars once believed that concepts like romantic anguish and longing for one particular person—and the accompanying concepts of romantic love and passion—were limited to contemporary Europe and America. But we now know that these experiences are nearly universal, across contexts and cultures. One famous study demonstrated that people experience not just lust, but love, passion, and even romantic obsession in 147 out of 166 (89 percent) highly diverse cultures. (Specifically, this set of cultures is called the Standard Cross Cultural Sample, and it covers over two thousand years of history and every corner of the globe.) And the remaining 11 percent of cultures simply had incomplete data. In other words, the powerful desire and longing to be with one specific person seems to be a pervasive human experience. For more details, see Jankowiak, W., *Romantic Passion: A Universal Experience?*, (New York: Columbia University Press, 1995); Jankowiak, W. and E. Fischer, "A Cross-cultural Perspective on Romantic Love," *Ethnology* 31, no. 2 (April 1992): 149–155. See also Sandel, A. A., "The Search for Love in Human Evolution: Primate Social Bonds and a New Science of Emotion," *American Journal of Biological Anthropology* 187 (2025).
8. Locke, D.P., et al., "Comparative and Demographic Analysis of Orangutan Genomes," *Nature* 469 (2011): 529–533.
9. Fraley, R.C., C.C. Brumbaugh, and M.J. Marks, "The Evolution and Function of Adult Attachment: A Comparative and Phylogenetic Analysis," *Journal of Personality and Social Psychology* 89 (2005): 731–746.

10. Bryant, J.V., et al., "Identifying Environmental versus Phylogenetic Correlates of Behavioural Ecology in Gibbons: Implications for Conservation Management of the World's Rarest Ape," *BMC Evolutionary Biology* 15 (August 2015): 1–13.
11. Bales, K.L., et al., "What Is a Pair Bond?," *Hormones and Behavior* 136 (November 2021); Eastwick, P.W., "Beyond the Pleistocene: Using Phylogeny and Constraint to Inform the Evolutionary Psychology of Human Mating," *Psychological Bulletin* 135, no. 5 (2009): 794–821; Fletcher, G.J.O., et al., "Pair-Bonding, Romantic Love, and Evolution: The Curious Case of *Homo sapiens*," *Perspectives on Psychological Science* 10, no. 1 (January 2015): 20–36.
12. Eastwick, "Beyond the Pleistocene," 794–821; Fletcher et al., "Pair-Bonding, Romantic Love, and Evolution," 20–36.
13. Bohannon, C., *Eve: How the Female Body Drove 200 Million Years of Human Evolution* (New York: Knopf, 2023); Prum, R.O., *The Evolution of Beauty: How Darwin's Forgotten Theory of Mate Choice Shapes the Animal World—and Us* (New York: Doubleday, 2017); Stanyon, R. and F. Bigoni, "Sexual Selection and the Evolution of Behavior, Morphology, Neuroanatomy and Genes in Humans and Other Primates," *Neuroscience & Biobehavioral Reviews* 46 (October 2014): 579–590.
14. Hazan and Diamond, "The Place of Attachment in Human Mating," 186–204.
15. Gettler, L.T., A.H. Boyette, and S. Rosenbaum, "Broadening Perspectives on the Evolution of Human Paternal Care and Fathers' Effects on Children," *Annual Review of Anthropology* 49 (2020): 141–160; Gray, P.B. and A.N. Crittenden, "Father Darwin: Effects of Children on Men, Viewed from an Evolutionary Perspective," *Fathering* 12, no. 2 (2014): 121–142; Hrdy, S.B., "The Optimal Number of Fathers: Evolution, Demography, and History in the Shaping of Female Preferences," *Annals of the New York Academy of Sciences* 907, no. 1 (April 2000): 75–96; Lew-Levy, S., et al., "How Do Hunter-Gatherer Children Learn Subsistence Skills?," *Human Nature* 28, no. 4 (December 2017): 367–394; Winking, J., et al., "The Goals of Direct Paternal Care among a South Amerindian Population," *American Journal of Physical Anthropology: The Official Publication of the American Association of Physical Anthropologists* 139, no. 3 (2009): 295–304.
16. Stewart-Williams, S. and A. Thomas, "The Ape That Thought It Was a Peacock: Does Evolutionary Psychology Exaggerate Human Sex Differences?," *Psychological Inquiry* 24, no. 3 (2013): 137–168.
17. Feeney, B.C. and N.L. Collins, "A New Look at Social Support: A Theoretical Perspective on Thriving Through Relationships," *Personality and Social Psychology Review* 19, no. 2 (May 2015): 113–147.

18. Feeney and Collins, "A New Look at Social Support," 113–147.
19. Diamond, L.M., "What Does Sexual Orientation Orient? A Biobehavioral Model Distinguishing Romantic Love and Sexual Desire," *Psychological Review* 110, no. 1 (February 2003): 173–192.
20. The scoring bins are rough approximations based on the means and standard deviations reported in table 1 for "attachment to partner" in Tancredy, C.M. and R.C. Fraley, "The Nature of Adult Twin Relationships: An Attachment-Theoretical Perspective," *Journal of Personality and Social Psychology* 90, no. 1 (January 2006): 78–93.
21. In a reanalysis of $N = 279$ people currently in relationships, safe haven and secure base correlated between $r = .64$ and $r = .73$ with satisfaction, commitment, and passion. These effect sizes are even larger than "large"; data from study 3 of Eastwick, P.W., E.J. Finkel, and A.H. Eagly, "When and Why Do Ideal Partner Preferences Affect the Process of Initiating and Maintaining Romantic Relationships?," *Journal of Personality and Social Psychology* 101, no. 5 (2011): 1012–1032. See also Joel, S., et al., "Machine Learning Uncovers the Most Robust Self-Report Predictors of Relationship Quality across 43 Longitudinal Couples Studies," *Proceedings of the National Academy of Sciences* 117, no. 32 (August 2020): 19061–19071.
22. Safe haven and secure base correlated at approximately $r = .30$ with romantic interest in a new prospective dating partner, a medium effect size that was larger than most of the other predictors of romantic interest in developing relationships, in appendix B in Eastwick, P.W., et al., "Predicting Romantic Interest during Early Relationship Development: A Preregistered Investigation Using Machine Learning," *European Journal of Personality* 37, no. 3 (May/June 2023): 276–312.
23. Of course, adults receive safe haven and secure base support from other people besides romantic partners: close friends, siblings, and even parents. If you don't have a romantic partner, that doesn't mean that you are out of luck. But it is also true that people who are partnered tend to believe that their romantic partners offer them the *most* safe haven and secure base support, on average, see Heffernan, M.E., et al., "Attachment Features and Functions in Adult Romantic Relationships," *Journal of Social and Personal Relationships* 29, no. 5 (August 2012): 671–693; Tancredy and Fraley, "The Nature of Adult Twin Relationships: An Attachment-Theoretical Perspective," 78–93.
24. Van Anders, S.M., "Beyond Sexual Orientation: Integrating Gender/Sex and Diverse Sexualities via Sexual Configurations Theory," *Archives of Sexual Behavior* 44, no. 5 (July 2015): 1177–1213.
25. Conley, T.D., et al., "Investigation of Consensually Nonmonogamous Relationships: Theories, Methods, and New Directions," *Perspectives on*

Psychological Science 12, no. 2 (March 2017): 205–232; Fletcher et al., "Pair-Bonding, Romantic Love, and Evolution," 20–36.

26. Girme, Y.U., Y. Park, and G. MacDonald, "Coping or Thriving? Reviewing Intrapersonal, Interpersonal, and Societal Factors Associated with Well-Being in Singlehood from a Within-Group Perspective," *Perspectives on Psychological Science* 18, no. 5 (2023): 1097–1120.
27. Diamond, "What Does Sexual Orientation Orient?," 173–192; Hazan and Diamond, "The Place of Attachment in Human Mating," 186–204; Jankowiak and Fischer, "A Cross-cultural Perspective on Romantic Love," 149–155; Van Anders, "Beyond Sexual Orientation," 1177–1213.
28. Perel, E., *Mating in Captivity: Reconciling the Erotic and the Domestic* (New York: Harper Collins, 2006).
29. Feeney and Collins, "A New Look at Social Support," 113–147.
30. Gable, S.L. and H.T. Reis, "Good News! Capitalizing on Positive Events in an Interpersonal Context," *Advances in Experimental Social Psychology*, ed. M.P. Zanna, vol. 42 (San Diego: Academic Press, 2010), 195–257.
31. Bradbury, T.N. and B.R. Karney, *Intimate Relationships*, 4th ed. (New York: Norton, 2024).
32. A meta-analysis found that strong social relationships increased the likelihood of survival, $r = .11$. That may be only a small effect, but keep in mind that all the predictors of mortality are modest by the standards of our ruler (exercise and quitting smoking are also small), see Holt-Lunstad, J., T.B. Smith, and J.B. Layton, "Social Relationships and Mortality Risk: A Meta-analytic Review," *PLOS Medicine* 7, no. 7 (2010).

CHAPTER 5

1. The effect size of this manipulation was medium-to-large, $r = .37$ on average across study 1 (the "conflict is good" study) and study 2 (the "differences are good" study) in Murray, S.L. and J.G. Holmes, "Seeing Virtues in Faults: Negativity and the Transformation of Interpersonal Narratives in Close Relationships," *Journal of Personality and Social Psychology* 65, no. 4 (October 1993): 707–722.
2. The effect size for this manipulation was large ($r = .48$) in Rusbult, C.E., et al., "Perceived Superiority in Close Relationships: Why It Exists and Persists," *Journal of Personality and Social Psychology* 79, no. 4 (2000): 521–545.
3. The association between "yes, butting" and relationship stability was $r = .29$— a medium effect size—in Murray, S.L. and J.G. Holmes, "The (Mental) Ties That Bind: Cognitive Structures That Predict Relationship Resilience," *Journal of Personality and Social Psychology* 77, no. 6 (1999): 1228–1244.

4. Heffernan, M.E., et al., "Attachment Features and Functions in Adult Romantic Relationships," *Journal of Social and Personal Relationships* 29, no. 5 (August 2012): 671–693; Joel, S. and G. MacDonald, "We're Not That Choosy: Emerging Evidence of a Progression Bias in Romantic Relationships," *Personality and Social Psychology Review* 25, no. 4 (November 2021): 317–343; Joel, S., R. Teper, and G. MacDonald, "People Overestimate Their Willingness to Reject Potential Romantic Partners by Overlooking Their Concern for Other People," *Psychological Science* 25, no. 12 (December 2014): 2233–2240.

5. Joel, S., et al., "Machine Learning Uncovers the Most Robust Self-Report Predictors of Relationship Quality across 43 Longitudinal Couples Studies," *Proceedings of the National Academy of Sciences* 117, no. 32 (August 2020): 19061–19071.

6. Cassidy, J. and P.R. Shaver, eds., *Handbook of Attachment: Theory, Research, and Clinical Applications,* 2nd ed. (New York: Guilford Press, 2008).

7. Levine, A., and R. Heller, *Attached: The New Science of Adult Attachment and How It Can Help You Find—and Keep—Love* (New York: Tarcher/Penguin Random House, 2012).

8. A given person's satisfaction in one relationship correlated with their satisfaction in a different relationship at $r = .21$ (on average), which has the same meaning as a 60/40 split, across three studies: Bühler, J.L. and U. Orth, "How Relationship Satisfaction Changes within and across Romantic Relationships: Evidence from a Large Longitudinal Study," *Journal of Personality and Social Psychology* 126, no. 5 (May 2024): 930–945; Johnson, M.D. and F.J. Neyer, "(Eventual) Stability and Change across Partnerships," *Journal of Family Psychology* 33, no. 6 (February 2019): 711–721; Robins, R.W., A. Caspi, and T.E. Moffitt, "It's Not Just Who You're with, It's Who You Are: Personality and Relationship Experiences across Multiple Relationships," *Journal of Personality* 70, no. 6 (December 2002): 925–964.

9. Bühler and Orth, "How Relationship Satisfaction Changes within and across Romantic Relationships," 930–945. Also, the effect of going to therapy on perceiving close others to be more supportive was $r = .19$ in this meta-analysis: Park, M., et al., "The Effects of Psychotherapy for Adult Depression on Social Support: A Meta-analysis," *Cognitive Therapy and Research* 38, no. 6 (2014): 600–611.

10. Across a variety of longitudinal studies, the predictive effect of early childhood attachment experiences on adult attachment style is about $r = .15$, which is a small effect: Fraley, R.C. and G.I. Roisman, "The Development of Adult Attachment Styles: Four Lessons," *Current Opinion in Psychology* 25 (February 2019): 26–30.

11. Fraley, R.C., O. Gillath, and P.R. Deboeck, "Do Life Events Lead to Enduring Changes in Adult Attachment Styles? A Naturalistic Longitudinal

Investigation," *Journal of Personality and Social Psychology* 120, no. 6 (June 2021): 1567–1606.

12. A given person's attachment avoidance in one relationship correlated with their avoidance in a different relationship at $r = .16$ (a small effect), and their attachment anxiety in one relationship correlated with their anxiety in a different relationship at $r = .31$ (a medium effect), in Moors, A.C., W. Ryan, and W.J. Chopik, "Multiple Loves: The Effects of Attachment with Multiple Concurrent Romantic Partners on Relational Functioning," *Personality and Individual Differences* 147 (September 2019): 102–110.

13. Lydon, J.E. and J.C. Karremans, "Relationship Regulation in the Face of Eye Candy: A Motivated Cognition Framework for Understanding Responses to Attractive Alternatives," *Current Opinion in Psychology* 1 (February 2015): 76–80. One of the first demonstrations of this phenomenon found that men and women in dating relationships thought that opposite-gender people depicted in ads from popular magazines were less attractive and less sexually desirable than single people did, $r = .25$ for both men and women in Simpson, J.A., S.W. Gangestad, and M. Lerma, "Perception of Physical Attractiveness: Mechanisms Involved in the Maintenance of Romantic Relationships," *Journal of Personality and Social Psychology* 59, no. 6 (1990): 1192–1201.

14. The extent to which relationship status predicted the attractiveness of the recalled sketch (in the attractive face condition) was $r = .41$, a medium-to-large effect, in Karremans, J.C., R. Dotsch, and O. Corneille, "Romantic Relationship Status Biases Memory of Faces of Attractive Opposite-Sex Others: Evidence from a Reverse-Correlation Paradigm," *Cognition* 121, no. 3 (December 2011): 422–426.

15. The extent to which relationship status predicted the tendency to exhibit inviting body language (in this case, to "mimic" the interaction partner) ranged from medium to very large, $r = .65$ (study 1), $r = .37$ (study 2), and $r = .30$ (study 3), in Karremans, J.C. and T. Verwijmeren, "Mimicking Attractive Opposite-Sex Others: The Role of Romantic Relationship Status," *Personality and Social Psychology Bulletin* 34, no. 7 (July 2008): 939–950.

16. The participants who recalled a time when they felt especially in love with their partner paid less attention to the attractive, opposite-gender faces than participants who simply recalled a time when they felt happy. The difference between these two groups was $r = .19$—a small-to-medium effect—in Maner, J.K., D.A. Rouby, and G.C. Gonzaga, "Automatic Inattention to Attractive Alternatives: The Evolved Psychology of Relationship Maintenance," *Evolution and Human Behavior* 29, no. 5 (September 2008): 343–349.

17. Participants who engaged in a brief fantasy about an alternative partner reported more sexual desire for their current partner with a medium-size effect, $r = .28$.

Especially fascinating is that this effect is a little larger than the effect of engaging in a brief fantasy about an alternative partner *on sexual desire for the alternative partner*, which was $r = .21$. In other words, a sexual fantasy about an alternative partner caused sexual desire to rebound onto an existing partner more strongly than it boosted sexual desire for the alternative partner in the first place, data from table 5 in Peters, S.D., J.K. Maner, and A.L. Meltzer, "Sexual Desire Is Not Partner-Specific: Evidence for a Positive Association between Desire for One's Romantic Partner and Desire for Alternative Partners," *Human Nature* 35 (2024): 323–346.

18. The extent to which commitment is associated with believing you have poor alternatives to your current partner ranges from $r = .50$—.60, which is a large effect. In other words, highly committed people tend not to have eyes for others, see meta-analysis in Le, B. and C.R. Agnew, "Commitment and Its Theorized Determinants: A Meta-analysis of the Investment Model," *Personal Relationships* 10, no. 1 (March 2003): 37–57.

19. Cohas, A. and D. Allainé, "Social Structure Influences Extra-Pair Paternity in Socially Monogamous Mammals," *Biology Letters* 5, no. 3 (2009): 313–316; Fletcher, G.J.O., et al., "Pair-Bonding, Romantic Love, and Evolution: The Curious Case of *Homo sapiens*," *Perspectives on Psychological Science* 10, no. 1 (January 2015): 20–36; Griffith, S.C., I.P. Owens, and K.A. Thuman, "Extra Pair Paternity in Birds: a Review of Interspecific Variation and Adaptive Function," *Molecular Ecology* 11, no. 11 (November 2002): 2195–2212; Larmuseau, M.H.D., K. Matthijs, and T. Wenseleers, "Cuckolded Fathers Rare in Human Populations," *Trends in Ecology & Evolution* 31, no. 5 (May 2016): 327–329.

20. Ezra expressed some discomfort with the "relationships as transactional" concept, while citing the influence of the market metaphor, on Klein, E., "Dan Savage on Polyamory, Chosen Family and Better Sex," January 10, 2023, *The Ezra Klein Show* (podcast), https://www.nytimes.com/2023/01/10/podcasts/ezra-klein-show-transcript-dan-savage.html.

21. Clark, M.S., et al., "Communal Relational Context (or Lack Thereof) Shapes Emotional Lives," *Current Opinion in Psychology* 17 (2017): 176–183; Clark, M.S. and J. Mills, "The Difference between Communal and Exchange Relationships: What It Is and Is Not," *Personality & Social Psychology Bulletin* 19, no. 6 (December 1993): 684–691.

22. Call, J., "Social Knowledge in Primates," in *The Oxford Handbook of Evolutionary Psychology*, ed. L. Barrett and R. Dunbar (New York: Oxford University Press, 2007), 71–81.

23. Burkart, J.M., S.B. Hrdy, and C.P. Van Schaik, "Cooperative Breeding and Human Cognitive Evolution," *Evolutionary Anthropology: Issues, News, and Reviews* 18, no. 5 (September/October 2009): 175–186.

24. Participants who ate a tasty chocolate with someone else liked it more (and found it more flavorful) than participants who did not eat it with someone else, $r = .27$ (a medium-size effect), in Boothby, E.J., M.S. Clark, and J.A. Bargh, "Shared Experiences Are Amplified," *Psychological Science* 25, no. 12 (December 2014): 2209–2216.
25. Burkart, Hrdy, and Van Schaik, "Cooperative Breeding and Human Cognitive Evolution," 175–186; Gergely, G. and G. Csibra, "The Social Construction of the Cultural Mind: Imitative Learning as a Mechanism of Human Pedagogy," *Interaction Studies* 6, no. 3 (January 2005): 463–481; Rossignac-Milon, M. and E.T. Higgins, "Epistemic Companions: Shared Reality Development in Close Relationships," *Current Opinion in Psychology* 23 (October 2018): 66–71.
26. When thinking about an ideal marriage, people were more likely to believe that partners "should pay attention to the other person's needs ... [such that] when one person does something for the other, the other should not owe the giver anything" than they were to believe that partners "should benefit [each] other with the expectation of receiving a benefit of similar value in return ... [and] keep track of benefits given and received in order to keep them in balance." The effect size between the first (communal) and second (exchange) description was $r = .89$, which is the largest effect size in this book. When couples completed these same questions about their current relationship, the effect size was $r = .82$, which is the second largest effect in this book, see Clark, M.S., et al., "Ways of Giving Benefits in Marriage: Norm Use, Relationship Satisfaction, and Attachment-Related Variability," *Psychological Science* 21, no. 7 (July 2010): 944–951. (Effect sizes were converted from *df* and *t* to *r* using the calculator at https://lbecker.uccs.edu/.) See also Clark, M.S. and O.R. Aragón, "Communal (and Other) Relationships: History, Theory Development, Recent Findings, and Future Directions," in *The Oxford Handbook of Close Relationships*, ed. J.A. Simpson and L.E. Campbell (New York: Oxford University Press, 2013), 255–280.
27. The average correlation between current relationship satisfaction and the extent to which participants felt that they themselves and/or their partner took an exchange approach to their relationship was $r = -.23$, a small-to-medium size negative effect, across two time points in table S1 in Clark et al., "Ways of Giving Benefits in Marriage," 944–951. In a meta-analysis across dozens of studies, the average association of communal strength ("How high a priority for you is meeting the needs of your partner?") with relationship satisfaction was $r = .44$ (a large effect), and the average association of communal strength with one's own personal well-being was $r = .16$ (a small effect), see Le, B.M., et al., "Communal Motivation and Well-Being in Interpersonal Relationships: An Integrative Review and Meta-analysis," *Psychological Bulletin* 144, no. 1 (2018): 1–25.

28. Fitzsimons, G.M., E.J. Finkel, and M.R. vanDellen, "Transactive Goal Dynamics," *Psychological Review* 122, no. 4 (2015): 648–673.
29. The intertwining of goals predicts relationship satisfaction at $r = .29$, a medium-size effect, in Fitzsimons, G.M. and E.J. Finkel, "Testing Transactive Goal Dynamics Theory" (unpublished raw data, Duke University, 2019), personal communication.
30. Gottman, J.M., "Psychology and the study of marital processes," *Annual Review of Psychology* 49 (1998): 169–197.
31. The average effect of daily stress (beyond what a person typically experiences) on daily "negative behaviors" was $r = .28$—a medium-size effect—in Buck, A.A. and L.A. Neff, "Stress Spillover in Early Marriage: The Role of Self-Regulatory Depletion," *Journal of Family Psychology* 26, no. 5 (October 2012): 698–708. The average effect of stress on marital satisfaction was $r = -.19$, which is a small-to-medium-size effect, in SI table 2 in McNulty, J.K., et al., "How Both Partners' Individual Differences, Stress, and Behavior Predict Change in Relationship Satisfaction: Extending the VSA Model," *Proceedings of the National Academy of Sciences* 118, no. 27 (July 2021). See also Neff, L.A. and B.R. Karney, "Acknowledging the Elephant in the Room: How Stressful Environmental Contexts Shape Relationship Dynamics," *Current Opinion in Psychology* 13 (February 2017): 107–110.
32. Waddell, N., et al., "Gendered Division of Labor During a Nationwide COVID-19 Lockdown: Implications for Relationship Problems and Satisfaction," *Journal of Social and Personal Relationships* 38, no. 6 (June 2021): 1759–1781.
33. The intersection of stress and communal norms has implications for the way we think about gender differences in housework. When times are good, couples tend to divvy up household tasks based on their relative preferences. If your partner truly hates doing the dishes, you're happy to do it. They're a great cook, so it's to your mutual benefit for them to handle the meals most of the time. When couples do this, the reality is that women end up taking on more of the housework in mixed-gender relationships on average. In fact, the gender difference in the extent to which women take on more household tasks ($r = .44$ gender difference in who *does* "indoor cleaning") is considerably larger than the gender difference in the preference for those tasks ($r = .14$ gender difference in *liking* "indoor cleaning"). It's quite possible that when waters are calm, neither couple member has concerns about this imbalance. But it becomes a problem when the stress hits: Someone is laid off, a family member gets sick, or parenthood becomes imminent, and now the pattern that once fit everyone's preferences now feels notably unfair to the underbenefited party, which is usually the woman. Effect sizes from Bleske-Rechek, A. and M.M. Gunseor, "Gendered

Perspectives on Sharing the Load: Men's and Women's Attitudes toward Family Roles and Household and Childcare Tasks," *Evolutionary Behavioral Sciences* 16, no. 3 (2022): 201–219. See also Carlson, D., R. Petts, and J. Pepin, "Men and Women Agree: During the COVID-19 Pandemic Men Are Doing More at Home," Council on Contemporary Families, May 20, 2020.

34. Buss, D.M., *When Men Behave Badly: The Hidden Roots of Sexual Deception, Harassment, and Assault* (New York: Little Brown Spark, 2021). For the original Dr. Irven DeVore quote, see "Behavior: Sociobiology and Sex," *Time*, August 1, 1977. Available at https://content.time.com/time/subscriber/article/0,33009,915182,00.html.

35. Prum, R.O., *The Evolution of Beauty: How Darwin's Forgotten Theory of Mate Choice Shapes the Animal World—and Us* (New York: Doubleday, 2017).

CHAPTER 6

1. Fisher, H.E., "*The Brain in Love*," TED Talk, February 2008, https://www.ted.com/talks/helen_fisher_the_brain_in_love?language=en; Fisher, H.E., "Technology hasn't changed love. Here's why," June 2016; https://www.ted.com/talks/helen_fisher_technology_hasn_t_changed_love_here_s_why/transcript?language=en.
2. Kenny, D.A., *Interpersonal Perception: The Foundation of Social Relationships*, 2nd ed. (New York: Guilford Press, 2019).
3. Eastwick, P.W. and L.L. Hunt, "Relational Mate Value: Consensus and Uniqueness in Romantic Evaluations," *Journal of Personality and Social Psychology* 106, no. 5 (March 2014): 728–751.
4. Joel, S., et al., "Machine Learning Uncovers the Most Robust Self-Report Predictors of Relationship Quality across 43 Longitudinal Couples Studies," *Proceedings of the National Academy of Sciences* 117, no. 32 (August 2020): 19061–19071.
5. Eastwick and Hunt, "Relational Mate Value," 728–751.
6. Feeney, B.C. and N.L. Collins, "A New Look at Social Support: A Theoretical Perspective on Thriving Through Relationships," *Personality and Social Psychology Review* 19, no. 2 (May 2015): 113–147; Lakey, B. and E. Orehek, "Relational Regulation Theory: A New Approach to Explain the Link between Perceived Social Support and Mental Health," *Psychological Review* 118, no. 3 (July 2011): 482–495.
7. Eastwick and Hunt, "Relational Mate Value," 728–751.
8. Houts, R.M., E. Robins, and T.L. Huston, "Compatibility and the Development of Premarital Relationships," *Journal of Marriage and the Family* 58, no. 1 (February 1996): 7–20; Youyou, W., et al., "Birds of a Feather Do Flock

Together: Behavior-based Personality-Assessment Method Reveals Personality Similarity among Couples and Friends," *Psychological Science* 28, no. 3 (March 2017): 276–284; Watson, D., et al., "Match Makers and Deal Breakers: Analyses of Assortative Mating in Newlywed Couples," *Journal of Personality* 72, no. 5 (November 2004): 1029–1068.

9. Luo, S., "Assortative Mating and Couple Similarity: Patterns, Mechanisms, and Consequences," *Social and Personality Psychology Compass* 11, no. 8 (August 2017).

10. Iyengar, S., T. Konitzer, and K. Tedin, "The Home as a Political Fortress: Family Agreement in an Era of Polarization," *The Journal of Politics* 80, no. 4 (October 2018): 1326–1338.

11. The difference in attraction between the $N = 32$ dyads who sat next to each other and the $N = 1302$ dyads who did not sit next to each other was $r = .62$, which is an enormous effect size (and when converted to an odds ratio is 17.6, or nearly 20 times higher). Data from Back, M.D., S.C. Schmukle, and B. Egloff, "Becoming Friends by Chance," *Psychological Science* 19, no. 5 (May 2008): 439. When two individuals shared no acquaintances but at least one class, they were on average 140 times more likely to interact than if they shared no acquaintances and no classes in Kossinets, G. and D.J. Watts, "Empirical Analysis of an Evolving Social Network," *Science* 311, no. 5757 (January 2006): 88–90.

12. Reis, H.T., et al., "Familiarity Does Indeed Promote Attraction in Live Interaction," *Journal of Personality and Social Psychology* 101, no. 3 (2011): 557–570.

13. These studies all calculate similarity in different ways, with different traits and attributes. There is not a single trait, value, or preference that consistently shows similarity effects across these studies, and the average effect size of similarity on attraction for the studies that report all tests is less than small, $r = .03$: Humberg, S., et al., "Is (Actual or Perceptual) Personality Similarity Associated with Attraction in Initial Romantic Encounters? A Dyadic Response Surface Analysis," *Personality Science* 4, no. 1 (April 2023): 1–25; Kurzban, R. and J. Weeden, "HurryDate: Mate Preferences in Action," *Evolution and Human Behavior* 26, no. 3 (May 2005): 227–244; Luo, S. and G. Zhang, "What Leads to Romantic Attraction: Similarity, Reciprocity, Security, or Beauty? Evidence from a Speed-Dating Study," *Journal of Personality* 77, no. 4 (July 2009): 933–964; Tidwell, N.D., P.W. Eastwick, and E.J. Finkel, "Perceived, Not Actual, Similarity Predicts Initial Attraction in a Live Romantic Context: Evidence from the Speed-Dating Paradigm," *Personal Relationships* 20, no. 2 (June 2013): 199–215; Wurst, S.N., S. Humberg, and M.D. Back, "The Impact of Mate Value in First and Subsequent Real-Life Romantic Encounters" (preprint, submitted January 26, 2018), https://osf.io/adej3/. Critically, all of these studies examine

similarity one trait at a time, but the same story emerges if you use an approach that estimates the effect of all traits simultaneously. In a reanalysis of the data in Tidwell, Eastwick, and Finkel, "Perceived, Not Actual, Similarity Predicts Initial Attraction," 199–215, the effect of overall similarity on attraction—using a statistically appropriate approach that captures all attributes—was less than small ($r = .02$).

14. Eastwick, P.W., et al., "Consistency and Inconsistency among Romantic Partners over Time," *Journal of Personality and Social Psychology* 112, no. 6 (March 2017): 838–859.

15. As with the attraction studies, these studies calculate similarity in different ways and with different attributes. Again, there is no trait, value, or preference for which similarity consistently predicts attraction. Across all the studies that report all tests, the similarity-satisfaction effect size on average is less than small, $r = .03$: Chopik, W.J. and R.E. Lucas, "Actor, Partner, and Similarity Effects of Personality on Global and Experienced Well-Being," *Journal of Research in Personality* 78 (February 2019): 249–261; Dyrenforth, P.S., et al., "Predicting Relationship and Life Satisfaction from Personality in Nationally Representative Samples from Three Countries: The Relative Importance of Actor, Partner, and Similarity Effects," *Journal of Personality and Social Psychology* 99, no. 4 (August 2010): 690–702; Gordon, A.M., M. Luciani, and A. From, "I Love You but I Hate Your Politics: The Role of Political Dissimilarity in Romantic Relationships," *Journal of Personality and Social Psychology* (July 2024); Luo, S., "Partner Selection and Relationship Satisfaction in Early Dating Couples: The Role of Couple Similarity," *Personality and Individual Differences* 47, no. 2 (July 2009): 133–138; Malouff, J.M., et al., "The Five-Factor Model of Personality and Relationship Satisfaction of Intimate Partners: A Meta-analysis," *Journal of Research in Personality* 44, no. 1 (February 2010): 124–127; Watson et al., "Match Makers and Deal Breakers," 1029–1068; Weidmann, R., et al., "Trait and Facet Personality Similarity and Relationship and Life Satisfaction in Romantic Couples," *Journal of Research in Personality* 104 (2023).

16. In contrast to the infinitesimal effect sizes of actual similarity discussed above, the correlation between perceived similarity ("My partner and I have a lot in common") and attraction is a whopping $r = .75$, which is enormous. It doesn't matter whether you are actually similar to someone; it just matters that you *find* some similarities to focus on, see Tidwell, Eastwick, and Finkel, "Perceived, Not Actual, Similarity Predicts Initial Attraction," 199–215.

17. Goel, S., W. Mason, and D.J. Watts, "Real and Perceived Attitude Agreement in Social Networks," *Journal of Personality and Social Psychology* 99, no. 4 (2010): 611–621; Higgins, E.T., M. Rossignac-Milon, and G. Echterhoff, "Shared Reality: From Sharing-Is-Believing to Merging Minds," *Current Directions in*

Psychological Science 30, no. 2 (April 2021): 103–110; Morry, M.M., "Relationship Satisfaction as a Predictor of Similarity Ratings: A Test of the Attraction-Similarity Hypothesis," *Journal of Social and Personal Relationships* 22, no. 4 (August 2005): 561–584; Morry, M.M., M. Kito, and L. Ortiz, "The Attraction-Similarity Model and Dating Couples: Projection, Perceived Similarity, and Psychological Benefits," *Personal Relationships* 18, no. 1 (March 2011): 125–143.

18. Campbell, L., et al., "Ideal Standards, the Self, and Flexibility of Ideals in Close Relationships," *Personality and Social Psychology Bulletin* 27, no. 4 (April 2001): 447–462.

19. The scientific literature on this topic has historically been a huge mess. One of the problems is that if you ask people about their preferences, you get many of the same answers repeatedly: Everyone wants a partner who is hot, funny, and kind. Only some people want a partner who is shy, good with animals, and makes a dynamite grilled cheese. What if people tended to like hot/funny/kind guy more than shy/good-with-animals/grilled-cheese guy? Should we conclude that compatibility is explained by people liking partners who match their preferences? No, not really. It's the chapter 1 phenomenon "we are initially attracted to people with great traits." All else equal, being hot is more appealing than being shy, being funny is more appealing than being good with animals, and being kind is more appealing than the ability to make a great grilled cheese. There are statistical and analytical approaches that dodge this issue and get at the true "matching" component, but not many studies have historically used the correct approaches. For more details, see Eastwick, P.W., E.J. Finkel, and J.A. Simpson, "Best Practices for Testing the Predictive Validity of Ideal Partner Preference-Matching," *Personality and Social Psychology Bulletin* 45, no. 2 (February 2019): 167–181; Wood, D. and R.M. Furr, "The Correlates of Similarity Estimates Are Often Misleadingly Positive: The Nature and Scope of the Problem, and Some Solutions," *Personality and Social Psychology Review* 20, no. 2 (May 2016): 79–99.

20. The correlation of the "corrected pattern metric" (i.e., the statistically appropriate choice) with attraction was $r = .19$ for people who were single and $r = .17$ for people who were partnered in Eastwick, P.W., et al., "A Worldwide Test of the Predictive Validity of Ideal Partner Preference-Matching," *Journal of Personality and Social Psychology* 128, no. 1 (2025), 123–146.

21. The average effect size was $r = .03$—which is extremely small—in Sparks, J., et al., "Negligible Evidence That People Desire Partners Who Uniquely Fit Their Ideals," *Journal of Experimental Social Psychology* 90 (September 2020).

22. Da Silva Frost, A. and P.W. Eastwick, "Experimental Tests of the Role of Ideal Partner Preferences in Relationships," *Personality and Social Psychology Bulletin*,

in press; Eastwick, P.W., E.J. Finkel, and A.H. Eagly, "When and Why Do Ideal Partner Preferences Affect the Process of Initiating and Maintaining Romantic Relationships?," *Journal of Personality and Social Psychology* 101, no. 5 (2011): 1012–1032.

23. Chapman, G.D., *The Five Love Languages: How to Express Heartfelt Commitment to Your Mate* (Chicago: Northfield Publishing, 1992).

24. Canary, D.J. and L. Stafford, "Relational Maintenance Strategies and Equity in Marriage," *Communication Monographs*, 59, no. 3 (1992): 243–267; Impett, E.A., H.G. Park, and A. Muise, "Popular Psychology through a Scientific Lens: Evaluating Love Languages from a Relationship Science Perspective," *Current Directions in Psychological Science* 33, no. 2 (April 2024): 87–92.

25. Egbert, N. and D. Polk, "Speaking the Language of Relational Maintenance: A Validity Test of Chapman's Five Love Languages," *Communication Research Reports* 23, no. 1 (2006): 19–26. The idea that love languages are "lovely things that partners do for each other" is captured by the simple correlation between each person's "expressed" love language and their partner's relationship satisfaction. Those values, averaged across all people in the dataset, were: quality time $r = .25$; words of affirmation $r = .23$; gifts $r = .19$; physical touch $r = .15$; acts of service $r = .08$. Data from Mostova, O., M. Stolarski, and G. Matthews, "I Love the Way You Love Me: Responding to Partner's Love Language Preferences Boosts Satisfaction in Romantic Heterosexual Couples," *PLOS One* 17, no. 6 (2022).

26. A wonderful thing about the Mostova, Stolarski, and Matthews paper "I Love the Way You Love Me" is that the data are openly available to anyone who would like to reanalyze them. As it happens, this article did not report the proper test of a matching hypothesis, which is commonly called a "corrected pattern metric" test (see Eastwick, Finkel, and Simpson, et al., "Best Practices for Testing the Predictive Validity of Ideal Partner Preference-Matching," 167–181). I conducted the test myself on the raw data, and the effect of similarity on satisfaction was $r = .07$ ($r = .05$ for men and $r = .09$ for women). In other words, the effect of love-language matching is less than small. For an accessible discussion of the science of love languages, see Impett, "Popular Psychology through a Scientific Lens," 87–92.

27. Shamshiri, P. and M. Hobbes, "The 5 Love Languages," April 20, 2023, *If Books Could Kill* (podcast), https://www.buzzsprout.com/2040953/episodes/12684857-the-5-love-languages.

28. Finkel, E.J., et al., "Online Dating: A Critical Analysis from the Perspective of Psychological Science," *Psychological Science in the Public Interest* 13, no. 1 (January 2012): 3–66.

29. Le, B.M., et al., "Communal Motivation and Well-Being in Interpersonal Relationships: An Integrative Review and Meta-analysis," *Psychological Bulletin* 144, no. 1 (2018): 1–25.
30. Finkel, et al., "Online Dating," 3–66.
31. Joel, S., P.W. Eastwick, and E.J. Finkel, "Is Romantic Desire Predictable? Machine Learning Applied to Initial Romantic Attraction," *Psychological Science* 28, no. 10 (October 2017): 1478–1489.
32. Lakey, B., et al., "When Forecasting Mutually Supportive Matches Will Be Practically Impossible," *Psychological Science* 32, no. 5 (May 2021): 780–788.
33. The Joel et al. study "Machine Learning Uncovers the Most Robust Self-Report Predictors of Relationship Quality" has many analyses, but here we're focused on whether partner 2's attributes—all of his/her traits, values, and personality attributes—explain partner 1's relationship satisfaction and commitment above and beyond partner 1's own attributes. In these machine learning models, if certain couples were especially compatible with each other based on their attributes, then adding partner 2's attributes should boost predictive power, relative to models that only contained partner 1's attributes. But these boosts were tiny; adding partner 2's attributes boosted the models by only about 2 percent when predicting relationship satisfaction and about 1 percent when predicting commitment.
34. Tiffany, K., "The Woman Who Made Online Dating into a 'Science,'" *The Atlantic*, December 11, 2022.

CHAPTER 7

1. Eastwick, P.W., E.J. Finkel, and S. Joel, "Mate Evaluation Theory," *Psychological Review* 130, no. 1 (2023): 211–241; Eastwick, P.W., et al., "Consistency and Inconsistency among Romantic Partners over Time," *Journal of Personality and Social Psychology* 112, no. 6 (March 2017): 838–859; Johnson, M.D. and F.J. Neyer, "(Eventual) Stability and Change across Partnerships," *Journal of Family Psychology* 33, no. 6 (February 2019): 711–721; Robins, R.W., A. Caspi, and T.E. Moffitt, "It's Not Just Who You're with, It's Who You Are: Personality and Relationship Experiences across Multiple Relationships," *Journal of Personality* 70, no. 6 (December 2002): 925–964.
2. Eastwick, P.W., E.J. Finkel, and J.A. Simpson, "Relationship Trajectories: A Meta-Theoretical Framework and Theoretical Applications," *Psychological Inquiry* 30, no. 1 (2019): 1–28; Eastwick, P.W., et al., "What Do Short-Term and Long-Term Relationships Look Like? Building the Relationship Coordination and Strategic Timing (ReCAST) Model," *Journal of Experimental Psychology: General* 147, no. 5 (May 2018): 747–781.

3. Prum, R.O., *The Evolution of Beauty: How Darwin's Forgotten Theory of Mate Choice Shapes the Animal World—and Us* (New York: Doubleday, 2017).
4. Prum, *The Evolution of Beauty*. For more details, see Hazan, C. and L.M. Diamond, "The Place of Attachment in Human Mating," *Review of General Psychology* 4, no. 2 (June 2000): 186–204.
5. Smith, E.R. and E.C. Collins, "Contextualizing Person Perception: Distributed Social Cognition," *Psychological Review* 116, no. 2 (2009): 343–364.
6. Smith and Collins, "Contextualizing Person Perception," 343–364; Weigel, D. and C. Murray, "The Paradox of Stability and Change in Relationships: What Does Chaos Theory Offer for the Study of Romantic Relationships?," *Journal of Social and Personal Relationships* 17, no. 3 (June 2000): 425–449.
7. Showalter, S., November 18, 2022, https://www.tiktok.com/@thesam_show/video/7167426202792217898.
8. Finkel, E.J., "Romantic Relationships," in *The Handbook of Social Psychology*, ed. Gilbert, D., et al., 6th ed. (Cambridge, MA: Situational Press, 2025).
9. The association between the vividness, intensity, and ease-of-recall of people's relationship origin stories was associated with marital satisfaction at $r = .23$—a medium-size effect—in Alea, N. and S.C. Vick, "The First Sight of Love: Relationship-Defining Memories and Marital Satisfaction across Adulthood," *Memory* 18, no. 7 (2010): 730–742.
10. Inclusion of the other in the self-predicted staying together with a medium-size effect of $r = .33$ in Le, B., et al., "Predicting Nonmarital Romantic Relationship Dissolution: A Meta-analytic Synthesis," *Personal Relationships* 17, no. 3 (2010): 377–390. Self-expansion predicted (a) greater satisfaction and commitment in two studies (with a large effect size $r = .56$), and (b) a lower likelihood of emotional and sexual infidelity (with a medium-size effect of $r = -.22$) in Mattingly, B.A., G.W. Lewandowski Jr., and K.P. McIntyre, "'You Make Me a Better/Worse Person': A Two-Dimensional Model of Relationship Self-Change," *Personal Relationships* 21, no. 1 (March 2014): 176–190. For additional discussion, see Aron, A., M. Paris, and E.N. Aron, "Falling in Love: Prospective Studies of Self-Concept Change," *Journal of Personality and Social Psychology* 69, no. 6 (1995): 1102–1112.
11. Berscheid, E., "Compatibility, Interdependence, and Emotion," in *Compatible and Incompatible Relationships,* ed. W. Ickes (New York: Springer, 1985), 143–161.
12. Bradbury, T.N. and B.R. Karney, *Intimate Relationships,* 4th ed. (New York: Norton, 2024).
13. Alcser-Isais, A.N. and P.W. Eastwick, "Liking Different People for Different Reasons" (unpublished Raw Data, University of California, Davis, 2023), https://osf.io/bp3xr?view_only=c5ea928f02d74364ad605c8ec6ed4e20; Hall, J.A.,

"Humor in Romantic Relationships: A Meta-analysis," *Personal Relationships* 24, no. 2 (2017): 306–322.

14. Eastwick, Finkel, and Joel, "Mate Evaluation Theory," 211–241.
15. Knee, C.R., "Implicit Theories of Relationships: Assessment and Prediction of Romantic Relationship Initiation, Coping, and Longevity," *Journal of Personality and Social Psychology* 74, no. 2 (February 1998): 360–370.
16. The difference in closeness between the 36 escalating-intimacy questions and the 36 small-talk questions was $r = .40$—which is a medium-to-large effect—in Aron, A., et al., "The Experimental Generation of Interpersonal Closeness: A Procedure and Some Preliminary Findings," *Personality and Social Psychology Bulletin* 23, no. 4 (April 1997): 363–377.
17. Across the (many!) studies that captured the extent to which people incorrectly estimate how awkward, connected, and happy they feel when talking to strangers in dyads, the average effect size for this misestimation effect was large ($r = .59$) in Kardas, M., A. Kumar, and N. Epley, "Overly Shallow?: Miscalibrated Expectations Create a Barrier to Deeper Conversation," *Journal of Personality and Social Psychology* 122, no. 3 (2022): 367–398.
18. Hill, F., "Can You Ever Really Escape Your Ex?," *The Atlantic*, March 27, 2024.
19. Joel, S. and G. MacDonald, "We're Not That Choosy: Emerging Evidence of a Progression Bias in Romantic Relationships," *Personality and Social Psychology Review* 25, no. 4 (November 2021): 317–343.
20. Bühler, J.L. and U. Orth, "How Relationship Satisfaction Changes within and across Romantic Relationships: Evidence from a Large Longitudinal Study," *Journal of Personality and Social Psychology* 126, no. 5 (May 2024): 930–945.
21. A clear example of the challenges of teaching relationship skills at scale comes from the Supporting Healthy Marriage program spearheaded by the U.S. Department of Health and Human Services. This yearlong program delivered about twenty-five hours of a relationship-skills curriculum to thousands of couples in a workshop-type setting. The skills reinforced by this program are certainly "good things to do" in relationships: don't be contemptuous of your partner, validate their experiences, take responsibility for your contributions to the conflict, etc. But the results showed that you can't really imbue people with these skills in a nontherapeutic, classroom setting: After couples completed the program, they experienced a very tiny gain in marital happiness, with a near-zero effect size of $r = .06$ above and beyond a control group who did not go through the program in Hsueh, J., et al., *The Supporting Healthy Marriage Evaluation: Early Impacts on Low-Income Families* (New York: Office of Planning, Research and Evaluation, Administration for Children and Families, 2012). For additional discussion of this study, see Bradbury and Karney, *Intimate Relationships*; Rogge, R.D., et al., "Is Skills Training Necessary for the Primary Prevention of Marital

Distress and Dissolution? A 3-Year Experimental Study of Three Interventions," *Journal of Consulting and Clinical Psychology* 81, no. 6 (2013): 949–961.
22. Bradbury and Karney, *Intimate Relationships.*
23. Burkart, J.M., S.B. Hrdy, and C.P. Van Schaik, "Cooperative Breeding and Human Cognitive Evolution," *Evolutionary Anthropology: Issues, News, and Reviews* 18, no. 5 (September/October 2009): 175–186; Clark, M.S., et al., "Communal Relational Context (or Lack Thereof) Shapes Emotional Lives," *Current Opinion in Psychology* 17 (2017): 176–183; Clark, M.S. and J. Mills, "The Difference between Communal and Exchange Relationships: What It Is and Is Not," *Personality & Social Psychology Bulletin* 19, no. 6 (December 1993): 684–691; Coomes, N.L., "Marriage Isn't Hard Work; It's Serious Play," *The Atlantic,* March 24, 2023.

CHAPTER 8

1. Rosenfeld, M.J., R.J. Thomas, and S. Hausen, "Disintermediating Your Friends: How Online Dating in the United States Displaces Other Ways of Meeting," *Proceedings of the National Academy of Sciences* 116, no. 36 (August 2019): 17753–17758; Rosenfeld, M.J., R.J. Thomas, and S. Hausen, "How Couples Meet and Stay Together 2017 v1.1" (computer files, Stanford University Libraries, 2019), https://data.stanford.edu/hcmst2017.
2. Rosenfeld, Thomas, and Hausen, "How Couples Meet and Stay Together 2017 v1.1," https://data.stanford.edu/hcmst2017.
3. Stinson, D.A., J.J. Cameron, and L.B. Hoplock, "The Friends-to-Lovers Pathway to Romance: Prevalent, Preferred, and Overlooked by Science," *Social Psychological and Personality Science* 13, no. 2 (March 2022): 562–571.
4. Ahuvia, A.C. and M.B. Adelman, "Formal Intermediaries in the Marriage Market: A Typology and Review," *Journal of Marriage and the Family* 54, no. 2 (May 1992): 452–463; Finkel, E.J., et al., "Online Dating: A Critical Analysis from the Perspective of Psychological Science," *Psychological Science in the Public Interest* 13, no. 1 (January 2012): 3–66.
5. McKenna, K.Y.A., A.S. Green, and M.E.J. Gleason, "Relationship Formation on the Internet: What's the Big Attraction?," *Journal of Social Issues* 58, no. 1 (Spring 2002): 9–31.
6. Goñi, M., "Assortative Matching at the Top of the Distribution: Evidence from the World's Most Exclusive Marriage Market," *American Economic Journal: Applied Economics* 14, no. 3 (July 2022): 445–87.
7. As we noted back in chapter 3, the online vs. offline effect on future likelihood of breaking up is $r = .02$, and the effect on future satisfaction is $r = .05$, in Cacioppo, J.T., et al., "Marital Satisfaction and Break-ups Differ across On-line

and Off-line Meeting Venues," *Proceedings of the National Academy of Sciences* 110, no. 25 (June 2013): 10135–10140. In other words, it doesn't ultimately matter how you meet your partner.

8. Chernev, A., U. Böckenholt, and J. Goodman, "Choice Overload: A Conceptual Review and Meta-analysis," *Journal of Consumer Psychology* 25, no. 2 (April 2015): 333–358; Greifeneder, R., B. Scheibehenne, and N. Kleber, "Less May Be More When Choosing Is Difficult: Choice Complexity and Too Much Choice," *Acta Psychologica* 133, no. 1 (January 2010): 45–50; Iyengar, S.S. and M.R. Lepper, "When Choice Is Demotivating: Can One Desire Too Much of a Good Thing?," *Journal of Personality and Social Psychology* 79, no. 6 (2000): 995–1006.

9. Pronk, T.M. and J.J. Denissen, "A Rejection Mind-Set: Choice Overload in Online Dating," *Social Psychological and Personality Science* 11, no. 3 (April 2020): 388–396.

10. Heino, R.D., N.B. Ellison, and J.L. Gibbs, "Relationshopping: Investigating the Market Metaphor in Online Dating," *Journal of Social and Personal Relationships* 27, no. 4 (June 2010): 427–447.

11. Relative to non-Tinder users, Tinder users were more likely to (a) compare their appearance to others' appearances, (b) internalize social media depictions of attractiveness, (c) monitor their appearance, and (d) feel greater shame about their bodies, with effect sizes ranging from $r = .11$ to $r = .18$, in Strubel, J. and T.A. Petrie, "Love Me Tinder: Body Image and Psychosocial Functioning among Men and Women," *Body Image* 21 (June 2017): 34–38.

12. Sassler, S. and A.J. Miller, "The Ecology of Relationships: Meeting Locations and Cohabitors' Relationship Perceptions," *Journal of Social and Personal Relationships* 32, no. 2 (March 2015): 141–160.

13. The Tinder-user vs. non-Tinder-user difference was $r = .16$ for Machiavellianism, $r = .14$ for narcissism, and $r = .35$ for psychopathy, in Sevi, B., "The Dark Side of Tinder: The Dark Triad of Personality as Correlates of Tinder Use," *Journal of Individual Differences* 40, no. 4 (June 2019): 242–246. Tinder users were higher on all three variables.

14. Vogels, E.A. and C. McClain, "Key Findings about Online Dating in the U.S.," Pew Research Center, February 2, 2023; Valentine, J.L., et al., "Dating App Facilitated Sexual Assault: A Retrospective Review of Sexual Assault Medical Forensic Examination Charts," *Journal of Interpersonal Violence* 38, no. 9–10 (May 2023), 6298–6322.

15. The preference-matching vs. mismatching experimental effect was a medium size of $r = .28$ when participants looked at a profile but a tiny $r = .03$ when participants met the partner face-to-face, averaged across studies 1 and 2 in Eastwick, P.W., E.J. Finkel, and A.H. Eagly, "When and Why Do Ideal Partner Preferences Affect the Process of Initiating and Maintaining Romantic

Relationships?," *Journal of Personality and Social Psychology* 101, no. 5 (2011): 1012–1032.

16. Eastwick et al., "When and Why Do Ideal Partner Preferences Affect the Process of Initiating and Maintaining Romantic Relationships?," 1012–1032.

17. Eastwick, P.W. and L.K. Smith, "Sex-Differentiated Effects of Physical Attractiveness on Romantic Desire: A Highly Powered, Preregistered Study in a Photograph Evaluation Context," *Comprehensive Results in Social Psychology* 3, no. 1 (2018): 1–27; Hitsch, G.J., A. Hortaçsu, and D. Ariely, "What Makes You Click?—Mate Preferences in Online Dating," *Quantitative Marketing and Economics* 8 (2010): 393–427; Jonason, P.K. and A.G. Thomas, "Being More Educated and Earning More Increases Romantic Interest: Data from 1.8 M Online Daters from 24 Nations," *Human Nature* 33, no. 2 (2022): 115–131; Lee, L., et al., "If I'm Not Hot, Are You Hot or Not? Physical-Attractiveness Evaluations and Dating Preferences as a Function of One's Own Attractiveness," *Psychological Science* 19, no. 7 (July 2008): 669–677.

18. Eastwick, P.W., et al., "The Predictive Validity of Ideal Partner Preferences: A Review and Meta-analysis," *Psychological Bulletin* 140, no. 3 (2014): 623–665; Kurzban, R. and J. Weeden, "HurryDate: Mate Preferences in Action," *Evolution and Human Behavior* 26, no. 3 (May 2005): 227–244. This is not to say that all attributes are equally desired by men and women in real-life attraction settings. In a study of speed-daters, the broadness of one's shoulders predicted men's attractiveness more than women's; a smaller waist predicted women's attractiveness more than men's. However, inconsistent with what men and women said they wanted, tall men *and women* were preferred (although the effects of height were generally small), see Sidari, M.J., et al., "Preferences for Sexually Dimorphic Body Characteristics Revealed in a Large Sample of Speed Daters," *Social Psychological and Personality Science* 12, no. 2 (March 2021): 225–236.

19. The very large speed-dating study, "HurryDate" by Kurzban, R. and J. Weeden, found that men said yes 49 percent of the time and women said yes 34 percent of the time, which translates to an effect size of $r = .15$. This effect precisely matches the meta-analytic effect size reported in Fletcher, G.J.O., et al., "Predicting Romantic Interest and Decisions in the Very Early Stages of Mate Selection Standards, Accuracy, and Sex Differences," *Personality and Social Psychology Bulletin* 40, no. 4 (April 2014): 540–550. Relatedly, retrospective studies, in which men and women describe how they felt after a first face-to-face meeting, reveal a similarly small gender difference. For the first two events that participants recalled, the gender difference in romantic interest was nearly identical to the speed-dating gender difference: $r = .12$ for relationships that would become "long-term" and $r = .09$ for relationships that would become

"short-term," in Eastwick, P.W., et al., "What Do Short-Term and Long-Term Relationships Look Like? Building the Relationship Coordination and Strategic Timing (ReCAST) Model," *Journal of Experimental Psychology: General* 147, no. 5 (May 2018): 747–781.

20. A difference of this size translates to an effect size of $r = .53$, which is quite large. Gerrard, B., "Why Do Women Have the Upper Hand on Tinder? Explaining the Two Worlds of the Dating App," The Bold Italic, Medium, March 8, 2021.

21. Levy, J., D. Markell, and M. Cerf, "Polar Similars: Using Massive Mobile Dating Data to Predict Synchronization and Similarity in Dating Preferences," *Frontiers in Psychology* 10 (2019); Fellizar, K., "Here's How Many Hours We Really Spend on Dating Apps per Week—vs. What Experts Recommend," *Bustle*, January 31, 2018.

22. Kelley, L., "America Is Sick of Swiping: Dating Apps Are Falling Back to Earth," *The Atlantic*, April 10, 2024.

23. Ury, L., *How to Not Die Alone: The Surprising Science That Will Help You Find Love* (New York: Simon and Schuster, 2021), 121.

24. Eastwick, P.W., et al., "Predicting Romantic Interest during Early Relationship Development: A Preregistered Investigation Using Machine Learning," *European Journal of Personality* 37, no. 3 (May/June 2023): 276–312.

25. Figure 8.3 draws from the data in Eastwick et al., "Predicting Romantic Interest during Early Relationship Development," 276–312. It charts the correlations between (a) participants' romantic-interest judgments about each crush at one time point, and (b) the average of the participants' romantic-interest judgments about the same crush at the subsequent *four* time points. (Using different averages of subsequent time points did not meaningfully change the pattern.) For example, at time 1 (first impression), the correlation is between participants' romantic interest judgments at time 1 and the average of their romantic-interest judgments at times 2–5. (The figure charts Fisher z-transformed correlations.) For the third impression (i.e., the correlation between participants' romantic interest judgments at time 3 and the average of their romantic interest judgments at times 4–7), this estimate is $r = .75$, which means that this third impression remains consistently high or low about 87 percent of the time and would change about 13 percent of the time.

26. Orben, A. and A.K. Przybylski, "The Association between Adolescent Well-Being and Digital Technology Use," *Nature Human Behaviour* 3, no. 2 (February 2019): 173–182; Twenge, J.M., et al., "Underestimating Digital Media Harm," *Nature Human Behaviour* 4, no. 4 (April 2020): 346–348.

27. Twenge, J.M., B.H. Spitzberg, and W.K. Campbell, "Less In-Person Social Interaction with Peers among US Adolescents in the 21st Century and Links to

Loneliness," *Journal of Social and Personal Relationships* 36, no. 6 (June 2019): 1892–1913.

28. Atalay, E., "A Twenty-First Century of Solitude? Time Alone and Together in the United States" (working paper, no. 22-11, Federal Reserve Bank of Philadelphia, April 2022), http://dx.doi.org/10.21799/frbp.wp.2022.11. The effect of smartphone and social media use on negative outcomes like loneliness is controversial and unclear. But the effect of *in-person socializing* on loneliness is extremely clear: People are less lonely to the extent that they spend time socializing in person with friends with a small effect size, $r = .15$, in Twenge, Spitzberg, and Campbell, "Less In-Person Social Interaction with Peers among US Adolescents," 1892–1913. So regardless of what you think about the effects of smartphones specifically—many of us have good social media habits—it's pretty clear that a lack of in-person socializing is not ideal.
29. Frost, J.H., et al., "People Are Experience Goods: Improving Online Dating with Virtual Dates," *Journal of Interactive Marketing* 22, no. 1 (2008): 51–61.
30. Ury, *How to Not Die Alone*.
31. Campodonico, C., "Who Will Vouch for This Bro? SF Singles Now Want References for Romantic Connections," *The San Francisco Standard*, February 13, 2024.
32. Stinson, Cameron, and Hoplock, "The Friends-to-Lovers Pathway to Romance," 562–571.
33. Reis, H.T., et al., "Familiarity Does Indeed Promote Attraction in Live Interaction," *Journal of Personality and Social Psychology* 101, no. 3 (2011): 557–570.

CHAPTER 9

1. Fox, J. and R. Ralston, "Queer Identity Online: Informal Learning and Teaching Experiences of LGBTQ Individuals on Social Media," *Computers in Human Behavior* 65 (December 2016): 635–642; McKenna, K.Y.A. and J.A. Bargh, "Plan 9 from Cyberspace: The Implications of the Internet for Personality and Social Psychology," *Personality and Social Psychology Review* 4, no. 1 (February 2000): 57–75.
2. Beauchamp, Z., "Our Incel Problem," *Vox*, April 23, 2019; Bydlowska, J., "The Woman Who Accidentally Started the Incel Movement," *Elle*, March 1, 2016.
3. "Alana's Personal Home Page," which was original upper level: https://web.archive.org/web/20020803035728/http://www.ncf.ca/~ad097/invcel.html.
4. Bates, L., *Men Who Hate Women: From Incels to Pickup Artists: The Truth About Extreme Misogyny and How It Affects Us All* (Naperville, IL: Sourcebooks, 2021);

Beauchamp, "Our Incel Problem"; Kelly, M., A. DiBranco, and J.R. DeCook, "Misogynist Incels and Male Supremacist Violence" in *Male Supremacism in the United States: From Patriarchal Traditionalism to Misogynist Incels and the Alt-Right*, ed. E.K. Carian, A. DiBranco, and C. Ebin (New York: Routledge, 2022), 164–180; Vogt, P.J., and A. Goldman, "INVCEL," May 10, 2018, *Reply All* (podcast), https://www.globalplayer.com/podcasts/42KrMm/.

5. Bates, *Men Who Hate Women*; Blake, K.R. and R.C. Brooks, "Societies Should Not Ignore Their Incel Problem," *Trends in Cognitive Sciences* 27, no. 2 (February 2023): 111–113; Kelly, DiBranco, and DeCook, "Misogynist Incels and Male Supremacist Violence," 164–180.

6. Regehr, K., "In(cel)doctrination: How Technologically Facilitated Misogyny Moves Violence off Screens and on to Streets," *New Media & Society* 24, no. 1 (January 2022): 138–155. People with "late sexual onset"—or late bloomers—are remarkably similar to people who self-identify as incels in terms of their anxiety, loneliness, and challenges forming relationships. But the major difference is that the misogynist rhetoric is vastly more pronounced among the incels than the classic late bloomers, see Stijelja, S. and B.L. Mishara, "Psychosocial Characteristics of Involuntary Celibates (Incels): A Review of Empirical Research and Assessment of the Potential Implications of Research on Adult Virginity and Late Sexual Onset," *Sexuality & Culture* 27, no. 2 (April 2023): 715–734.

7. Peterson, J. and J. Densley, *The Violence Project Database of Mass Shootings in the United States, 1966–2019* (Saint Paul, MN: The Violence Project, November 2019), https://www.theviolenceproject.org/wp-content/uploads/2019/11/TVP-Mass-Shooter-Database-Report-Final-compressed.pdf; Silva, J.R., "Global Mass Shootings: Comparing the United States against Developed and Developing Countries," *International Journal of Comparative and Applied Criminal Justice* 47, no. 4 (2023): 317–340.

8. Kassam, A., "Woman Behind 'Incel' Says Angry Men Hijacked Her Word 'As a Weapon of War,'" in *The Guardian*, April 25, 2018.

9. Castle, L., *The Blackpill Theory: Why Incels Are Right & You Are Wrong* (self-pub., 2019). To be clear, incels draw from scientific ideas without being bound by scientific conventions or decorum. For example, an incel might say "it is in [a woman's] best interest to not be attached to a single man in particular, but keep monkey branching to a stronger, better provider," from Ging, D., "Alphas, Betas, and Incels: Theorizing the Masculinities of the Manosphere," *Men and Masculinities* 22, no. 4 (October 2019): 649. In contrast, an evolutionary psychologist might write about how women should have evolved to remain somewhat open to "mate switching" in cases where "a higher value man might become unmated, rendering him newly available on the mating market," Buss,

D.M., et al., "The Mate Switching Hypothesis," *Personality and Individual Differences* 104 (January 2017): 144. The incel rhetoric is cruder, but note that these two quotes illustrate precisely the same idea. Incels are channeling the science correctly while infusing it with venom and misogyny.

10. Bates, *Men Who Hate Women*; Ging, "Alphas, Betas, and Incels," 638–657; Vallerga, M. and E.L. Zurbriggen, "Hegemonic Masculinities in the 'Manosphere': A Thematic Analysis of Beliefs about Men and Women on The Red Pill and Incel," *Analyses of Social Issues and Public Policy* 22, no. 2 (August 2022): 602–625; Van Brunt, B. and C. Taylor, *Understanding and Treating Incels: Case Studies, Guidance, and Treatment of Violence Risk in the Involuntary Celibate Community* (New York: Routledge, 2020).

11. Harden, K.P., "Genetic Determinism, Essentialism and Reductionism: Semantic Clarity for Contested Science," *Nature Reviews Genetics* 24, no. 3 (March 2023): 197–204.

12. Donovan, B.M., et al., "Sex and Gender Essentialism in Textbooks," *Science* 383, no. 6685 (February 2024): 822–825.

13. Harden, "Genetic Determinism, Essentialism and Reductionism," 197–204; Prentice, D.A. and D.T. Miller, "Essentializing Differences between Women and Men," *Psychological Science* 17, no. 2 (February 2006): 129–135.

14. Haslam, N., L. Rothschild, and D. Ernst, "Essentialist Beliefs about Social Categories," *British Journal of Social Psychology* 39, no. 1 (March 2000): 113–127.

15. Wood, W. and A.H. Eagly, "Biosocial Construction of Sex Differences and Similarities in Behavior," in *Advances in Experimental Social Psychology*, ed. M.P. Zanna and J.M. Olson, vol. 46 (San Diego: Academic Press, 2012), 55–123.

16. Kimmel, M., *Angry White Men: American Masculinity at the End of an Era* (New York: Bold Type Books, 2013); Messner, M.A., "The Limits of 'The Male Sex Role': An Analysis of the Men's Liberation and Men's Rights Movements' Discourse," *Gender & Society* 12, no. 3 (June 1998): 255–276.

17. Bowles, N., "Jordan Peterson, Custodian of the Patriarchy," *The New York Times*, May 18, 2018; Ging, "Alphas, Betas, and Incels," 638–657; Kimmel, *Angry White Men*.

18. Bernstein, J., "The 'Manosphere'? It's Planet Earth," *The New York Times*, February 1, 2025.

19. McBride, J., "The Pronoun Warrior," *Toronto Life*, January 25, 2017.

20. Butker, H., "Harrison Butker of Kansas City Chiefs Graduation Speech," May 11, 2024, https://www.ncregister.com/news/harrison-butker-speech-at-benedictine.

21. Radford, A., "Who is Andrew Tate? The Self-Proclaimed Misogynist Influencer," BBC News, August 4, 2023; Moran, C., *What about Men?: A Feminist Answers the Question* (New York: Harper, 2023).

22. Bernstein, "The 'Manosphere'? It's Planet Earth"; French, "The Atmosphere of the 'Manosphere' Is Toxic," *The New York Times,* April 14, 2024; Ging, "Alphas, Betas, and Incels," 638–657; Kimmel, *Angry White Men.*
23. Girlguiding, *Girls' Attitudes Survey 2023: Girls' Lives over 15 Years* (London: Girlguiding, 2023); Moran, *What about Men?*
24. Cheryan, S., et al., "Why Are Some STEM Fields More Gender Balanced Than Others?," *Psychological Bulletin* 143, no. 1 (2017): 1–35; Galos, D.R. and A. Coppock, "Gender Composition Predicts Gender Bias: A Meta-reanalysis of Hiring Discrimination Audit Experiments," *Science Advances* 9, no. 18 (2023); Moss-Racusin, C.A., et al., "Science Faculty's Subtle Gender Biases Favor Male Students," *Proceedings of the National Academy of Sciences* 109, no. 41 (October 2012): 16474–16479; Reeves, R.V., *Of Boys and Men: Why the Modern Male Is Struggling, Why It Matters, and What to Do About It* (Washington, DC: Brookings Institution Press, 2022); Wood and Eagly, "Biosocial Construction of Sex Differences and Similarities in Behavior," 55–123.
25. Barkow, J.H., L. Cosmides, and J. Tooby, *The Adapted Mind: Evolutionary Psychology and the Generation of Culture* (New York: Oxford University Press, 1992); Eagly, A.H. and W. Wood, "The Origins of Sex Differences in Human Behavior: Evolved Dispositions versus Social Roles," *American Psychologist* 54, no. 6 (1999): 408–423.
26. Lloyd, E., S. Rao, D.S. Wilson, and E. Sober, "Evolutionary Mismatch and How to Evaluate It: A Basic Tutorial," *This View of Life,* October 22, 2024, https://www.prosocial.world/posts/evolutionary-mismatch-and-how-to-evaluate-it-a-basic-tutorial.
27. Marcotte, A., "The Insidious Rise of 'Tradwives': A Right-Wing Fantasy Is Rotting Young Men's Minds," *Salon,* November 27, 2023.
28. Harden, "Genetic Determinism, Essentialism and Reductionism," 197–204.
29. Kale, S., "50 Years of Pickup Artists: Why Is the Toxic Skill Still So in Demand?," *The Guardian,* November 5, 2019.
30. Bates, *Men Who Hate Women;* Van Brunt and Taylor, *Understanding and Treating Incels.*
31. Sometimes, in the scientific literature, this loose form is referred to as *biological essentialism.* But technically, the idea that biological causes lead to less changeable outcomes (vs. social or cultural causes) is a form of determinism, not essentialism. Essentialism is about whether different category members (like men and women) have one or more deep underlying characteristics that make them "what they are," see Harden, "Genetic Determinism, Essentialism and Reductionism," 197–204.
32. Nettle, D., W.E. Frankenhuis, and K. Panchanathan, "Biology, Society, or Choice: How Do Non-experts Interpret Explanations of Behaviour?," *Open*

Mind 7 (2023): 625–651. According to the raw data provided in Nettle, Frankenhuis, and Panchanathan, "Inferred Malleability and Explanations for Behavior" (unpublished raw data, Open Science Framework, November 2022), https://osf.io/yc8dw/ (study 2), participants rated the nine "sociocultural" and "psychological" behaviors as easier to change than the three "biological" behaviors with an effect size of $r = .40$ (i.e., a medium-to-large effect size).

33. Specifically, participants read that "Evolutionary psychologists are discovering that biology does have a strong influence on what we do and how we think. This applies to humans in general, but is also true for differences between men and women." Participants then read about four areas where evolutionary psychologists have documented gender differences: mating-related preferences, aggressiveness, nurturing tendencies, and the motivation to pursue a career vs. childcare. Reading this vignette (compared to a vignette where these issues were up for debate) reduced people's beliefs in the possibility of social change with an effect size of $r = .16$ (a small effect) in Morton, T.A., et al., "Theorizing Gender in the Face of Social Change: Is There Anything Essential about Essentialism?," *Journal of Personality and Social Psychology* 96, no. 3 (March 2009): 653–664.

34. Stewart-Williams, S., *The Ape That Understood the Universe: How the Mind and Culture Evolve* (Cambridge: Cambridge University Press, 2018), 89; Symons, D., *The Evolution of Human Sexuality* (New York: Oxford University Press, 1979), 250 ; Buss, D.M., *The Evolution of Desire: Strategies of Human Mating* (New York: Basic Books, 1994), 71.

35. Conroy-Beam, D., "How the Incels Warped My Research," *The Boston Globe*, May 16, 2024; *Truth Wins Out*, "Dr. Lisa Diamond: 'NARTH Distorted My Research,'" August 18, 2008, https://www.youtube.com/watch?v=64A2HrvYdYQ. As evolutionary biologist Dr. D.S. Wilson points out, our understanding of what constitutes a "natural" behavior informs legal culpability, and it has done so for centuries. In other words, imagine that science "discovers" an evolved basis for a particular behavior that harms the general welfare (e.g., an evolved tendency for men to make sexual advances toward women who work for them, for example). If this tendency is supposedly evolved and natural, then people—not just laypeople, but judges and lawyers, too—will tend to think that the behavior deserves a lighter punishment. In short, claims about humans' evolved nature carry downstream ethical implications because deterministic beliefs are widespread and consequential: Wilson, D.S., E. Dietrich, and A.B. Clark, "On the Inappropriate Use of the Naturalistic Fallacy in Evolutionary Psychology," *Biology and Philosophy* 18 (November 2003): 669–681.

36. Clark, C. and B. Winegard, "Sex and the Academy," *Quillette*, October 8, 2022.

37. Wood and Eagly, "Biosocial Construction of Sex Differences and Similarities in Behavior," 55–123.

38. Freese, J., "The Arrival of Social Science Genomics," *Contemporary Sociology* 47, no. 5 (September 2018): 524–536; Harden, "Genetic Determinism, Essentialism and Reductionism," 197–204. There was a glut of findings about ten to twenty years ago that purported to find single genes that had very large effects on complex psychological attributes, like depression. As it turned out, none of those studies held up to scrutiny. Today, here is how scientists talk about genetic effects: Hundreds or thousands of genes work together, in conjunction with developmental and environmental forces, to *probabilistically predict* that someone will possess a complex psychological attribute. There is not "a gene for" something behavioral or psychological in humans.
39. Stroop, J.R., "Studies of Interference in Serial Verbal Reactions," *Journal of Experimental Psychology* 18, no. 6 (1935): 643–662.
40. In the best-case scenario ("sexual arousal prime"), it was harder for participants to turn their attention away from attractive (vs. average) opposite-sex targets by about 30 milliseconds—a small effect size, $r = .11$—in table 1 in Maner, J.K., et al., "Can't Take My Eyes off You: Attentional Adhesion to Mates and Rivals," *Journal of Personality and Social Psychology* 93, no. 3 (2007). In contrast, the Stroop effect (interference minus baseline) is about 300 milliseconds for younger participants (and it's even larger for older participants). This is an enormous effect size, $r = .73$, see table 1 in Verhaeghen, P. and L. De Meersman, "Aging and the Stroop effect: A Meta-analysis," *Psychology and Aging* 13, no. 1 (1998): 120–126.
41. Stinson, D.A., J.J. Cameron, and L.B. Hoplock, "The Friends-to-Lovers Pathway to Romance: Prevalent, Preferred, and Overlooked by Science," *Social Psychological and Personality Science* 13, no. 2 (March 2022): 562–571; Eastwick, P.W., E.J. Finkel, and J.A. Simpson, "Relationship Trajectories: A Meta-Theoretical Framework and Theoretical Applications," *Psychological Inquiry* 30, no. 1 (2019): 1–28; Eastwick, P.W., et al., "What Do Short-Term and Long-Term Relationships Look Like? Building the Relationship Coordination and Strategic Timing (ReCAST) Model," *Journal of Experimental Psychology: General* 147, no. 5 (May 2018): 747–781.
42. Eastwick, P.W. and L.L. Hunt, "Relational Mate Value: Consensus and Uniqueness in Romantic Evaluations," *Journal of Personality and Social Psychology*, 106, no. 5 (March 2014): 728–751; Epley, N., et al., "Undersociality: Miscalibrated Social Cognition Can Inhibit Social Connection," *Trends in Cognitive Sciences* 26, no. 5 (2022): 406–418.
43. Miller, C.C., "How the Last Eight Years Made Young Women More Liberal," *The New York Times,* September 15, 2024.
44. Carothers, B.J. and H.T. Reis, "Men and Women Are from Earth: Examining the Latent Structure of Gender," *Journal of Personality and Social Psychology* 104,

no. 2 (2013): 385–407; Conley, T.D., "Perceived Proposer Personality Characteristics and Gender Differences in Acceptance of Casual Sex Offers," *Journal of Personality and Social Psychology* 100, no. 2 (February 2011): 309–329; Feeney, B.C. and N.L. Collins, "A New Look at Social Support: A Theoretical Perspective on Thriving Through Relationships," *Personality and Social Psychology Review* 19, no. 2 (May 2015): 113–147.

45. Clark, M.S. and J.R. Mills, "A Theory of Communal (and Exchange) Relationships," in *The Handbook of Theories of Social Psychology*, ed. P.A.M. Van Lange, A.W. Kruglanski, and E.T. Higgins, vol. 2 (London: SAGE, 2012): 232–250; Eastwick, P.W., E.J. Finkel, and S. Joel, "Mate Evaluation Theory," *Psychological Review* 130, no. 1 (2023): 211–241; Joel, S., et al., "Machine Learning Uncovers the Most Robust Self-Report Predictors of Relationship Quality across 43 Longitudinal Couples Studies," *Proceedings of the National Academy of Sciences* 117, no. 32 (August 2020): 19061–19071.

46. French, "The Atmosphere of the 'Manosphere' Is Toxic"; Moran, *What about Men?*

47. Stijelja and Mishara, "Psychosocial Characteristics of Involuntary Celibates (Incels)," 715–734.

48. Lankford, A. and J.R. Silva, "Sexually Frustrated Mass Shooters: A Study of Perpetrators, Profiles, Behaviors, and Victims," *Homicide Studies* 28, no. 2 (May 2024): 196–219.

49. Cox, D.A. and S. Pressler, "Disconnected: The Growing Class Divide in American Civic Life," Survey Center on American Life, August 22, 2024.

50. Cox and Pressler, "Disconnected."

CHAPTER 10

1. 46 percent of women and 73 percent of men reported sexual attraction higher than "none" for their closest other-gender friend in Kaplan, D.L. and C.B. Keys, "Sex and Relationship Variables as Predictors of Sexual Attraction in Cross-Sex Platonic Friendships between Young Heterosexual Adults," *Journal of Social and Personal Relationships* 14, no. 2 (April 1997): 191–206. See also Baumeister, R.F., S.R. Wotman, and A.M. Stillwell, "Unrequited Love: On Heartbreak, Anger, Guilt, Scriptlessness, and Humiliation," *Journal of Personality and Social Psychology* 64, no. 3 (1993): 377–394; LeFebvre, L.E., et al., "Conceptualizing the Friendzone Phenomenon," *Imagination, Cognition and Personality* 42, no. 1 (September 2022): 42–76; Motley, M.T., H. Reeder, and L.J. Faulkner, "Behaviors That Determine the Fate of Friendships After Unrequited Romantic Disclosures," in *Studies in Applied Interpersonal Communication*, ed. M.T. Motley (Thousand Oaks, CA: SAGE, 2008), 71–93.

2. Shields, G.L., "A place where every decent guy will find himself eventually:

Delineating the friend zone as a site of sexual violence" (master's thesis, University of Texas at Austin, 2017), https://repositories.lib.utexas.edu/bitstreams/7877ed46-0ff4-4fd0-96e0-83470d622e3c/download.

3. Erosheva, E. A., H. Kim, C. Emlet, and K. I. Fredriksen-Goldsen, "Social networks of lesbian, gay, bisexual, and transgender older adults," *Research on Aging* 38, no. 1 (2016): 98-123.

4. There is a pervasive assumption that using online dating must follow a quick "meet, hook up, start dating" sequence if it's going to work out. That isn't actually true. In this representative U.S. sample, among people who met their partner online, the median amount of time between meeting and forming a relationship was a full month. For some pairs, it was months or even years. Suffice to say that many of these pairs were friends in the meantime. Data from Rosenfeld, M.J., R.J. Thomas, and S. Hausen, "How Couples Meet and Stay Together 2017 v1.1" (computer files, Stanford University Libraries, 2019), https://data.stanford.edu/hcmst2017. See also Stinson, D.A., J.J. Cameron, and L.B. Hoplock, "The Friends-to-Lovers Pathway to Romance: Prevalent, Preferred, and Overlooked by Science," *Social Psychological and Personality Science* 13, no. 2 (March 2022): 562–571.

5. In the Stinson, Cameron, and Hoplock "Friends-to-Lovers-Pathway" data, it took a *median* of 12 months from the formation of the friendship until the formation of the romantic relationship. (The *average* is even higher—21 months—some people wait a decade or more!) Also, 70 percent of friends-to-lovers "just became friends and then became attracted/romantically interested after getting to know each other," whereas in 30 percent, one party "intentionally became friends" with the other person because they were attracted to them.

6. Eastwick, P.W., et al., "Predicting Romantic Interest during Early Relationship Development: A Preregistered Investigation Using Machine Learning," *European Journal of Personality* 37, no. 3 (May/June 2023): 276–312.

7. For men, the effect size of the number of female friends on hostile sexism was $r = -.33$, and the effect size of the number of female friends on sexual objectification was $r = -.37$, which are medium-to-large effects (more female friends predicts less sexism). The effect size of the number of male friends on hostile sexism was $r = .31$, and the effect size of the number of male friends on sexual objectification was $r = .27$, which are medium effects (more male friends predicts more sexism), in Jenkins, D.L., S.X. Xiao, and C.L. Martin, "Does the Gender of Your Friends Matter for Sexist Attitudes about Women?," *Emerging Adulthood* 11, no. 2 (April 2023): 380–393. A handy heuristic from this study: If you ask a man "How many of your closest friends are women?" and "How many of your closest friends are men?" he is likely to be low in hostile sexism and sexual objectification if he lists as many (or more) women as men.

8. Across all the time points in this study, the average association of the size of a person's *other*-gender network and forming a romantic relationship was $r = .23$, which is a medium-size effect. The average association of the size of a person's *same*-gender network and forming a romantic relationship was $r = .07$ (which is smaller than small) in Connolly, J., W. Furman, and R. Konarski, "The Role of Peers in the Emergence of Heterosexual Romantic Relationships in Adolescence," *Child Development* 71, no. 5 (September/October 2000): 1395–1408.

9. LGBTQ folks were more likely to be friends with exes than straight men and women, with a medium effect size of $r = .25$, in Griffith, R.L., et al., "Staying Friends with Ex-romantic Partners: Predictors, Reasons, and Outcomes," *Personal Relationships* 24, no. 3 (September 2017): 550–584. The motive to stay in touch with an ex because you share a network with them was not meaningfully associated with commitment/satisfaction to a current partner, $r = .08$. The motive to stay in touch with an ex because you view them as a backup partner was negatively associated with commitment/satisfaction to a current partner with a medium effect size, $r = -.36$, in Rodriguez, L.M., et al., "Communication with Former Romantic Partners and Current Relationship Outcomes among College Students," *Personal Relationships* 23, no. 3 (September 2016): 409–424.

10. Eastwick, P.W., E.J. Finkel, and S. Joel, "Mate Evaluation Theory," *Psychological Review* 130, no. 1 (2023): 211–241; Robins, R.W., A. Caspi, and T.E. Moffitt, "It's Not Just Who You're with, It's Who You Are: Personality and Relationship Experiences across Multiple Relationships," *Journal of Personality* 70, no. 6 (December 2002): 925–964; Park, M., et al., "The Effects of Psychotherapy for Adult Depression on Social Support: A Meta-analysis," *Cognitive Therapy and Research* 38, no. 6 (2014): 600–611.

11. Hill, F., "Nostalgia for a Dating Experience They've Never Had," *The Atlantic*, April 15, 2024.

12. Eastwick, P.W., et al., "Selective versus Unselective Romantic Desire: Not All Reciprocity Is Created Equal," *Psychological Science* 18, no. 4 (April 2007): 317–319; Girme, Y.U., Y. Park, and G. MacDonald, "Coping or Thriving? Reviewing Intrapersonal, Interpersonal, and Societal Factors Associated with Well-Being in Singlehood from a Within-Group Perspective," *Perspectives on Psychological Science* 18, no. 5 (2023): 1097–1120; Kenny, D.A., *Interpersonal Perception: The Foundation of Social Relationships,* 2nd ed. (New York: Guilford Press, 2019).

13. Kristof, N., "How We Can Fix Our Loneliness Epidemic," *The New York Times*, September 7, 2023.

14. Cacioppo, J.T. and S. Cacioppo, "Loneliness in the Modern Age: An Evolutionary Theory of Loneliness (ETL)," in *Advances in Experimental Social Psychology,* ed. J.M. Olson, vol. 58 (Cambridge, MA: Academic Press, 2018),

127–197; Maner, J.K., et al., "Does Social Exclusion Motivate Interpersonal Reconnection? Resolving the 'Porcupine Problem,'" *Journal of Personality and Social Psychology* 92, no. 1 (2007): 42–55.
15. Reis, H.T., et al., "Familiarity Does Indeed Promote Attraction in Live Interaction," *Journal of Personality and Social Psychology* 101, no. 3 (2011): 557–570.
16. Cacioppo, S., et al., "Loneliness: Clinical Import and Interventions," *Perspectives on Psychological Science* 10, no. 2 (March 2015): 238–249. The effect of social cognitive interventions on reducing loneliness was a medium size $r = .29$ in Masi, C.M., et al., "A Meta-analysis of Interventions to Reduce Loneliness," *Personality and Social Psychology Review* 15, no. 3 (August 2011): 219–266.
17. O'Day, E.B. and R.G. Heimberg, "Social Media Use, Social Anxiety, and Loneliness: A Systematic Review," *Computers in Human Behavior Reports* 3 (January–July 2021). The positive effects of face-to-face communication on mental health during the Covid-19 pandemic was a medium-size $r = .24$, whereas effects were much smaller for videoconferencing/texting/telephone, average $r = .06$, in Stieger, S., D. Lewetz, and D. Willinger, "Face-to-Face More Important Than Digital Communication for Mental Health During the Pandemic," *Scientific Reports* 13, no. 1 (2023).
18. Ury, L., *How to Not Die Alone: The Surprising Science That Will Help You Find Love* (New York: Simon and Schuster, 2021).
19. Aron, A., et al., "The Experimental Generation of Interpersonal Closeness: A Procedure and Some Preliminary Findings," *Personality and Social Psychology Bulletin* 23, no. 4 (April 1997): 363–377. You can find all thirty-sex escalating-intimacy questions in Jones, D., "The 36 Questions That Lead to Love," *The New York Times*, January 9, 2015, https://www.nytimes.com/2015/01/09/style/no-37-big-wedding-or-small.html.
20. Aron, "The Experimental Generation of Interpersonal Closeness," 363–377.
21. People who relied on their preprepared topics with strangers enjoyed their conversations more, with a small-to-medium effect size $r = .20$, in study 3 in Abi-Esber, N., et al., "The Power of Forethought: Brainstorming Possible Topics Before Conversations Begin" (working paper, London School of Economics, London, 2023); Brooks, A. W., *TALK: The Science of Conversation and the Art of Being Ourselves* (New York: Crown, 2025).
22. Emery Thompson, M., "How Can Non-human Primates Inform Evolutionary Perspectives on Female-Biased Kinship in Humans?," *Philosophical Transactions of the Royal Society B: Biological Sciences* 374, no. 1780 (September 2019).
23. Kramer, K.L., R. Schacht, and A. Bell, "Adult Sex Ratios and Partner Scarcity Among Hunter–Gatherers: Implications for Dispersal Patterns and the

Evolution of Human Sociality," *Philosophical Transactions of the Royal Society B: Biological Sciences* 372, no. 1729 (July 31, 2017).

CONCLUSION

1. Emba, C., "Men Are Lost. Here's a Map out of the Wilderness," *The Washington Post*, July 10, 2023; Reeves, R.V., *Of Boys and Men: Why the Modern Male Is Struggling, Why It Matters, and What to Do About It* (Washington, DC: Brookings Institution Press, 2022); Sitman, M. and S. Adler-Bell, "What's Wrong With Men?," June 6, 2023, *Know Your Enemy* (podcast), https://know-your-enemy-1682b684.simplecast.com/episodes/whats-wrong-with-men.
2. Moran, C., *What about Men?: A Feminist Answers the Question* (New York: Harper, 2023).
3. Hazan, C. and L.M. Diamond, "The Place of Attachment in Human Mating," *Review of General Psychology* 4, no. 2 (June 2000): 186–204.

· INDEX ·

acts of service, 162–63
Adam case studies, 92–96, 97–99
affirmation, words of, 162–63
age preferences, gender differences and, 66–67
aggression, proactive, 188
Ainsworth, Mary, 107–8
Alana, 214–17
Alana's Involuntary Celibacy Project, 215–16
Alex and Marco, 179–83
algorithmic matching, 165–66
alpha males, 77
alternatives, derogation of, 134–36
Amanda, 193–95
Andre and Erica, 133, 134, 142
Angie, 237, 238, 240–41, 242
Anna, 25–28, 49–50
Annie Hall, 71
anxious attachment style, 130–32
Aron, Art, 247–49
Attached, 130
attaching phase, 97–98
attachment bonds/styles
  anxious, 130–32
  avoidant, 130–32
  biases and, 126–46
  case study and, 105–6
  changes in over time, 131–33
  compatibility and, 13
  compatibility factor and, 151
  evolution of, 111–16
  in humans, 107–11
  long-term mating/relationships and, 101
  monogamy versus, 111
  secure, 130
  speed of forming, 128–29
  support and, 107
  time needed for, 125
attraction
  author's study on, 44–45
  compatibility and, 184–86
  compatibility factor and, 150, 151*fig*
  field of close relationships and, xi
  friends/friendships and, 240, 241*fig*
  mate choice and, 172–77
  popularity and, 82–83
  preference-matching and, 203–5, 204*fig*
  similarity-attraction hypothesis and, 154–57
  Social Relations model (SRM) and, 34–37, 35*fig*
  speed-dating research on, 58–62, 88, 165–66
  third impressions and, 207–9
attractiveness
  attractiveness-exchange script and, 48
  changes in over time, 40
  fading power of, 43–47
  matching, 31–33, 43–44, 64
  mismatches in, 46

Austin, 105–6, 110
avoidant attachment style, 130–32

Bates, Laura, 218n
Bear, The, 138–39
belonging, need for, 124
Berman, Laura, 5
biases
   changes in, 126–27
   impact of on relationships, 127–33
   other possible partners and, 133–36
   positive, 128
   study on, 127–28
biological determinism, 224–30
biological essentialism, 219–24, 227–30
biosocial role perspectives, 228–29
bisexual women, casual sex and, 69–70. *See also* LGBTQ community
Black Mirror, 166–67
black pills, 225–26, 227
bodily symmetry
   as health-signaling attribute, 82–83
   long-term relationships and, 84
body language, 134
bonobos, 112
Bowlby, John, 107–8
brain size, human, 113–14
breakups, 105–6, 110, 147, 242
Buss, David, 16n, 54–55
Butker, Harrison, 221

callbacks, 183
Cannon, Nick, 5
caregiving bonds, 107–10, 120, 130
casual sex
   gender differences and, 68–71
   Zero-Sum model and, 83–84
celebrity relationships, 30–31
chaos theory, 175
Chapman, Gary, 162, 163n
Chemistry.com, 149, 165
chimpanzees, 112, 113, 137, 174, 250
choice overload, 199, 200
close relationships, science of, 107

cognitive dissonance, 127
collective needs, 142
commitment, 62–63, 69
communal interdependence, 13
communal norms, 139–41
communal relationships, 125, 136, 138–45, 164
compatibility
   algorithmic matching and, 165–66
   assessing, 99, 146, 147–49
   attraction and, 151*fig*
   bonding and, 11–14, 17
   challenges of creating, 184–88
   consensus factor and, 35–36, 35*fig,* 38–39, 38*fig*
   construction of, xv, 170
   cultivating, 101
   description of, 34
   importance of, 42, 48, 49, 150–52, 236
   love languages and, 162–63
   opposites-attract theory and, 164–65
   preference matching and, 158–61
   Relationship Trajectories models and, 97
   similarity and, 152–57
   Social Relations model (SRM) and, 170–72
   unpredictability of, 166–68, 181–82
consensus factor, 34–37, 35*fig,* 38*fig,* 39, 41–42, 43, 46, 150, 170–72
conversations, chaotic nature of, 176–77
cooperative breeders, 137–38
couples therapy, 187
Covid-19 pandemic, 144
culture wars, 9–10
cultures, relationships as, 177–84
curiosity, 122

Darwin, Charles, 52
Darwinian principles, 3, 4
dating histories, similarity-attraction hypothesis and, 154–55
Davison, Jake, 10

INDEX

demographic assortative mating, 46–47, 155, 198
derogation of alternatives, 134–36
destiny beliefs, 184
determinism, 213–14, 218–19, 224–30
DeVore, Irven, 145
Diamond, Lisa, 228n
distractions, 233–34
distress-depression-detachment sequence, 110
dopamine, 149

Eagly, Alice, 16n
earning potential, gender differences and, 57, 58–60, 59*fig*, 60*fig*, 63–65
economic model, 136, 168
education levels, gender differences and, 65–66
effect sizes
  as "guessing game," 261–62
  scale for, 20*fig*
  use of, 19–20
eharmony, 90, 165
80/20 rule, 9–10
Emma and Sara, 116–18
Erica and Andre, 133, 134, 142
escalating intensity questions, 247–48*t*, 247–49
essentialism, 213–14, 218–24, 227–30
estrogen, 149
evolutionary mismatches, 56
evolutionary psychology
  approach of, xiii–xiv
  author's experience with, 3, 14–15
  biological determinism and, 226–27
  Buss's 37-cultures study and, 54–55
  culture wars and, 9–10
  Independent Strategies and, 86
  lack of robust studies in, 16
  overview of, 3–6
  as reckless, 213–14
  social role theory and, 222–23
  speed-dating and, 62
  weaknesses of, 15
  Zero-Sum model and, 82
EvoScript
  central pillars of, 7–9
  consensus factor and, 36
  culture wars and, 9–10
  description of, 4, 5
  determinism and, 224
  gender differences and, 52–54
  incels and, 217–18
  long-term relationships and, 79–80
  mate value and, 42, 47–48
  as misleading, 100
  orgasms and, 174
  reproductive success and, 28–29
  skepticism of, 6
  testosterone and, 85
exchange norms, 139, 140–41
experienced (revealed) preferences, 58–62, 158
Ezra Klein Show, The, 136

family-systems therapists, 182, 183
"fast friends" procedure, 247–49
FBoy Island, 78
feminism
  bending gender rules and, 254
  men's rights advocates and, 220–21, 235
Finkel, Eli, 57–58, 248–49
first impressions, 208
Fisher, Helen, 5, 149, 164
(500) Days of Summer, 126–27
flexibility, 251–52
found families, 243
4Chan, 216
Frances Ha, 178
Friends, 237
friends/friendships
  friends-first approach and, 238–40
  meeting partners through, 193–94, 195–96, 195*fig*
  mixed-gender, 237–42, 241*fig*
  number of close, 234, 234*fig*

friendzone, 237–38, 240–41
Fuentes, Nick, 221

Galloway, Scott, 65
Game, The, 225
gamification, online dating and, 210
gender, essentialism and, 219–22
gender cliff in income, 65, 66*fig*
gender differences
  age preferences and, 66–67
  casual sex and, 68–71
  EvoScript and, 52–54, 55
  general belief in, 51–52
  incels and, 218
  in income, 65, 66*fig*
  intimacy and, 5
  mate value and, 6
  online dating and, 205–6
  in partner trait preferences, 54–62, 56*fig*
  physical attractiveness and, 61, 63–65
  political divide and, 232
  social role theory and, 222
genetic propensities, 229
Gerwig, Greta, 178
gibbons, 112–13
gifts, 162–63
Goldblum, Jeff, 175
gorillas, 112, 113, 114, 174, 250
growth beliefs, 184

Hamill, Mark, 47n
Harden, Paige, 224n
health-signaling attributes, 82–83
High Fidelity, 47
Hinge, 210n
Hitch, 5–6
Homo erectus, 113–15
Hönekopp, Johannes, 39
Hunt, Lucy, 41
hunter-gatherers
  gender roles and, 53–54
  group size among, 12–13
  individual differences trade-off and, 80, 81

investment in offspring and, 115–16
migration/moving and, 249–50

incels, 9, 10, 213, 215–16, 224–26, 227–28
income levels, gender differences and, 65, 66*fig*
Independent Strategies, 86–92, 87*fig*, 91*fig*, 98
individual differences trade-off, 80
infants
  attachment bonds and, 108
  brain size and, 114
infidelity, 84, 135
inside jokes, 183
instability in relationship satisfaction, 131, 186–87
intimacy, gender differences regarding, 5
IQ, impact of on marriage rates, 53

Joel, Samantha, 72–73, 88–90, 165–66
Julian and Lloyd, 176–77
Jurassic Park, 175

La La Land, 169–70
Lauren, 147–49, 167
learning your place, 25–28
LGBTQ community
  casual sex and, 69–70
  conversion-therapy agenda and, 228n
  differences related to, 18
  earning potential and, 60n
  EvoScript and, 18–19
  friends-to-lovers pathway and, 196, 239
  mixed-gender networks and, 238n
  online dating and, 198
  relationships with exes and, 242
life history strategy, 81
life-stage trade-offs, 79–80
listening, 123
Lloyd and Julian, 176–77
Lobster, The, 156

loneliness, 210, 235, 236, 244–49
long-term mating/relationships
  desire and preparedness for, 76–79
  EvoScript and, 8–9
  Independent Strategies and, 86–92, 87*fig*, 91*fig*
  mate-value matching and, 47–49
  men and, 80–81
  physical attractiveness and, 84
  Relationship Trajectories model and, 96–100, 98*fig*, 121
  women and, 81
  Zero-Sum model and, 81–86
love languages, 162–63, 167

Machiavellianism, 201
Marco and Alex, 179–83
marriage, delay in, 197
Marshall, J. Howard, 55
masculinity, reimagined version of, 253–54
mass shootings, 217
matching, concept of, 149
matching phenomenon, 31–33, 43–44, 64
mate choice, 172–77
mate value
  as assessment of potential reproductive success, 28–29
  celebrity relationships and, 30–31
  compatibility and, 14
  description of, 1–2
  ephemerality of, 39–42, 88
  EvoScript and, 6
  feedback and, 29–30
  incels and, 218
  as inherent, 7
  long-term relationships and, 47–49
  online dating and, 39
  shifts in, 30–31
  short-term versus long-term, 87–88
  understanding your, 27–28
  use of, 25n
maternal deprivation, 108
mating effort, 79–80

mating market concept/metaphor, 1–2, 20, 21, 136, 144–45, 167, 207, 224–25, 231
Matrix, The, 9, 224
Men Who Hate Women (Bates), 218n
men's rights advocates, 213, 214, 219–24, 227, 235
#MeToo, 198, 232
migration/moving, 249–52
Miller, Geoffrey, 7
Minassian, Alek, 10, 217
mind-reading abilities, 137–38
minimization process, 156–57
misogyny. *See also* incels
  biological determinism and, 227
  men's rights advocates and, 221–22
  shootings motivated by, 217
monogamy, 111
Moral Animal, The (Wright), 4
Moran, Caitlin, 254
mutual friends, meeting partners through, 193–94, 195–96, 195*fig*
mystery, 122

narcissism, 201
natural selection, xiii, 4, 52, 112, 114, 116, 130, 188
Nettle, Daniel, 226
networks. *See also* socializing
  building mixed-gender, 236–44
  regaining, 233–35
norms, differences in, 74–75

offspring, investment in, 52, 68, 113–16, 226
OkCupid, 67n
one-night stands, 92–93, 93*fig*
online dating
  age preferences and, 66–67
  algorithmic matching and, 165
  attractiveness matching and, 44
  cases for and against, 197–206
  choice overload and, 199, 200
  commodification and, xii–xiii

online dating (*cont'd*)
   consensus factor and, 39
   as demeaning, 200
   depressing nature of, 189
   description of, 194–95
   as dominant method of meeting partners, 195–96, 195*fig*
   filtering and, 202–3
   gender differences and, 205–6
   lack of accountability and, 201
   live interactions versus, 210–11
   mate value and, 39
   "mating market" concept and, 2
   negative aspects of, 199–200
   partner trait preferences and, 55–56
   pluses and minuses of, 196–97
   positive aspects of, 197–99
   rejection and, 200–201
   safety and, 201–2
   similarity and, 153
   time between meeting and forming a relationship and, 40
   ways to improve, 206–11
opposites-attract theory, 164–65
orangutans, 112, 113
orgasms/orgasm gap, 69, 174
overconfidence, 100
ovulation, concealed, 173

pair-bonding
   in adult mating partners, 111–13
   attachment bonds and, 130
   biases and, 126
   extra-pair fathers and, 135
   in gibbons, 112–13
   investment in offspring and, 113–16
   scarcity of, 106–7
   seasonal, 107
   work needed for, 125
parental investment, 52, 68, 113–16, 226
parenting effort, 79–80
Parks and Recreation, 46
partible paternity, 81

partners, gender differences in traits of, 54–62, 56*fig*
patterns
   creation of, 181
   entrenched, 177–78
   shifts in, 182–83
   as unique to each relationships, 184
penises, human versus other primate, 173–74
perceived superiority, 128
Perel, Esther, 122
Peterson, Jordan, 10, 53, 221
Pew Research Center, 201–2
photo-rating design, 37–39, 37*fig*
physical attractiveness
   fading power of, 43–47
   gender differences and, 61, 63–65
   as health-signaling attribute, 82–83
   long-term relationships and, 84
   matching phenomenon and, 31
physical touch, 162–63
pickup artistry, 225
pill-curious men, how to talk to, 230–33, 230*fig*
political differences, gender divide and, 232
polyamorous communities, 121, 132, 171
polygyny, 121
porcupine problem, 245–46
preference matching, 158–61, 167, 203–5, 204*fig*
preferences, revealed, 58–62, 158
primates, 111–12, 112*fig*, 137–38. *See also individual primates*
proactive aggression, 188
productivity, gender and, 74
progression bias, 128–29, 186
prosociality, 137–38, 188–89
proximity, impact of, 153, 159
Prum, Richard, 173–74
psychopathy, 201

quality time, 162–63
questions, escalating intensity, 247–48*t*, 247–49

Rachel, 76–77
reactive patterns, 188
reciprocity, 136
red pill worldview, 213–14, 224–25
Reeves, Keanu, 233
registered reports, 159
rejection
    EvoScript and, 10
    incels and, 216
    mindset for, 199–200
    online dating and, 200–201
    student experiences of, xii
    understanding your mate value and, 27–28
relationship satisfaction, 62–63, 72–73, 131, 155, 162–63, 186–87
relationship security, 132
relationship skills, 187
relationship stability, 63
Relationship Trajectories model, 96–101, 98*fig*, 121
re-mating preferences, 174
reproductive success, 7–8, 28–29
revealed preferences, 58–62, 158
risk-aversion, 100
Rodger, Elliot, 217
Roe v. Wade, 232
Rogan, Joe, 6, 16
Rosefeld, Michael, 195
Rules, The, 4–5, 6

safe haven support, 107, 116, 117*fig*, 118–21, 119*t*, 122–23, 151
safety, 240–41
same-sex relationships
    casual sex and, 69–70
    differences related to, 18
    earning potential and, 60n
    EvoScript and, 18–19
    friends-to-lovers pathway and, 196, 239
    mixed-gender networks and, 238n
sandbox metaphor, 188–89
Sara and Emma, 116–18
Savage, Dan, 136

Savannah Pumé hunter-gatherers, 250
Schneider, Sherrie, 6
secure attachment style, 130
secure base support, 107, 116, 117*fig*, 118–21, 119*t*, 122–24, 151
selectivity factor, 34–36, 38–39, 42, 170–72
self-esteem, 29–30
self-expansion, 181
self-partner overlap, 181
self-protection, 140
serotonin, 149
service, acts of, 162–63
sexual desire
    attachment bonds and, 118–19, 121–22
    gender differences and, 67–73
    Zero-Sum model and, 81–86
sexual dimorphism, 114–15
sexual intercourse, mate choice and, 173–75
sexual pleasure, 174–75
sexual selection, 52
sexual violence, 74
sexy phase, 97–98
shootings, 217
short-term mating/relationships
    case studies on, 91*fig*, 92–96, 96*fig*
    EvoScript and, 8–9
    Independent Strategies and, 86–92, 87*fig*, 91*fig*
    Relationship Trajectories model and, 96–100, 98*fig*, 121
    strategies regarding, 76–77
    women and, 81
    Zero-Sum model and, 81–86
Showalter, Sam, 178, 179
similarity, compatibility factor and, 152–57
similarity-attraction hypothesis, 152–57, 164, 167
smartphones, impact of, 209–10
Smith, Anna Nicole, 55

social confidence
    as health-signaling attribute, 82–83
    long-term relationships and, 84
social essentialism, 219–20, 222
Social Relations model (SRM), 33–39, 42, 170–72
social role theory, 222–23
social-engagement innovations, 234
socializing. *See also* networks
    smartphones' impact on, 209–10
    young men and, 231–32
sociosexuality, 68–71, 83–84
speed-dating, studies using data from, 39, 57, 62, 67, 83, 165–66, 205, 248–49
stable traits and attributes, 87–90, 89*fig*
Star Is Born, A, 51, 65, 75
stay-at-home girlfriend trend, 55
"story of us," 180
strangers, fear of, 70–71
stress, effects of, 143–44
Stroop task, 229–30
successes, sharing, 123–24
support
    attachment bonds and, 107
    safe haven, 107, 116, 117*fig,* 118–21, 119*t,* 122–23, 151
    secure base, 107, 116, 117*fig,* 118–21, 119*t,* 122–24, 151

Tate, Andrew, 221–22
testosterone, 85, 149
therapy/therapists
    couples, 187
    family-systems, 182, 183

third impressions, 207–9, 209*fig*
Time magazine, 3, 4, 47–48
time required for relationships, 92–96
Tinder, 201, 206
touch, physical, 162–63
tradwife trend, 55, 64, 213, 223, 232
traits that support strong relationships, 186
Trivers, Robert, 52
Trump, Donald, 221
trust, 123

uncertainty, 101, 123
Ury, Logan, 207
"used date" parties, 210

"vast breeding experiment" comment, 145–46
Victoria, Queen, 198
virtue ethics, 233

When Harry Met Sally . . . , 77
words of affirmation, 162–63
workplaces, meeting partners at, 198–99
Wright, Robert, 4

"yes, but" responses, 128
York, Marilou, 47n

Zach, 76–77
zebra finches, 80–81
Zero-Sum model, 81–86

ABOUT THE AUTHOR

PAUL EASTWICK is a professor of psychology at UC Davis, where he serves as the head of the Social-Personality Psychology program and the director of the Attraction and Relationships Research Laboratory. Thousands of undergraduate students have taken his course on attraction and close relationships, and he has published over one hundred scientific articles and chapters and won numerous early career awards. His research and writing have been featured in outlets like *The New York Times, The Atlantic,* NPR, and *Scientific American Mind.* He hosts the popular podcast *Love Factually* with his longtime colleague Eli Finkel, where they analyze rom-coms and romantic dramas from the perspective of relationship science. He earned his bachelor's degree at Cornell University and his PhD at Northwestern University.